FEDERAL
INCOME TAXATION

FEDERAL INCOME TAXATION

Second Edition

DAVID M. HUDSON

Professor of Law, University of Florida

STEPHEN A. LIND

Professor of Law, University of Florida and
Hastings College of the Law

BLACK LETTER SERIES

WEST PUBLISHING CO.
ST. PAUL, MINN.
1987

COPYRIGHT © 1985 By WEST PUBLISHING CO.
COPYRIGHT © 1987 By WEST PUBLISHING CO.
      50 West Kellogg Boulevard
      P.O. Box 64526
      St. Paul, Minnesota 55164–0526

Library of Congress Cataloging-in-Publication Data

Hudson, David M.
 Federal income taxation.

 (Black letter series)
 1. Income tax—Law and legislation—United States—Outlines, syllabi, etc. I. Lind, Stephen A. II. Title. III. Series.

KF6369.3.H83 1987   343.7305′2   87–13352

ISBN 0–314–59191–5   347.30352

  Hudson & Lind-Fed. Income Tax. 2nd Ed. BLS

   1st Reprint—1988

PUBLISHER'S PREFACE

This "Black Letter" is designed to help a law student recognize and understand the basic principles and issues of law covered in a law school course. It can be used both as a study aid when preparing for classes and as a review of the subject matter when studying for an examination.

Each "Black Letter" is written by experienced law school teachers who are recognized national authorities in the subject covered.

The law is succinctly stated by the author of this "Black Letter." In addition, the exceptions to the rules are stated in the text. The rules and exceptions have purposely been condensed to facilitate quick review and easy recollection. For an in-depth study of a point of law, citations to major student texts are given. In addition, a **Text Correlation Chart** provides a convenient means of relating material contained in the Black Letter to appropriate sections of the casebook the student is using in his or her law school course.

If the subject covered by this text is a code or code-related course, the code section or rule is set forth and discussed wherever applicable.

FORMAT

The format of this "Black Letter" is specially designed for review. (1) **Text.** First, it is recommended that the entire text be studied, and, if deemed necessary, supplemented by the student texts cited. (2) **Capsule Summary.** The Capsule Summary is an abbreviated review of the subject matter which can be used both before and after studying the main body of the text. The headings in the Capsule Summary follow the main text of the "Black Letter." (3) **Table of Contents.** The Table of Contents is in outline form to help you organize the details of the subject and the Summary of Contents gives you a final overview of the materials. (4) **Practice Examination.** The Practice Examination in Appendix B gives you the opportunity of testing yourself with the type of question asked on an exam, and comparing your answer with a model answer.

In addition, a number of other features are included to help you understand the subject matter and prepare for examinations:

Short Questions and Answers: This feature is designed to help you spot and recognize issues in the examination. We feel that issue recognition is a major ingredient in successfully writing an examination.

Perspective: In this feature, the authors discuss their approach to the topic, the approach used in preparing the materials, and any tips on studying for and writing examinations.

Analysis: This feature, at the beginning of each section, is designed to give a quick summary of a particular section to help you recall the subject matter and to help you determine which areas need the most extensive review.

Examples: This feature is designed to illustrate, through fact situations, the law just stated. This, we believe, should help you analytically approach a question on the examination.

Glossary: This feature is designed to refamiliarize you with the meaning of a particular legal term. We believe that the recognition of words of art used in an examination helps you to better analyze the question. In addition, when writing an examination you should know the precise definition of a word of art you intend to use.

We believe that the materials in this ''Black Letter'' will facilitate your study of a law school course and assure success in writing examinations not only for the course but for the bar examination. We wish you success.

The Publisher

SUMMARY OF CONTENTS

APPENDIX

TABLE OF CONTENTS

III. Deductions and Allowances—Continued | Page

APPENDIX

CAPSULE SUMMARY

I. PERSPECTIVE

An individual's income tax liability involves a series of computations according to the following *general* schematic:

	Gross Income
Less	IRC § 62 Deductions
	Adjusted Gross Income
Less	Personal Exemptions & either the Standard Deduction or Itemized Deductions
Equals	Taxable Income
Times	Tax Rate
	Gross Tax Liability
Less	Tax Credits
Equals	Net Tax Liability

II. GROSS INCOME

Gross income includes virtually any economic benefit realized by a taxpayer, including salaries, many fringe benefits, and gains from the sale or exchange of property. In order to clarify the law, Congress sometimes provides by statute for specific inclusion of some items in gross income. For example, alimony payments and most prizes or awards are specifically included in gross income. In addition,

1

Congress has provided by statute that some economic benefits are to be excluded from gross income. Examples include proceeds from life insurance, certain fringe benefits, gifts and inheritances, interest paid on certain state and local bonds, compensation for injuries or illness and damages for personal injuries, some income from the discharge of indebtedness, and some scholarships and fellowship grants.

III. DEDUCTIONS AND ALLOWANCES

Various deductions and allowances may be subtracted from Gross Income in arriving at Taxable Income. A deduction may be taken only if a statute specifically allows it and only if all the requirements of the statute are met and if no other statute disallows the deduction. Deductions may be separated into two classifications: deductions related to profit seeking activities and deductions related to non-profit seeking activities. Profit related deductions and allowances include ordinary and necessary expenses incurred in carrying on a trade or business, such as salaries, traveling expenses, rents and certain education expenses. In addition, ordinary and necessary expenses incurred in connection with the production or collection of income, or in the management of income producing property are deductible even though the activity is not a "trade or business." An individual may deduct losses incurred in a trade or business or in any transaction entered into for profit. Property which is used in profit-seeking activities sometimes qualifies for depreciation deductions and related tax benefits.

As a general rule, no deductions are allowed for personal, living or family expenses or for capital expenditures. However, some deductions are allowed even though they are not connected with a trade or business or other profit-seeking activity. Some personal expenses such as some payments of interest, some state and local taxes, personal casualty and theft losses, charitable contributions, extraordinary medical expenses, alimony, and moving expenses are deductible.

Congress sometimes specifically disallows deductions of items which otherwise would be deductible. For example, deductions are disallowed for certain illegal activities, expenses relating to tax exempt income, and some transactions between related taxpayers. Statutory guidelines are provided for determining the extent to which deductions may be taken with respect to activities not engaged in for profit, business meals and entertainment expenses, the business use of one's residence and the rental of vacation homes. Deductions with respect to most profit-seeking activities are limited by the amount the taxpayer has invested in the venture according to "at risk" rules. Further, deductions attributable to passive investment activities, such as a business in which the taxpayer does not materially participate or rentals, are allowed in a taxable year only to the extent of the taxpayer's income derived from passive investment activities that year.

IV. TIMING

Tax liability is determined annually either on a calendar year or a fiscal year. The computation of a taxpayer's tax liability is made with regard to the items of income, deductions and credits properly attributable to the taxpayer's taxable year. An item is attributed to a year according to the taxpayer's accounting method or convention. The cash method of accounting in essence looks to cash flow and a taxpayer generally includes in gross income items when he actually or constructively receives them and takes deductions for expenditures when he pays them. An accrual method taxpayer generally includes items in gross income when her right to the amount becomes fixed and the amount is reasonably certain (the "all events" test), and she generally takes deductions when the all events test is met and economic performance occurs. In some circumstances both accrual method and cash method taxpayers may defer the recognition of gain from the sale of property under an installment method of reporting and other special rules apply to annuities and deferred compensation. In addition to the general rules, the claim of right doctrine and the tax benefit rule may affect the timing of income and deductions.

Although gross income includes gains on property as the gains are realized, in some circumstances the property received in the realization, or the reinvestment of proceeds received in a realization, essentially involves a continuation of the old investment. In such situations Congress provides a series of rules allowing nonrecognition of such realized gain. Nonrecognition rules may apply, for example, to exchanges of like kind property, to involuntary conversions, and to the sale of a taxpayer's principal residence.

Special rules involving timing of income are applicable to certain loans or installment purchases of property if no interest is called for, or if the amount of interest called for is too low. These rules not only create or impute interest to both parties but also provide for the timing of such imputed interest.

V. WHO IS THE PROPER TAXPAYER

The amount of tax imposed on any dollar of gross income, or the utility of any dollar of deduction, is determined by the applicable tax rate which, in turn, is a function of who is the proper taxpayer. Generally, income is taxed to the taxpayer who performs income producing services or the taxpayer who owns income producing property, and it is not permissible for one taxpayer to give or assign his right to receive income to another taxpayer. A taxpayer may, however, give income producing property to another taxpayer, or she may sell for its present value a right to receive income in the future, and the income received thereafter will be taxed to the recipient. In addition, determination of who is the proper taxpayer may be affected when income producing activities or property are engaged in or are owned by a partnership, a corporation or a trust. If transactions take place between related taxpayers, the I.R.S. may reallocate items of income and deductions among them in order to clearly reflect each of their respective incomes.

Alimony and child support are subject to special treatment. Payments which qualify as alimony are included in the gross income of the recipient spouse, and are deductible by the paying spouse. Payments of child support, however, may not be deducted and they are not included in the recipient's gross income. Transfers of property between spouses, or to a former spouse if the transfer is incident to a divorce, do not result in gain or loss to the transferring spouse and they are not included in gross income of the recipient spouse.

VI. CHARACTERIZATION OF INCOME AND DEDUCTIONS

After items of gross income and deduction have been properly identified and the year of their inclusion and deduction as well as the proper taxpayer who is taxed on them or allowed to deduct them is determined, each item of income and deduction must be characterized. Gain (or loss) from the sale or exchange of a capital asset is a capital gain (or loss); it is a long-term capital gain (or loss) if the asset has been held for more than 6 months, and if the holding period is not that long, it is a short-term capital gain (or loss). Unless a statute provides to the contrary, any gain or loss on property which is not a capital asset or lacks a sale or exchange is an ordinary gain or loss.

Although long-term and short-term capital gains are currently taxed at the same rate as ordinary income, there are limitations on the amount of capital losses which may be deducted in a taxable year. In general terms, capital assets are property other than inventory, depreciable property or real property used in a trade or business, certain copyrights and similar property, certain accounts receivable, and property which is an integral part of a taxpayer's trade or business.

In addition to the general rules, there are some situations in which property (a "quasi-capital asset") which is not a capital asset or which lacks a sale or exchange may give rise to a capital gain or loss. And sometimes gain on property which would otherwise be a capital gain may be recharacterized in whole or in part as ordinary income under the recapture rules, if certain depreciation deductions have been taken with respect to property which is sold or exchanged.

VII. COMPUTING TAX LIABILITY

Once a taxpayer's Gross Income for a taxable year and the deductions properly attributable to that year have been determined, computation of Taxable Income is a two-step process. First, if certain deductions already allowed by another section are also described in IRC § 62 they are then subtracted from Gross Income to arrive at Adjusted Gross Income. The Adjusted Gross Income concept is significant in computing other items of income and deduction. Second, deductions for personal exemptions as well as *either* the standard deduction *or* the itemized deductions (some of which are subjected to a 2% floor) are subtracted from Adjusted Gross Income in computing Taxable Income.

The next step in computing a taxpayer's tax liability is to multiply the Taxable Income by the appropriate rate, determined with reference to the taxpayer's classification. A taxpayer's classification is determined by his marital status and, if he is married, whether he files a joint return with his spouse, or, if he is not married, whether he is a surviving spouse, a head of household, or simply an unmarried taxpayer. In addition a taxpayer may increase his regular tax liability if he is subject to the alternative minimum tax.

For taxable years beginning after 1987, tax on taxpayers other than corporations will be imposed at two rates, 15% and 28% and tax on corporations will be imposed at three rates, 15%, 25% and 34%. However, some high income taxpayers will have all of their income taxed at the highest (28% or 34%) marginal rate; for these taxpayers the income tax is a flat-rate tax.

The final step in determining the Net Tax Liability is to subtract the amount of any Tax Credits available to the taxpayer from the tax liability determined above. Each dollar of credit offsets one dollar of tax liability. Some credits are "refundable," i.e., if the amount of the credit exceeds the precredit tax liability, a refund is paid to the taxpayer. Other credits are not refundable, but some of them may be carried back or forward to other taxable years if the full amount cannot be used in the current taxable year.

VIII. PROCEDURE

An annual income tax return for taxpayers whose taxable year is a calendar year must be filed on or before April 15 of the following year; fiscal year taxpayers must file a return by the 15th day of the fourth month following close of the year. Penalties are provided for failure to file a return and for failure to timely pay a tax liability.

A taxpayer may dispute the amount of his liability with the Internal Revenue Service, either because he feels he should be allowed a refund or because the Service feels he paid too little. Such disputes are first handled administratively within the Service. If the administrative process is unsuccessful and the Service asserts that a taxpayer owes additional taxes, the taxpayer may litigate the asserted deficiency in the Tax Court prior to paying the taxes. In the alternative, if a taxpayer claims and is denied a refund from the Service, he may litigate the issue in the Federal District Court or the Claims Court. Appeals from any of the three trial courts may be taken to the Circuit Court of Appeal, with ultimate review by certiorari in the Supreme Court.

*

PERSPECTIVE

Analysis

A. INTRODUCTION

1. THE SUBJECT IN GENERAL

Federal income tax law is one of the most complex subjects likely to be encountered in a law school curriculum or by a practicing attorney. Federal income tax law is complex for two basic reasons. First, the ever-changing variety of sources of the law, including administrative pronouncements, judicial interpretations, and legislative enactments, often make it difficult to ascertain what the law is in a particular situation. The second reason the Federal income tax is complex is because it is superimposed on various transactions and relationships, such as corporate reorganizations or international sales transactions, which are themselves complex and difficult to understand. Federal income tax law is important because tax considerations permeate virtually every other course in a law school curriculum, and virtually every facet of the practice of law as well. Lawyers who are not tax specialists are nonetheless likely to be confronted with Federal income tax problems in a variety of settings, ranging from divorce proceedings to zoning controversies.

Because of the importance of Federal income tax law, and in acknowledgment of its complexity, the objective of a basic law school tax course (and of this outline) is to concentrate on the fundamental aspects of the law as it pertains to individuals. In this manner, students are provided with a sturdy skeletal framework which can be fleshed out by other tax courses, such as corporate tax or partnership tax, as desired, or by self-study as the need arises in practice. Entities such as trusts, estates, and corporations, often are "taxpayers," but they receive little attention here because the fundamental rules affecting them are the same fundamental rules applicable to individuals, and because the special rules pertaining to entities as well as nonentities such as partnerships are sufficiently complex that generally separate law school courses are devoted to them. For similar reasons, the tax treatment of foreign persons, or of foreign transactions engaged in by domestic persons, are not addressed in this outline.

The complexity of Federal income tax law is, at times, overwhelming, especially to the new student. Concepts and terms which are encountered early in the study of taxation cannot be fully comprehended until after later concepts are learned; conversely, later concepts cannot be digested unless the student has grasped the principals dealt with earlier. This conundrum may be frustrating, but it is not unresolvable. It is important to review material periodically during a term not only to ensure that fundamental concepts dealt with at the beginning have been learned, but also so that material covered more recently can shed light on the earlier matters. This outline provides numerous cross references between various sections to assist the student in tying together various related concepts, regardless of the time they may be covered in class, or in the outline itself. At times there will be cross references to materials which have not yet been covered. We have no choice but to do this and only assure you that when the entire course is completed all the cross references will fit like putting together a puzzle.

2. PREPARING FOR EXAMINATIONS

The Internal Revenue Code (the Code, or IRC) is the quintessence of Federal income tax law. Tax law is fundamentally statutory, and it is essential that students become adept at reading statutory language—the skills learned in this regard in a tax course are transferrable skills, useful in any other area of the law where statutes may be encountered. Therefore, it cannot be overemphasized that this outline should only supplement, not supplant, study of the Code. Indeed, whenever a student is reading their casebook, a judicial opinion, a Treasury Regulation, even this outline, or any other discussion of a provision of the Code, the student's copy of the Code should be close at hand, so that the explanation can be scrutinized alongside the Code, thereby enhancing the student's understanding of the statutory provision.

It is common practice for tax law professors to use hypothetical fact situations or problems, with appropriate dollar amounts, to illustrate and explain various concepts of tax law throughout the course. Because of the frequent use of numbers and computations during the term, many law students who do not have a background in accounting or business become apprehensive about a tax law examination, fearful that they will be called upon to be as adept with calculations on the examination as the professor was during class. In preparing for the examination in tax law, students should keep in mind that this is a *law* course being taught in a *law* school, as part of the training for *lawyers*. It is *not* a course in accounting, or economics, or math. Therefore, the basic approach in preparing for an examination in tax law is the same as the basic approach in preparing for an examination in any other law school subject:

1. Prepare all assignments and attend all class sessions. If the professor or a research assistant conducts help sessions or review sessions, attend them as well.

2. Review periodically during the term. The table of contents of your casebook should be consulted frequently, to keep you oriented as to where you are in relation to the material which has already been covered, and the material yet to come. Appropriate break-points, at the end of a Chapter, Part or Unit, should come every two or three weeks, and should comprise a digestible body of material to review. If you do not understand a point (or several points) in the material you have reviewed, consult with your professor *now* to clear up the matter while the material is still relatively fresh in your mind (and in the professor's!)

Techniques and tactics in actually taking a tax law examination are once again basically the same as those employed in taking an examination in any other law school course:

1. Read each question thoroughly before beginning your answer. Identify the pertinent facts involved, the issues which are raised, and the questions which are asked.

2. Be certain to answer the questions which are asked; conversely, do not waste time by attempting to answer questions which have *not* been asked.

3. If a problem involves computations, do not get bogged down and waste time on the mathematics. Rather than precisely adding together

several items, and computing the extent to which that sum exceeds a percentage of the sum of yet another group of items, you will undoubtedly do much better if you explain what computations should be made, in what order and why, while simply giving a rough approximate of the numerical solution. If the professor permits you to use a calculator while taking the examination, by all means, do so.

4. There are many situations in which there is not *a* correct answer. For example, there may be conflicting opinions from different circuit courts of appeal on the issue. These issue areas are often tax law professors' favorites for examination questions; thus they deserve a bit more attention in study and review. When such an issue is raised in an examination question, be certain to discuss both (or more) views of the correct treatment. If you have been asked to arrive at a conclusion regarding the issue, do so and explain why the approach you have taken is preferable to other alternatives.

3. ADDITIONAL READING

In most circumstances, the Code, the casebook, and assigned portions of the Treasury Regulations will be all that a student in an introductory Federal income tax course will need to consult. Indeed, it may be counterproductive for a student in such a course to consult a treatise or loose-leaf service which has been written for, and at the level of, a more experienced practitioner. There are, however, four collateral sources which students may find helpful. *Federal Income Taxation* (4th ed. 1985) by Marvin A. Chirelstein provides a useful discussion of the major concepts from a slightly different perspective than is found in most casebooks. *Federal Income Taxation* (1983) by Daniel Q. Posin is one of the West Publishing Company's "Hornbook Series" and it provides an excellent discussion of most of the topics covered in the introductory Federal income tax course. Professor Borris I. Bittker's *Fundamentals of Federal Income Taxation* (student ed. 1983) provides a relatively detailed discussion of not only basic income tax topics, but more advanced subjects as well. Finally, *The Federal Income Tax* (student ed. 1986) by Joyce Stanley and Richard Kilcullen provides a section-by-section discussion of the Code. In light of the major tax revision legislation enacted in 1986, it is likely that more recent editions of each of these sources will be forthcoming in the near future.

B. HISTORY OF THE U.S. INCOME TAX

The income tax has occupied a permanent, and increasingly prominent, place in the economic and social fabric of the United States since 1913. Attempts were made to impose a Federal income tax during the Civil War years, but it was not until 1894 that an income tax was enacted under the Constitutional authority to "lay and collect taxes, duties, imposts and excises. . . ." [U.S. Const. art. 1, § 8, cl. 1.] The 1894 Act was held to be unconstitutional, however, in 1895 because of the rule of apportionment.

Direct taxes must be "apportioned among the several states in accordance with their respective populations . . . ." [U.S. Const. art. 1, § 9, cl. 4.] Income subject to tax under the 1894 Act included income derived from renting real property and the Supreme Court held that because a tax on land is a direct tax, a tax imposed on rental income from land is also a direct tax; because the 1894 Act was not properly apportioned, it was unconstitutional. [*Pollock v. Farmers' Loan & Trust Co.*, 157 U.S. 429, *on remand* 158 U.S. 601 (1895).] Although the reasoning of the Court in *Pollock* was criticized, subsequent Congressional efforts to enact an income tax were stalled by arguments that the Constitution needed an Amendment specifically authorizing the Congress to impose an income tax without it having to be apportioned. The Sixteenth Amendment became effective on February 25, 1913, and the infant form of the modern income tax was born on October 3, 1913.

Between 1913 and 1939 Congress enacted numerous laws dealing with the income tax, as well as other taxes, and in 1939, these internal revenue laws were collected, codified and enacted as the law in the Internal Revenue Code of 1939. The internal revenue laws, including provisions dealing with the income tax, were dramatically revised in 1954 with the enactment of the Internal Revenue Code of 1954. There have been a number of major tax acts enacted in the past thirty years, and that trend can be expected to continue. In 1986 the Congress dramatically revised the internal revenue laws and redesignated the Internal Revenue Title of the U.S. Code the "Internal Revenue Code of 1986" (commonly referred to as the Code, or IRC). Virtually all legislation affecting the income tax may be found in the Code.

C. SOURCES OF TAX LAW

The primary source of tax law is, of course, the Internal Revenue Code of 1986, as amended (the Code, or IRC). In addition to the bare language of the statute, interpretations of the statute and its application in a variety of fact situations are provided by both the judicial and the executive branches of government.

The Treasury Department is the executive agency which has the authority and responsibility to administer and enforce the provisions of the Code, and it is generally the Internal Revenue Service (the I.R.S.) within the Treasury Department which deals with the income tax. The Income Tax Regulations (the Regulations, or Regs.) are promulgated by the Treasury Department, generally in accordance with the Federal Rules of Administrative Procedure, and they may be found in the Federal Register and the Code of Federal Regulations although they are published separately by several private publishers. Regulations are either "interpretive" or "legislative." Interpretive regulations are promulgated under the general authority to interpret the Code as necessary for the proper administration of the statute.

[IRC § 7805.] Legislative regulations are promulgated under more specific guidelines when Congress delegates authority to legislate in certain prescribed situations. [See IRC § 7872(g).] There is a trend toward increased use of legislative regulations in recent years.

The Treasury Department also issues Rulings in which it expresses its opinion of the proper tax consequences of a particular fact situation. Formal rulings are issued in response to requests either by taxpayers or by various personnel within the I.R.S.; they are released weekly in the Internal Revenue Bulletin (I.R.B.) and are collected semi-annually in the Cumulative Bulletin (C.B. or Cum.Bull.). Formal rulings may be relied on by other taxpayers whose circumstances coincide with the facts addressed in the ruling. Informal, "private letter" rulings are issued to taxpayers who request them; the rulings are made public, although the identity of the taxpayer is not revealed, but they may not be relied on as precedent by other taxpayers.

The judicial branch also has a role in determining tax law. The Tax Court, the U.S. Claims Court, the Federal District Courts, the U.S. Courts of Appeal, and, of course, the U.S. Supreme Court all have jurisdiction, in varying circumstances, over tax cases. [See discussion, VIII. E., at page 326, *infra.*]

II

GROSS INCOME

Analysis

A. The Nature of Gross Income
   1. Economists' Concept of Income
   2. Tax Law Concept of Income
B. Examples of Gross Income   *$61*
   1. Compensation for Services
   2. Gains Derived From Dealings in Property *$1001 – $1016*
   3. Items Specifically Included in Gross Income by Statute *72 – 86, 82,*
C. Items Specifically Excluded From Gross Income by Statute
   1. Death Benefits *$101 – 135*
   2. Gifts and Inheritances
   3. Interest on State and Local Bonds
   4. Compensation for Injuries or Sickness and Damages
   5. Income From Discharge of Indebtedness
   6. Scholarships, Tuition Reductions and Educational Assistance Programs
   7. Meals and Lodging
   8. Miscellaneous Items Excluded From Income by Statute

A. THE NATURE OF GROSS INCOME

1. ECONOMISTS' CONCEPT OF INCOME

Economists have defined income as

the algebraic sum of (1) the market value of rights exercised in consumption and (2) the change in the value of the store of property rights between the beginning and end of the period in question.

This definition of income (referred to as the "Haig-Simons" definition of income) is useful as an economic concept, but it is incomplete, or at best troublesome, when used to describe the *tax base* (the dollar amount subject to tax) of an income tax system.

a. Imputed income

The first part of the Haig-Simons definition of income refers to consumption. "Imputed income" refers to the monetary value of goods and services which someone produces and consumes within the family unit, as well as the monetary value of using property which someone owns.

Example: Andy grows vegetables in his back-yard garden, and he and his wife and children consume produce which would cost $200 in a grocery store. Betty is a carpenter who usually works for $20 an hour, and she spends 10 hours building bookshelves in her own house. Clarence owns a house in which he lives with his family, but if they did not occupy the house, he could rent it to someone else for $12,000 per year. Andy and Betty each has imputed income from the consumption of the goods and services which they produce, and Clarence has imputed income from consuming the rental value of his house.

An income tax imposed on imputed income would be difficult for taxpayers to comply with, and difficult for the I.R.S. to enforce. Thus, imputed income is not included in the concept of income within the U.S. income tax system. [*See Helvering v. Independent Life Ins. Co.,* 292 U.S. 371, 54 S.Ct. 758 (1934).]

b. Accretion in value

The second portion of the Haig-Simons definition of income refers to accumulations of wealth during a particular period of time.

Example: Debbie buys a painting on January 1 for $3,000, and on December 31 of the same year, someone offers to buy it from her for $4,000. The Haig-Simons definition of income includes the $1,000 increase in the value of Diane's painting regardless of whether she sells the painting or keeps it.

Although increases in the value of property are within an economic concept of income, they are not included in the income tax concept of income for two basic reasons. First, there would be considerable practical problems of compliance, administration and enforcement because of the need to annually determine the value of virtually all of a taxpayer's property. Second, there is a liquidity problem. If an income tax is computed by reference to the increase in value of an individual's property, a particular taxpayer may be required to pay income tax even though he has not received any money or other property during the year.

Example: Elijah owns real estate which increases $100,000 in value during a year. If the $100,000 increase in value is included in his income tax base, he might be required to pay, say, $30,000 of tax as a consequence of that appreciation even though he has no other income during the year.

Because of the problems of enforcement, compliance and liquidity, the income tax concept of income departs from the Haig-Simons definition of income by requiring that any appreciation in the value of property must be *realized* before it is included in gross income. [See II. A. 2. a., at page 16, *infra,* and *Comm'r v. Glenshaw Glass Co.,* 348 U.S. 426, 75 S.Ct. 473 (1955).]

2. TAX LAW CONCEPT OF INCOME

The determination of an individual's income tax liability involves a series of computations according to the following schematic:

	Gross Income
Less	Section 62 Deductions
Equals	Adjusted Gross Income
Less	Personal Exemptions & either the Standard Deduction or Itemized Deductions
Equals	Taxable Income
Times	Tax Rate
Equals	Gross Tax Liability
Less	Credits
Equals	Net Tax Liability

Section 61 purports to define gross income: "Except as otherwise provided in this subtitle, gross income means all income from whatever source derived, including (but not limited to) . . ." fifteen items, such as compensation for services, rents and interest. However, there is no true definition of "income" contained in the Code, nor has there been such a definition in any of the income tax laws dating back to the Revenue Act of 1913. It has been the judiciary, rather than the Congress, which has provided the gloss on the concept of income as that term is used in the income tax statutes.

a.) Realization requirement

For income tax purposes, income does not include the mere increase in value of an item of property between two points in time. Instead, early in the history of the income tax in this country, the Supreme Court confined the concept of income to "gain derived from" property or labor. [*Eisner v. Macomber,* 252 U.S. 189, 40 S.Ct. 189 (1920).] Similarly, today the Code enumerates as an item of gross income "[g]ains derived from dealings in property." [IRC § 61(a)(3).] There must be some sale or other disposition of an item of property before the appreciation is "realized" and becomes gain included in gross income. [See discussion, II. B. 2. c., at page 41, *infra.*]

b.) Receipt of an economic benefit

Gross income may arise indirectly if someone receives an economic benefit, even though there is no direct receipt of money or other property.

Example: William is employed by a company which, in addition to paying him a cash salary, pays his federal income tax liability. William has gross income in the amount of the income taxes paid on his behalf, even though he does not directly receive money or other property from his employer. [*Old Colony Trust Co. v. Comm'r,* 279 U.S. 716, 49 S.Ct. 499 (1929).] Similarly, Frances, an accountant, agrees to prepare an income tax return for Geoffrey, a dentist who agrees to fill a few of Frances' cavities. Frances and Geoffrey each receive an economic benefit, the value of which is included in their respective gross incomes. [Rev.Rul. 75–24, 1979–1 C.B. 60.]

If someone receives an economic benefit, it is generally appropriate to include it in their tax base, even though the amount of the economic benefit is not attributable to capital, or labor, or both combined.

Example: In 1957, Ermenegildo purchased a used piano for $15 and in 1964 he discovered $4,500 in old currency hidden in the back of the piano. Under local law, the currency became his property in 1964, the year in which he found it. Ermenegildo had $4,500 of gross income for his 1964 taxable year. [*Cesarini v. U.S.,* 296 F.Supp. 3 (N.D.Ohio 1969).]

i. Borrowing

Gross income does not include amounts of money (or the value of other property) which is borrowed, because there is a concurrent obligation to repay that which was borrowed. The borrower does not have any *net* "accession to wealth;" the borrowed assets may increase the value of his "store of wealth," but it is completely offset by an equal liability, his obligation to repay the loan. If the obligation to repay ceases to exist, however, because the lender "forgives" the indebtedness, or because the statute of limitations for enforcing the debt expires, then the borrower will have an "accession to wealth," and gross income, at that time. [See discussion, II. C. 5., at page 55, *infra.*]

ii.   Illegal gains

Money or other property which is illegally gotten is included in gross income. Thus, if a thief has "actual command" over stolen money, he has gross income even though he may, under local law, be obligated to return the money to its rightful owner. [*James v. U.S.,* 366 U.S. 213, 81 S.Ct. 1052 (1961).]

iii. Rebates

If the seller of an item of property provides a rebate of a portion of the purchase price to a purchaser, the amount of the rebate is not income to the purchaser; rather, it is a reduction of the purchase price of the item of property. [Rev.Rul. 76–96, 1976–1 C.B. 23.]

iv.   Damages

Amounts received as damages may provide an economic benefit to the recipient, and thus the amount received may be included in gross income. In some situations, damages merely serve to "make the plaintiff whole," thus there is no element of gain to the recipient and the amount should not be included in gross income. [See discussion of exclusion of certain damage awards from gross income, II. C. 4., at page 51, *infra.*]

> *Example:* The G.G. Company filed suit against the H.E. Company, alleging fraud and violation of the antitrust laws. The parties ultimately settled the lawsuit and the H.E. Company paid the G.G. Company $325,000 in punitive damages for fraud and the antitrust violations. The G.G. Company received an economic benefit in the amount of the punitive damages which were an accession to wealth, clearly realized, over which the G.G. Company had complete dominion. The G.G. Company must include the $325,000 punitive damages in gross income. [*Comm'r v. Glenshaw Glass Co.,* 348 U.S. 426, 75 S.Ct. 473 (1955).]

B. EXAMPLES OF GROSS INCOME
1. COMPENSATION FOR SERVICES

Compensation received for services, including fees, commissions, most fringe benefits, and similar items, are gross income to the recipient. [IRC § 61(a)(1); see Reg. § 1.61–2(a)(1).] Compensation includes salary or wages paid in cash, as well as the value of property and other economic benefits received because of services which the recipient has performed, or will perform in the future, unless excluded by statute.

a. Payments "in kind"

Compensation includes the receipt of property or services, as well as the receipt of money. Such noncash payments are referred to as having been made "in kind," and are included in gross income in the amount of their fair market value. [Reg. § 1.61–2(d)(1); see *Comm'r v. Smith*, 324 U.S. 177, 181, 65 S.Ct. 591, 593 (1945).]

b. Bargain-Purchase

The full value of property need not be transferred to an employee as an in kind payment. If, as part of an employee's compensation, an employer sells an item of property to an employee for a price less than the property's fair market value, the difference between the price paid and the value of the property acquired in the "bargain purchase" is compensation income to the employee unless the amount is excluded as a qualifying employee discount fringe benefit. [Reg. § 1.61–2(d)(2)(i); see discussion of fringe benefits, II. B. 1. e., at page 19, *infra.*]

c. Compensation without the receipt of cash or property

The touchstone of the concept of gross income is "economic benefit." If, as compensation for services rendered, an employee receives an economic benefit, she has income even though she does not directly receive any cash or other property. [*Old Colony Trust Co. v. Comm'r*, 279 U.S. 716, 49 S.Ct. 499 (1929).]

An employee may have compensation income by virtue of being permitted to use property which belongs to her employer.

Example: John and his wife are permitted to live in a house which is owned by his employer. The fair rental value of the home is included in John's gross income. [*Dean v. Comm'r*, 187 F.2d 1019 (3d Cir.1951).] This is so even though John owns the corporation which employs him. John and his wholly owned corporation are treated as two different persons for Federal tax purposes and consequently this is not imputed income. [See discussion, II. A. 1. a., at page 14, *supra.*]

Congress has provided that an employee who receives an interest-free or below market interest loan from his employer generally has gross income in the amount of interest the Federal government would have had to pay to borrow the money less any interest paid. [IRC § 7872; see discussion, IV. E. 1. b., at page 233, *infra.*]

d. Excessive compensation

Not all payments, whether cash or in kind, made by an employer to an employee are compensation. The central issue is whether the payment is, in fact, being paid in consideration for services rendered, or whether there is another motive for the payment which affects its tax status. If the payment is made to an individual who is both an employee and a shareholder in the corporate-employer, the payment may be a dividend, rather than compensation. The characterization of a payment as a dividend, rather than as compensation, makes no difference to the employee/shareholder; the classification is significant, however, to the employer/corporation which may take a deduction for compensation paid to its employees, but it is not entitled to a deduction for the payment of a dividend to its shareholders.

e. Fringe benefits

i. In general

Compensation income includes the value of any property or services or other economic benefit received in exchange for the performance of services. Congress, however, has provided a number of specific provisions to exclude the value of certain "fringe benefits" from the gross income of employees. The term "fringe benefit" is generally used to describe an economic benefit, other than cash salary or wages, which is provided to an employee by her employer as compensation for services.

Until 1984, the I.R.S. permitted certain employees to receive a variety of economic benefits from their employers without including their value in gross income. The exclusion of such items was not authorized by the Code; thus, they were referred to as "non-statutory fringe benefits." Congress in 1984 provided for the statutory exclusion of certain fringe benefits, providing further that fringe benefits which do not qualify under one of the statutory exclusion provisions must be included in gross income.

Section 132 provides rules for excluding five categories of fringe benefits from gross income: (1) no-additional-cost services, (2) qualified employee discounts, (3) working condition fringe benefits, (4) de minimis fringe benefits, and (5) on the premises athletic facilities.

ii. No-additional-cost services

The economic benefit of a service provided to an employee by her employer is excluded from the employee's gross income if the service is of a type offered for sale to customers in the ordinary course of the employer's line of business in which the employee is performing services, and if the employer incurs no substantial additional cost in providing the service to the employee. [IRC § 132(a), (b).] The amount of revenue an employer loses because of providing the service to an employee rather than to a paying customer, and the amount of time spent by employees in providing a service for an employee are factors taken into consideration in determining whether the no-additional-cost services fringe benefit exclusion applies.

Example: XYZ Corporation is engaged in two separate businesses, providing airline services and hotel accommodations. Gabriel works for XYZ as an airplane pilot, and when he is off-duty he is entitled to fly for no charge on XYZ's scheduled airline flights, on a space available basis. He is also entitled to free lodging in XYZ's hotels if a room is available after 6 p.m. Gabriel may exclude from gross income the value of the airline services which he receives, but he may not exclude the value of the hotel services because he does not perform services for XYZ in the line of business of providing hotel accommodations.

No-additional-cost services generally must be provided by an employee's own employer to qualify for the exclusion. Provision is made, however, for two or more employers engaged in the same line of business to enter into a written reciprocal agreement under which services may be provided to an employee of another employer if none of the employers incurs any substantial additional cost (including lost revenue) in providing the services under the agreement. [IRC § 132(g) (2).]

Example: XYZ Corporation, the same corporation in the previous Example, enters into a written agreement with QST Corporation, another corporation engaged in the airline business, under which XYZ's employees may fly free, on a space-available basis, on QST's scheduled flights, and QST's employees may fly on XYZ's flights on the same terms. Gabriel takes advantage of free flights on both XYZ and QST flights. The value of the flights is not included in Gabriel's gross income.

iii.   Qualified employee discounts

An exclusion from gross income is provided for the amount of a "qualified employee discount," which is the "employee discount" with respect to "qualified property or services." [IRC § 132(c)(1).] "Qualified property or services" includes services or property (other than real property or investment property) which are offered for sale by the employer to nonemployee customers in the ordinary course of the employer's line of business in which the employee works. [IRC § 132(c)(4).] An "employee discount" is the difference in the price of property or services which are provided to employees, and the price at which the same property or services are offered to nonemployee customers. [IRC § 132(c)(3).]

a. Qualified employee discounts for property   *GP%*

The exclusion of an employee discount with respect to qualified property may not exceed an amount equal to the "gross profit percentage" of the price at which the property is offered for sale to customers. The "gross profit percentage" is essentially the employer's average mark-up on his goods, and is determined by dividing the difference between the aggregate sales price of such property sold to customers by the employer, less the cost of the goods, divided by the aggregate sales price of the property. [IRC § 132(c)(2), (4).]

> ***Example:*** Harriet is employed as a salesclerk in a clothing store. She is entitled to receive a discount of 50% of the normal retail price of merchandise, and she pays $50 for a blouse which retails for $100. Her employer's total sales of clothing during a year were $1 million, and the employer's aggregate cost for the goods was $600,000. The employer's gross profit percentage for the year is 40% [($1,000,000 – 600,000 = $400,000)/$1,000,000]. The employee discount is excluded from Harriet's gross income only to the extent of 40% of the selling price of the blouse ($40); the excess discount on the purchase ($10) is included in her gross income.

b. Qualified employee discounts for services   *20%*

The exclusion of an employee discount with respect to qualified services may not exceed 20% of the price at which the services are offered to customers in the ordinary course of business, regardless of the employer's gross profit percentage. [IRC § 132(c)(1)(B).]

> ***Example:*** Irving is an employee of a corporation engaged in providing life insurance; an insurance policy is considered a service rather than property. A particular policy normally requires a premium payment of $100, but Irving is entitled to the coverage for only $75. Irving may exclude only $20 of the employee discount with respect to the insurance coverage; the excess discount on the purchase of the insurance ($5) is included in his gross income.

iv.   Working condition fringe benefits

Gross income does not include the value of any property or services provided to an employee by her employer to the extent that, if the employee paid for the property or services herself, she would be entitled to a deduction under IRC §§ 162 or 167. [IRC § 132(d) see discussion of IRC §§ 162 and 167, III. A. 1. and III. A. 5., respectively, at pages 70 and 104, *infra*.] In addition, parking provided to an employee on or near the business premises of her employer is considered to be a working condition fringe benefit, excluded from gross income.   [IRC § 132(h)(4).]

Example: Janet is employed as a broker by a brokerage house which provides her with subscriptions to business periodicals. Janet could have deducted the cost of the periodicals as a business expense if she had paid for the subscriptions. The cost of the periodicals is excluded from Janet's gross income. In addition, Janet commutes to work by driving her own automobile and her employer provides a parking space for her in a lot across the street from her office. Even though Janet would not be able to deduct the cost of parking her car, because it is a personal commuting expense, she may exclude the value of the parking space from her gross income.

v.   De minimis fringe benefits

A "de minimis fringe" is defined as any property or service which is so small as to make accounting for it unreasonable or administratively impracticable. In determining whether the de minimis rule applies, consideration is given to the frequency with which similar benefits are provided to employees. [IRC § 132(e)(1).] An eating facility operated by an employer for its employees is treated as a de minimis fringe if the facility is located on or near the business premises of the employer and if the price charged to employees for meals is equal to or greater than the costs of operating the facility. [IRC § 132(e)(2).]

Example: Kevin is employed as the personnel officer of a large corporation. Examples of de minimis fringes which Kevin might receive, and exclude from gross income, include the typing of personal letters by his secretary, occasional personal use of the company copying machine, occasional company cocktail parties or employee picnics, occasional supper money or taxi fare because of overtime work, and coffee and doughnuts furnished to him and other employees.

vi.   Athletic facilities

Gross income does not include the value of using a gym or other athletic facility provided to an employee by his employer. The athletic facility must be on the premises of the employer, it must be operated by the employer, and substantially all of the use of the facility must be by employees. [IRC § 132(h)(5).]

Example: Lisa is employed by a corporation which owns a parcel of land across the street from its business offices on which is located a swimming pool, a track, two handball courts as well as locker rooms and shower facilities; use of the facilities is restricted to employees. Lisa's gross income does not include the value of using the athletic facilities provided by her employer.

vii. Additional considerations
a.   Nondiscrimination rules

If a benefit is provided under an arrangement which discriminates in favor of the employer's highly compensated employees, the exclusions for some of the above fringe benefits do not apply to those highly compensated employees. Those fringes are no-additional-cost services, qualified employee discounts, employer provided eating facilities, and athletic facilities. [IRC §§ 132(e)(2), (h)(1), and 274(e)(5).]

b.   Definition of "employee"

No-additional-cost services, qualified employee discounts, and employer provided gyms or other athletic facilities may be provided to an employee, as well as the spouse and dependent children of an employee. With respect to the above fringes only, an employee includes: (1) an individual who is currently employed, (2) former employees who were separated from service by retirement or disability, and (3) widows and widowers of individuals who died while employed or while a retired or disabled former employee. [IRC § 132(f).]

2.   GAINS DERIVED FROM DEALINGS IN PROPERTY

Gross income includes gains derived from dealings in property. [IRC § 61(a)(3).] In keeping with the concept of "income" that only *gain* is subject to tax, there are two factors considered in determining *whether* a transaction produces gain, and, if so, *how much* gain. The first factor is the *amount realized* from the disposition of the property; that is, how much, in money or money's worth (including economic benefit), did the property owner receive for the property. The second factor is the *adjusted basis* of the property. There are several rules for determining the initial basis of property, and adjustments which may need to be made to the basis; the basic thrust of these rules is to determine the amount which the property owner has invested (in a tax sense) in the property. Thus, gain realized from the disposition of property is the excess of the amount realized over the adjusted basis of the property. [IRC § 1001(a).] *Gain = AR - AB*

a. Basis

i. Introduction

The basis of an item of property is the amount which a taxpayer has invested, in a tax sense, in the property. A taxpayer's basis in an item of property is determined initially upon acquiring the property, and may be adjusted as a consequence of subsequent events. The *adjusted basis* of an item of property is used to calculate several important tax consequences with respect to the property, including the amount of depreciation deductions which may be allowed and the amount of a loss deduction allowable if the property is stolen or destroyed.

ii. Cost basis

The Code contains several rules for determining the basis of property prior to making any required adjustments. The first statutory rule is that "[t]he basis of property shall be the cost of such property . . .." [IRC § 1012.] If property is purchased for cash, it is clear that the "cost basis" of the property is the amount which was paid. [See Reg. § 1.1012–1(a).] However, property may be acquired in transactions other than a cash purchase, and still have a cost basis. The costs of acquiring property, such as sales commissions which are paid by the purchasers are properly included in the property's cost basis, even though such amounts are not paid to the seller.

Example: Kathy purchases a parcel of unimproved real property for $10,000 cash; the cost basis of the property is $10,000. If Kathy pays a real estate agent a commission of $200 for finding the land, in addition to $10,000 which Kathy pays to the seller of the land, her cost basis for the land is $10,200.

a. Deferred payment

The cost basis of property is generally determined at the time the property is acquired, based upon the amount the party acquiring the property pays at the time of acquisition, or agrees to pay in the future (not including interest). This rule is based on the assumption that the purchaser will ultimately pay the full purchase price agreed upon; if the seller later agrees to accept a lesser amount, the cost basis of the property is reduced. [See discussion, II. C. 5. b. i., at page 57, *infra.*]

Example: Lance purchases a desk. Lance's cost basis for the desk is $1,000 if (i) he pays the seller $1,000 cash, or (ii) he borrows $800 from a bank and transfers the loan proceeds plus $200 of his own cash to the seller, or (iii) he pays the seller $200 cash and agrees to pay the seller the remaining $800 in equal monthly installments (plus interest) over the next 2 years. If Lance purchases the desk under the terms of (iii), and subsequently the seller agrees to accept $700 in full payment for the desk, Lance's cost basis for the desk is reduced to $900.

b. Exchanges

Property is often acquired for consideration other than money (cash) or its equivalent (such as a check) such as when one item of property is exchanged for another item of property. In determining the cost basis of property received in an exchange, it seems logical to look at the fair market value of the property which is given up in the exchange. However, in an exchange of two items of property, there are tax consequences with respect to *both* items of property involved. With regard to the property which is given up, it has an adjusted basis to the transferor, and thus there will be gain or loss depending on what the "amount realized" is in the exchange. The amount realized for the property which is given up is the fair market value of the property received. [IRC § 1001(b); see discussion, II. B. 2. b., at page 37, *infra.*] In the exchange, it is necessary to determine both the proper cost basis of the property received, and the tax consequences of the property given up at the same time. Because it is the fair market value of the property *received* in an exchange which determines the amount realized with regard to the property given up, it is appropriate in an income tax context to determine the "cost" of property received in a taxable exchange to be the fair market value of the property *received,* rather than the fair market value of the property given up. [*Philadelphia Park Amusement Co. v. U.S.,* 125 F.Supp. 184 (Ct.Cl. 1954).] Note the above rules become significant only if the properties exchanged have different values; if, as is usually the case, they have equal values the above issue does not arise.

Example: Mary purchases an automobile from Ned for her personal use which has a sticker price of $15,000, but instead of paying that amount, she exchanges her truck, which has a fair market value of $15,000, and an adjusted basis to her of $10,000. Mary's cost basis for the automobile received in the exchange is

[Handwritten margin notes:]

(B)

M
AB 10 Truck
AR 15
G +5

Auto
AB 15
AR

N   Auto
AB 15
AR 14
G -1   Truck
AB 15
AR

$15,000, the fair market value of the property received in the exchange. [In addition, Mary has a realized gain of $5,000 ($15,000 – $10,000) with respect to her truck.] *(B)* If Mary made a good deal and her truck was worth only $14,000 but the automobile was worth $15,000, (her gain is still $5,000) and the cost basis of the automobile is still $15,000, while Ned has an amount realized and a cost basis of $14,000 for the truck. *(limited to lower of 2 Amts to prevent loss?)*

There are some situations in which an exchange might be entitled to special treatment (nonrecognition of gain) and different rules apply to determine the basis of property acquired in such transactions. [See discussion, IV. D., at page 214, *infra.*]

c.   **"Tax cost" basis**
A person may receive property without transferring cash or other property to the transferor, and yet receipt of the property results in tax consequences to the transferee. The cost basis of the property received is its fair market value.

> ***Example:*** Duberstein performs services for his employer, and his compensation includes $25,000 cash and a motorcycle worth $4,000. Duberstein's gross income includes the fair market value of the motorcycle. Because the motorcycle is included in his gross income at its fair market value of $4,000, he has a "tax cost" basis in the motorcycle of $4,000. [See Reg. § 1.61–2(d)(2).] Note that if Duberstein were not allowed the $4,000 basis and he immediately sold the motorcycle, he would have $4,000 gain on the sale and he would in effect be taxed twice on the $4,000 amount.

iii.   **Property acquired from a decedent**
The basis of property acquired from a decedent is generally the fair market value of the property as of the date of the decedent's death. (IRC § 1014.) Because the date-of-death fair market value of property is often higher than its adjusted basis just prior to the decedent's death, it is common to refer to such property as receiving a "stepped-up basis." The effect of this rule permits the appreciation in the value of property which occurs during the life of a decedent to totally escape income tax.

[Handwritten margin note: Good explanation]

> ***Example:*** Olivia bought a parcel of real estate 50 years ago for $2,000, and on the date she died it was worth $1,002,000. Peter, Olivia's son, receives the property by devise under

her will; his basis for the property is $1,002,000. If Peter immediately sells the land for $1,002,000, he does not realize any gain.

a.   **General fair market value rule**
     The general rule for determining the basis of property acquired from a decedent is to use the fair market value as of the date of the decedent's death. This basis rule parallels the general rule of the estate tax for determining the value of property which is included in a decedent's gross estate. [IRC § 2031.]

b.   **Exceptions**
     The estate tax authorizes some exceptions to the general rule, and if one of those exceptions has been used in computing the decedent's estate tax, generally the income tax basis rule follows suit. Similarly, the estate tax law permits special valuation methods to be used for certain qualified real property; if a special valuation method is used in computing the estate tax, that value must be used to determine the income tax basis of the property. [IRC §§ 1014(a), 2032, and 2032A.]

     Example: The real property which Olivia owned in the previous Example is worth $1,002,000 on the date of her death, and $1,100,000 6 months later. The $1,100,000 value on the "alternate valuation date" is used in computing Olivia's Federal estate tax. [See IRC § 2032.] Peter's adjusted basis for the property is also $1,100,000. [IRC § 1014(a)(2).]

c.   **Test of estate inclusion**
     Property is generally considered to be "acquired from a decedent" for purposes of IRC § 1014 if the property is includible in the decedent's gross estate for purposes of the estate tax. [IRC § 1014(b).] Under the estate tax rules, an item of property may be transferred during an individual's life under circumstances which require the value of the property to be included in his gross estate when he dies. The basis rules of IRC § 1014 will apply, unless the recipient has sold or otherwise disposed of the property before the decedent's death.

     Example: Robin gives Blackacre to her son, Stuart, but she retains a life estate. Robin dies and the value of Blackacre is included in her gross estate. [See IRC § 2036.] Stuart's adjusted basis for Blackacre is its fair market value as of the date of Robin's death.

However, if 4 years prior to Robin's death, Stuart had sold his remainder interest in Blackacre, he would have used a basis determined under IRC § 1015 to compute the amount of his realized gain or loss on the sale.

d.   Special community property rule

Only one-half of community property is included in a deceased spouse's gross estate, thereby receiving a date-of-death fair market value basis. However, IRC § 1014(b)(6) treats the surviving spouse's remaining one-half share in such community property as if it was also "acquired from a decedent," thus effectively permitting the surviving spouse to have a date-of-death fair market value basis in her one-half of the property.

Example: Stella and Ted were husband and wife, owning 100 shares of stock in XYZ Coronation as community property. Stella dies leaving her 50 shares to their son when the 100 shares of stock has a fair market value of $10,000. Both Son and Ted have a $5,000 basis for their 50 shares of stock.

e.   Section 1014(e) denial of stepped-up basis

The "stepped-up basis" rule presented an opportunity for abuse by family members or friends, one of whom was aged or ill and expected to die in the near future, and another who held appreciated property. If appreciated property was given to the ill individual, who would then bequeath it back to the donor, the property would return to the hands of the initial donor with a stepped-up basis. Alternatively, the property might be sold by the estate of the donee/decedent (producing little or no gain because of the estate's stepped-up basis) with the will providing for the proceeds to be paid to the initial donor. IRC § 1014(e) was enacted to stem this abuse. Appreciated property will not receive a stepped-up basis if it is acquired by gift by a decedent within one year of his death and if it passes back to the initial donor or the donor's spouse. Instead, the property will take a transferred basis, equal to the donor's basis in the property prior to the gift to the decedent. [See IRC § 1015 and discussion below.]

Example: Donor gives some land with a basis of $5,000 and worth $10,000 to his sick mother who dies 9 months later and wills it to him. Donor's basis in the land is $5,000.

iv.   Property acquired by gift

A donor does not have any realized gain when he transfers property by gift.   In addition, a statutory exclusion provides that gross income does not include the value of property received as a gift by a donee.   [IRC § 102(a); see discussion, II. C. 2., at page 47, *infra*.] However, the donee is generally treated as stepping into the shoes of the donor with respect to the gift property and in doing so the adjusted basis of property acquired by the gift is the same in the hands of the donee as it was in the hands of the donor.   [IRC § 1015(a).]   Property acquired by gift is referred to as having a "transferred basis."   [IRC § 7701(a)(43).]

> *Example:*   Diane gives Ernie property which has a fair market value of $120 and an adjusted basis to Diane of $100.   One year later, Ernie sells the property for $150.   In computing Ernie's gain on the sale, Ernie has an adjusted basis for the property of $100; thus the amount of his realized gain is $50 ($150 amount realized − $100 adjusted basis).

a.)   Exception

The general rule does not apply if, (1) the donor's adjusted basis in the property is *greater than* the fair market value of the property, both amounts computed as of the date of the gift, *and* (2) the donee sells or otherwise disposes of the property in a transaction which would produce a *loss*.   If the exception applies, the property's basis (prior to any adjustments which might be necessary because of events which have transpired while the property was in the hands of the donee) is its *date-of-gift fair market value*.   [IRC § 1015(a), first sentence, "except clause."] This exception prevents one person who holds loss property from effectively transferring (i.e., assigning) that loss deduction to someone else.   The exception to the transferred basis rule produces a curious result if a donee disposes of gift property for an amount somewhere between the donor's adjusted basis and the date-of-gift fair market value.   In such a situation, the donee has neither any gain, nor any loss.

> *Examples:*   Diane gives Ernie property which has an adjusted basis to Diane of $100, but a fair market value of only $80.   One year later, Ernie sells the property for $50 cash.   In computing the *loss* (defined by IRC § 1001(a) as "the *excess* of the adjusted basis . . . over the amount realized") on the sale, Ernie has an adjusted basis for the property of $80, and thus the amount of the loss is $30 ($80 − $50).

Alternatively, Ernie sells the gift property for $90, which is the "amount realized." The adjusted basis for determining *gain*, under the general rule, is $100 (the donor's adjusted basis); however, there is not any *excess* amount realized over the adjusted basis, and thus there is no gain. The adjusted basis for determining *loss*, under the exception to the general rule, is $80 (date-of-gift fair market value); however, there is not any *excess* adjusted basis over the amount realized ($90), and thus there is no loss. [See IRC § 1001(a).] Hence, Ernie has neither gain nor loss on a sale at a price between $80 and $100 [Reg. § 1.1015–1(a)(2) Example.]

b. Effect of gift tax

The basis of gift property may be modified if a *gift tax* is incurred on the transfer. The basis rule of IRC § 1015 is confined to property which is received under the income tax concept of a "gift," and even though the gift tax concept differs from the income tax concept, many transfers will be a "gift" under *both* the income tax and the gift tax. [See discussion, II. C. 2., at page 47, *infra*.] A donor may incur a transaction cost, in the form of a gift tax, upon making a gift of property to a donee. Historically, this transaction cost was reflected in the basis of gift property by increasing the property's basis (up to the date-of-gift fair market value of the property) by the full amount of gift tax paid on the transfer. [IRC § 1015(d)(1).] In 1976, the rule was changed on the theory that the gift tax basis adjustment is appropriate only *to the extent* that both the gift tax and the income tax are imposed on the same portion of the economic value of the property. The gift tax disregards the donor's adjusted basis in gift property and is computed, generally, with regard to the property's fair market value. The income tax is imposed only on gain, the excess of the amount realized (generally, the property's fair market value) over its adjusted basis. Thus, it is only to the extent that a gift tax is imposed on the excess of the date-of-gift fair market value of the property over the donor's adjusted basis that the two taxes overlap. This difference is defined as the "net appreciation in the value of the gift," and the basis of gift property may be increased only by the amount of the gift tax which is attributable to the net appreciation. [IRC § 1015(d)(6).]

Example: Fred gives Geraldine property which has an adjusted basis to Fred of $150 and a fair market value of $200, and the transfer results in a gift tax to Fred of

$20. Under the post-1976 rule, Geraldine's transferred basis of $150 is increased by only $5, the amount of the gift tax ($20) multiplied by the ratio of the net appreciation in the value of the property $200 – 150 = $50) over the amount of the gift ($200). If Fred's basis in the property were $200 Geraldine's IRC § 1015(a) basis would be $200; however, since there is no appreciation on the property Geraldine gets no increase in basis even though Fred pays $20 of gift tax.

c. Part gift-part sale—in general

If the transfer of property is in part a gift and in part a sale, rules provided in the regulations work to the benefit of the transferor-donor if property has appreciated, but not if it has declined in value. First, the transferor-donor recognizes gain only to the extent that her amount realized on the sale exceeds her total adjusted basis in the property. [Reg. § 1.1001–1(e).] However, the transferee-donee takes the property with a basis equal to the *larger* of: (1) the amount the transferee pays for the property, or (2) the amount of the transferor's basis in the property. [Reg. § 1.1015–4(a).] The transferee's basis may be further adjusted on account of gift tax incurred on the transfer, if any. [See discussion, II. B. 2. a. iv. *b.*, at page 30, *supra.*] If the transferee is determining a loss upon a later disposition of the property, its unadjusted basis is also limited to the date-of-gift fair market value of the property. [See discussion, II. B. 2. a. iv., at page 29, *supra.*]

Examples: Heather transfers property, which has an adjusted basis to her of $20,000 and a fair market value of $60,000, to her son, Irving, for $30,000. Heather has a gain of $10,000 and Irving has a basis for the property of $30,000.

If the property had an adjusted basis to Heather of $40,000 (instead of $20,000), she will not have a loss, and Irving takes the property with a basis of $40,000.

If the property had an adjusted basis to Heather of $90,000 (instead of $20,000), she will not have a loss; Irving takes the property with a basis for determining a gain of $90,000, and a basis for determining a loss of $60,000. [Reg. § 1.1015–4(b) Example (4).]

d.   Bargain sale to charitable organization

Generally, if property is transferred for consideration equal to the property's adjusted basis there will be no realized gain or loss. Further, if property is transferred to a charitable organization, the transferor is generally entitled to a deduction equal to the fair market value of the property less any consideration received for the property. [IRC § 170; see discussion, III. B. 6., at page 140, *infra*.] The combination of these two general rules would permit property to be transferred to a charitable organization in return for consideration up to the amount of the transferor's adjusted basis in the property without the transferor realizing any gain on the transaction, but receiving the benefit of a charitable deduction on the excess. In addition, the unrealized appreciation might never be taxed, because the transferee is an exempt organization. For example, without IRC § 1011(b), if property with a basis of $10,000 and a fair market value of $30,000 was sold to a charitable organization for $10,000, the seller would have had her initial investment of $10,000 returned to her, she would have had no gain on the transfer, and she would have been entitled to a charitable deduction of $20,000.

IRC § 1011(b) requires the transferor in a bargain sale of property to a charitable organization to apportion the basis of the property between the "sale" and the "gift" portions of the transaction. The adjusted basis for purposes of determining gain is computed by multiplying the entire adjusted basis of the property by a fraction, the numerator is the amount realized and the denominator is the property's fair market value. The effect of this rule is to bifurcate the transaction, treating the taxpayer as if he had disposed of the property in two separate transactions, one a sale and the other a charitable contribution.

Example: Joyce sells property with an adjusted basis of $10,000 and a fair market value of $30,000 to a charitable organization for $10,000 cash. Joyce must apportion her basis between the sale and gift elements of the transaction; $3,333 of her basis of $10,000 [$10,000 × ($10,000 amount realized/$30,000 fair market value)] will be apportioned to the sale element of the transaction. Joyce will realize a gain of $6,667 ($10,000 amount realized less $3,333 adjusted basis). The gift portion of the property will carry with it the remaining $6,667 adjusted basis of the property. Note that the adjusted basis of the gift portion of the property may be significant in determining the amount of the charitable deduction allowable. [See discussion, III. B. 6. c., at page 142, *infra.*]

v. Property acquired from a spouse

When property is transferred from an individual to her spouse (or to her former spouse, if the property is transferred incident to their divorce), the property is treated as received by the transferee as a gift, and its value is thereby excluded from his gross income. [IRC § 1041(b)(1) see further discussion, V. C. 3., at page 265, *infra.*] The adjusted basis of such property in the hands of the recipient is the same as the transferor's adjusted basis. [IRC § 1041(b)(2).] This special rule applies for transfers of property between spouses (or former spouses); the "gift" basis rules of IRC § 1015 do not apply. [IRC § 1015(e).]

> *Example:* Ramsey transfers property which has an adjusted basis of $100 and a fair market value of $80 to his wife, Stacey. Stacey takes the property with a basis of $100 under IRC § 1041(b)(2). If she later sells the property for $90, she has a loss of $10.

vi. Adjustments to basis

The adjusted basis for determining the gain or loss upon the disposition of property is the property's basis determined under the appropriate provisions of IRC §§ 1012–1015, adjusted as provided by IRC § 1016. [IRC § 1011(a).] In general, adjustments called for under IRC § 1016 are necessary in order to accurately measure the amount of the property owner's investment, in a tax sense, in the property. Therefore, property's basis is increased in the amount of any capital additions to the property and decreased in the amount of any deductions which have been taken reflecting a return to the taxpayer of his investment in the property.

a. Increases

The basis of property is increased by the amount of capital expenditures, such as the cost of capital improvements made to the property.

> *Example:* Kent purchased a lot and a house 2 years ago for $100,000. Last year, he had a swimming pool installed in the back yard at a cost of $15,000, and a garage built at a cost of $10,000. Kent's adjusted basis for the property is $125,000. [See Reg. § 1.1016–2(b) Example.]

b.   Reductions

The amount of the reduction in basis on account of deductions for depreciation, amortization or depletion is the greater of the amount "allowed" (taken) or the amount "allowable" (could have been taken). [IRC § 1016(a)(2).] The basis of property must be reduced by the amount such a deduction was "allowable," even though no deduction was actually taken, in order to discourage taxpayers from taking depreciation deductions only in taxable years in which it is advantageous for them to do so. The effect of the "allowable" basis reduction rule is to force the taxpayer to take the depreciation deduction in each taxable year the property qualifies for the deduction. [See discussion, III. A. 5. a. v., at page 110, *infra.*]

Alternatively, the basis of property must be reduced to the extent such a deduction was "allowed" and resulted in a reduction in the taxpayer's income tax. A deduction is "allowed" if it was claimed on the taxpayer's return, and it was not challenged by the IRS. [*Virginian Hotel Corp. v. Helvering,* 319 U.S. 523, 63 S.Ct. 1260 (1943).]. The "tax benefit" element requires a reduction in the property's basis only when the taxpayer has had an *effective* return of his investment, in a tax sense. [IRC § 1016(a)(2)(B); see Reg. § 1.1016–3(e).]

vii. Allocation of basis

When an item of property is acquired, the appropriate basis rule is generally applied to determine the basis of the entire property; however, later transactions may make it necessary to allocate the entire basis between component parts of the property.

Example: Laura purchases a 640 acre section of farmland for $1,280,000 cash, and later sells 64 acres of it for $300,000 cash. The $1,280,000 cost basis is allocated according to the relative fair market values, determined as of the date of acquisition, of the components of the property. If all of the land in the section was equal in value at the time of acquisition, then $^{64}/_{640}$, or 10%, of the total cost basis, or $128,000 (10% of $1,280,000) is allocated to the portion being sold, resulting in a gain of $172,000 ($300,000 – 128,000) to Laura. If the parcel being sold is located on a lake, however, it would have had a greater fair market value at acquisition than the balance of the section, resulting in the allocation of, perhaps, 20% of the total cost basis to it, or $256,000 (20% of $1,280,000). Laura would thus have a gain of $44,000 ($300,000 – 256,000).

Similarly, if land and a building is purchased for use in a trade or business for a lump sum, the total purchase price must be allocated between the land and the building for purposes of computing the proper depreciation deductions for the building. [See discussion, III. A. 5., at page 104, *infra.*]

In most situations it will be possible to determine the relative fair market values of components of an item or parcel of property, and the various associated property rights, and thus an allocation of basis will have to be made if a portion of the property or property rights is sold. If an easement over real property is sold, however, it may be impossible to determine precisely what portion of the property is being sold, and thus impossible to make a proper allocation of basis. In such a case, the taxpayer may be permitted to treat the entire amount received for the easement as a recovery of capital, up to the amount of the entire basis, and the basis of the property must be reduced by a like amount. [See *Inaja Land Co. v. Comm'r*, 9 T.C. 727 (1947), and discussion, IV. B. 3. d. iii., at page 211, *infra.*]

viii. Uniform basis rule

The basis of property acquired by gift or bequest must be uniform, or the same, in the hands of various persons who might have legal title to the property from time to time. Thus, if property is held by a decedent, and title initially passes to the personal representative, and later to a trustee, before finally vesting in a beneficiary, the beneficiary ultimately takes the property with a date-of-death fair market value basis, appropriately adjusted for any intervening events. [Regs. §§ 1.1014–4 and 1.1015–1(b).]

Property acquired by gift or bequest has a uniform basis even though several interests may have been created in the property. If one of the interests is disposed of, the uniform basis of the entire property is apportioned between the interest disposed of and the balance of the property determined *as of the date of the disposition.*

Example: Linda dies and devises a building used in her trade or business to Mike for 10 years, remainder to Nancy; the building has a date-of-death fair market value of $1 million. Mike and Nancy *together* take the property with a basis of $1 million. [IRC § 1014.] Ten years later, Nancy will take the property with a basis of $1 million, adjusted for depreciation deductions and other events which have occurred during the intervening 10 years. However, if 3 years after Linda dies, Nancy sells her remainder interest, her adjusted basis for determining gain or loss is her proportion, determined as of the date of sale, of the property's uniform basis. Viewed from another perspective, Nancy has an adjusted basis for her remainder interest equal to the entire uniform basis less the proportionate value of Mike's term interest, which still has 7 years to run. A 7 year term interest has a present value of roughly 50% of the total value of the property. [See Regs. §§ 1.1014–5 and 20.2031–7(f) Table B.] Thus, if no adjustments have been made to the uniform basis (*e.g.,* for depreciation deductions), Nancy has an adjusted basis of $500,000 (50% of $1 million) when she sells her remainder interest at the end of Year Three.

There is an exception to the rule for apportioning the uniform basis of property acquired by gift or bequest if a "term interest" (life estate, term of years, or income interest in a trust) in property is disposed of. [IRC § 1001(e).] In such situations, the portion of the uniform basis apportioned to the term interest is disregarded, with the result that the person disposing of such an interest has gain in the full amount of the amount realized. This rule is necessary to prevent property from having "too much basis" involved in various transactions. This exception does not apply if both interests are simultaneously transferred (because in this situation there is no duplicate use of the same basis). [IRC § 1001(e)(2).]

Example: If Mike, in the preceding Example, sells his term interest to Ophelia for $600,000, he has $600,000 gain. If he was able to offset the amount realized by 50% of the uniform basis ($500,000) in computing his gain, the uniform basis rule would still permit Nancy, the remainderman, to take the property with 100% of the uniform basis ($1 million) when the term interest ends after 10 years. Under the exception if both Mike and Nancy sold their interests to Ophelia at the time of the preceding Example, each would be able to use $500,000 of basis and Mike would have only a $100,000 gain.

ix. **Personal-use property converted to business-use**
Property which is used in a trade or business, or held for the production of income, may qualify for deductions for depreciation or losses, while property which is used for personal purposes does not qualify for such deductions. [See discussion, III. A. 3. and 5., at pages 96 and 104, *infra.*] If property is purchased initially for personal use, and is subsequently converted to use in a trade or business, or held for the production of income, the basis of the property for computing depreciation or loss deductions is the lower of its cost basis or the date-of-conversion fair market value. [Reg. §§ 1.167(g)–1, 1.165–9(b)(2).]

This rule requires the depreciation and loss deductions to be limited to the value of the property which is used in profit-seeking endeavors, if the date-of-conversion fair market value is lower than the taxpayer's adjusted basis in the property. Failure to provide this rule would result in a deduction (through depreciation or loss deductions) for the decline in value during the time the property was held for personal use.

> *Example:* Paul purchases an automobile for $15,000 and uses it for personal purposes. One year later, when the fair market value of the automobile has dropped to $10,000, he begins using it exclusively in his business. Because the automobile was not subject to depreciation deductions while it was used for personal purposes, the adjusted basis of the automobile as of the date of conversion to business use remains $15,000, its cost basis. Nonetheless, the basis used to compute depreciation deductions after the automobile begins being used for business purposes is $10,000, its date-of-conversion fair market value.

b. Amount realized

Income in the nature of gain derived from the disposition of property is the excess of the amount realized over the property's adjusted basis. [IRC § 1001(a).] In general terms, the amount realized is the consideration received for the property; it includes the sum of any money plus the fair market value of any other property received in the transaction. [IRC § 1001(b).]

i. Fair market value of consideration received

The fair market value of property received as consideration for the sale or other disposition of property is included in the amount realized. The determination of the fair market value of an item of property is a question of fact, involving a search for "the price at which the property would change hands between a willing buyer and a willing seller, neither being under any compulsion to buy or to sell and both having reasonable knowledge of relevant facts." [Reg. § 20.2031–1(b).] If the value of property received in a taxable exchange cannot be determined directly, it is presumed to be equal to the value of the property given up in the exchange. [See *Philadelphia Park Amusement Co. v. U.S.*, 130 Ct.Cl. 166, 126 F.Supp. 184 (1954).] Only in rare and unusual circumstances, however, will it not be possible to ascertain the fair market value of property and thus compute an amount realized. [Reg. § 1.1001–1(a); see discussion, IV. B. 3. e. iii., at page 211, *infra.*]

The amount realized includes the receipt of services and other economic benefits, including being relieved of a liability. [See *Crane v. Comm'r,* 331 U.S. 1, 67 S.Ct. 1047 (1947).]

Example: Steve bought a truck several years ago, borrowing part of the purchase price from a finance company. Today, he transfers the truck to Tina, who is a dentist. In addition to paying Steve $3,000 cash, Tina repairs Steve's bridgework (a service for which she would normally charge $200), and she assumes Steve's remaining $1,500 debt to the finance company. Steve's amount realized on the sale of the truck is $4,700.

ii. Selling expenses

Commissions, and other expenses connected with the disposition of property which are incurred by a non-dealer seller reduce the amount realized. Generally, the type of expenditures which reduce the amount realized, if paid by the seller, are the same expenditures which would be included in the cost basis of property if paid by the purchaser. [See discussion, II. B. 2. a., at page 24, *supra.*] Examples of such expenditures include appraisal fees, fees for abstracts of title, brokerage fees, legal fees, recording fees, title insurance, title opinions and transfer taxes. It should be emphasized that the proper treatment of selling expenses is to reduce the amount realized; *they are not deductions.* The significance of this treatment, and the tax consequences flowing from it, become clearer after one understands the treatment accorded capital gains and capital losses. [See discussion VI. B. 1., at page 270, *infra.*]

Example: Ursula sells property, which has an adjusted basis of $5,000, to Victor for $10,000 cash and Ursula pays a sales commission of $1,000. Ursula has an amount realized of $9,000 and a gain of $4,000 ($9,000 amount realized over $5,000 adjusted basis); she does *not* have an amount realized of $10,000, a gain of $5,000, and a deduction of $1,000.

iii. Allocation

If several items of property are sold for one lump sum, the purchase price must be allocated among the various items being sold so that the amount of gain or loss with respect to each item may be computed. A lump sum purchase price is generally allocated according to the relative fair market values of the items of property being sold.

Example: Willeane sells her business, a sole proprietorship, for a lump sum. The sale of a sole proprietorship is not the sale of a single asset, but is the sale of each of the component parts of the business, including fixtures, accounts receivable, trucks, inventory, and goodwill. It is necessary, therefore, to compute the amount and character (capital or ordinary) of gain or loss with respect to each item. [*Williams v. McGowan*, 152 F.2d 570 (2d Cir.1945).] If in addition to selling the assets of her business, Willeane enters into a covenant not to compete with the buyer in the same line of business in the same state for a period of five years for a payment of $5,000, this additional sum is ordinary income to Willeane as income from services (and the buyer may deduct the $5,000 over five years, the identifiable life of the covenant).

iv.   Mixed motive transactions

Generally, if consideration received when property is sold is greater than (or less than) the fair market value of the property, the discrepancy is disregarded. It is assumed that the buyer and seller negotiate at arm's length, and that the tax consequences should not be altered if the seller (or the buyer) is the better negotiator and thus receives more (or less) than the property is worth. If the facts indicate that a portion of the payment is being made for purposes other than the sale of the property, however, such amount will not be included in the amount realized for the disposition of the property.

Example: Xenos agrees to sell a machine worth $8,000 for $10,000, and as part of the contract, he agrees to keep the machine in good repair for a period of 3 years. Only $8,000 of the purchase price is allocated to the amount realized for the machine, while the remaining $2,000 is compensation for the services which Xenos has agreed to perform.

Conversely, property may be transferred for a purchase price less than its fair market value. Facts surrounding the transaction may have to be examined to determine the nature and tax consequences of the transaction. For example we have already seen a part gift, part sale. [See discussion II. B. 2. a. iv. *c.*, at page 31, *supra.*] In addition assume an employer makes a "bargain sale" to an employee of property not normally sold to customers. Here it is likely that the seller is transferring a portion of the value of the property to compensate the buyer for services rendered by the buyer. In such situations, the value of the services is included in the seller's amount realized; the seller's total amount realized is the fair market value of his property. Note that the value of the property, less consideration paid, is also included in the gross income (as compensation) of the buyer.

Example: X Corporation, which is in the restaurant business, sells a personal computer to Yuri, one of its employees, for $1,250 cash. The computer has an adjusted basis to X Corporation of $1,000 and a fair market value of $3,000. Surrounding facts make it clear that X Corporation is selling the computer to Yuri at a bargain price as compensation for services Yuri has rendered to X Corporation. Yuri has compensation income of $1,750 ($3,000 – $1,250); this is not an excluded fringe benefit because this is not an employee discount related to qualified property. [See IRC § 132(c)(4) and discussion, II. B. 1. e. iii., at page 20, *supra.*] X Corporation has an amount realized of $3,000 ($1,250 + $1,750 value of Yuri's services) and a gain of $2,000 ($3,000 – $1,000).

v. Role of liabilities

If property which is encumbered by a liability is sold or otherwise disposed of and the liability is either assumed by the buyer (personal liability) or the property is taken subject to the liability (nonrecourse liability), the amount of the liability is included in the seller's amount realized. If a taxpayer borrows money and mortgages property which he owns as security for the loan, he does not have gain or gross income because borrowing is not a taxable event as there is no accession to wealth. [See discussion, II. A. 2. b. i., at page 16, *supra.*]

Example: Zachary owns a parcel of real property which has an adjusted basis of $5,000 and a fair market value of $20,000 when he borrows $10,000, mortgaging the property as security for the debt. Zachary does not have gain or gross income because he does not have any accession to wealth (he must repay the loan). [*Woodsam Associates, Inc. v. Comm'r*, 198 F.2d 357 (2d Cir.1952).] Several years later after no repayment of principal on the loan Zachary transfers the property to Alice for $25,000 cash in addition to her agreement to assume the $10,000 mortgage. Zachary's amount realized is $35,000. The result would be the same if Alice merely took the property subject to the mortgage, rather than assuming it. [*Crane v. Comm'r*, 331 U.S. 1, 67 S.Ct. 1047 (1947).] Alternatively, if the property had a fair market value of $9,000 but it was encumbered by a mortgage of $10,000, and Zachary transferred it to Alice subject to the mortgage, Zachary's amount realized is still $10,000. [*Comm'r v. Tufts,* 461 U.S. 300, 103 S.Ct. 1826 (1983).]

c. Realized gain (loss) vs. recognized gain (loss)

The entire amount of a realized gain or loss is required to be recognized, unless a specific provision provides otherwise. [IRC § 1001(c).] If a realized gain is recognized, it is included as an item of gross income. We'll consider this later, but a realized loss, even if it is a recognized loss, must find statutory authority before it may be deducted in computing taxable income. [See discussion, III. A. 3., at page 96, *infra.*] Further, in some situations a loss may be realized and recognized, but a deduction for the loss may be disallowed. [*E.g.,* IRC § 267(a)(1); see discussion, III. C. 5. c. at page 160, *infra.*] All or a portion of a realized gain or loss may be entitled to non-recognition under certain circumstances. [See discussion, IV. D., at page 214, *infra.*]

3. ITEMS SPECIFICALLY INCLUDED IN GROSS INCOME BY STATUTE   *irreg of whether they're comp or gifts, etc*

Congress has not left questions of what should be included in gross income to be answered exclusively by the I.R.S. and the courts; there are a few situations where Congress has specifically provided that certain economic benefits must be included in gross income. These provisions were enacted to clarify the law, to make the law uniform, or to set the stage for permitting some exclusion from gross income.

a. Prizes and awards
i. In general

Gross income includes amounts received as prizes or awards. [IRC § 74(a).] If the prize or award is made in goods or services, the fair market value of the goods or services is included in gross income. This provision effectively precludes the recipient from asserting that a prize or an award is a "gift" excludable from gross income under IRC § 102. The line as to whether an economic benefit is a prize, and thus included in gross income, can generally be drawn by asking *TEST* whether the employee could refuse the benefit.

> *Example:* The fair market value of a color television set awarded to a contestant in a television game show is included in the recipient's gross income. Similarly, the fair market value of an automobile awarded to an exceptional baseball player is included in his gross income. [*Wills v. Comm'r.,* 411 F.2d 537 (9th Cir.1969).] However, the value of a trip to Hawaii which an employee is required to make for bona fide business reasons is not a prize merely because he is selected at random from among co-workers of equal status to take the trip which was primarily for the

employer's benefit. [*Allen J. McDonell*, 26 T.C.M. 115 (1967).]

ii.   Exceptions
    a.   Qualified Scholarships

An amount which is a qualified scholarship and is excluded from gross income under IRC § 117 remains excluded even if it is received as a prize or an award. [See discussion, II. C. 6., at page 59, *infra.*]

> ***Example:*** Deborah wins a beauty contest and receives a fur coat with a fair market value of $2,000, and a $10,000 scholarship. The $2,000 value of the coat is included in her gross income; the $10,000 value of the scholarship is excluded from her gross income under IRC § 117 and is not required to be included under IRC § 74. [*Wilson v. U.S.*, 322 F.Supp. 830 (D.Kan. 1971).]

    b.   Prizes and awards transferred to charities $74(b)

A prize or an award is *excluded* from gross income if it is made primarily in recognition of religious, charitable, scientific, educational, artistic, literary or civic achievement, and it is transferred directly by the payor to a charity or governmental unit designated by the recipient without any possession or use by the recipient. [IRC § 74(a).] The exclusion does not apply to an award made in recognition of athletic achievement. [*Hornung v. Comm'r*, 47 T.C. 428 (1967).] Further, the exclusion applies only if the recipient is selected without any action on her part to enter the contest and if she is not required to render substantial future services as a condition to receiving the prize or award. If a qualifying assignment is made and the prize or award is excluded from the winner's gross income, no charitable contribution deduction is allowed.

> ***Example:*** An amount received as a Pulitzer prize or a Nobel prize is excluded from gross income if a qualifying assignment is made to a charitable organization or governmental unit, even though the recipient is expected to make a speech at the award ceremonies. [Reg § 1.74–1(b); Rev.Rul. 58–89, 1958–1 C.B. 40.]

    c.   Employee achievement awards

An employee achievement award is excluded from the recipient's gross income if the cost to the employer of providing the award (and all other awards during the taxable year) to that employee does not exceed certain dollar limits; the dollar limits are also the maximum amounts the employer may deduct in computing its taxable income. [IRC §§ 74(c) and 274(j).] An "employee achievement award" is an item of tangible personal property transferred as part of a meaningful presentation by an employer to an employee in recognition of length of service or safety achievement, but it does not include disguised compensation. [IRC § 274(j)(3)(A).]

b. Alimony and separate maintenance payments

Amounts received as alimony or separate maintenance payments are included in the gross income of the recipient spouse; a corresponding deduction is generally available to the paying spouse. [IRC §§ 71(a) and 215(a); see discussion, V. C. 1., at page 261, *infra*.]

c. Services of a child

Amounts received for services performed by a minor child are included in the gross income of the child, not her parents. [IRC § 73(a).] This rule applies even though the amounts are received by the parent, and even though state law makes the parent the legal owner of such amounts. Expenditures made by the parent which are attributable to amounts included in the child's gross income are deductible by the child. [IRC § 73(b); see discussion, V.A., at page 244, *infra.*]

d. Reimbursement for expenses of moving

Amounts received, as compensation for services, in payment for or reimbursement of expenses of moving from one residence to another are included in gross income. [IRC § 82.] The recipient, however, may be entitled to a deduction for the moving expenses for which he is being reimbursed. [IRC § 217, see discussion, III. B. 9., at page 152, *infra.*

Example: Elmer is required by his employer to move from Denver to San Diego. Elmer receives $500 cash from his employer to cover motels and food for himself and his family while they drive to San Diego, and he is reimbursed $1,000 for food and lodging expenses incurred in San Diego while they look for a new house. In addition, the employer pays a moving company $2,500 to move Elmer's household goods. Several months after Elmer makes the move, he sells his old house in Denver at a loss of $1,500 and his employer reimburses him for the loss. Elmer must include $5,500 ($500 + 1,000 + 2,500 + 1,500) in gross income. [See Reg. § 1.82–1(a).] Note that these amounts may also be deductible by Elmer. [IRC § 217, see discussion, III. B. 9., at page 152, *infra.* See also IRC §§ 63 and 67(b)(6).]

e. Transfer of appreciated property to a political organization

Gross income includes the gain which is deemed to arise under the circumstances described in IRC § 84. Under that section, if a taxpayer transfers property whose fair market value exceeds its adjusted basis (appreciated property) to a political organization, a sale of the property is deemed to take place, and the taxpayer is treated as having an amount realized equal to the fair market value of the property. [IRC § 84(a); see IRC § 527(e)(1). Compare the results of transfers to charitable organizations; see discussion, III. B. 6. c. ii., at page 143, *infra.*]

f. Social security payments

Although social security benefits are generally excluded from gross income, a *maximum* of one-half of such payments may be included in gross income. Social security benefits are subject to tax if, within a taxable year, the sum of the "modified adjusted gross income" plus one-half of the social security benefits received exceeds the recipient's "base amount." [IRC § 86(a) and (b).] A taxpayer's modified adjusted gross income for a taxable year is his adjusted gross income computed without reduction for certain exclusions relating to foreign activities, or for the two-earner married couple exclusion, and including interest received which is exempt from tax. [IRC § 86(b)(2).] The base amount is $25,000 for individuals, $32,000 for married taxpayers filing a joint return, and zero for a married taxpayer filing a separate return if he lived with his spouse for a portion of the year. [IRC § 86(c).] The amount required to be included in gross income is one-half of the smaller of the social security benefits received or the modified adjusted gross income less the base amount.

g. Unemployment compensation

Gross income includes amounts received under federal or state law as unemployment compensation. [IRC § 85.]

h. Annuities

Gross income includes amounts received as an annuity under an annuity, endowment or life insurance contract. [IRC § 72(a).] There is, however, an important exception which permits the recipient to exclude from gross income the portion of annuity payments received which is attributable to his cost of purchasing the annuity. [IRC § 72(b).] Annuities are related to timing of income and are therefore considered later in this Outline. [See discussion, IV. F. 1., at page 239, *infra.*]

C. ITEMS SPECIFICALLY EXCLUDED FROM GROSS INCOME BY STATUTE

In addition to specifying certain economic benefits which must be included in gross income, Congress has designated, for varying policy reasons, certain economic benefits which are excluded from gross income.

1. DEATH BENEFITS

IRC § 101 excludes from gross income two categories of death benefits: proceeds of life insurance, and amounts paid by an employer to a deceased employee's estate or beneficiaries.

a. Proceeds of life insurance

i. In general

Proceeds paid under a "life insurance contract," including amounts received as death benefits under workmen's compensation insurance contracts, endowment contracts, health and accident insurance contracts, or other contractual death benefit payments, are excluded from gross income. [IRC § 101(a)(1); Reg. § 1.101–1(a)(1).]

Insurance involves shifting the economic risk of the death of the insured. Thus, the exclusion does not apply to a contract providing for payment of a future annuity, but providing further that if the annuitant dies before the first annuity payment is due, his estate is to receive the greater of the premiums paid for the contract or its cash surrender value; the contract does not involve any risk with regard to the annuitant's death. [Rev.Rul. 55–313, 1955–1 C.B. 219; see discussion, IV. F. 1., at page 239, *infra.*]

Excludable benefits must be paid "by reason of the death of the insured." [IRC § 101(a)(1).] The exclusion is not applicable to payments made under an insurance policy for reasons *other than* the death of the insured, such as when the insured "cashes in" on the policy and receives its cash surrender value during her life, or when she elects to receive annuity payments or other lifetime benefits. Similarly, if a creditor is entitled to life insurance proceeds in satisfaction of the insured's obligation to the creditor (such as "credit-life insurance"), the proceeds are considered to be received in payment of the debt, not "by reason of" the insured's death, and thus the proceeds are not excludable. [Rev.Rul. 70–254, 1970–1 C.B. 31.]

ii. Installment payments of proceeds

Qualified insurance proceeds are excludable whether they are paid in a lump sum, or in several payments. [IRC § 101(a)(1).] The exclusion, however, is available only in the amount of the lump sum payable at the date of the insured's death, or, if payments are to be made in the future, the date-of-death present value of such future payments. If future payments are to be made, the excludable amount is computed as of the date of the insured's death, and prorated over the future payments. The effect of this rule is to exclude the principal amount payable at the death of the insured, but to require the beneficiary to be taxed on amounts earned by that principal sum.

Example: A life insurance policy gives the beneficiary, Charlotte, the choice of receiving a lump sum of $100,000 cash, or annual payments of $12,000 for 10 years. The maximum amount Charlotte may exclude is $100,000; if she elects to receive the annual payments, the $100,000 excludable amount is prorated over the 10 year period, or $10,000 to each year. For each $12,000 annual payment, Charlotte will exclude $10,000 from gross income, and she will include the remaining $2,000. The same result occurs if Charlotte elects to take an annuity for her life and she has a 10 year life expectancy. However, if she lives beyond 10 years the exclusion continues to apply. Compare the results if Charlotte had purchased an annuity, taxable under the rules of IRC § 72; see discussion at IV. F. 1., at page 239, *infra.*

An alternative rule applies if the insurance company retains all or part of the principal sum, and the beneficiary receives primarily interest earned on the principal sum. In such circumstances, the proration rule of IRC § 101(d) does not apply, and the interest payments are included in gross income in full. [IRC § 101(c).] The regulations provide that the question of whether a payment falls within IRC § 101(c) or (d) depends on whether there is a "substantial diminution of the principal amount during the period when such interest payments are being made . . . ." [Reg. § 1.101–3(a).]

iii. Transfer of policy for valuable consideration
    The general rule for excluding the proceeds of life insurance does not apply if the policy has been "transfer[red] for a valuable consideration . . . ." [IRC § 101(a)(2).]

Example: Donald pays a $5,000 premium for a $100,000 life insurance policy on his own life, and sells the policy to his sister, Ella, for $5,000. Ella may not exclude the $100,000 proceeds when Donald dies; she must include in her gross income the $100,000 less the $5,000 which she paid for the policy, and less the amount of any additional premiums she paid.

There are two exceptions to this exception: (1) if the transferee of the policy has a transferred basis in the policy; or (2) if the transferee is the insured, the insured's partner or a partnership in which the insured is a partner, or a corporation in which the insured is a shareholder or an officer. [IRC § 101(a)(2)(A), and (B).]

Example: On the facts of the preceding Example, the $100,000 insurance proceeds may be excluded if Donald sells the policy to a corporation of which he is the president. If Donald sells the policy to Ella and she, in turn, gives the policy to her son, Frank, the policy is tainted by the earlier transfer-for-value, and only $5,000 (plus any additional premiums paid by Ella or Frank) of the $100,000 proceeds is excludable by Frank when Donald dies. [Reg. § 1.101–1(b)(3), (5) Example (6).]

b.   Employees' death benefits

The estate or beneficiaries of an employee may exclude amounts paid by the employer by reason of the death of the employee, up to $5,000. [IRC § 101(b).] This provision effectively permits an exclusion, up to the $5,000 limit even though the former employer made a "gift."

An excludable amount must be "paid by reason of the death of the employee." Payment of an employee's accrued, but unpaid, back wages, bonuses, or payments for unused vacation or sick leave, therefore, is not excludable. [Reg. § 1.101–2(a)(2).] Self-employed individuals generally are not considered to be "employees" for purposes of this exclusion. [IRC § 101(b)(3).]

2.   GIFTS AND INHERITANCES

Amounts received as a gift, or by bequest, devise or inheritance, are excluded from gross income. [IRC § 102(a).] The exclusion does not apply, however, to *income from* the property received by gift or inheritance; nor does the exlusion apply to a gift or devise *of income* from property [IRC § 102(b)]; nor does it apply to a gift from an employer to an employee [IRC § 102(c)(1)].

Example: Gloria receives shares of stock of Xerox Corporation as a gift. The value of the shares are excluded from Gloria's gross income, but the amount of dividends she receives thereafter is included in her gross income. Alternatively, Harry gratuitously transfers shares of Ford Motor Company stock to a trust, providing that all income from the trust (the income interest) is to be paid to his daughter, Irene, for 10 years, and then the trust corpus (the remainder interest) is to be transferred to his son, Jack. Irene may not exclude the payments which she receives from the trust, but Jack may exclude the value of the corpus which he receives.

a. Gifts

IRC § 102(a) excludes from gross income the value of property "acquired by gift," but the Code does not define "gift," as that term is used in IRC § 102 (exclusion from gross income) and § 1015 (basis of property acquired by gift). The Supreme Court has declined to prescribe a definition of gift, or a test for determining whether a particular transfer is a gift, but the Court has concluded that a "gift" is made if the trier of fact determines that the dominant reason for the transfer (the transferor's intention) was "out of affection, respect, admiration, charity or like impulses," or from the transferor's "detached and disinterested generosity." [*Comm'r v. Duberstein*, 363 U.S. 278, 80 S.Ct. 1190 (1960).] When property is transferred to a spouse (or to a former spouse, if the transfer is incident to a divorce), however, there is no need to determine the transferor's motive; the property is treated as received by the transferee as a gift, and thus it is excluded from the transferee's gross income. [IRC § 1041(b)(1); see discussion, V. C. 3., at page 265, *infra*.]

For purposes of the *gift tax,* the transfer of property "for less than an adequate and full consideration in money or money's worth" is a gift. [IRC § 2512(b).] The gift tax definition of a gift, however, is not the same as the income tax concept of a gift. [See *Farid-Es-Sultaneh v. Comm'r,* 160 F.2d 812 (2d Cir.1947).]

The issue of whether the receipt of an economic benefit is an excludable gift arises most often when the recipient has performed some service for the transferor. "Tips" received by waiters, taxicab drivers, barbers and others in similar occupations are not excludable gifts, nor are "tokes" received by casino craps dealers from gamblers who are motivated by impulsive generosity and superstition. [See *Roberts v. Comm'r,* 176 F.2d 221 (9th Cir.1949); and *Olk v. U.S.,* 536 F.2d 876 (9th Cir.1976).] No amount received by an employee from his employer is excluded from gross income as a gift, although some employer provided economic benefits, such as fringe benefits, are excluded under other provisions of the Code. [IRC § 132; see discussion, II. B. 1. e., at page 19, *supra.*]

The exclusion for gifts does not apply to prizes, awards or scholarships which are provided for by specific inclusion or exclusion provisions. [Reg. § 1.102–1(a); see IRC §§ 74 and 117 and discussions, II. B. 3. a. and II. C. 6., at page 41, *supra,* and at page 59, *infra.*]

b. Inheritances

The value of property acquired by bequest, devise or inheritance is excludable from gross income. [IRC § 102(a).] None of the three terms used in the statute (referred to collectively in this outline as "inheritance") are defined in the Code; the Regulations refer to property "received under a will or under statutes of descent and distribution

. . . ." [Reg. § 1.102–1(a).] The statute has been broadly construed, however, to exclude from gross income virtually all acquisitions made with donative intent in the devolution of a decedent's estate.

Example: Mary receives property from her grandfather's estate in compromise of her claim as one of his heirs. Because her claim is based upon her status, under state law, as an heir of the estate, the amount she receives in the settlement of the will contest is excluded from her gross income. [*Lyeth v. Hoey,* 305 U.S. 188, 59 S.Ct. 155 (1938).]

An amount is not excluded from gross income, however, merely because it is provided for in a will; the exclusion does not apply if the legacy is not of a donative nature and instead is compensation for services, payment for property, or some other payment which would be included in income if received directly rather than by means of a will.

Example: Ned, an attorney, performs legal services for a client who, in lieu of paying attorney fees during her lifetime, provides in her will for property to be transferred to Ned after her death. A transfer of property which is compensation for services is not excludable merely because the parties choose to pay the compensation in the form of a bequest. [*Wolder v. Comm'r,* 493 F.2d 608 (2d Cir.1974).]

3. INTEREST ON STATE AND LOCAL BONDS

Generally, gross income does not include interest paid on obligations issued by or on behalf of the government of the District of Columbia, any State or possession of the United States, or any of their political subdivisions (State or local bonds). [IRC § 103(a); Reg. § 1.103–1(b).] A "political subdivision" includes a governmental unit which has the authority to exercise sovereign powers, and thus may include municipalities, sewer districts, road districts, and school districts. Interest paid on obligations issued by the Federal government, however, does not qualify for this exclusion and must be included in gross income.

Example: The Massachusetts Turnpike Authority is a political subdivision. [Rev.Rul. 57–308, 1957–2 C.B. 94.] A state university which lacks the power to tax, the power of eminent domain, or police power is not a political subdivision. [Rev.Rul. 77–165, 1977–1 C.B. 21.]

The exclusion from gross income for interest on state and local bonds was provided initially because of some concern that the federal government could not constitutionally impose a tax which would burden the borrowing power of the states. Today, most commentators believe a tax on such interest would be constitutional, but the exclusion is justified as providing Federal assistance to state and local governments by effectively permitting them to pay interest on borrowed funds at a lower rate than they would have to pay if the interest was taxable to the recipient.

Example: Olivia, who is subject to income tax at a marginal rate of 28%, seeks to maximize her after-tax return on an investment of $100. She will prefer to purchase a municipal bond paying 10% interest, tax free, than to purchase a bond issued by Chrysler Corporation paying 12% interest, assuming that each investment carries equal risk. Viewing the situation from the perspective of the municipality, it will need to pay only $10 to borrow funds which General Motors must pay $12 to borrow.

In recent years, Congress has enacted several complex provisions to stem perceived abuses of this exclusion. The exclusion does not extend to interest paid on any State or local bond which is a private activity bond which is not a qualified activity bond, an arbitrage bond, or a bond which is not in registered form. [IRC § 103(b).]

a. Private activity bond which is not a qualified bond

In general terms, a private activity bond is a bond issued by a State or local government to provide financing for activities other than traditional governmental operations. More technically, the Code defines a private activity bond in terms of applying either a "private loan financing test" or a "private business use test" plus a "private security or payment test". [IRC § 141(a).] The objective of these tests is to identify those bonds which are being sold by a State or local government to raise money to be used directly or indirectly by private, nongovernmental individuals or businesses. Unless a private activity bond is a qualified bond, interest paid on the bond is *not* excluded from the recipient's gross income. [IRC § 103(b)(1).]

Interest paid on a private activity bond which is a qualified bond is excluded from the recipient's gross income, as long as none of the other disqualifying provisions are applicable. In general terms, a "qualified bond" is a private activity bond which is in one of seven statutorily defined categories. The categories include exempt facility bonds, qualified veterans' mortgage bonds and qualified student loan bonds. [IRC § 141(d); see IRC §§ 142, 143, 144, and 145.] The details of these provisions are far beyond the scope of this outline, but the general thrust is that in these specified and circumscribed situations a State or local government may sell bonds, use the proceeds to benefit private individuals or businesses, and the interest received by the owners of the bonds is excluded from gross income.

b.   Arbitrage bond

The exclusion of interest paid on State or local bonds does not apply to arbitrage bonds. [IRC § 103(b)(2).] Generally, an arbitrage bond is a State or local bond where the proceeds are reasonably expected to be used, directly or indirectly, by the State or local government to acquire higher yielding investments. [IRC § 148(a).]

> *Example:* If a municipality sells bonds paying 10% interest, and uses the proceeds to purchase bonds issued by Chrysler Corporation paying 12% interest, the municipal bond is an arbitrage bond, and the interest paid thereon is not excludable from gross income.

c.   Registration requirement

State and local bonds with a maturity of one year or more must be in registered form for the interest exclusion to apply. [IRC § 103(b)(3).] This provision requires the bond issuer to submit to the I.R.S. not only information which can be used to determine if the bond is a State or local bond qualifying for the interest exclusion but also the names of the owners of the bonds thereby improving the ability of the I.R.S. to enforce income, gift and estate taxes on the bond itself. [See IRC § 149(a).]

4.)   COMPENSATION FOR INJURIES OR SICKNESS AND DAMAGES
a.   Introduction $104

When a taxpayer receives compensation for personal injuries or sickness, or when he receives an award of damages (or an amount in settlement of a claim), determination of whether such an amount is includible in gross income involves concepts of the fundamental nature of "gross income" as well as the application of specific statutory provisions. Generally, the tax consequences of receiving an award of damages (or an amount to settle a claim) will be determined by the nature of the underlying claim. If the underlying claim is based on an alleged injury to a taxpayer's business or profession, an award of damages generally adds to his wealth, rather than merely compensating him for a loss. Damages for lost business profits, therefore, are included in gross income, as are liquidated damages for the breach of a contract to sell property, as well as punitive or exemplary damages under antitrust statutes. [*Comm'r v. Glenshaw Glass Co.,* 348 U.S. 426, 75 S.Ct. 473 (1955).] If an award of damages "makes the plaintiff whole" by compensating her for a loss, she does not have gross income to the extent the compensation does not exceed her adjusted basis in the damaged property.   Similarly, a recovery which is in the nature of recovery of capital is excluded from gross income.

> *Examples:* In Year One, Ursula loaned her friend, Victor, $10,000 cash. Victor did not repay the loan in accordance with the terms of

the loan, so Ursula filed suit against her ex-friend. In Year Five, before the case went to trial, Victor settled the action by paying Ursula $12,000, $2,000 of which was interest. The $10,000 repayment of the principal amount of the loan is not included in Ursula's gross income; the $2,000 interest payment is included in her gross income for Year Five. If the suit had gone to trial and Ursula had recovered $12,000, the results would be the same.

Nicholas was an inventor who obtained a patent for a shoe manufacturing machine. Several years after obtaining the patent, he filed suit for infringement of his patent against the United Shoe Machinery Corporation. Nicholas prevailed in the lawsuit, and he was awarded $63,000 in damages for patent infringement. The damages were to compensate him for unrealized profits from the exploitation of his patent by United Shoe, and they were includible in his gross income. [*Mathey v. Comm'r,* 177 F.2d 259 (1st Cir.1949).]

b. Compensation for injuries or sickness

In general terms, IRC § 104 excludes from gross income amounts received, from several enumerated sources, as compensation for personal injuries or sickness. The exclusion is not available, however, if the recipient has taken a deduction, in any taxable year prior to receiving the compensation, on account of the medical expenses for which he is now being compensated. [IRC § 104(a).] This rule prevents a taxpayer from obtaining a double benefit for medical expenses, once by taking a deduction under IRC § 213 in the year the expense is paid, and again by excluding amounts received to compensate for the expenditure. The corresponding rule in the medical expense deduction provision disallows a deduction to the extent the taxpayer has been compensated for medical expenses. [IRC § 213, see discussion, III. B. 7, at page 150, *infra.*]

Example: Paul takes a deduction for a medical expense in Year One, and receives reimbursement for the expense in Year Two. The reimbursement is not excluded from Paul's gross income for Year Two. If the reimbursement is received in Year One, no IRC § 213 deduction is allowable, but the reimbursement is excluded from Paul's gross income for Year One.

i. Workmen's compensation

Amounts received for personal injuries or sickness under workmen's compensation acts are excluded from gross income. [IRC § 104(a)(1).] A "workmen's compensation act" is a statute which provides compensation to employees for sickness or personal injuries incurred in the course of employment; the exclusion, however, does not extend to amounts paid under such statutes as a retirement pension or annuity, or amounts paid for nonoccupational injury or sickness. Amounts paid as compensation to the survivors of a deceased employee under a workmen's compensation act are also excludable.

Amounts received by certain governmental employees and retired armed forces personnel for personal injuries or sickness are excludable under provisions conceptually similar to the exclusion for workmen's compensation benefits. [IRC § 104(a)(4) and (5).]

ii. Damages for personal injuries or sickness

Amounts received as damages for personal injuries or sickness are excluded from gross income. [IRC § 104(a)(2).] The exclusion applies to recoveries for either intentional or unintentional torts. The I.R.S. contends it does not apply to punitive damages. [Rev.Rul. 84–108, 1984–2 C.B. 32.] Amounts received to settle potential lawsuits for personal injuries are excludable to the extent that the nature of the claim settled is for personal injuries. [*Seay v. Comm'r*, 58 T.C. 32 (1972).] The concept of personal injuries has been expanded by the courts to include non-physical injuries such as those resulting from libel, slander of personal character, invasion of privacy, and alienation of affection. Damages for injury to a taxpayer's professional reputation, however, are excludable. [See Threlkeld v. Comm'r, 87 TC No. 76 (1987).]

iii. Recoveries under accident or health insurance

Amounts received from accident or health insurance for personal injuries or sickness are excludable from gross income. [IRC § 104(a) (3).] There is no limit on the amount which may be excluded under this provision. However, exclusion does not apply if the payments are made to an employee either: (1) under an accident or health plan to which the employer made contributions which were excluded from the employee's gross income under IRC § 106, or (2) by the employer. Amounts received by an employee which do not qualify for this exclusion may qualify, however, for exclusion under IRC § 105. [See discussion, II. C. 4. c., below.]

Example: Susan develops pneumonia and receives $100 for each day she is hospitalized under an insurance policy on which she paid the premiums. The $100 daily payments are excludable, regardless of the amount of her medical expenses.

c. Payments for and recoveries under employer-provided accident or health plans

An employee may exclude from gross income amounts which his employer contributes on his behalf to accident or health plans to compensate the employee for personal injuries or sickness. [IRC § 106.] Payments made to an employee either directly by the employer, or under an accident or health plan to which the employer made contributions which were excluded from the employee's gross income under IRC § 106 are required to be *included* in gross income under IRC § 105(a), but may qualify for exclusion under another subsection of IRC § 105. An employer-provided accident or health plan may be provided directly by the employer or by insurance. [IRC § 105(e).] Generally, self-employed individuals are not considered to be "employees" for purposes of these exclusions. [IRC § 105(g).] Payments need not be made under a formal, written plan; the exclusion is available if it is the policy or custom of the employer to make such payments, but the exclusion is not available if payments are made under a plan which discriminates in favor of highly compensated employees. [IRC § 105(h).]

i.   Amounts spent for medical care

Amounts required to be *included* by IRC § 105(a) may be *excluded* under IRC § 105(b) to the extent they are paid, directly or indirectly, *to reimburse* the employee for medical expenses incurred for himself, his spouse and dependents. The exclusion does not apply if the employee has taken a deduction for the medical expenses in any prior year, nor does it apply to the extent the amount received is in excess of medical expenses. If an employee receives a recovery which qualifies for exclusion under IRC § 105(b), and also receives a recovery which qualifies for exclusion under IRC § 104(a)(3), an allocation of the medical expenses incurred must be made between the two recoveries to determine the amount excludable by IRC § 105(b).

Example: Tom incurred $900 of medical expenses for sickness and injuries to himself and his family. During the same year, he received a total of $1,200 in compensation for such injuries and sickness: $800 from a medical insurance policy provided by his employer, and $400 from a medical insurance policy he had paid premiums on. Two-thirds ($800/$1,200) of the employer-provided insurance recovery is considered to be reimbursement for Tom's medical expenses of $900; thus, $600 is excludable by IRC § 105(b) and $200 must be included in gross income. The $400 received under the policy Tom purchased is totally excludable under IRC § 104(a)(3). [Rev.Rul. 69–154, 1969–1 C.B. 46.]

ii.   Payments unrelated to absence from work

Amounts required to be *included* by IRC § 105(a) may be *excluded* under IRC § 105(c) to the extent they are payment for the permanent loss of a limb or disfigurement of an employee, her spouse or dependents, and are computed with reference to the nature of the injury, not the length of time the employee is absent from work.

5.   INCOME FROM DISCHARGE OF INDEBTEDNESS

Gross income generally includes income from the discharge of indebtedness.   [IRC § 61(a)(12).]

Example: In January of Year One, K.L. Company borrowed $12 million, by selling its bonds which called for the payment of interest at the prevailing rate of 10% per year and repayment of the principal amount in 25 years.   By December of Year One, the prevailing rate of interest had risen to 15%, and thus the market value of the K.L. bonds fell to $10 million.   K.L.'s cash position had improved by December, so it purchased all of the outstanding bonds for $10 million thereby eliminating the company's obligation to repay the $12 million face amount of the bonds.   The $12 million which K.L. borrowed in January was not gross income, because of the company's obligation to repay $12 million;   however, when the obligation to repay was satisfied in December, K.L. had income from the discharge of indebtedness in the amount of $2 million.   [*U.S. v. Kirby Lumber Co.*, 284 U.S. 1, 52 S.Ct. 4 (1931).]

There are several statutory and judicial exceptions to the general rule. [IRC § 108.]   If one of the exceptions applies, the taxpayer is generally required to reduce various tax attributes, or the basis of property, by the amount excluded from gross income.   [IRC §§ 108(b), (c) and 1017.]

a.   Bankruptcy and insolvency
i.   In general

Gross income does not include income from the discharge of indebtedness if the discharge occurs in bankruptcy (a Title 11 case) or to the extent the taxpayer is insolvent.   [IRC § 108(a)(1)(A) and (B).] If the discharge of indebtedness occurs in bankruptcy, and the discharge also qualifies for exclusion from gross income under one of the other statutory exceptions, the bankruptcy rules control.   [IRC § 108(a)(2)(A).]   The insolvency exception applies only to the extent the taxpayer's liabilities exceed the fair market value of his assets immediately prior to the discharge.   [IRC § 108(a)(3), (d)(3).]   The discharge of indebtedness of a taxpayer engaged in the business of farming may qualify for this gross income exclusion rule even though the taxpayer is not insolvent.   [IRC § 108(g).]

Example: On December 1 of Year One Winifred's creditor, to whom she owed $10,000, agreed to settle his claim in exchange for Winifred's *only* asset, a painting with a fair market value and an adjusted basis of $8,000. Winifred had income from the discharge of indebtedness in the amount of $2,000. Because Winifred was insolvent to the extent of $2,000, the $2,000 of income from the discharge is excluded from her gross income. Alternatively, if Winifred also had other assets with a total fair market value of $500, in addition to the painting, she would have been insolvent only to the extent of $1,500; she would have had $2,000 of income from the discharge of indebtedness of which only $1,500 would be excluded from gross income. However, Winifred must pay for the exclusion by a reduction of tax attributes and she may be able to exclude the additional $500. [See following discussion.]

ii.   Reduction of tax attributes

If income from the discharge of indebtedness is excluded from gross income under the bankruptcy or insolvency exceptions, various tax attributes of the taxpayer must be reduced by the amount so excluded. [IRC § 108(b)(1).] The tax attributes which must be reduced are as follows: (1) net operating losses, (2) certain tax credit carryovers, (3) capital loss carryovers, (4) adjusted basis of property, and (5) foreign tax credit carryovers. [IRC § 108(b)(2).] As an alternative to the statutory ordering of tax attribute reductions, the taxpayer may elect to any extent to first reduce the basis of *depreciable* property and real property inventory. [IRC § 108(b)(5).]

Example: In Year Two, Adam has $4,000 of income from the discharge of indebtedness excluded from gross income under the insolvency exception, and he has a $5,000 net operating loss carryover from Year One. Adam must reduce his net operating loss carryovers down to $1,000. In the alternative, he may elect to have all or any portion of the $4,000 used to reduce the basis of his depreciable property and real property inventory, and the other tax attributes (his net operating loss) will not be reduced to that extent.

iii.   Reduction of basis

If the basis of property is *required* to be reduced under the provisions of IRC § 108, the special rules of IRC § 1017 *must* be applied to effect the reduction in the basis of property which the taxpayer holds at the beginning of the taxable year following the year in which the discharge occurs. The taxpayer is required to reduce his basis only to the extent of the excess of the total adjusted bases of the taxpayer's property immediately after the discharge over the total liabilities immediately after the discharge. [IRC § 1017(b)(2).] This limitation does not apply, however, if the taxpayer elects to reduce the basis of depreciable property and real property inventory in lieu of reducing net operating losses and other tax attributes. [*Id.*]

Example: On November 1 of Year One, Betty had liabilities of $20,000, and property with a total adjusted basis and fair market value of $15,000. On that date, one of her creditors settled his $3,000 claim against her for one of her items of property which had a fair market value and an adjusted basis of $2,000. Betty has $1,000 of income from the discharge of indebtedness which is excluded from gross income under the insolvency exception. Assuming that Betty does not have any tax attributes, other than the basis of her property, subject to reduction under IRC § 108(b), the basis of property which she holds on January 1 of Year Two, must be reduced by $1,000, subject, however, to the limitation of IRC § 1017(b)(2). Under that limitation, the total bases of her property after the discharge ($13,000) does not exceed her total liabilities after the discharge ($17,000); therefore, the basis of her property is not reduced. If Betty had tax attributes, such as net operating loss carryovers, but made the IRC § 108(b)(5) election to reduce the basis of depreciable property and real property inventory, the limitation will not apply, and the basis of property which she holds on January 1 of Year Two, will be reduced by $1,000. [IRC § 1017(b)(2).]

b. Solvency or partial solvency

If a taxpayer is solvent or partially solvent, gross income *includes* income from the discharge of indebtedness except to the extent the taxpayer is insolvent. [IRC § 108(a)(3).] However, there are some judicial and statutory exceptions.

i. Purchase price adjustment

If indebtedness arising out of the purchase of property is reduced or discharged by the seller of the property, the reduction is treated as a reduction in the purchase price of the property rather than as income from the discharge of indebtedness. [IRC § 108(e)(5).] If the purchase price of an item of property is reduced under this rule, the cost basis of the property must also be reduced.

> ***Example:*** Diane purchases a parcel of unimproved real property from Ed for $20,000, paying $3,000 in cash and agreeing to pay the remaining $17,000, plus interest, one year later. On the date the final payment is due, Diane is not insolvent nor has she filed a bankruptcy petition, but she is short on cash and Ed agrees to accept $16,000, plus interest, as payment in full for the land. Diane does not have income from the discharge of indebtedness; the purchase price of the land, however, is reduced to $19,000 as is her cost basis.

ii. Gratuitous debt forgiveness

    A debt cancellation which constitutes a gift or bequest is not included in gross income of the recipient.

iii. Equity for debt

    Generally, a corporation will not have gross income from the discharge of indebtedness if it issues shares of its own stock to a creditor. However, the exception does not apply if only a nominal amount of stock is issued for the debt, or in certain situations where a corporation in financial difficulty is significantly restructuring its debt obligations. [IRC § 108(e)(8).]

iv. Student loans

    Gross income does not include income from the discharge of all or a portion of certain student loans, if the debt is discharged because the taxpayer works for a certain period of time in certain professions for any of a broad class of employers. [IRC § 108(f).]

> ***Example:*** Frank receives a loan from a state agency to help defray his expenses of attending medical school. Under the terms of the loan, $5,000 is forgiven for each year a loan recipient practices medicine in a rural area of the State. Upon completing his medical education, Frank does practice medicine in a rural area of the State for 2 years, and $10,000 of his loans are forgiven. The amounts forgiven under this program are excluded from Frank's gross income.

v. Qualified farm indebtedness

    The discharge of indebtedness of a taxpayer engaged in the business of farming may qualify for exclusion from gross income even though the taxpayer is not insolvent, but he will be subject to the reduction of tax attributes rules described above. [IRC § 108(g).]

6. SCHOLARSHIPS, TUITION REDUCTIONS AND EDUCATIONAL ASSISTANCE PROGRAMS

a. Qualified scholarships

Amounts received as a qualified scholarship by a candidate for a degree at an educational institution are excluded from gross income. [IRC § 117(a).] The tax treatment of scholarships is provided for exclusively by IRC § 117. To the extent that a qualified scholarship is not totally excluded from gross income under IRC § 117, the excess amount may not be excluded as a gift under IRC § 102. [Reg § 1.117–1(a).]

A payment or allowance is not considered as a scholarship and thus is includible in gross income if the amount is compensation for past, present or future employment services, or if the amount is paid to enable the recipient to pursue studies or research which primarily benefits the grantor. [Reg. § 1.117–4(c); *Bingler v. Johnson,* 394 U.S. 741, 89 S.Ct. 1439 (1969).] This is the threshold inquiry, because if the payment is in the nature of compensation, the exclusion provided by IRC § 117 will not apply.

A "qualified scholarship" is an amount paid as a scholarship or fellowship grant to the extent it is spent in accordance with the grant for tuition and fees required for enrollment at an educational institution and for fees, books, supplies, and equipment required for courses of instruction. [IRC § 117(b).] Amounts provided for meals, lodging, laundry, travel and other purposes are not considered part of a qualified scholarship and are not excluded from gross income. Further, amounts received as compensation for services, such as teaching or research, rendered by the recipient as a condition of receiving the scholarship do not qualify for the exclusion. [IRC § 117(c).]

Example: Edgar receives a $10,000 scholarship to attend graduate school at State University; the terms of the scholarship require him to use the funds to pay for tuition, fees, books, room and board. Edgar actually spends $4,000 for tuition and books, and the remaining $6,000 for room and board. Only $4,000 of the scholarship may be excluded from Edgar's gross income. In addition, if as a condition of receiving the scholarship Edgar is required to perform part-time teaching services for which the University would normally pay $10,000, none of the scholarship may be excluded from gross income.

To be considered as a "candidate for a degree," an individual must be enrolled at an educational organization which normally maintains a regular faculty and curriculum and normally has a regularly enrolled body of pupils or students in attendance at the place where the educational activities are regularly carried on. [IRC §§ 117(a) and 170(b)(1)(A)(ii).] There is no maximum amount or duration limit for the exclusion of qualified scholarships received by an individual who is a candidate for a degree.

b. Qualified tuition reduction

The amount of a qualified tuition reduction is excluded from gross income. [IRC § 117(d).] "Qualified tuition reduction" is the amount of any reduction in tuition provided to an employee of an educational institution for education (below the graduate level) at that institution or at another educational institution. [IRC § 117(d)(2); see IRC § 170(b)(1)(A)(ii).] This exclusion applies to reductions in tuition not only for the employee himself, but also for tuition reductions for the employee's spouse, dependent children and, in some cases, the surviving spouse of a deceased employee. [See IRC § 132(f).] An educational institution's tuition reduction plan may not discriminate in favor of any highly compensated employee. [IRC § 117(d)(3).]

c. Educational assistance programs

An employee may exclude from gross income up to $5,250 of the value of benefits received from his employer under an educational assistance program. [IRC § 127(a).] Although this exclusion expires automatically [IRC § 127(d)], the expiration date has been postponed by Congress several times since the provision was first enacted and it is possible that it will be postponed again.

An "educational assistance program" is an employer's written plan providing educational assistance exclusively for his employees. [IRC § 127(b).] "Educational assistance" is the payment by the employer of the costs of tuition, fees, books, supplies and equipment relating to the education of the employee, or the value of the employer himself providing the educational instruction for the employee; the term does not include the payment for tools or supplies which the employee may keep after completing the course of instruction, or for meals, lodging or transportation, or for courses involving sports, games or hobbies. [IRC § 127(c)(1).] "Education" is instruction which improves or develops the capabilities of the employee; it is not limited to job related courses and the employee is not required to be a candidate for a degree. [Reg § 1.127–2(c)(4).] A program will be disqualified if it is not available to a broad class of employees or if it discriminates in favor of highly compensated employees. [IRC § 127(b)(2) and (3).]

7. MEALS AND LODGING

An exclusion from gross income is provided for the value of meals and lodging provided to an employee for the convenience of his employer on the employer's business premises. [IRC § 119(a).] Beginning shortly after the enactment of the income tax, the I.R.S. and the courts recognized various situations where the value of meals and lodging should not be included in gross income. [*E.g.,* O.D. 265, 1 C.B. 21 (1919) (value of meals and lodging furnished to seamen while on board ship excluded from gross income because furnished "for the convenience of the employer").] Congress enacted IRC § 119 in 1954 to clarify earlier law and to bring uniformity to the treatment of meals and lodging provided by employers to their employees.

a. Exclusion of meals

The value of meals furnished to an employee by her employer may be excluded from gross income only if the meals are furnished on the business premises of the employer and if they are furnished for the convenience of the employer.

i.   Business premises of the employer

The "business premises" of an employer is generally the place of employment of the employee; it is the place where the employee carries on significant employment duties or the employer conducts a significant portion of his business.

Example: Meals furnished to a domestic servant in the employer's home are furnished "on the business premises" of his employer. [Reg. § 1.119–1(c)(1).]

ii. Convenience of the employer

Meals are furnished to an employee "for the convenience of the employer" only if there is a substantial noncompensatory business purpose for providing the meals and if the meals are furnished without charge or if a flat fee for the meals is charged. If the employee has a choice of accepting the meals and paying for them, or of not paying and providing her meals in some other way, any meals which are furnished are *not* "for the convenience of the employer." [Reg. § 1.119–1(a)(3)(i).] If there is a substantial noncompensatory business purpose for providing the meals, they are considered to be furnished for the convenience of the employer even though the meals may also be furnished as compensation. [Reg. § 1.119–1(a)(2)(i).] An employer furnishes meals for a substantial noncompensatory business purpose if they are furnished to an employee during his working hours in order to have the employee available for emergency calls or because the nature of the employer's business requires that meal periods be too short to reasonably expect employees to eat elsewhere. [Reg. § 1.119–1(a)(2)(ii).]

Example: Jake is a waiter who works from 6 a.m. to 3 p.m. at a restaurant which provides him with breakfast and lunch, without charge, each day. He is not required to eat breakfast before work begins (he could eat at home before going to work), but he is required to remain at the restaurant during his lunch break. Jake may exclude from his gross income the value of both the breakfasts and the lunches. If Jake is also allowed to have free breakfasts and lunches at the restaurant on his days off, these meals are not furnished for the convenience of his employer and their value is included in his gross income. [Reg. § 1.119–1(d) Examples (1) and (2).]

iii. Additional considerations

a. "Meals"

The exclusion provided by IRC § 119 is only for "meals" furnished to an employee; it does not authorize the exclusion of cash allowances or reimbursements for meals. [See *Comm'r v. Kowalski,* 434 U.S. 77, 98 S.Ct. 315 (1977).] Authority is mixed whether provision of groceries qualifies as "meals;" it likely is not.

b. Employee's family

The value of meals furnished to an employee's spouse or any of his dependents may be excluded from the employee's gross income if the meals satisfy the business premises and convenience of the employer requirements, *supra.*

c. Meals and lodging

If the value of lodging furnished to an employee is excluded from her gross income, the value of any meal furnished without charge to the employee, her spouse and dependents is also excluded from her gross income. [Reg. § 1.119–1(a)(2)(i).]

b. **Exclusion of lodging**

The value of lodging furnished to an employee by his employer may be excluded from gross income only if the lodging is furnished on the business premises of the employer, if it is furnished for the convenience of the employer, and if the employee is required to accept the lodging as a condition of his employment. [IRC § 119(a)(2).]

i. Business premises of the employer

As in the case of meals, the "business premises" of an employer is generally the place of employment of the employee; it is the place where the employee carries on significant employment duties, or the employer conducts a significant portion of his business.

Examples: Jack is the manager of a hotel who lives in a house located on property owned by the hotel, but located across the street from the hotel. Jack, however, can observe the hotel from the house, and he otherwise makes business use of the house. The house is part of the business premises of the employer, and the value of the lodging furnished to Jack there is excluded from his gross income. [*Lindeman v. Comm'r,* 60 T.C. 609 (1973).]

Charles, who is also a hotel manager, lives in a house owned by the hotel, but located two blocks away from the hotel. Charles does not perform any significant part of his employment duties at the house. The value of the lodging is not excluded from Charles' gross income. [*Comm'r v. Anderson,* 371 F.2d 59 (3d Cir.1966).]

ii. **Convenience of the employer**
In the case of lodging, the statute not only requires that the lodging must be furnished for the convenience of the employer, but also that the employee must be required to accept such lodging "as a condition of his employment." [IRC § 119(a)(2).] This additional statutory language seems to be surplusage, however, rather than imposing an additional, different test or requirement. The regulations list the two as separate requirements, but indicate that they are satisfied if the employee is "required to accept the lodging in order to enable him properly to perform the duties of his employment." [Reg. § 1.119–1(b).]

Example: Herbert is the manager of a funeral home, and he lives in an apartment located on the business premises of his employer. It is a customary business practice in this community for a funeral home to have someone in attendance 24 hours a day to take care of the business. The value of the lodging furnished to Herbert by his employer is excludable from his gross income. [*Herbert G. Hatt,* 28 T.C.M. 1194 (1969).]

c. **Faculty housing**
Gross income does not include the value of qualified campus lodging furnished to an employee of an educational institution. [IRC § 119(d).] "Qualified campus lodging" is lodging, the value of which is not already excluded from gross income under IRC § 119(a), located on or near the campus and furnished for use as a residence by the employee, his spouse or dependents. [IRC § 119(d)(3).] An exception to this exclusion, thereby requiring an amount to be *included* in gross income, applies to the extent the employee pays rent which is less than the average rent paid by nonemployees and nonstudents to the institution for use of comparable lodging (or 5% of the appraised value of the lodging, if less). [IRC § 119(d)(2).]

d.   Rental value of parsonages

A "minister of the gospel" may exclude from gross income the rental value of a home furnished to him, or a rental allowance paid to him to the extent he uses the allowance for housing. [IRC § 107.] The language of the statute notwithstanding, the exclusion is *not* confined to Christians; the Tax Court has held that the exclusion is available to a Cantor of the Jewish faith, there being no legislative intent to exclude non-Christian faiths or persons who perform religious duties equivalent to ministers. [*Abraham A. Salkov,* 46 T.C. 190 (1966).] An excludable rental allowance may include amounts used to pay for utilities at the residence [Rev.Rul. 59–350, 1959–2 C.B. 45], and may be used to purchase a residence [Reg. § 1.107–1(c)]; however, because the rental allowance must be "paid to him as part of his compensation," it is necessary for the employer/church to designate the amount of the minister's compensation which is the rental allowance. [Reg. § 1.107–1(b)].

8.   MISCELLANEOUS ITEMS EXCLUDED FROM INCOME BY STATUTE

Congress has expressly provided for the exclusion from gross income of various items which have relatively less significance than the items discussed in previous sections.

a.   Improvements by lessee on lessor's property

Gross income does not include the value of improvements to real property made by a lessee and left on the property at the termination of the lease if the improvements were not part of the rent for the use of the property. [IRC § 109.] If the value of improvements is excluded from gross income, the basis of the property may *not* be increased on account of the improvements. [IRC § 1019.] This effectively postpones recognition of gain and does not actually result in an exclusion.

Example: Godfrey rents a house to Holly and Ivy, two second-year law students, on a month-to-month lease for a rent of $500 per month. Holly and Ivy decide to remove the linoleum covering the kitchen floor and they have a brick floor installed in its place for $5,000. In addition, they have a hot-tub constructed in the back yard at a cost of $2,500. When Holly and Ivy graduate from law school and move out of Godfrey's house, the brick floor and the hot-tub remain in place. The value of the improvements is not included in Godfrey's gross income, nor is the basis of the house increased because of the improvements. The value of the house, however, has been increased because of the improvements, so if Godfrey subsequently sells the house, he will have a larger gain than if the improvements had not been made.

b. **Armed forces personnel**

Certain members of the U.S. armed forces may exclude all or a portion of their compensation received while serving in a combat zone or while hospitalized as a result of injuries received while serving in a combat zone. [IRC § 112.] In addition, mustering-out payments and certain qualified military benefits are excluded from gross income [IRC §§ 113 and 134.]

c. **Amounts received under insurance contracts for certain living expenses**

Amounts received under insurance contracts to pay for living expenses when an individual's principal residence is rendered uninhabitable by a fire or other casualty are excludable to the extent the amounts received exceed the amount of normal living expenses the individual would have incurred absent the calamity. [IRC § 123.]

d. **Certain foster care payments**

Certain amounts received for providing care for a qualified foster individual are excludable from gross income. [IRC § 131.]

REVIEW QUESTIONS

Q# 1: Clint's employer pays Clint $20,000 a year in cash and gives him a new car worth $10,000. How much gross income does Clint have and what is his basis in the car?

Q# 2: Burt buys a painting for $10,000 and he sells it several years later for $12,000. What sections of the IRC are relevant in determining the amount of gain or loss from the sale?

Q# 3: Assume Burt, from Question # 2, receives the painting as a gift from his father, who bought the painting several years ago for $10,000. The painting is worth $5,000 when father gives it to Burt. What is Burt's gain (or loss) when he sells the painting several years later for $12,000? What if he sells it for $4,000? What if he sells it for $8,000?

Q# 4: Sally bought a house in Year One for $50,000. In Year Three, she had a swimming pool built behind the house at a cost of $8,000 and she also repaired a portion of the roof at a cost of $2,000. What is Sally's basis in the house?

Q# 5: Susan operated an ice cream business as a sole proprietor until she sold it to Meryl for a total purchase price of $10,000. The assets of the business consisted of equipment worth $5,000, inventory of $4,000 and goodwill of $1,000. How is Meryl's basis in the ice cream business calculated?

Q# 6: In the current year, Tom receives the following amounts: $2,000 interest from a money market account; $1,500 interest on a New York state bond;

$5,000 from an inheritance; $20,000 salary from his job; and a $30,000 damage award to compensate him for personal injuries sustained in an automobile accident. What is Tom's gross income for the current year?

Q# 7: Rodney receives a $10,000 scholarship from a local university where he is enrolled in a program leading to a bachelor's degree in business administration. What additional information is needed to determine the proper tax treatment of this scholarship?

Q# 8: Ron rents an office building from Nancy for an annual rental of $5,000. Ron decides to build an additional office onto the building which increases the fair market value of the building by $5,000. Ron continues to pay his $5,000 annual rental to Nancy. Is the value of the improvement included in Nancy's gross income? What is the effect on Nancy's basis?

Q# 9: Madeline works for an insurance company; all employees are allowed to buy insurance at a 30% discount from the normal premiums charged to customers. In the current year, Madeline obtains liability insurance for her automobile, a homeowners policy for her house, and a life insurance policy insuring her own life. She pays a total of $700 in premiums, while a nonemployee customer would have been charged $1,000. Is this discount taxable to Madeline in the current year, and if so, to what extent?

Q# 10: Gene inherits stock from his mother in the current year. The basis of the stock to Gene's mother was $20,000 and the fair market value of the stock as of the date of her death was $10,000. If Gene later sells the stock for $5,000 what is the amount of Gene's gain or loss?

Q# 11: Terri sells a building for $75,000 cash down payment and she accepts a note from the purchaser for an additional $50,000, to be paid one year later (plus a reasonable rate of interest). In addition, the building is mortgaged for $100,000 (Terri is not personally liable under the mortgage) and the purchaser agrees to assume the mortgage. What is Terri's amount realized on the sale?

Q# 12: Although Marty is solvent, he owes various business creditors a total of $50,000. Marty's creditors agree to accept $40,000 in complete satisfaction of Marty's debts to them. What are the tax consequences of this transaction? What additional information is relevant?

Q# 13: Dudley works as a waiter at a restaurant. Dudley's employer requires Dudley to eat his evening meal at the restaurant in order to keep dinner breaks for employees as short as possible. Dudley is paid a $10,000 salary and he receives $3,000 in tips and $2,000 in meals. What is his gross income?

Q# 14: Rosie entered a sweepstakes contest and won the grand prize of $200,000. In the same year, Rosie also received an award of $10,000 in recognition of her literary talents, evidenced by the best selling novel she wrote a few years ago. Rosie did not seek to enter the literary competition, and she is not required to perform any services as a condition of receiving the $10,000. How much is included in Rosie's gross income?

Q# 15: Perry takes out a $100,000 whole-life insurance policy on his life. Several years later, at a time when Perry has paid a total of $15,000 in premiums, he sells the policy to his wife, Sadie, for $20,000; in January of the next year, Perry dies and the insurance company pays the $100,000 to Sadie. How much must Sadie include in her gross income?

Q# 16: Joseph is a minister at a protestant church. As compensation for the services he performs as a minister, the church pays Joseph $1,500 per month, plus a housing allowance of $500 per month. Joseph rents an apartment for $450 per month and pays utility bills of $100 per month. How much must Joseph include in his gross income each month?

Q# 17: Earl's business is defamed by a malicious competitor and Earl receives a $100,000 recovery. This recovery represents $25,000 in lost profits, $40,000 to injured goodwill of the business (in which Earl had a $30,000 basis), and $35,000 in punitive damages. What is Earl's gross income as a result of the recovery?

Q# 18: Jan purchases a piece of depreciable property paying $20,000 of cash and incurring a nonrecourse liability of $80,000. When the property appreciates in value, she takes out another $50,000 liability on the property. Several years later, when she has properly taken $40,000 of depreciation on the property and the liabilities on the property are $45,000 and $25,000, she sells it for $60,000 of cash and the buyer assumes the liabilities. What is Jan's gain on the sale?

Q# 19: Al operates an illegal loan-sharking business from which he derives a profit of $100,000 in the current year. Is Al subject to income tax on this profit? Are Al's expenses deductible?

Q# 20: Richard, an accountant, has the following tax realizations during the year; what is his gross income for the year:

(1) He is paid a $35,000 salary, receives a $10,000 cash bonus, and a $5,000 car to be used for personal purposes.

(2) He sells for $10,000 some stock purchased for $2,000, and he sells for $9,000 some municipal bonds whose interest is tax exempt which he purchased for $6,000.

(3) He wins a $1,000 vacation in a raffle.

(4) He has an income interest in a trust established by his deceased mother and he collects $5,000 of dividends from the trust.

(5) His uncle wills him $2,000 as agreed compensation for services he rendered to the uncle prior to his death.

(6) He recovers $5,000 of damages for defamation to his personal character.

(7) He collects on a $2,500 loan he made to a friend along with $500 of interest.

(8) He fills out his family's income tax return; H & R Block would have charged $300 to do it.

(9) His employer pays $50 a month for a parking space for Richard in the basement of the building in which they rent their offices.

(10) He buys a $10,000 boat and gets a $1,000 rebate.

III

DEDUCTIONS AND ALLOWANCES

Analysis

Various deductions and allowances may be subtracted from gross income to arrive at taxable income; taxable income is the tax base against which the appropriate rate is applied to arrive at a taxpayer's tax liability before the application of any tax credits. Deductions and allowances may be broadly classified into those which are related to profit-related activities and those which are not. Finally, there are some restrictions imposed on otherwise allowable deductions.

A. PROFIT RELATED DEDUCTIONS AND ALLOWANCES

The basic, fundamental concept of the income tax in the United States is that the tax is imposed on net income, not gross receipts. Therefore, it is appropriate to offset gross income by expenditures incurred in earning the income. The deductions and allowances covered in this section are within this broad classification. The Code sections dealt with here identify deductible expenses and provide rules for measuring the amount of the deductions. [Discussion of the proper time to take deductions is found at IV. B. 1. b. and 2. c., at pages 188 and 196, *infra.*]

1. TRADE OR BUSINESS EXPENSES

A deduction is allowed for ordinary and necessary expenses paid or incurred during a taxable year in carrying on a trade or business. [IRC § 162(a).]

a. "Ordinary and necessary"

An otherwise qualified expenditure must be both "ordinary" and "necessary" to be deductible. An expenditure is "ordinary" if it is one which is common within the business community to which the taxpayer belongs, even though the expenditure may be "extraordinary" to a particular taxpayer in the sense that it is a once-in-a-lifetime event.

> *Example:* A tort action is filed against Anita's business, and in order to preserve and protect her business, Anita incurs an expense for attorney fees to defend the lawsuit. She has never been involved in such a lawsuit before, and it is of such a nature that it is unlikely she will ever be involved in such an action again. Nonetheless, it is common and accepted in the business community to incur attorney fees for defending such lawsuits.

The expense for the attorney fees is ordinary. [*Welch v. Helvering*, 290 U.S. 111, 54 S.Ct. 8 (1933).]

An expenditure is "necessary" if it is appropriate and helpful to the trade or business. An expenditure is not necessary, and thus it is not deductible, if the taxpayer could be compensated or reimbursed for the expense or if the amount of the expense is unreasonable in light of the circumstances.

The determination of whether an expenditure is both ordinary and necessary is ultimately a question of fact, determined by surrounding facts and circumstances. Because the attitudes and norms of the business community may change over time, the trier of fact may conclude that an expenditure is not ordinary and necessary at one time and may arrive at a contrary conclusion at a different time. Lines here are hard to draw and cases are not necessarily consistent.

Examples: In 1922, Tom was an officer of a corporation which filed for bankruptcy and was discharged from its debts. In subsequent years, he paid some of the corporation's discharged debts because he continued to be involved in the same line of business and he wanted to solidify his own credit rating and reputation in the business community. The trial court sustained the IRS's assertion that Tom could not deduct the payment of the corporation's discharged debts as ordinary and necessary expenses. [*Welch v. Helvering*, 290 U.S. 111, 54 S.Ct. 8 (1933).]

In 1968, Conway Twitty started a fast food restaurant chain, and several of his friends and business associates invested in the enterprise. In 1970, the corporation encountered financial difficulties and it was decided to cease operations and to close all of the franchise outlets. In 1973 and 1974, Conway repaid some of the investors because he wanted to protect his personal business reputation and earning capacity. The court held that the repayments were ordinary and necessary business expenses. [*Harold L. Jenkins*, ¶ 83,667 P–H Memo TC.]

b.   "Expenses"

A deduction is allowed only for an item of "expense", as contrasted with a "capital expenditure." Generally, no deduction is allowed for a capital expenditure at the time the amount is paid; however, a capital expenditure may give rise to deductions for depreciation at a later time. [IRC §§ 263, 167 and 168; see discussion, III. A. 5., at page 104, *infra*.]

i.   Capital expenditures vs. repairs

Items of capital *expenditure,* which are therefore not deductible *expenses,* generally include the costs of acquiring or constructing buildings, machinery, equipment and other property which has a useful life substantially beyond the taxable year. [Reg. § 1.263(a)–2.] However, the cost of some items which have a short life or small cost may be deductible. [See Reg. § 1.162–6.] The amount of a capital expenditure is added to the basis of the property. [IRC § 1016(a)(1).]

Capital expenditures also include amounts paid which add to the value of property, substantially prolong the useful life of the property, or adapt the property to a new or different use. In contrast, amounts spent for the incidental repair or maintenance of business property are *expenses* (immediately deductible) and are not capital expenditures (thus, no effect on the property's basis). [Reg. § 1.263(a)–1(b).] An expenditure *to repair* property does not materially add to the value of the property (if the property were new), nor does it appreciably prolong the life of the property (beyond its expected life at acquisition); rather, a repair merely keeps the property in its ordinarily efficient operating condition. If the expenditure arrests the deterioration and appreciably prolongs the life of property, it is not a deductible expense, but is a capital expenditure. [Reg. § 1.162–4.] The determination of whether a particular expenditure is a deductible repair or a capital expenditure is essentially a question of fact, made on the basis of surrounding facts and circumstances. Again, the lines are often hard to draw in this area.

Examples: M.E.P., Inc., has operated a meat packing plant for 25 years. Recently, oil from a neighboring refinery began to leak into the basement, creating a fire hazard and making the basement unusable in its meat packing business. M.E.P. pays to oilproof the basement. The expenditure does not add to the value of the building, nor does it prolong the building's expected useful life; rather, the expenditure merely keeps the property in its ordinary operating condition. The expenditure is a "repair," deductible as an expense. [*Midland Empire Packing Co.,* 14 T.C. 635 (1950).]

Drive-In, Inc., constructed an open-air theater on sloping land formerly covered with vegetation without including in the construction any drainage system. Three years later, the taxpayer constructed a drainage system. At the time the theater was initially constructed, it was obvious that a drainage system would be required to properly dispose of normal rainfall; thus, the taxpayer's capital investment was incomplete until the drainage system was added. The expenditure for the drainage system did not merely restore, rearrange or repair the original capital asset. The expenditure created a new capital asset and thus is a nondeductible capital expenditure. [*Mt. Morris Drive-In Theatre Co. v. Comm'r,* 25 T.C. 272 (1955).]

ii. Advertising

Generally, expenditures for advertising a taxpayer's products or services are deductible expenses. [Reg. § 1.162–1(a).] In addition, expenditures for "institutional or 'goodwill'" advertising, such as newspaper advertisements encouraging contributions to the Red Cross, are deductible. [Reg. § 1.162–20(a)(2).] Advertising expenses are generally deductible even though the benefits of the advertising may extend substantially beyond the taxable year in which the expenditure is incurred. However, if the medium of the advertising material is such that it will have a useful life significantly more than one year, the amount may be a capital expenditure, not a deductible expense.

> *Example:* Amounts spent by a corporation to outfit and support a local baseball team which represents the corporation are deductible. [Rev.Rul. 70–393, 1970–2 C.B. 34.] Amounts spent by a corporation for signs, clocks, and scoreboards bearing the company's name are not currently deductible because they have a useful life of 5 years, but amounts spent for magazine advertising are deductible. [*Alabama Coca-Cola Bottling Co.,* ¶ 69,123 P–H Memo TC.]

c. "Carrying on"

Ordinary and necessary expenses are deductible only if incurred while "carrying on" a trade or business. Expenses incurred in acquiring or starting a *new* trade or business are generally not deductible because they are incurred when the taxpayer is not "carrying on" the trade or business. In contrast, ordinary and necessary expenses incurred in expanding an *existing* trade or business which is being "carried on" are deductible. Generally, expenditures which are not deductible because of this rule are added to the basis of the new trade or business.

i. Expenses incurred as an entrepreneur

Expenses incurred in *investigating* a *new* trade or business are treated as capital expenditures and are not currently deductible; however, if the investigation reaches a *transactional* stage and is dropped before a trade or business is developed or acquired, the transactional expenditures may give rise to a loss deduction. [IRC § 165(c)(2), see discussion, III. A. 3., at page 96, *infra.*]

Some expenses incurred in acquiring or starting a new trade or business may be deducted as "start-up expenditures" if the taxpayer so elects. [IRC § 195.] Qualifying expenditures include amounts paid while investigating the creation or acquisition of an existing active trade or business or in creating a new active trade or business, which are not deductible because they violate the "carrying on" requirement of IRC § 162. If the election is made, the total amount of the start-up expenditures is deducted ratably over a period selected by the taxpayer. The period must be at least 60 months (5 years) in length, and it begins with the month in which the active business begins.

Example: Morton and his wife Agnes travel throughout the United States to examine various newspapers and radio stations which they are interested in acquiring and operating as a business. Ultimately, they purchase a newspaper business in Ohio, after incurring expenses for travel, telephone and legal expenses. The expenses are not deductible because they are incurred at a time when they are not engaged in the newspaper business. [*Morton Frank,* 20 T.C. 511 (1953).] If these expenses had been incurred after the enactment of IRC § 195, Morton and Agnes could elect to deduct them over a period of not less than 5 years. If Morton and Agnes already owned a newspaper publishing business and incurred expenses to acquire another, those expenses would be currently deductible as Morton and Agnes are "carrying on" a newspaper publishing business.

ii.   Expenses incurred in obtaining employment as an employee

An individual may be in the trade or business of providing services as an employee. Thus, expenses incurred in obtaining another job in the same line of work are deductible because they are incurred while carrying on a trade or business. However, expenses incurred in obtaining employment in a *new* line of work, or in obtaining a *first* job are not deductible, because a trade or business is not being carried on at the time the expenditure is incurred. Furthermore, IRC § 195 seemingly may not be used by a taxpayer in employee status after she acquires employment to amortize her prior expenses.

Example: Adam, who has previously worked as a licensed electrician, incurs expenses traveling to union halls seeking employment as an electrician. Adam's expenses are deductible. Betty, a recent graduate of Undergrad University, incurs expenses traveling to a nearby city seeking employment as a teacher. Betty's expenses are not deductible. [Rev.Rul. 75–120, 1975–1 C.B. 55.]

d. "Trade or business"

Ordinary and necessary expenses are deductible pursuant to IRC § 162 only if they are paid or incurred while carrying on a "trade or business." The issue of whether an individual's profit-seeking activities constitute a "trade or business," for the purpose of determining the deductibility of expenses, does not often arise today because IRC § 212 authorizes deductions for ordinary and necessary expenses incurred either in the production or collection of income, or in dealing with property which is held for the production of income, even if the taxpayer is not carrying on an active "trade or business." [See discussion, III. A. 2., at page 93, *infra.*] There are other situations where the distinction between a "trade or business" and other profit-seeking activities is significant, such as the determination of adjusted gross income [IRC § 62(a)(1); see discussion, VII. A., at page 304, *infra*], deductions relating to the business use of portions of a personal residence [IRC § 280A(c)(1)(A); see discussion, III. C. 7. b., at page 164 *infra*], the limitations on passive investment activities [IRC § 469; see discussion, III. C. 10., at page 171, *infra*], limits on the deductibility of investment interest [IRC § 163(d); see discussion, III. B. 2., at page 131, *infra*], and the treatment of "quasi-capital assets" [IRC § 1231; see discussion, VI. C. 2., at page 292, *infra*]. The "trade or business" requirement of IRC § 162 is important today primarily to emphasize that expenses incurred for personal purposes are not deductible, and in this regard, the touchstone is that the taxpayer must have a profit motive for engaging in the activity which gives rise to the expense. [IRC § 262; see also IRC § 183 and discussion at III. C. 3., at page 157, *infra.*]

Example: Eugene had extensive investments in corporate stocks and bonds, and a large number of parcels of rental real estate. He spent a considerable amount of his time overseeing his interests, he hired several employees to assist him, and he leased office space for them to work in. In 1932 and 1933, he paid salaries and expenses incident to looking after his properties. The expenditures were deductible to the extent they were attributable to his real estate rental activities, because those activities constituted the conduct of a business. Eugene's investment activities in corporate stocks and bonds, no matter of what magnitude, however, did not constitute a trade or business, and thus the expenses associated with those activities were not deductible under the predecessor to IRC § 162. [*Higgins v. Comm'r*, 312 U.S. 212, 61 S.Ct. 475 (1941).] Alternatively, if the investment expenses were incurred in the current year, they would be deductible under IRC § 212.

e. Salaries

i. Reasonable compensation

Reasonable salaries or compensation paid for personal services actually rendered may be deducted. [IRC § 162(a)(1).] Two issues which frequently arise are whether the amount of the compensation is "reasonable," and whether the payments are, in fact, purely for services. [Reg. § 1.162–7(a).] The determination of whether the amount of compensation is reasonable is made in light of the nature and extent of the services performed and in comparison with amounts paid in similar circumstances. If compensation is paid pursuant to an agreement providing for the amount to be contingent upon future events, such as a percentage of the employer's profits, the amount of compensation actually paid is generally considered reasonable if the agreement was made at arm's length and if the terms of the agreement were reasonable when the agreement was made. [Reg. § 1.162–7(b)(2).]

Example: Fifteen years ago, Raymond agreed to provide management services to H.C. Corporation, for which he was to be paid an annual salary of $10,000 plus a bonus of 20% of the corporation's net profits each year. It was not unusual for employers engaged in the same line of business as the H.C. Corporation to enter into similar percentage compensation contracts, but the sole stockholders of H.C. Corporation were Raymond's two sons whom he dominated. Last year, H.C. Corporation paid Raymond a total of $500,000 under the contract. Because the agreement between Raymond and H.C. Corporation was not the result of a "free bargain," the reasonableness of his compensation is measured in the light of the circumstances in the year in which he is paid, rather than in light of the reasonableness of the agreement at the time it was made 15 years ago. A trier of fact concludes that someone performing similar services last year in similar circumstances would ordinarily be paid only $300,000. The $200,000 paid to Raymond in excess of $300,000 may not be deducted by H.C. Corporation. [*Harolds Club v. Comm'r*, 340 F.2d 861 (9th Cir.1965).]

Only compensation paid for "personal services actually rendered" may be deducted. If a payment is made to an employee as partial payment for property, or as a distribution of a dividend by a corporate employer to a shareholder/employee, the tax consequences will be determined accordingly; the amount will not be deductible as payment of salary.

> *Example:* Charles and Deborah were partners in the C & D partnership. In 1984, they sold their partnership to Acquiring Corporation for $100,000 cash. In addition, they each agreed to become employees of Acquiring at a "salary" of $50,000 per year for the next 5 years. Salaries ordinarily paid for similar services in similar circumstances are only $30,000 per year. The $20,000 excess paid to each of the former partners in each of the 5 years are part of the purchase price Acquiring pays for the partnership and may not be deducted by Acquiring as salary expenses. [Reg. § 1.162–7(b)(1).]

ii. Golden parachute payments

In the early 1980's Congress became increasingly concerned about the size and number of large corporate take-overs, mergers and acquisitions. One technique which facilitated a take-over was for a potential target corporation to provide its officers or directors (who would likely be fired by the new owners after the take-over) with a bonus salary payment which was contingent upon a take-over; such a bonus was referred to as a "golden parachute." If the ownership of the corporation did subsequently change, the officers so protected would be handsomely compensated and knowing this, they would be less inclined to fight against a take-over attempt.

The 1984 Tax Reform Act enacted IRC § 280G which disallows any deduction for the excess of *any* "parachute payment" over a "base amount" which is paid to a "disqualified individual," unless the parachute payment is shown to be for reasonable compensation. A "disqualified individual" is a corporate officer, shareholder or highly-compensated employee or any other employee or independent contractor who performs personal services for a corporation. [IRC § 280G(c).] Generally, a "parachute payment" is any payment in the nature of compensation which is contingent on the change of ownership or effective control of the corporate employer, or upon a change in the ownership of a substantial portion of its assets, *if* the present value of such payments exceeds 3 times the disqualified individual's "base amount." [IRC § 280G(b)(3).] The "base amount" is, generally, a disqualified individual's average compensation over the previous 5 years. [IRC § 280G(b)(3).] If an excess parachute payment is made, the payor is denied a deduction for the full amount of the parachute payment except to the extent it is reasonable compensation. In addition, the recipient is subject to a 20% excise tax on such amount. [IRC § 4999.] The rules do not apply, however, if the corporate employer is a small business corporation whose stock is not readily tradeable on an established securities market and if the payment has been approved by the shareholders. [IRC § 280G(b)(5).

Example: Prexy, a corporate president, receives an $800,000 severance payment when his corporation is acquired in a corporate take-over. His normal salary for the past 5 years has averaged $200,000 per year, a reasonable salary in light of the size and nature of the corporation's business and Prexy's duties and responsibilities as president. The parachute payment is $800,000; assuming that Prexy does not establish that any portion of it is for reasonable compensation for services he has actually rendered, the excess parachute payment is $600,000 ($800,000 less the base amount of $200,000). The corporation may not deduct the $600,000 excess parachute payment and Prexy must pay an excise tax of $120,000 (20% of $600,000) on receipt of the excess parachute payment. If the payment was $500,000, instead of $800,000, it would not be a "parachute payment" because it would not exceed 3 times Prexy's base amount of $200,000; the corporation would not be denied a deduction under IRC § 280G, and Prexy would not be subject to the excise tax under IRC § 4999.

f. Traveling expenses

A deduction is allowed for traveling expenses, including lodging and a portion of the cost of meals, incurred while a taxpayer is *away from home* in the pursuit of a trade or business. [IRC § 162(a)(2).] Because of the inherently personal nature of expenditures for food and a place to sleep, for which no deduction is allowed in normal circumstances [IRC § 262], the I.R.S. and the courts have been careful in limiting the circumstances in which a deduction is appropriate. Three conditions must be satisfied before a traveling expense deduction is allowable: (1) the expense must be a reasonable and necessary traveling expense, (2) the expense must be incurred while away from home, and (3) the expense must be incurred in the pursuit of business. [*Comm'r v. Flowers,* 326 U.S. 465, 66 S.Ct. 250 (1946).] The further limitations on deductions for the cost of meals are discussed at III. A. 1. g., at page 84, *infra.*

i. In general

"Travel expenses" include the costs of travel itself, such as for airplane tickets and taxicabs, as well as meals, lodging, and other expenses incident to travel. Incidental travel expenses include expenditures for telephone calls, public stenographers, sample rooms, tips, baggage charges, laundry, and helpers for handicapped travelers. [Reg. § 1.162–2(a).] The amount of the expenditure must be reasonable, a notion underscored by the parenthetical language in IRC § 162(a)(2) that a deduction will not be allowed for amounts "which are lavish or extravagant under the circumstances." All deductible travel expenses, of course, must be "ordinary and necessary," and paid or incurred "in carrying on [a] trade or business." [IRC § 162(a).]

Example: Daisy is a lawyer who resides with her family in Mississippi, and who is employed in Alabama. The expenses incurred in traveling from her home to her place of employment are not incurred while carrying on the trade or business of the taxpayer or of her employer; they are in essence non-deductible personal expenses for commuting to work. [*Comm'r v. Flowers,* 326 U.S. 465, 66 S.Ct. 250 (1946).]

ii.   "Away from home"

Travel expenses are deductible only if they are incurred while the taxpayer is "away from home." This requirement has been interpreted in a variety of contexts, but has never been specifically interpreted by the Supreme Court. If a taxpayer does not have a permanent residence or abode, she does not have a "home" and thus she cannot be "away from home."

Example: Robert is a jewelry salesman who spends some 300 days each year traveling throughout his sales territory in the midwest. He does not have any permanent residence of his own; he uses his brother's address in New York City to register to vote, to license his automobile and to file his income tax returns. Several times a year he visits his employer's headquarters in New York City, but he always stays in hotels, rather than at his brother's house. Robert may not deduct the costs of his meals and lodging incurred while traveling throughout the midwest, nor those incurred while in New York City, because he does not have a "home" to be away from. [*Rosenspan v. U.S.,* 438 F.2d 905 (2d Cir.1971).]

If a taxpayer has both an abode and a principal place of business, the I.R.S. considers his "tax home" to be the location of the principal place of business. If a taxpayer has more than one place of business, the location of the "principal" business is the tax home. The determination of which of two or more places of business is the "principal" one is a question of fact, determined by considering factors such as the amount of income earned in each location, the nature and extent of the business activities which take place in each location, and the amount of time spent in each location.

Example: Francis resides in Ohio where he operates a business as a consultant and development engineer and he is also employed by General Motors in Michigan. Last year, he spent 5 days each week for 50 weeks working in Michigan, returning to Ohio on the weekends, and he earned most of his income from his employment in Michigan. His "tax home" is in Michigan and he cannot deduct his expenses for meals and lodging while there. He may, however, deduct the transportation costs for driving from Michigan to Ohio and his lodging and 80% of meals while there on those few occasions when it was necessary for him to be in Ohio to manage his business enterprises there. [*Markey v. Comm'r,* 490 F.2d 1249 (6th Cir.1974); see also *Comm'r v. Flowers,* 326 U.S. 465, 66 S.Ct. 250 (1946).]

If a taxpayer has a principal place of business, and is assigned to work in another location for a *temporary* period, reasonably expected to last less than one year, he is "away from home" while on the assignment. If a taxpayer, however, is assigned to work at a new location on a *permanent* basis, or for an *indefinite* period of time, her tax home changes to the new location, which is her new "principal place of business"; her travel expenses incurred while at the new tax home are not deductible under IRC § 162(a)(2), even though her abode remains at the old location. [But some deduction for moving expenses may be available; see IRC § 217 and discussion, III. B. 9., at page 152, *infra.*]

Example: Philip is a systems analyst who lives with his family in Buffalo, NY and who works there for a major corporation. His employer sends him to San Francisco for an 18-month training program. His family remains in Buffalo in the house which they own there, and he is expected to return to his job in Buffalo at the conclusion of the training program. If a taxpayer anticipates employment at a new location to last for 1 year or more, and the employment does, in fact, last more than 1 year, it is presumed that the employment is indefinite, not temporary, and thus Philip's travel expenses in San Francisco would not be deductible. Philip may overcome this presumption, however, if his employment in San Francisco is expected to last for more than 1 year, but less than 2 years, and if objective factors demonstrate that he realistically expects to return to Buffalo. Here, the facts that Philip's family remains in their house in Buffalo, and that Philip's employer expects him to return to his job in Buffalo would overcome the presumption that his stay in San Francisco is indefinite; his stay in San Francisco is temporary and his travel expenses are deductible. If a taxpayer's actual or anticipated stay in a new location is 2 years or more, it will be considered an indefinite stay, and not a stay away from home, regardless of any other facts or circumstances. [Rev.Rul. 83–82, 1983–1 C.B. 45; see *Peurifoy v. Comm'r,* 358 U.S. 59, 79 S.Ct. 104 (1958).]

iii. Overnight rule

Expenses incurred for lodging and 80% of meals are deductible only if the taxpayer is away from her tax home long enough to require her to stop for substantial sleep or rest no matter what distance she travels or what mode of transportation she uses; otherwise, the expenditures are nondeductible personal expenses under IRC § 262.

> *Example:* Robert is a traveling salesman for a wholesale grocery company in Tennessee. He customarily leaves home early in the morning, eats breakfast and lunch on the road, and returns home in time for dinner. Because Robert is not away from home long enough to require sleep or rest, the cost of his breakfasts and lunches are not deductible traveling expenses; they are nondeductible personal expenses. [*U.S. v. Correll,* 389 U.S. 299, 88 S.Ct. 445 (1967).]

iv. Travel for business and personal reasons

If a taxpayer travels away from home and engages in both business and personal activities, the expenses of traveling to and from the distant location are deductible only if the *primary* reason for the trip relates to his trade or business. If the primary reason for the travel is to engage in personal activities, none of the expenses for travel are deductible. The determination of the primary reason for travel is a question of fact. In addition, expenses incurred at the location away from home which are properly allocable to the trade or business are deductible, even though the expenses of traveling there are not deductible, and vice versa. [Reg. § 1.162–2(b).]

> *Example:* Gale travels from her home and principal place of employment in Washington, DC, to New York City. While in New York, she spends 1 week on activities directly related to her business and 3 weeks on vacation. The travel is primarily for personal reasons, and the costs of her airplane ticket and other travel expenses are not deductible. However, expenses, including lodging and 80% of meals, incurred during the week she is engaged in business activities are deductible. [See Reg. § 1.162–2(b).]

v. Foreign travel

Deductions for expenses incurred while traveling outside the United States are subject to additional limitations. If travel outside the United States lasts more than one week, or if the non-business activities constitute 25% or more of the time traveling outside the United States away from home, only a portion of the travel expenses are deductible even though the primary reason for the travel is for business purposes. In applying this rule, travel outside the United States does not include any travel from one point in the United States to another point in the United States. [IRC § 274(c).] Deductions for expenses incurred in attending conventions in certain locations outside the United States are subject to additional restrictions. [See IRC § 274(h).]

Example: Hal flies from Chicago to New York where he spends 6 days on business. He then spends one day flying to London for 4 days of business meetings. The primary reason for Hal's overseas trip is to attend the business meetings in London, but once he is there he decides to fly to Paris for a 3 day vacation, after which he spends one day flying back to New York, where he changes planes to return to Chicago. Travel outside the United States away from home, including 2 days travel en route, exceed one week, and the nonbusiness activities exceeded 25% of the total time spent on such travel. (The time spent in New York on business is disregarded.) Nine days were spent outside the United States away from home, of which 3 days were spent on nonbusiness activities; thus, ³⁄₉ths (or ⅓) of the travel costs incurred between New York and London are not deductible because of the limitation of IRC § 274(c). The expense of meals and lodging while engaged in business in London are deductible; the expenses of traveling to Paris from London and expenses for meals and lodging while in Paris are personal and are not deductible in any event. [Reg. § 1.274–4(g) Example (7).]

vi. Water transportation

Restrictions apply to the deductibility of expenses incurred for transportation by water or in attending a convention, seminar or other meeting on a cruise ship. If otherwise deductible travel involves transportation by water, the amount of the deduction for each day of such travel is limited to two times the highest per diem allowance for Federal employees for travel within the United States. [IRC § 274(m)(1).] This limitation does not apply to the expense of attending a convention, seminar or other meeting on a cruise ship, however, other requirements must be satisfied or *no* deduction will be allowed. Cruise ship meeting expenses are deductible only if the meeting is directly related to the taxpayer's trade or business, the cruise ship is registered in the United States, all ports of call are in the United States or possessions, and certain reporting requirements are complied with. [IRC § 274(h)(2) and (5).]

vii. Spouse traveling with taxpayer

Traveling expenses incurred to enable the spouse (or other family members) of a taxpayer to travel with her on a business trip are deductible only if the spouse's presence on the trip has a bona fide business purpose. [Reg. § 1.162–2(c).]

Examples: For bona fide business reasons, Irene travels to a convention in Atlanta accompanied by her husband, John. While Irene attends the scheduled meetings at the convention, John goes shopping and visits with friends. He also spends a few minutes each evening typing up the notes which Irene has taken at the meetings that day and he accompanies her to the dinners scheduled each evening. John's traveling expenses to Atlanta are not deductible; Irene may deduct the cost of her hotel room at the single rate. [Rev.Rul. 56–168, 1956–1 C.B. 93.]

Roy is an employee and an officer of a corporation which produces "family-type" motion pictures. Longstanding company policy requires corporate executives to travel with their spouses when their presence will enhance the company's image or otherwise promote its interests. Edna, Roy's wife, travels with him on business trips, attending luncheons, dinners, film screenings, meetings of employees, exhibitors, distributors, business associates, the press and the public. In addition, she helps entertain at various social gatherings, she makes arrangements for some social functions, she is interviewed at some press conferences and she makes goodwill visits to people in the company's industry. The dominant purpose for Edna's travel is to serve Roy's business purposes in making the trips; thus, Edna's traveling expenses are deductible. [*U.S. v. Disney*, 413 F.2d 783 (9th Cir.1969).]

viii. Legislators

The "tax home" of a U.S. Senator or Representative is his residence in the district which he was elected to represent. Expenses for meals and lodging incurred while he is in Washington, DC, therefore, are incurred while he is "away from home," and are deductible, up to $3,000 per year. [IRC § 162(a), last sentence.]

A State legislator whose residence is more than 50 miles from the State capitol building may elect to treat her residence within the legislative district she represents as her "tax home." A State legislator who makes this election is deemed to have expenditures for meals and lodging in an amount equal to the number of "legislative days" for the taxable year, multiplied by the appropriate per diem rate. The amount of her deduction for food and lodging is computed under the statutory formula; the amount she actually spends is irrelevant. [IRC § 162(h).]

g. Meals

No deduction for the cost of food or beverages is allowed if, under the circumstances, the expenditure is lavish or extravagant or if the taxpayer or an employee is not present when the food or beverages are furnished. [IRC § 274(k).] The amount which may be deducted for the cost of food or beverages is generally limited to 80% of such cost. [IRC § 274(n)(1).] Further, unless the taxpayer is traveling away from home on business, the cost of food and beverages is treated as an entertainment expense and is deductible only if the meal is directly related to or associated with his trade or business. [IRC § 274(a); see discussion, III. C. 6. b., at page 161, *infra*.] Food and beverage expenses incurred by a taxpayer who is traveling away from home on business will also be treated as entertainment expenses unless she eats alone or with persons, such as family members, who are not business-connected (and then, only 80% of the cost of the taxpayer's meal qualifies for a deduction).

> ***Example:*** Stanley, an attorney who lives in New York, travels on business to Miami with his wife, June. The first night in Miami Stanley pays $100 for dinner for himself and June, of which $40 is attributable to June's meal. Stanley has a potential deduction of $48 (80% of $60). The second night, Stanley invites a client and his wife to dinner in order to maintain a good relationship with the client and Stanley picks up the tab of $200. Stanley may not deduct any portion of the second night's meal.

h. Rentals
i. In general

Expenditures for rentals or other payments required to be made for the use of property in a taxpayer's trade or business are deductible. [IRC § 162(a)(3).] The property being used may be real property, tangible personal property or intangible personal property; deductible payments include royalties for the use of intangible personal property, or royalties paid for the right to extract minerals from real property. The deduction is available for payments made for the "continued use or possession" of property, but payments made to acquire title to or an equity interest in property are not deductible.

Example: Delano has a fire sprinkler system installed in his manufacturing plant under an agreement which provides for him to make annual rental payments of $1,240 for 5 years. At the end of five years, Delano has the right to use the sprinkler system for an additional 5 years at an annual rental of $32, but if he does not elect to extend the lease, the lessor has the right to remove the system. Fire sprinkler systems are generally tailor-made for a specific location, and if an installed system is removed, its salvage value is negligible. Even though the parties structure the transaction as a "lease," and even though only a lessor/lessee relationship is established under local law, the *substance* of the transaction must be examined to determine whether the payments are for the "use or possession" of property, and thus are deductible as rental payments or whether the payments are made to acquire the property, and thus are nondeductible capital expenditures. The practical effect of the agreement is that Delano is purchasing the sprinkler system; therefore, the annual payments are not deductible as rent. Note, however, that depreciation deductions will be available for the cost of the sprinkler system and a portion of each annual payment may be deductible as interest. [*Estate of Starr v. Comm'r,* 274 F.2d 294 (9th Cir.1959).]

ii. Transfer and lease-back

Only "ordinary and necessary" business expenses are deductible. [See discussion, III. A. 1. a., at page 70, *supra.*] The statute provides that a deduction is available for "rentals, or other payments *required* to be made as a condition to the continued use or possession" of property. [IRC § 162(a)(3) (emphasis added).] When there is a gift and leaseback, the nature of the transaction is a negative assignment of income by means of a deduction (for rent) on the donor's part. The issue boils down to whether general assignment of income principles apply [see discussion, V. B., at page 245, *infra*] or whether a stricter requirement is applied due to the fact there is a deduction which contains the term "necessary." Some courts have denied a deduction on grounds of a sham or lack of business purpose. [See *White v. Fitzpatrick,* 193 F.2d 398 (2d Cir.1951).]

> ***Example:*** Lewis is a doctor whose office is located in a building which he owns. He transfers the building to an irrevocable trust for the benefit of his children. Lewis pays a reasonable monthly rent for the use of the building in his medical practice. Under the terms of the trust, Lewis does not retain substantially the same control over the building after transferring it to the trust, the trustee is independent, and the property is not used for the benefit of the donor because Lewis uses it strictly in his capacity as a lessee. The rental payments are deductible under IRC § 162. [*Cf. Quinlivan v. Comm'r,* 599 F.2d 269 (8th Cir.1979); and see *Rosenfeld v. Comm'r,* 706 F.2d 1277 (2d Cir.1983); but see *Mathews v. Comm'r,* 520 F.2d 323 (5th Cir.1975) (transfer of business assets to trust and lease-back disregarded and deduction for "rental" payments disallowed apparently because of lack of business purpose for the overall transaction, not just the lease-back).]

i.   Expenses for education

i.   In general

Expenses for education are not addressed in IRC § 162. The regulations, however, do attempt to describe situations where such expenditures satisfy the fundamental requirements of IRC § 162, and thus a deduction is allowable, and to distinguish them from situations where expenditures have a predominantly personal character, and thus no deduction is allowed. [Reg. § 1.162–5.] Generally, expenses incurred by an individual for education, whether or not the education leads to a degree, are deductible if one of two tests of deductiblity are satisfied and if neither of two tests of nondeductiblity are violated.

ii.   Tests of deductibility

Expenses for education may be deducted *either* if the education maintains or improves skills required by a taxpayer in his employment or other trade or business *or* if the education meets express requirements imposed by law or the taxpayer's employer as a condition to the retention of the taxpayer's employment, status, or rate of compensation. [Reg. § 1.162–5(a).]

a.   Maintaining or improving skills

Expenses for education may be deductible if skills which are used in the taxpayer's employment, or other trade or business, are maintained or improved by the education. [See Reg. § 1.162–5(c)(1).]

Examples: George is an attorney whose practice involves considerable work in matters pertaining to Federal taxation. He attends an Institute on Federal Taxation, sponsored by New York University, where he learns about trends, thinking and developments in Federal taxation from experts accomplished in that field. The costs of attending the Institute are deductible. [*Coughlin v. Comm'r,* 203 F.2d 307 (2d Cir.1953).]

James is a Chicago police detective. He enrolls in courses in Philosophy, English, History and Political Science at a local university. James is unable to demonstrate that his skills as a policeman are improved or maintained by the education, and thus the education expenses are not deductible. [*Carroll v. Comm'r,* 418 F.2d 91 (7th Cir.1969).]

b.   **Meeting requirements of employer or law**
   Expenses for education undertaken to satisfy requirements imposed by a taxpayer's employer, or by law, may be deductible. If the employer imposes the requirement, it must be for a bona fide business purpose of the employer. [Reg. § 1.162–5(c)(2).]

Example: Nora is engaged in the business of teaching school in Virginia, where state law requires teachers to have a valid teaching certificate. Regulations promulgated under the statute require teachers to renew their certificates every few years, and require a teacher to either pass an examination or acquire credits for taking certain college courses in order to renew her certificate. Although most teachers use the examination alternative, Nora enrolls in two college courses so that she can qualify to have her teaching certificate renewed. Nora's expenses for taking the two courses are deductible. [*Hill v. Comm'r,* 181 F.2d 906 (4th Cir.1950).]

iii. **Tests of nondeductiblity**
   Expenses for education must be incurred while carrying on a trade or business. They are not deductible, even though they satisfy either of the two tests of deductibility, if the education *either* is required in order to meet minimum educational requirements for the taxpayer's employment or other trade or business *or* is part of a program of study which will lead to qualifying the taxpayer for a new trade or business. [Reg. § 1.162–5(b).]

a.   Minimum educational requirements

Expenses for education are nondeductible if applicable laws, regulations, or professional standards require a taxpayer to obtain the education in order to meet the minimum educational requirements for his employment or other trade or business. If a taxpayer satisfies the minimum educational requirements for a particular job when he is first employed in the position, he is considered to continue to satisfy them even though they are subsequently changed. [Reg. § 1.162–5(b)(2)(i).]

Example: Donald, who has a B.A. degree, obtains a temporary job as an Instructor at Y University and at the same time he enrolls in graduate courses leading to a Ph.D. degree. Under University policy, Donald may not become a full time faculty member unless he has a Ph.D. degree, and he may hold his position as an Instructor only while he continues to make satisfactory progress towards his graduate degree. The graduate courses which Donald takes are to satisfy the minimum educational requirements for qualification in Donald's trade or business; the expenditures for the graduate courses, therefore, are not deductible. [Reg. § 1.162–5(b)(2)(iii) Example (2).]

b.   Qualification for new trade or business

Expenses for education may not be deducted if the education is part of a program of study leading to qualifying the taxpayer for a new trade or business. This rule does not apply if an employee obtains education to qualify her to perform *new duties,* if the new duties involve the *same general type of work* as is involved in her present employment. Generally, all teaching and related duties are considered to involve the same general type of work. [Reg. § 1.162–5(b)(3).]

Example: Ella is a high school mathematics teacher. She enrolls in college courses so that she may teach high school science courses. The education qualifies her for new duties involving the same general type of work, not a new trade or business; the expenses of the education, therefore, are deductible. Frank is self-employed as an accountant, and he enrolls in law school. Frank's expenditures in attending law school are not deductible because the course of study qualifies him for a new trade or business. Gloria is engaged in the private practice of psychiatry. She attends a program of study which qualifies her to practice psychoanalysis. Gloria may deduct her educational expenses because the education maintains or improves skills required by her trade or business and the education does not qualify her for a new trade or business. [Reg. § 1.162–5(b)(3) Examples (1) and (4).]

c. The "carrying on" requirement

The deduction for educational expenses must satisfy the fundamental requirements of IRC § 162, including the requirement that the expense be incurred while the taxpayer is "carrying on" a trade or business. [See discussion, III. A. 1. c., at page 73, *supra.*] This requirement may preclude the deduction for educational expenses incurred when a taxpayer has not yet begun a trade or business, or when he has abandoned his trade or business.

Examples: C.B. enrolls in a graduate tax program immediately after he graduates from law school with his J.D. degree. His expenses in attending the graduate tax program are not deductible because, even though he is admitted to the Louisiana bar, he has never actively engaged in the profession of law. [*Johnson v. U.S.,* 332 F.Supp. 906 (E.D.La.1971).]

Irene has been engaged in the practice of anesthesiology for several years, however, she suspends her practice indefinitely because of increases in her premiums for malpractice insurance. While her practice is suspended, she attends educational sessions, medical meetings, and conventions to maintain her professional competence in the field of anesthesiology. Irene's educational expenses incurred while her practice is suspended are not deductible because they are not incurred while she is carrying on the trade or business of anesthesiology. [Rev.Rul. 77–32, 1977–1 C.B. 38.]

iv. Travel *as* education

Expenses for travel as a form of education are not deductible. [IRC § 274(m)(2).]

Example: Edith is a high school world history teacher. During the summer vacation, she travels to France where she spends 8 weeks visiting various places which have an important part in the history, art or architecture of France. Even though Edith can demonstrate that the major portion of her activities during the trip are directly related to maintaining or improving the skills required in her employment as a world history teacher, her travel expenses are not deductible.

v.   Travel *to obtain* education

If a taxpayer travels away from home primarily to obtain education, and the education expenses are deductible, then the traveling expenses, including lodging and 80% of the cost of meals, are also deductible. [Reg. § 1.162–5(e).]

Example: Harold is a lawyer who lives and practices law in Washington, DC. He takes a leave-of-absence from his law firm and travels to Gainesville, FL, to attend a 9 month graduate law program leading to an LL.M. degree in Federal taxation. While enrolled in school in Florida, he flies to Boston for a vacation during a 3 week semester break. Harold's expenses incurred in traveling from Washington to Florida and returning at the end of the year are deductible, as are his expenses for lodging and 80% of the cost of meals while in Gainesville; his expenses for traveling to Boston for vacation purposes over semester break, however, are not deductible. [See Reg. § 1.162–5(e)(2) Example (1).]

j.   **Miscellaneous business deductions**

IRC § 162 authorizes the deduction of business expenses in general terms, enumerating by way of illustration only three specific types of expenses which may qualify: salaries, traveling expenses, and rent. [See discussions, III. A. 1. e., f., and h., at pages 76, 78 and 84, *supra.*] Several categories of deductible business expenses occur with sufficient frequency to be mentioned here.

i.   Entertainment

Expenses incurred for meals and entertaining may be deducted if there is a demonstrable business benefit to be derived from the expenditure, and if the expenditure is "ordinary and necessary." It is customary to entertain customers, prospective customers or suppliers in most businesses, and thus such expenditures are generally deductible. Deductions for expenditures for entertainment are subject to additional restrictive rules of IRC § 274 [see discussion, III. C. 6., at page 161, *infra*], and generally only 80% of the cost of deductible entertainment as well as 80% of the cost of food and beverages may be deducted [see discussion, III. A. 1. g., at page 84, *supra*].

ii.   Uniforms

A deduction is allowable for the cost of uniforms and work clothing, if they are specifically required as a condition of employment and if they are not adaptable to general use. [Rev.Rul. 70–474, 1970–2 C.B. 34.] Law enforcement personnel, fire fighters, nurses, and baseball players may, therefore, generally deduct the cost of their uniforms. Military uniforms of full-time active duty personnel generally take the place of civilian clothing, and, thus, their cost is not deductible. If the cost of the uniform or work clothing is deductible, so is the cost of maintaining it, including dry cleaning or laundry expenses.

iii.   Dues

A deduction is generally allowed for the payment of dues to an organization which is directly related to a taxpayer's employment or other trade or business. Thus, dues paid to a local chamber of commerce, trade association, or professional society are generally deductible. Likewise, dues paid by a plumber to her local union or annual dues paid by an attorney to the state bar are deductible. However, dues paid to social, athletic, or sporting clubs or organizations are subject to the restrictive rules of IRC § 274. [See discussion, III. C. 6. c., at page 162, *infra.*]

iv.   Periodicals

Amounts spent for periodicals and books whose useful life is short may be deducted if they relate to the taxpayer's business and otherwise satisfy the deductibility requirements of IRC § 162.

Example: Lloyd is an executive of 6 corporations conducting substantial and profitable businesses. He subscribes to *Time* magazine and the *Wall Street Journal* newspaper. He may not deduct the cost of the *Time* subscription, a periodical of general interest, but he may deduct the cost of the *Wall Street Journal,* because it is more exclusively of business interest. [*Noland v. Comm'r,* 269 F.2d 108 (4th Cir.1959).]

v.   Utilities

The costs of water, electricity, telephone and other utilities are deductible if they are ordinary and necessary and incurred in carrying on a trade or business.

Example: Thomas is a fireman who is required by his employer to be on call 24 hours a day and to have a telephone so that he may be called in emergencies or for extra duty. He is allowed a deduction for a portion of the expense of maintaining the telephone; he is not allowed a deduction to the extent the telephone is used for personal purposes. [*Thomas C. Banks,* ¶ 81,480 P–H Memo TC.]

vi. Taxes

Deductions for payment of certain, specifically enumerated state, local and foreign taxes are authorized under IRC § 164. [See discussion, III. B. 3., at page 135, *infra.*] Payment of taxes which are not listed in IRC § 164, and for which deductions are not specifically disallowed under IRC § 275, may be deducted if incurred as an ordinary and necessary business expense. [Reg. § 1.164–3(f).] No deduction is allowed, however, for any tax paid in connection with acquiring or disposing of property; instead, the amounts of such taxes are added to the cost basis of the property, if paid by the buyer, or subtracted from the amount realized for the property, if paid by the seller. [IRC § 164(a), last sentence.]

Examples: Taxidriver pays a state sales tax on items such as oil and tires purchased in conjunction with running his taxi. Although the tax is not specifically deductible under IRC § 164, it is deductible under IRC § 162. [See also the last sentence of IRC § 164(a).]

Leo purchases for $1 million a building from Melanie for use in his business. Leo pays a $1,000 State intangibles tax and Melanie pays a $1,500 State documentary stamp tax. Neither Leo nor Melanie may deduct the State taxes they paid. Leo's basis for the building is $1,001,000 and Melanie's amount realized is $998,500.

k.   Substantiation requirements

As a matter of tax planning, taxpayers should be prepared to prove that they actually incurred, and paid, an expenditure for which they expect to take a deduction. If the I.R.S. disallows a deduction and if a taxpayer does not have substantiating proof of an expenditure, the taxpayer may be able to obtain a deduction for an approximate amount which would have been spent in light of the surrounding circumstances, unless a statute requires more specific substantiation.

Example: Jasper leases a small store where he is engaged in the business of selling children's clothing at retail. He takes a deduction for his expenses for rent and utilities at the store, but the IRS disallows the deductions because he does not have any receipts or other records reflecting the amounts he spent. Because it is reasonable for someone to pay $300 per month rent, and $75 per month for utilities, for a store of the same size and general location as Jasper's, a court may allow him a deduction in those amounts, notwithstanding his lack of substantiation. [*Cohan v. Comm'r,* 39 F.2d 540 (2d Cir.1930).]

IRC § 274(d), initially enacted in 1962, provides an exception to the *Cohan* estimate rule and specifically disallows deductions for traveling expenses (including meals and lodging while away from home), business gifts, entertainment expenses, business meals and certain "listed property" including automobiles and personal computers, unless the taxpayer substantiates by adequate records or other evidence the amount of the expense, the time and place of the travel or entertainment, or the date and description of the gift, the business purpose of the expenditure, and the business relationship to the taxpayer of the person entertained or receiving the gift. [See also IRC § 280F(d)(4).] The regulations specify the details of acceptable substantiating records or other evidence. [Reg. § 1.274–5.] This provision precludes a taxpayer from attempting to deduct an expenditure for one of the enumerated categories of expenses unless he can produce the prescribed substantiation; a court cannot allow an estimated or approximate amount as a deduction, regardless of the surrounding circumstances and the reasonable likelihood that the taxpayer, in fact, actually incurred an expense.

2. NONBUSINESS EXPENSES

An individual may deduct all ordinary and necessary expenses paid or incurred during a taxable year: (1) for the production or collection of income, (2) for the management of property held for the production of income, or (3) for dealing with tax matters. [IRC § 212.] The first two provisions were enacted in response to a decision of the Supreme Court that someone who invests in corporate stocks and bonds is not "carrying on a trade or business," and, thus, his expenses related to such investments are not deductible under IRC § 162. [*Higgins v. Comm'r,* 312 U.S. 212, 61 S.Ct. 475 (1941); see discussion, III. A. 1. d., at page 75, *supra.*] Concepts developed under IRC § 162 are pertinent to the deduction allowed by IRC § 212 as well. [See *Bingham's Trust v. Comm'r,* 325 U.S. 365, 65 S.Ct. 1232 (1945).] To be deductible, therefore, an item must be "ordinary and necessary," it must be an "expense," and it must not be inherently personal in nature. Congress has denied deductions for the costs of attending a convention, seminar, or similar meeting relating to IRC § 212 activities although expenses of attending such an event which relates to a trade or business generally are deductible. [IRC § 274(h)(7).] In addition, these deductions authorized under IRC § 212 are generally miscellaneous itemized deductions, deductible only if a taxpayer elects to itemize deductions and then only to the extent the total amount of miscellaneous itemized deductions exceeds 2% of the taxpayer's adjusted gross income. [IRC § 67; see discussion at VII. A, at page 304, *infra.*]

Even though the statute only authorizes a deduction to "an individual," qualifying nonbusiness expenses incurred by an estate or a trust may be deducted by the personal representative or trustee. A corporation is not entitled to deductions under the authority of IRC § 212, but a corporation's activities generally are presumed to qualify as "carrying on a trade or business," and thus a corporation's expenses are deductible under IRC § 162.

Examples: Jack purchases common stock of a major corporation for $300,000, believing that it is a good long-term investment. Later, he learns that the corporate management is not operating the business very well, so he and some other shareholders form a Committee and attempt to change the corporation's management by engaging in a proxy battle. Jack contributes $17,000 to the Committee as his share of its expenses in waging the proxy battle. The Committee succeeds in replacing one third of the Directors of the corporation. The corporation's profits increase, as do the dividends paid to Jack, and he subsequently sells his stock at a $50,000 gain. The expenditure is "ordinary and necessary" and is proximately related to the production of income; the $17,000, therefore, is deductible. [*Surasky v. U.S.,* 325 F.2d 191 (5th Cir.1963); Rev.Rul. 64–236, 1964–2 C.B. 64.]

Samuel owned 100 shares of stock in a major corporation. When he died, he left 50 shares to a charitable trust, and the remaining 50 shares to his wife, Karen. Subsequent to Samuel's death, Karen purchased the shares of stock which had been left to the charity for $255,000. The State Attorney General filed suit to invalidate the sale, and Karen spent $30,000 for attorney's fees in a successful defense of the litigation. The deductibility of litigation expenses, including attorney's fees, turns on the "origin of the claim" involved in the litigation. The $30,000 expenditure for attorney's fees is not a deductible "expense" because it is incurred in defending or perfecting her title to the shares of stock; the $30,000 is a capital expenditure and must be added to her basis for the shares of stock. [*Bowers v. Lumpkin,* 140 F.2d 927 (4th Cir.1944); Reg. § 1.212–1(k).]

Meyer entered into an antenuptial agreement with his wife-to-be, Joan, providing that in the event of divorce, Meyer would pay Joan $5,000, and Joan would release all marital rights she might otherwise have to Meyer's property. Six years later, Joan filed for divorce, and sought to have the antenuptial agreement set aside. Meyer incurred $3,000 in legal expenses defending Joan's suit. The "origin of the claim" filed by Joan arose out of the marital relationship; thus, the expenses which Meyer incurred in defending the action were inherently personal in nature and not deductible. [*Meyer J. Fleischman*, 45 T.C. 439 (1966).]

a. Production or collection of income

Ordinary and necessary expenses paid or incurred in a taxable year for the production or collection of income are deductible by an individual taxpayer. [IRC § 212(1).] An expense may be deductible even though the income to which it relates is not realized in the same taxable year as the expense is paid or incurred. [Reg. § 1.212–1(b).] Further, "income" includes rents, dividends, interest, alimony and other current receipts, as well as income in the nature of gain from the disposition of property. Expenses incurred in protecting or asserting one's rights to property, or income from property, as an heir or beneficiary are capital expenditures and are not deductible. [Reg. § 1.212–1(k).] Although attorney's fees incurred incident to a divorce are generally nondeductible personal expenses, they may be deductible to the extent they are attributable to obtaining alimony or are related to tax advice in the divorce proceedings. [Reg. § 1.262–1(b)(7); I.R.C. § 212(3).]

b. Management of income producing property

Ordinary and necessary expenses paid or incurred in a taxable year for the management, conservation, or maintenance of property held for the production of income are deductible. [IRC § 212(2).]

Example: Mary died leaving shares of stock in a trust which provided that the trust income was to be paid to certain beneficiaries for a number of years, at which time the trust would terminate and the trust assets would be distributed to other beneficiaries. In the year of termination, the trust incurs expenses associated with the final distribution of the trust assets. The expenditures are for managing the trust fund, which consists of property held for the production of income during the term of the trust, and, therefore, the expenses are deductible. [*Bingham's Trust v. Comm'r*, 325 U.S. 365, 65 S.Ct. 1232 (1945).]

Expenses paid or incurred for managing, conserving, or maintaining investment property are deductible even though the property is not currently producing income, and even though it is unlikely that the property will be disposed of at a gain; it is sufficient if the property is being held in order to minimize an unrealized loss in its value. [Reg. § 1.212–1(b).] Deductions are not allowed for expenses incurred with respect to property which is held for personal purposes. It is possible, however, to change one's relationship to property; qualifying expenses incurred while property is held for the production of income are deductible even though the property was formerly held for personal use.

Example: Ed owns a house at the seashore, which he used for personal purposes as a summer residence until 3 years ago when he listed the house with a real estate broker, attempting to sell it. He bought the house 6 years ago for $100,000, and his asking price for the house is $150,000. During the current year, he incurs expenses for maintenance and repairs to the house. If he also puts the house up for *rent* while attempting to sell it, it is held for the production of income. [*William C. Horrmann*, 171 T.C. 903 (1951).] Even if he holds the house solely for sale, the expenses may be deductible if he is no longer holding the house for personal use and he is holding the house for the production of income, *i.e.*, an anticipated *postconversion* profit when he sells it. [*Lowry v. U.S.*, 384 F.Supp. 257 (D.N.H.1974).] In addition, in both situations above, he may take depreciation deductions. [See discussion, III. A. 5., at page 104, *infra*, and compare deductibility of losses on sales of converted residences at III. A. 3. b. iii., at page 98, *infra*.]

c. **Expenses in connection with taxes**

Expenses incurred or paid in connection with the determination, collection, or refund of *any tax* (not just income taxes) are deductible. [IRC § 212(3).] The tax may be imposed by the Federal government, or a State or local government; the expenses may be for preparing tax returns, contesting a tax liability, or determining the tax consequences of anticipated action. [Reg. § 1.212–1(l).]

Example: Wilma pays $1,000 in attorneys fees to unsuccessfully contest a property tax assessment on her residence. The expenses are deductible.

3. **LOSSES**
a. **In general**

A deduction is allowed for any loss sustained during a taxable year which is not compensated for by insurance or otherwise. [IRC § 165(a).] Just as unrealized appreciation in the value of property does not give rise to gain, a loss must be "sustained" to be deductible. Some "closed and completed transaction," such as a sale or exchange, or some "identifiable event," such as a theft or a fire, must occur before a deductible loss arises; an unrealized decline in the value of property does not give rise to a deductible loss. [Reg. § 1.165–1(b).] Individuals may take deductions only for losses which are incurred in a trade or business, losses incurred in transactions entered into for profit, and certain casualty losses. [IRC § 165(c); see discussion of casualty losses, III. B. 4., at page 136, *infra*.] Different rules of deductibility apply to losses which arise in a business or profit-seeking context and to personal losses.

In addition if losses are capital losses, they may be deducted only within the limitations of IRC §§ 1211 and 1212. [See discussion, VI. B. 2., at page 271, *infra*.]

b. Amount of loss
i. In general

The amount of a loss from the sale or other disposition of property is the excess of the adjusted basis of the property over the amount realized. [IRC § 1001(a).] If there is no realization event, however, such as when property is damaged or destroyed by a fire or other casualty, the amount of the loss is the *lesser* of the difference between the fair market values of the property immediately before and immediately after the damage is done *and* the adjusted basis of the property; thus the amount of the loss *deduction* may never exceed the amount of the property's adjusted basis. [IRC § 165(b).] In addition, if property used in a business or profit-seeking activity is *totally destroyed* and its fair market value immediately before destruction is less than its adjusted basis, the amount of the loss is the property's adjusted basis. [Reg. § 1.165–7(b)(1).]

Example: Elliot purchases a delivery truck for use in his business for $20,000, and he takes $11,000 in depreciation deductions over the next several years, thereby reducing the truck's adjusted basis to $9,000. At a time when the truck's fair market value is $12,000, it is damaged by a hit-and-run driver. Elliot pays $10,000 to fix the damages, for which he is not compensated. The work done on the truck only takes care of the damage suffered and merely restores the truck to its pre-accident condition and fair market value. [See Reg. § 1.165–7(a)(2)(ii).] The amount of Elliot's loss is $10,000, but he may deduct only $9,000, the amount of the truck's adjusted basis immediately prior to the accident. [Elliot's basis in the truck after the transaction is $10,000 ($9,000 pre-accident basis less $9,000 loss deduction plus $10,000 capital expenditure).] In the alternative, if the truck had a fair market value of $6,000 and an adjusted basis of $9,000 and it was totally destroyed in an accident, the amount of the loss would be $9,000; but if the truck were not totally destroyed and was worth $2,000 after the accident, Elliot's loss would be limited to $4,000.

ii. "Compensated for by insurance or otherwise"

A deduction may be taken with respect to a loss only to the extent that it is "*not* compensated for by insurance or otherwise." If a taxpayer has insurance covering damaged or stolen property, however, the deduction is allowable even if he does not file a claim with his insurance company for reimbursement. This does not apply, however, to personal casualty losses. [IRC § 165(h)(4)(E); see discussion at III. B. 4., at page 136, *infra.*]

> *Example:* If Elliot, whose truck was damaged in the first part of the preceding Example, recovered $8,000 in insurance or in a lawsuit, his loss would be limited to $1,000, $9,000 less the recovery. If he recovered $10,000 he would not have any loss and would have a $1,000 casualty gain (the excess of his insurance amount realized less his adjusted basis in the property). If Elliot's only prospect for reimbursement, however, was to file a claim under his own comprehensive motor vehicle insurance policy, but he does not file such a claim, a loss would be sustained and a deduction would be allowed. [*Hills v. Comm'r,* 76 T.C. 484 (1981).]

iii. Losses on property converted from personal use to business use

If property is acquired and initially used for personal purposes before being converted to business use, and if its fair market value is less than its adjusted basis on the date of conversion, a loss which is subsequently sustained is limited to the fair market value of the property.

> *Example:* Ivan purchased an airplane for personal use at a cost of $40,000. Two years later, when the fair market value of the airplane was $25,000, Ivan began using the airplane exclusively in his business and the next day the airplane was completely destroyed in a tornado. The amount of Ivan's loss is $25,000. [See Reg. § 1.165–7(a)(5).] Allowance of a $40,000 loss would in effect allow Ivan a deduction for the decline in value during the time the airplane was held for personal use. If the loss had occurred at a later time, the amount of Ivan's loss would be $25,000 reduced by any depreciation taken on the airplane.

c. Classification of losses

i. Trade or business losses

Losses realized from the sale or other disposition of property which is used in a trade or business are deductible. Whether one is "engaged in a trade or business" turns on the same concepts explored in IRC § 162. [See discussion, III. A. 1. d., at page 75, *supra.*]

Examples: Gordon buys a computer which he uses exclusively for business purposes. At a time when the computer has an adjusted basis of $5,000, he sells it for $3,500. Gordon has a deductible loss of $1,500 on the sale.

Hester buys an apartment building and operates a business of renting the apartments for several years. At a time when the building has an adjusted basis of $200,000 and it is subject to liabilities of $150,000, she abandons it because rental income has dropped and she does not want to pay for improvements to the building so that it will comply with various building codes and housing ordinances. Hester has a loss of $50,000 on the abandonment of the building. [See Reg. § 1.167(a)–8(a)(4).]

Ian's uninsured truck used in his trade or business is destroyed in a wreck. His adjusted basis in the truck was $5,000 and it was worth $6,000 prior to the wreck. He may deduct a $5,000 loss. [Reg. § 1.165–7(b)(1).]

a.   Demolition losses

No deduction is allowed for a loss sustained upon a taxpayer's demolition of a building or other structure regardless of the capacity in which the structure is held. The amount of such a loss, plus the costs of demolition, must be added to the basis of the land. [IRC § 280B.]

Example: Julia buys some improved real estate for $100,000; $95,000 of the purchase price is allocated to the land and $5,000 is allocated to a warehouse which was built many years ago. A year later, Julia decides to tear down the warehouse and build an office building on the land. It costs $2,000 to demolish the warehouse. Julia may not deduct either the $5,000 loss of the warehouse or the $2,000 demolition expenses; $7,000 is added to the basis of Julia's land.

b.   Gambling losses

Losses arising from gambling, even if the gambling activities are arguably a trade or business or "transactions entered into for profit," are limited to the extent of gains derived from gambling during the taxable year. [IRC § 165(d).]

Example: Fritzie devotes 50 hours a week to playing the ponies; during the current year, she wins $85,000 with some well-placed bets at the racetrack, but she also loses

$90,000 on other bets. Fritzie may only deduct $85,000 of her wagering losses.

ii.   Losses incurred in a transaction entered into for profit

Losses are also allowed with respect to transactions entered into for profit. [IRC § 165(c)(2).]

Example: William purchased some stock at a cost of $8,000 which he sells for $6,000 and some tax exempt bonds purchased for $10,000 which he sells at $9,500. William has deductible losses of $2,000 and $500, respectively.

The threshold for deducting losses in a "transaction entered into for profit" is higher than the threshold for deducting expenses paid or incurred for the production or collection of income, or for managing property held for the production of income. [See IRC § 212, and discussion, III. A. 2., at page 93, *supra.*]

Example: William's mother died and left him a house which he lived in for several years. He decided that the house was too large for him, so he moved out and attempted to either rent or sell the property. The house was never rented, and it was ultimately sold at a loss. William incurred expenses for maintaining the house while it was being held for sale or rent. Because the house was being "held for the production of income," the maintenance expenses and depreciation are deductible even though no income was currently being produced, and even though the house was ultimately sold at a loss. The loss incurred on the sale is not deductible, however, because there was no *transaction* entered into for profit. Merely abandoning the personal use of the house, and listing it for sale or rent, is not sufficient. [*William C. Horrmann,* 17 T.C. 903 (1951).] If the house had been rented there would have been a *transaction* with respect to the house and the loss would be deductible.

Some restrictions are imposed on the deductibility of losses arising in connection with investments in stocks, securities, and certain debt obligations.

a.   Worthless securities

If a taxpayer owns a security which is a capital asset, and if the security becomes worthless during a taxable year, it is deemed to be disposed of in a sale or exchange transaction occurring on the last day of the taxpayer's taxable year. [IRC

§ 165(g); see discussion, VI. B. 4. b. i., at page 283, *infra.*] A "security" means: (1) a share of stock in a corporation, (2) a right to subscribe for a share of stock in a corporation, or (3) a bond or other evidence of indebtedness issued by a corporation or by a governmental authority, but only if it has interest coupons or is in registered form. [IRC § 165(g)(2).]

b. Registration requirement

The loss deduction is denied for losses incurred with respect to certain debt obligations which have not been issued in registered form. [IRC § 165(j).] Generally, the obligations subject to the disallowance rule are ones which have been issued to the public by governmental entities after 1982; such obligations are also subject to restrictions on the issuer's deduction for interest paid, and on the bearer for receiving tax-free interest. [IRC §§ 163(f) and 103(j); see discussions, III. B. 2., at page 131, *infra,* and II. C. 3., at page 49, *supra.*]

iii. Casualty losses

The theft or destruction of property which is used in a trade or business or profit-seeking activities may give rise to a loss deduction using the principles above. Special rules may apply to determine the character of all such losses. [IRC § 1231; see discussion, VI. C., at page 291, *infra.*] In addition, special rules apply to casualty losses with respect to property used for personal purposes, known as personal casualty losses. [IRC § 165(c)(3) and (h); see discussion, III. B. 4., at page 136, *infra.*]

d. Timing of losses

Losses are deductible in the year in which sustained following normal accounting rules. Special rules apply to the timing of business, profit seeking, or personal casualty losses. [See discussion, III. B. 4. d., at page 140, *infra.*]

4. BAD DEBTS
a. In general

A deduction is allowed for any debt which becomes worthless during a taxable year. [IRC § 166(a).] The manner in which the deduction is allowed depends upon the nature of the debt, i.e., whether the debt is a business debt, a nonbusiness debt, or a security.

b. Bona fide debt requirement

Only a bona fide debt, arising from a debtor/creditor relationship based on a valid and enforceable obligation to pay a fixed or determinable sum of money, may provide a deduction if it becomes worthless. Whether a debtor/creditor relationship exists is a question of fact determined by the intention of the parties at the time the "debt" was created. Generally, if the lender had a reasonable expectation of being repaid at the time the funds were lent, the resulting debt is bona fide. If the facts indicate that a gift was intended, however, no debtor/creditor relationship exists and no deduction is allowed if the funds are not later repaid. "Loans" between family members or close friends, therefore, are closely scrutinized by the I.R.S.

Example: Howard owned and ran a beer parlor in Hermosa Beach. On several occasions over a period of years, Howard lent money to Paul, who was a friend and a steady customer at the beer parlor. Paul borrowed the money for various business ventures, none of which proved to be successful. The loans were evidenced by notes, and a reasonable rate of interest was also to be paid. Howard lent Paul the money because he believed Paul's business ventures would be successful and that he would be repaid; there was no indication that Howard was making gifts to Paul. A bona fide debtor/creditor relationship was established. [*Howard S. Bugbee,* 34 T.C.M. 291 (1975).]

c. Determination of worthlessness

A taxpayer has the burden of demonstrating that a debt becomes worthless in the taxable year in which the deduction is claimed. All pertinent evidence, including the value of any collateral securing the debt and the financial condition of the debtor, will be considered in determining whether a debt has become worthless. The creditor does not need to institute legal action against the debtor to demonstrate that the debt is worthless, and a debtor's declaration of bankruptcy is generally evidence that at least part of her unsecured debts are worthless. A deductible bad debt, however, must be worthless and uncollectible; a gratuitous forgiveness of a debt does not generate a bad debt deduction.

d. Amount of deduction

The amount of the deduction for any bad debt is limited to the adjusted basis of the debt. [IRC § 166(b).]

Example: Roxanna is a cash method taxpayer who works for a regional airline company. Her salary is generally paid to her every 2 weeks. However, her employer is in financial difficulty and files for bankruptcy at a time when she is owed $1,000 in unpaid salary. Even though it does not appear likely that she will ever be paid the $1,000, she may not take a bad debt deduction because she has not included the $1,000 in her gross income and, thus, she has a zero basis for her claim against her employer. [See Reg. § 1.166–1(e).] If Roxanna had used the accrual method of accounting, she would have included the

$1,000 salary in her gross income at the time her right to the amount became fixed, even though the amount remained unpaid. Thus, she would have had a basis of $1,000 in the claim against her employer and would be entitled to a bad debt deduction. [See discussions of the cash and accrual methods of accounting, IV. B. 1. b. and 2. c., at pages 188 and 196, *infra.*]

e. Special rules for business bad debts

The deduction which is allowed for a worthless business debt is an *ordinary* loss. [IRC § 165.] A "business debt" is not defined in the Code, but the term is used to refer to a debt which is *neither* a "nonbusiness debt," defined in IRC § 166(d), *nor* a "security," defined in IRC § 165(g). A deduction may be allowed for a business debt which becomes wholly worthless during a taxable year, or to the extent it becomes *partially* worthless during a taxable year. [IRC § 166(a)].

Example: X Corporation, an accrual method taxpayer, is in the business of selling appliances. During the current year, it sells a $1,000 refrigerator on credit ($200 cash down payment and a note for $800 plus interest) to a customer who, a few months later, files for bankruptcy. Initial proceedings in the bankruptcy court make it clear that creditors such as X Corporation will not be paid more than one half of their claims. X Corporation may deduct $400 for its partially worthless debt of $800.

f. Special rules for nonbusiness debts

With respect to taxpayers other than corporations, a "nonbusiness debt" is subject to different rules: (1) the nonbusiness debt must become *wholly* worthless before any deduction is allowable; and (2) the amount of a worthless nonbusiness debt is deemed to be a short-term capital loss and is deductible as such. [IRC § 166(d); see discussion, VI. B. 2., at page 271, *infra.*]

A "nonbusiness debt" is a debt *other than:* (1) a debt which was created or acquired in connection with a trade or business of the taxpayer; or (2) a debt which becomes worthless, producing a loss which is incurred in the taxpayer's trade or business. [IRC § 166(d)(2).]

Example: Thresa is engaged in the grocery business, and in Year One she extends credit to Walter. In Year Two, Thresa sells the business to Yvonne, but she retains the claim against Walter, which becomes worthless in Year Three. Thresa's claim against Walter is *not* a nonbusiness debt (it is a business debt) because the debt was created in connection with Thresa's business. Alternatively, Thresa dies, leaving the grocery business and the claim against Walter to her son, Alan. The debt is *not* a nonbusiness debt (again, it is a business debt) in Alan's hands because the loss, when the debt becomes worthless in Year Three, is sustained incident to the conduct of the grocery business at the time the debt becomes worthless. In the third alternative, Thresa dies, leaving the grocery business to her son, Alan, but she leaves the claim against Walter to her daughter, Betty, who is not engaged in any trade or business in Year Three. The debt *is* a nonbusiness debt in Betty's hands because it was not created or acquired in any trade or business of Betty, nor was the loss sustained as a proximate incident of any trade or business of Betty at the time the debt became worthless. [Reg. § 1.166–5(d) Examples (1), (3) and (4).]

g. Worthless securities

Debts which are issued by a corporation, a government or political subdivision and which are evidenced by a bond, certificate or other evidence of indebtedness with interest coupons or in registered form are treated as "securities." [IRC § 165(g)(2)(C).] If a security is a capital asset and it becomes worthless, the bad debt rules of IRC § 166 do not apply; the loss is characterized as a long-term or short-term capital loss under the loss rules of IRC § 165(g). [See discussion, III. A. 3. c. ii. *a.,* at page 100, *supra.*]

h. Debts owed by political parties

No deduction is allowed for the worthlessness of a debt owed by a political party because to allow deductions for such debts would indirectly provide a deduction for political contributions. [IRC § 271; see also IRC § 276.]

5. PROPERTY

The cost of acquiring property used in a trade or business or property held for the production of income is generally a nondeductible capital expenditure because such property has a greater than one year life. [IRC § 263.] Because the income tax is imposed on *net* income, however, it is appropriate to allow a deduction, in some manner and at some point in time, for the cost of items of property which is used up while producing income. The depreciation deduction has traditionally provided such treatment by spreading the cost of property used up in producing income (the basis of the property less its salvage value) over the number of taxable years it is used in producing income (the useful life of the property). [IRC § 167.] Beginning in 1981, depreciation deductions have been computed, for most items of property, under the "Accelerated Cost Recovery System" (ACRS), which permits the entire cost of qualifying property to be deducted over a period of time which is usually much shorter than the time the property will actually be used in producing income. [IRC § 168(e).] The Tax Reform Act of 1986 substantially altered the ACRS rules and the new rules are referred to as "current ACRS" while the rules enacted in 1981 are referred to as "old ACRS." In varying situations, property may be subject to the pre-ACRS rules of depreciation deductions under IRC § 167, the old ACRS rules, or the current ACRS rules. The basis of property which qualifies for depreciation deductions must be reduced by the amount of the deductions allowed or allowable for such deductions. [IRC § 1016(a)(2).] Other rules considered later such as IRC § 179 bonus depreciation and the limitations of IRC § 280F also interrelate with the depreciation rules.

a. Depreciation deductions (non-ACRS)

A depreciation deduction is allowed in the amount of a "reasonable allowance" for the exhaustion, wear and tear, or obsolescence of property which is either used in a trade or business or held for the production of income. [IRC § 167(a).] The "reasonable allowance" for most tangible property is provided under the Accelerated Cost Recovery System (ACRS). [ACRS is discussed at III. A. 5. b., at page 110, *infra.*] The discussion in this section is confined to property which is *not* subject to the ACRS rules.

The deduction for depreciation is not available for inventory or property held for sale to customers, nor does it apply to property used for personal purposes. A deduction may be taken only with respect to property which, by its nature, is subject to being exhausted, worn out, or becoming obsolete. The "reasonable allowance" for depreciation is a function of the property's basis, salvage value, and useful life, as well as the method of computation used; these concepts are explored further in the following paragraphs of this section.

Example: Abigail buys an apartment building to operate in her business of renting apartments. The building is of a character which is subject to the allowance for depreciation, and depreciation deductions may be taken with respect to its use in Abigail's business. The land on which the building is constructed, however, is not subject to exhaustion, to wear and tear, or to obsolescence, and, thus, no depreciation deductions may be taken with respect to the land.

i. Cost or other basis

The depreciation deduction for an item of property is generally computed with reference to its adjusted basis used for determining gain on the sale or other disposition of the property. [IRC § 167(g).] If the property has been used for personal purposes, however, before being used in income seeking activities, the fair market value of the property as of the date of conversion is used to compute the depreciation deduction, if that amount is lower than the property's adjusted basis.

> *Example:* Barney receives a computer, which he uses in his business, as a gift. The adjusted basis of the computer, determined under IRC § 1015, is $4,000; the allowance for depreciation is computed with reference to the $4,000 adjusted basis. Alternatively, Barney purchases a computer for $5,000 cash and uses it at home to play video games. Some time later, when the computer has a fair market value of $2,500, he takes it to his business office and thereafter uses it exclusively in his business. The basis for computing the depreciation deduction is $2,500. [Reg. § 1.167(g)–1.]

If an item of property is used partly for personal purposes and partly for business purposes during a taxable year, the property must be divided between its business and personal uses, and depreciation deductions are allowed only with respect to the property's basis allocated to the business use. Additional restrictions on the depreciation deduction may apply with respect to certain types of property if it is not used exclusively for business purposes. [IRC § 280F, See discussion, III. A. 5. d. vi., at page 121, *infra.*]

> *Example:* Hugh purchased an airplane for $54,000 which he used 25% for business purposes and 75% for personal purposes. Depreciation deductions are only allowed on the basis of $13,500 (25% of $54,000). [*Sharp v. U.S.*, 199 F.Supp. 743 (D.Del.1961).]

ii. Useful life

The useful life of an item of property is the length of time the property may reasonably be expected to be used in the taxpayer's particular income seeking activity; it is not the period of time the property might be actually, physically useful in some other trade or business or to some other taxpayer.

> *Example:* H. Corporation is in the business of renting and leasing automobiles. The average automobile which H. Corporation purchases can be expected to provide safe transportation for 8 years. Because automobile rental customers do not want to rent a car which is more than one model year old, H. Corporation's policy is to sell automobiles after they have been in use for only 2 years. For the purpose of computing depreciation deductions, the

useful life of an automobile to H. Corporation is 2 years. [*Hertz Corp. v. U.S.*, 364 U.S. 122, 80 S.Ct. 1420 (1960).]

The determination of the useful life of a particular item of property to a certain taxpayer is generally a question of fact. In an attempt to reduce controversies between taxpayers and the I.R.S. concerning the useful life of property, Congress authorized the I.R.S. to prescribe useful lives for various classes of property. If an item of property is described in one of the classes, the corresponding useful life may be used by the taxpayer without having to provide proof of its useful life to her in her particular income seeking activity. [IRC § 167(m).]

If the useful life of property is indefinite or unascertainable, such as for goodwill, a trademark or antique furniture, no depreciation deduction may be taken. Intangible assets which do have an ascertainable useful life, such as a contract not to compete for a certain number of years, a copyright or a patent whose lifespan is limited by law, may qualify for depreciation deductions, normally referred to as amortization, the writing off of their cost over their lives. In some situations, Congress has prescribed a time period over which deductions may be taken for certain expenditures. Some of these expenditures might not otherwise qualify for depreciation deductions, while others are simply being provided with a shorter deduction period than normal rules would provide. These are also referred to as "amortization deductions," and generally allow the expenditure to be deducted ratably over the period of time prescribed in the statute. [*E.g.*, IRC §§ 188 (capital expenditures for child care facilities may be amortized over period of 60 months); and 195 ("start-up" expenditures may be amortized over period of not less than 60 months; see discussion, III. A. 1. c. i., at page 73, *supra*).]

iii. Salvage value

The salvage value of property is the amount, determined at the time of acquisition, which is estimated the property could be sold for at the end of its useful life *to the taxpayer*. The salvage value of a particular item of property, therefore, may represent a significant portion of the value of the property and not merely its value as scrap.

Example: An automobile purchased by H. Corporation in the preceding Example cost $12,000. At the time it is purchased, it is estimated that it will be sold 2 years later for $9,000. The salvage value of the automobile to H. Corporation is $9,000.

The salvage value of personal property, other than livestock, with a useful life of 3 years or more may be reduced by an amount up to 10% of the basis of the property at the time it is placed in service. [IRC § 167(f).]

The salvage value of an item of depreciable property is significant because the total amount of deductions for depreciation under IRC § 167 may not exceed the excess of the cost or other basis for computing depreciation over the salvage value of the property.

Example: Edith purchases an item of depreciable property for use in her business at a cost of $10,000, and its salvage value to her is $8,000. Only $2,000 of deductions for depreciation may be taken, regardless of the method of computing depreciation deductions Edith uses. [Reg. § 1.167(a)–1(c)(1).]

iv. Methods of computing depreciation

For depreciable property which is not covered by the ACRS rules, there are three significant methods for computing depreciation deductions, each of which requires that the *depreciable base* of the property be multiplied by the *depreciation rate* for each taxable year in which a deduction is allowable. In addition to the three principal methods, other methods may be allowed in certain circumstances.

a. Straight line method

Essentially, under the straight line method, the *depreciable base* of the property is its cost or other basis less its salvage value, and the *depreciation rate* is a fraction, the numerator of which is 1 and the denominator is the number of years of the property's useful life. The straight line method of depreciation results in an equal amount of depreciation deduction in each of the years involved.

Example: An item of property cost $10,000, and it has a salvage value of $2,000 and a useful life of 5 years. Under the straight line method, the depreciation deduction in each of the 5 years is $1,600 [($10,000 – 2,000 = $8,000) × (⅕)]. [Reg. § 1.167(b)–1.] Thus over 5 years the total depreciation deductions are $8,000.

b. Declining balance method

Under the declining balance method, the *depreciable base* of the property is its cost or other basis reduced by depreciation deductions allowed or allowable in prior years (but not reduced by the salvage value). The *depreciation rate* is the same fraction which would be used in the straight line method (the numerator is 1 and the denominator is the number of years of the property's useful life) multiplied by a factor not exceeding 2. If the factor is 2, the method is the double declining balance method; if it is 1½, it is a 150% declining balance method, etc. Although the salvage value is not taken into consideration in determining the depreciable base, an item of property may not be depreciated below its salvage value. In each year of the property's useful life, the depreciable base changes, but the depreciation rate remains constant. [Reg. § 1.167(b)–2.]

Example: An item of depreciable property cost $10,000, and it has a salvage value of $2,000 and a useful life of 5 years. If the property qualifies for depreciation deductions under the declining balance method at a rate not exceeding twice the straight line rate (the double declining balance method), depreciation deductions will be computed as follows:

Year	Depreciable Base	Depreciation Rate	Depreciation Allowance
One	$10,000	40% (2 × ⅕)	$4,000
Two	$ 6,000	40%	$2,400
Three	$ 3,600	40%	$1,440
Four	$ 2,160	40%	$ 160 *
		Total deductions:	$8,000

* Even though the depreciation allowance in Year Four would seem to be $864 (40% of $2,160), it is limited to $160 because the salvage value of the property is $2,000. For the same reason, no depreciation deduction will be allowed in Year Five.

c. Sum of the years-digits method

Under the sum of the years-digits method, the *depreciable base* of the property is its cost or other basis reduced by its salvage value, and the *depreciation rate* is a fraction, the numerator of which changes each year to the number of years remaining in the useful life of the property (including the year for which the computation is being made), and the denominator is the sum of all the years digits in the useful life of the property. In each year of the property's useful life the depreciable base remains constant, but the depreciation rate changes. [Reg. § 1.167(b)–3.]

Example: An item of property costs $10,000, and it has a salvage value of $2,000 and a useful life of 5 years. If the property qualifies for depreciation deductions under the sum of the years-digits method, depreciation deductions will be computed as follows:

Year	Depreciable Base	Depreciation Rate	Depreciation Allowance
One	$8,000	5/15	$2,667
Two	$8,000	4/15	$2,133
Three	$8,000	3/15	$1,600
Four	$8,000	2/15	$1,067
Five	$8,000	1/15	$ 533
		Total deductions:	$8,000

d. Other methods

In some limited circumstances, another method of computing depreciation, such as the unit of production method or the sinking fund method, may be used if the taxpayer uses the method consistently and if it produces a "reasonable allowance" for depreciation. [See IRC § 167(b)(4); Reg. § 1.167(b)–0(b) and –4.]

v. Relationship of depreciation deductions to basis

The basis of property must be reduced to account for the amounts allowed (actually taken) or allowable (which could have been taken) for deductions for depreciation. [IRC § 1016(a)(2).] Thus if depreciation is actually taken on property, its basis is reduced by the amount of deductions taken (except to the extent there was no reduction in tax from the deductions). In the event an item of property was subject to a depreciation allowance, but no deduction was taken (i.e. in an "allowable" situation) the basis of the property must, nonetheless, be reduced by the amount of a deduction which would have been taken under the straight line method.

b. Accelerated Cost Recovery System (ACRS)

As part of the Economic Recovery Tax Act of 1981, Congress enacted the Accelerated Cost Recovery System (ACRS) provisions of IRC § 168. As the name implies, the general thrust of ACRS is to allow deductions in the nature of depreciation deductions to be taken at a rate faster than prior law permitted. The principal features of current ACRS, which distinguish it from the IRC § 167 depreciation deduction rules, follow: (1) the useful life of the property in the taxpayer's business is generally irrelevant; property is assigned to one of 8 classes and deductions are spread over periods ranging from 3 to 31.5 years; (2) the salvage value of the property is not taken into consideration in computing ACRS deductions, thus 100% of the cost of the property is deductible; (3) there is no distinction between old and new property; and (4) there are only two methods for computing ACRS deductions with respect to an item of property, either the accelerated rate prescribed by statute or a straight-line rate. Under current ACRS, certain property must be depreciated under an alternative depreciation system. [IRC § 168(g); see discussion, III. A. 5. d. iv. e., at page 119, *infra*.] Under old ACRS, applicable generally to property placed in service after 1980 and before 1987, there were only 6 classes of property and deductions were spread over periods ranging from 3 years to 19 years.

Deductions are allowed under current ACRS with respect to "any tangible property." [IRC § 168(a).] The deduction allowed under ACRS is deemed to be the "reasonable allowance" otherwise provided for the exhaustion, wear and tear or obsolescence of property under IRC § 167. In most situations, ACRS is mandatory, not elective, and, in any event, deductions may not be taken with respect to an item of property under both IRC §§ 167 and 168. The basis of recovery property is reduced by the amount of ACRS deductions (allowed or allowable.) [IRC § 1016(a)(2); see discussion, III. A. 5. a. v., at page 110, *supra.*]

i.   Tangible property
      The "reasonable allowance" for depreciation authorized by IRC § 167 is computed under the provisions of IRC § 168 for "any tangible property." However, concepts of the depreciation deduction previously discussed [*see* III. A. 5. a., at page 105, *supra*] are still pertinent under ACRS; thus, the property must be used in the taxpayer's trade or business or it must be held for the production of income, the property must by its nature be subject to being exhausted, worn out, or becoming obsolete, the property must have an ascertainable useful life, and it must otherwise be of a character subject to the allowance for depreciation. ACRS does not apply to intangible property, nor does it apply to certain public utility property, motion picture films and video tapes, sound recordings and property depreciated under the unit-of-production method. [IRC § 168(f)(1)–(5).] With respect to a particular taxpayer, property is not eligible for current ACRS if it was placed in service before January 1, 1987, and it is not eligible for old ACRS if it was placed in service before January 1, 1981.

      Congress enacted ACRS, in part, to stimulate the economy by encouraging taxpayers to invest in business machinery, equipment and buildings; Congress did not want to make the old ACRS or current ACRS rules applicable to property which was already in service in a taxpayer's business (or the business of a person related to the taxpayer) when the provisions were enacted in 1980 and 1986, respectively. Therefore, under "anti-churning" rules, a taxpayer may not use current ACRS with respect to property acquired from a "related person" who, in turn, had placed the property in service before 1987 if the deduction under current ACRS is greater than the deduction computed under the method the related person would have had to use (i.e., either IRC § 167 or old ACRS, depending, perhaps, on when the related person placed the property in service). [IRC

§ 168(f)(5).] A "related person" under the anti-churning rules means a taxpayer's spouse, children and other family members as well as corporations, partnerships and trusts or estates in which the taxpayer has an economic interest.

> ***Example:*** Lucy purchases a building in 1979 which she uses in her business. In 1988, Lucy sells the building to her father, Milo, who subsequently uses it in his business. The building cannot be depreciated under IRC § 168 either before the sale by Lucy or after the sale by Milo. If Milo sells the building to Nora, an unrelated third party, it is under current ACRS in her hands.

ii.   Classes of property

Property is divided into 8 classes for the purpose of computing deductions under current ACRS. [IRC § 168(e).] Six of the classes include primarily personal property and are discussed at III. A. 5. d. iv. *a.,* at page 116, *infra;* 2 of the classes are comprised of real property and are discussed at III. A. 5. e. i. *a.,* at page 124, *infra.* Although the useful life of property to a particular taxpayer is irrelevant under both old ACRS and current ACRS, some of the classes of property are described with reference to the "class life" of property. The "class life" of an item of property is determined by reference to the class lives for property established by the I.R.S. under the authority of IRC § 167(m). [IRC § 168(i)(1).]

iii.   Recovery period

The recovery period is the number of years during which depreciation deductions are taken under ACRS for an item of depreciable property. [See IRC § 168(a)(2).] The applicable recovery period for an item of property is determined by its classification which, as previously discussed, is determined with reference to the class life of the property. There are 8 different recovery periods corresponding with the 8 different classes of property. Property in the class of 3-year property has a recovery period of 3 years; property in the class of 10-year property has a recovery period of 10 years, and so on. [IRC § 168(c).]

iv.   Applicable convention

Depreciation deductions are authorized for property which is used in a trade or business or in the production of income for the period of time it is properly placed in service. Instead of requiring the computation of the exact number of days within a taxable year items of depreciable property are actually used in the taxable years in which they are placed in or removed from service, current ACRS uses several conventions, the half-year convention, the mid-month convention and the mid-quarter convention. [IRC § 168(d); see discussions at III. A. 5. d. iv. *d.,* at page 118, *infra,* and III. A. 5. e. i. *d.,* at page 124, *infra.*]

c.   Related concept of depletion
The depreciation deduction is a method for permitting a taxpayer to subtract from gross income an amount representing the cost of using up property which has an ascertainable useful life in income producing activities.   Taxpayers who are in the business of extracting oil, coal, gold or other natural resources, and selling them to produce income, also "use up" the income producing potential of their wells and mines with each barrel of oil, or ton of ore, extracted, but there is usually no reliable method to determine how long a particular well or mine will be productive.   Over the years, several different methods of providing such taxpayers with a rough equivalent to a depreciation deduction have been authorized.   Today, two general methods, cost depletion and percentage depletion, are permitted in varying situations.

Deductions are allowed under cost depletion according to a formula which takes into account the adjusted basis of the property, the number of units of the resource sold within a taxable year, and the number of units of the resource estimated to remain at the end of the taxable year.   [See IRC §§ 611 and 612.]   Cost depletion is often used for timber and minerals.

Deductions are allowed under the percentage depletion method by multiplying the gross income from the property by a percentage which varies according to the type of mineral (ranging from 5% for gravel to 22% for uranium).   [See IRC § 613.]   Special limitations, applicable primarily to the major oil companies, restrict the use of the percentage depletion method with respect to oil and natural gas.   [See IRC § 613A.]

d.   Special rules for personal property
i.   Introduction
Personal property used in a trade or business or held for the production of income may qualify for the bonus depreciation deduction under IRC § 179 as well as the ACRS deduction under IRC § 168.   In some instances, depreciation deductions with respect to personal property must be taken under IRC § 167, rather than the ACRS provisions of IRC § 168.   The rules applicable to personal property are interrelated and do not operate in isolation.   However, they will be initially explained separately in this Outline.

ii.   Section 179 bonus depreciation
A taxpayer may elect to deduct all or a portion of the cost of any "section 179 property" in the taxable year in which it is placed

in service. [IRC § 179.] This deduction is allowed in addition to the amount of depreciation deduction otherwise allowable under IRC § 168, hence, the commonly used description, "bonus depreciation." If deductions are taken under IRC § 179 with respect to an item of property, the property's basis must be reduced just like any other depreciation deduction and the basis of the property must be reduced *before* computing any further depreciation deductions under IRC § 168.

The total amount of deductions which may be taken with respect to section 179 property within a taxable year is subject to several limitations. If the basis of an item of section 179 property is determined by reference to other property which the taxpayer at any time held, such as when one item of property is exchanged for another item of a like kind, the "cost" of the newly acquired property does not include the amount of such exchanged basis. [IRC § 179(d)(3); see discussion of like kind exchanges, IV. D. 1., at page 215, *infra.*]

a.   Section 179 property
        "Section 179 property" is property which qualifies for current ACRS deductions and which is "section 38 property" (as defined in IRC § 48(a)); the concept is thus generally confined to tangible personal property. In addition, the property must be acquired by purchase for use in the active conduct of a trade or business. [IRC § 179(d)(1).] "Purchase" means any acquisition of property with a cost basis, unless the property is acquired from certain related individuals, or within a controlled group of corporations, and so long as the property does not have a substituted basis or a basis determined under the rules applicable to property acquired from a decedent. [IRC § 179(d)(2).] The property must be used in a trade or business; property which is merely held for the production of income does not qualify.

b.   Limitations
        Generally, a taxpayer may deduct a maximum of $10,000 annually under IRC § 179, but this limit is reduced, dollar for dollar, by the cost of section 179 property placed in service during the year which exceeds $200,000. [IRC § 179(b)(1) and (2).] Thus, if a taxpayer places in service section 179 property with a total cost of $210,000 or more, no bonus depreciation under IRC § 179 is allowed. In addition to the dollar limitation, the deduction otherwise allowable under IRC § 179 is limited in a taxable year to the amount of the taxpayer's taxable income (computed without regard to the cost of section 179 property) derived from the active conduct of any trade or business.

Amounts disallowed under the trade or business income limitation are carried over to the next taxable year. [IRC § 179(b)(3).] Only 50% of the maximum dollar limitation amount is allowed to a husband or a wife filing a separate return, unless the spouses elect to apportion the limitation on some other basis, such as $7,000 to the wife and the remaining $3,000 to the husband. [IRC § 179(b)(4).]

Example: In the current year, Franz, an unmarried taxpayer, purchases for use in his business a computer for $12,000 and office furniture for $8,000; these are the only items of section 179 property he purchases this year. He may apportion his maximum of $10,000 of deductions allowable under IRC § 179 between the computer and the furniture in whatever manner he chooses; if he deducts the full $10,000 with respect to the computer, none of the cost of the furniture may be deducted under IRC § 179. If taxable income from Franz's trade or business is only $7,000 in the current year (computed without regard to the cost of section 179 property), only $7,000 may be deducted under IRC § 179 in that taxable year; the remaining $3,000 will be treated as an expenditure incurred to purchase section 179 property in the next taxable year, deductible in the next taxable year subject to the dollar and trade or business income limitations applicable in the next taxable year.

c. Recapture

The deduction is allowed with respect to specific items of section 179 property which the taxpayer must identify on her income tax return. [IRC § 179(c)(1).] If a deduction is taken under IRC § 179 with respect to an item of property and if at any time the property ceases to be used predominantly in a trade or business, even though the property is not disposed of or sold, the taxpayer must include in income the tax benefit derived from the deduction. [IRC § 179(d)(10).]

Example: Franz, from the preceding Example, elects to deduct $5,000 under IRC § 179 with respect to the computer. Two years later he moves the computer to his home and uses it for personal purposes. Franz must include in his gross income for the latter taxable year an amount equal to the difference between $5,000 and the amount which would have been deductible under ACRS if the $5,000 had been capitalized.

iii. Regular investment tax credit

As an additional incentive for taxpayers to purchase business machinery and equipment, the Congress has provided a tax credit for the purchase of certain depreciable property used in a trade or business. Unlike the depreciation deduction, the investment tax credit has not been a constant feature of the income tax system; first enacted in 1962 it has been frequently amended, repealed and reenacted as a mechanism to "fine tune" the nation's economy. In general terms, immediately prior to its repeal in 1986 the regular investment tax credit was an amount equal to 10% of a taxpayer's qualified investment in tangible personal property used in a trade or business. The credit was elective and if it was taken the basis of the property generally had to be reduced by the amount of the credit prior to computing depreciation deductions with respect to the property, and if the property was disposed of before the ACRS recovery period expired, all or a portion of the investment tax credit was recaptured by adding an amount directly to the taxpayer's tax liability. It seems likely that some version of the investment tax credit will reappear in the U.S. income tax law.

iv. Section 168 Accelerated Cost Recovery System (ACRS)

Deductions under ACRS may be taken with respect to most tangible property. [IRC § 168(a); see discussion, III. A. 5. b. i., at page 111, *supra*.] ACRS deductions for an item of property are computed by using the depreciation method, recovery period and convention applicable to the property's classification, concepts which are discussed below. If property qualifies under ACRS, the provisions of IRC § 168(a) or (g) must be used to compute depreciation deductions; ACRS is mandatory, not elective, except for property depreciated under the unit-of-production method or any other method which is not expressed in a term of years (excluding the retirement-replacement-betterment method). [IRC § 168(f)(1).]

a. Classifications of personal property

There are 6 classifications of property which include personal property. [IRC § 168(e)(1).] Some items of real property are included within these 6 classifications, but they are discussed here because they are dealt with under ACRS in the same manner as personal property. The classifications are described with reference to the "class life" of property, a concept derived from the role played by property's useful life to a taxpayer in computing depreciation deductions. [IRC §§ 167(m) and 168(i)(1)(A); see discussion at III. A. 5. a. ii., at page 106, *supra*.] The class life of a particular item of property is determined by the I.R.S. according to the physical characteristics of the property itself and the nature of the trade or business in which it is used by the taxpayer. Property is assigned to a classification in accordance with its class life under the following table which is prescribed in IRC § 168(e)(1):

Property shall be treated as:	If such property has a class life (in years) of:
3-year property	4 or less
5-year property	More than 4 but less than 10
7-year property	10 or more but less than 16
10-year property	16 or more but less than 20
15-year property	20 or more but less than 25
20-year property	25 or more.

Some items of property are specifically assigned to a classification regardless of the class life of the property. For instance, race horses more than 2 years old when first placed in service are assigned to the 3-year property classification while automobiles and light general purpose trucks are specifically assigned to the 5-year property classification and single-purpose agricultural or horticultural structures (i.e., greenhouses) are deemed to be 7-year property. [IRC § 168(e)(3).]

b.   Applicable depreciation methods

The depreciation method applicable to most personal property is the double declining balance method, switching to the straight line method in the taxable year the straight line method (applied to the adjusted basis as of the beginning of the year) produces a deduction larger than that computed under the double declining balance method. [IRC § 168(b)(1); see discussion of the methods of computing depreciation deductions at III. A. 5. a. iv., at page 108, *supra*.] The 150% declining balance method is used initially (again switching to the straight line method when that produces the larger deduction) for property in the 15-year and 20-year classifications. [IRC § 168(b)(2).] As an alternative, a taxpayer may use the straight line method if he makes an irrevocable election, applicable to all items of property in the same classification placed in service during the taxable year. [IRC § 168(b)(5).] Depreciation deductions are computed under an alternative depreciation system for certain property. [IRC § 168(g); see discussion at III. A. 5. d. iv. e., at page 119, *infra*.] Regardless of the method of depreciation used, the salvage value of property is treated as zero. [IRC § 168(b)(4).]

c.   Applicable recovery period

The applicable recovery period for an item of property is determined by its classification which, in turn, takes its name from the recovery period; thus the recovery period for 3-year property is 3 years, the recovery period for 5-year property is 5 years, and so on. [IRC § 168(c).]

d.   Applicable convention

The depreciation deduction is allowed for property used in a trade or business or held for the production of income, and is confined to the time period while it is being so used; no deduction is appropriate or allowed before the property is placed in service (or after it is removed from service) in the trade, business or income producing activity. Because of the administrative and recordkeeping problems of keeping track on a day-to-day basis of numerous items of depreciable property, various conventions or rules-of-thumb have been developed to deal with the start-up and ending time periods; three of these conventions are now prescribed in the Code, of which two apply to personal property.

i.   Half-year convention

The half-year convention treats all personal property placed in service during a taxable year as if it was placed in service (or removed from service) precisely in the middle of the year. [IRC § 168(d)(4)(A).] Thus, a depreciation deduction for the taxable year in which property is first placed in service is computed for half of the year, regardless of the exact date during the year it is actually placed in service. Because of the half-year convention, the number of taxable years over which the recovery period runs is 1 year greater than the number of years in the recovery period.

Example: A light duty truck, which is 5-year property, is purchased for $10,000 and placed in service by a calendar year taxpayer on January 1 of Year One. The double declining balance method of depreciation allows 40% ($\frac{1}{5} \times 200\%$) of the adjusted basis, or $4,000, to be deducted, but the mid-year convention allows only half that amount because the truck is treated as being in service for only half of the year. The result would be the same if the truck is placed in service on December 31 of Year One (unless the mid-quarter convention, discussed below, applies). Depreciation deductions will be allowed for the truck in Year One through

Year Six because the 5 year recovery period begins at the mid-point of Year One and ends 5 years later at the mid-point of Year Six.

ii. Mid-quarter convention

Because the mid-year convention operates generously for property placed in service towards the end of a taxable year, allowing deductions as if the property had been used for a full 6 months, the mid-quarter convention was fashioned to forestall the tactic of placing a substantial amount of property in service at the end of a taxable year. The mid-quarter convention applies if the total basis of property placed in service during the last 3 months of a taxable year exceeds 40% of the total basis of property placed in service during the entire year; nonresidential real property and residential rental property are disregarded. [IRC § 168(d)(3).] The mid-quarter convention treats property placed in service during any quarter of the taxable year as if it were placed in service at the mid-point of the quarter. [IRC § 168(d)(4)(C).]

Example: On January 1 of the current year, Mary (a calendar year taxpayer) purchases for $6,000 and places in service an item of depreciable property, and on December 31 she purchases for $5,000 and places in service a second item of depreciable property. The mid-year convention applies because more than 40% of the depreciable property purchased in the current year is placed in service during the last 3 months of the year. The first item of property is treated as if it is placed in service at the mid-point of the first quarter of Mary's taxable year, effectively treating it as if it is used 87.5% (3 full quarters, or 75%, plus half of 1 quarter, or 12.5%) of the year. The second item of property is treated as if it is placed in service at the mid-point of the last quarter of Mary's taxable year, effectively treating it as if it is used 12.5% of the year.

e.   Alternative depreciation system

An alternative depreciation system must be used for certain items of personal property, such as property used predominantly outside the United States and property leased to a tax-exempt entity, and a taxpayer may make an irrevocable election to use the alternative depreciation system for all items in any classification of property placed in service during a taxable year. [IRC § 168(g)(1).] The alternative depreciation system uses the straight line method (disregarding salvage value), the applicable convention, and a recovery period equal to the class life (rather than the "applicable recovery period") of the property. [IRC § 168(g)(2).] Specific class lives are imposed for certain types of property such as automobiles, computer-based telephone central office switching equipment, and railroad track, and for property with no class life. [IRC § 168(g)(3).]

> ***Example:***   Fred purchases for $10,000 some office equipment which he uses in his business in Mexico. Office equipment has a class life of 10 years. Fred must compute depreciation deductions for the office equipment under the alternative depreciation system, using the straight line method (disregarding the salvage value), the half-year convention and a recovery period of 10 years. In the first year the office equipment is placed in service, a depreciation deduction of $500 ($10,000 × $\frac{1}{10}$ × 50%) is allowable. Assuming the property continues to be used in Fred's business in Mexico, deductions of $1,000 are allowable each year from Year Two through Year Ten; in Year Eleven, a deduction of $500 is allowed. Depreciation deductions totaling $10,000 are allowed from Year One through Year Eleven.

v.   Section 167 depreciation

Although most tangible property placed in service after December 31, 1980, is subject to either old ACRS or current ACRS, items of intangible personal property and some items of tangible personal property (when the anti-churning rules apply) do not qualify and deductions for depreciation must then be computed in accordance with IRC § 167. [See discussion of property which qualifies for ACRS at III. A. 5. b. i., at page 111, *supra.*]

Under IRC § 167, depreciation deductions are allowed to the extent the cost or other basis of the property exceeds the salvage value of the property, and they are spread out over the useful life of the property to the taxpayer. Deductions for depreciable intangible personal property must be computed according to the straight line method. [See IRC § 167(c).] Deductions for new tangible personal property with a useful life of 3 years or more may be computed under the straight line method, the declining balance method using a rate up to twice the straight line rate (the "double declining balance" method), or the sum of the years-digits method. [*Id.*] Used tangible personal property may be depreciated under the straight line method or the declining balance method using a rate up to 150% of the straight line rate.

vi. Section 280F limitations

Depreciation deductions are subject to further limitations with respect to "luxury automobiles" and certain "listed property" which is used for personal purposes. [IRC § 280F.]

a. "Luxury automobiles"

In an attempt to preclude big tax write-offs for luxury automobiles Congress imposed restrictions on the depreciation of such automobiles. Depreciation deductions with respect to a passenger automobile may not exceed $2,560 for the first taxable year it is placed in service, $4,100 for the second year, $2,450 for the third year and $1,475 for succeeding years in the recovery period. [IRC § 280F(a)(2)(A).] Because passenger automobiles are 5-year property, these limitations affect only "luxury" automobiles which cost more than $12,800 (subject to annual price inflation adjustment after 1988). [See IRC § 280F(d)(7).] If these limitations apply and the automobile continues to be used exclusively for business after the recovery period expires, a maximum of $1,475 may be deducted in each year following the recovery period until the basis is reduced to zero. [IRC § 280F(a)(2)(B).] Amounts deducted under the bonus depreciation provisions of IRC § 179 [see discussion at III. A. 5. d. ii., at page 113, *supra*] are treated as depreciation deductions for purposes of these limitations. [IRC § 280F(d)(1).]

Example: Gloria purchases a Porsche for $50,000 on July 1, 1987, to use exclusively in her business. Using the double declining balance method, a 5 year recovery period and the mid-year convention, a depreciation deduction of $10,000 would be allowed for 1987, but it is limited to $2,560 by IRC § 280F(a)(2). Assuming Gloria continues to use the Porsche exclusively in her business, she is limited to depreciation deductions of $4,100 in 1988, $2,450 in 1989, and $1,475 in each succeeding year.

b.   "Listed property"

Section 280F also imposes limitations on depreciation deductions with respect to certain "listed property" which is used in part for personal purposes during a taxable year. [IRC § 280F(b).] "Listed property" includes: (1) any passenger automobile; (2) any other property used as a means of transportation; (3) any property generally used for entertainment, recreation or amusement; (4) any computer or peripheral equipment; or (5) any other property specified in the regulations. [IRC § 280F(d)(4).]

If less than 50% of the use of an item of listed property is for a qualified business use during a taxable year, the depreciation deductions must be determined under the alternative depreciation system of IRC § 168(g) [see discussion at III. A. 5. d. iv. *e.*, at page 119, *supra*] for that taxable year and all subsequent taxable years. [IRC § 280F(b)(2).] In addition, if business use exceeds the 50% threshold in one or more taxable years, but falls below that line in the current taxable year, the excess of the amount of depreciation deductions taken in the earlier years over the amount which would have been allowed under the alternative depreciation system must be "recaptured" by being included in gross income in the current taxable year. [IRC § 280F(b)(3).]

In addition to the IRC § 280F limitations on depreciation deductions, IRC § 274(d) disallows any deduction or credit with respect to items of listed property if the taxpayer fails to substantiate the use of the property by adequate records.

Example: On July 1 of Year One, Homer purchases for $10,000 and places in service an item of listed property which has a class life of 8 years (thus, it is 5-year property). During Year One the property is used exclusively for a qualified business use. Using the double declining balance method of depreciation, a recovery period of 5 years and the mid-year convention, Homer is allowed a depreciation deduction of $2,000 for the property in Year One under IRC § 168(a). In Year Two, the property is used only 40% in a qualified business use and the remaining 60% for personal purposes. The depreciation deduction for Year Two is $500, computed under the alternative depreciation system of IRC § 168(g) using the straight line method (disregarding salvage value), the mid-year convention, an 8 year recovery period, and limited to the 40%

business use ($10,000 $\times$ ⅛ $\times$ 40%). In addition, Homer must include in gross income $1,375 for Year Two, the difference between the amount allowed as a depreciation deduction in Year One ($2,000) and the amount which would have been allowed if the alternative depreciation system had been used in Year One, remembering to apply the mid-year convention to the first year the property was placed in service [$625 ($10,000 $\times$ ⅛ $\times$ ½)]. Homer must continue to use the alternative depreciation system to compute depreciation deductions for this item of property even if the qualified business use exceeds 50% in succeeding years.

vii. Summary of interrelationship of special rules for personal property

The first step which should be taken in applying the special rules to depreciable personal property which is used in a trade or business or held for the production of income is to determine whether the item of property is subject to ACRS. If it is *not* subject to ACRS, it will not qualify for the bonus depreciation deduction of IRC § 179 or ACRS under IRC § 168; instead, depreciation deductions will be computed under IRC § 167.

If the item of property *is* subject to ACRS, the next step is to determine whether it qualifies for the bonus depreciation deduction under IRC § 179; if it does qualify and if the taxpayer elects to take advantage of the deduction, the basis of the property must be reduced by the amount of the deduction before computing the ACRS deductions.

Computation of the depreciation deductions ACRS deductions under IRC § 168 or under IRC § 167 is the third step.

Finally, consideration should be given to the limitations of IRC § 280F.

e. **Special rules for real property**

Real property does not qualify for the bonus depreciation deduction under IRC § 179. Most real property is classified under ACRS as either nonresidential real property or residential rental property. A few items of property which might be realty under local property law, such as a greenhouse or a municipal wastewater treatment plant, are specifically placed in ACRS classifications along with personal property. [E.g., IRC § 168(e)(3)(C)(ii) and (D)(i); see discussion at III. A. 5. d. iv. *a.* at page 116, *supra.*] Old ACRS applies to most real property placed in service after 1980 and before 1987 while current ACRS applies to most real property placed in service after 1986. The provisions of old ACRS were more generous to real property because they allowed deductions to be computed at a more accelerated rate than is permitted under current ACRS, and the time period for fully depreciating real property was substantially shorter than it is under current ACRS. In some circumstances, real property is depreciated under IRC § 167 rather than ACRS.

i.   Section 168 Accelerated Cost Recovery System (ACRS)
        Real property which qualifies as under ACRS must be depreciated under the accelerated cost recovery system of IRC § 168. As with personal property, ACRS deductions for an item of depreciable real property are computed by using the depreciation method, recovery period and convention applicable to the property's classification.

   a.   Classifications of real property

         Most real property is classified either as nonresidential real property or as residential rental property under current ACRS.

      i.   Residential rental property

             Residential rental property is defined as a building or other structure from which 80% or more of the rental income is rental income from dwelling units. [IRC §§ 167(j)(2)(B) and 168(e)(2)(A).] A dwelling unit is a house or apartment used to provide living accommodations other than on a transient basis. [IRC § 167(k)(3)(C).] Most apartment buildings, duplexes, townhouses and the like, whose occupants are tenants rather than owners, are residential rental properties.

      ii.   Nonresidential real property

             Depreciable real property other than residential rental property or property with a class life of less than 27.5 years is defined as nonresidential real property. [IRC §§ 168(e)(2)(B) and 1250(c).] Most office buildings, retail stores, shopping centers, factory buildings and the like are nonresidential real property.

   b.   Applicable depreciation method

         The applicable depreciation method for both residential rental property and nonresidential real property is the straight line method, but the salvage value is deemed to be zero. [IRC § 168(b)(3) and (4).]

c.   Applicable recovery period

The applicable recovery period for residential rental property is 27.5 years while it is 31.5 years for nonresidential real property.   [IRC § 168(c).]

d.   Applicable convention

The mid-month convention is the applicable convention for both nonresidential real property and residential rental property. [IRC § 168(d)(2).]   Under the mid-month convention, property is deemed to be placed in (or removed from) service at the mid-point of month in which it is placed in (or removed from) service. [IRC § 168(d)(4)(B).]

> ***Example:***   Charlotte, a calendar year taxpayer, buys an office building and places it in service in her business on March 2.   Under the mid-month convention, she is treated as using the building for 9.5 months.   The result is the same if the building is placed in service on March 31.

e.   Alternative depreciation system

As with personal property, an alternative depreciation system must be used for some real property, and a taxpayer may elect to use the alternative system for other real property.   [IRC § 168(g); see discussion at III. A. 5. d. iv. *e.,* at page 119, *supra.*] The recovery period for both nonresidential real property and residential rental property is 40 years.   [IRC § 168(g)(2)(C)(iii).] Unlike the election with respect to personal property, a taxpayer may make the election to use the alternative depreciation system separately for each item of nonresidential real property or residential rental property;   once made, an election is irrevocable. [IRC § 168(g)(7).]

f.   Anti-churning rules

ACRS is generally not available for computing depreciation deductions for certain property under the "anti-churning rules" where the property was acquired from a related person who, in turn, had placed the property in service before 1987.   [IRC § 168(f)(5)(A); see discussion at III. A. 5. b. i., at page 111, *supra.*] The anti-churning rules do not apply (thus, depreciation deductions must be computed under current ACRS) with respect to either residential rental property or nonresidential real property if for the first full taxable year the property is placed in service the amount computed under old ACRS or IRC § 167 (whichever is applicable) is greater than the amount computed under current ACRS. [IRC § 168(f)(5)(B).]

> *Example:* Betsy purchases residential rental property from her father in Year One; her father had purchased the property 2 years earlier and was computing depreciation deductions under old ACRS. For Year One, if Betsy computes depreciation deductions under new ACRS, a deduction of $5,000 will be allowable, but if she computes deduction under old ACRS, a deduction of $6,500 will be allowable. The anti-churning rules do not apply in this instance; Betsy must compute depreciation deduction under new ACRS.

ii.   Section 167 depreciation

Most real property which is placed in service subsequent to December 31, 1980, qualifies for depreciation deductions under either old ACRS or current ACRS. Depreciation deductions for depreciable real property which is not covered by ACRS are authorized under IRC § 167 to the extent the cost or other basis of the property exceeds its salvage value, and the deductions are spread out over the useful life of the property to the taxpayer. The straight line method may be used for computing depreciation deductions for all types of real property. In addition, the 150% declining balance method may be used for "new" nonresidential real property; "new" residential rental property may be depreciated under the 200% declining balance method and under the sum of the years-digits method; "used" residential rental property with a useful life of 20 years or more may be depreciated under the 125% declining balance method. Used nonresidential property qualifies only for straight line depreciation. [IRC § 167(j).] Property is "new" if its original use commences with the taxpayer. [See Reg. § 1.167(j)–1(a)(2)(ii).] Property is residential rental property if 80% or more of the gross rental income from the property is rental income from dwelling units. [IRC § 167(j)(2)(A).]

6.   NET OPERATING LOSS DEDUCTION

A deduction may be taken in a taxable year in the amount of the net operating loss carryovers and carrybacks to the year. [IRC § 172(a).] A "net operating loss" is the excess of allowable business deductions over gross income for a taxable year (the "loss year"). [IRC § 172(c).] With regard to individual taxpayers, the following deductions may not be taken into account in computing the net operating loss for a loss year: capital losses in excess of capital gains, personal exemptions authorized by IRC § 151, and other nonbusiness deductions. In addition, no net operating loss deduction, of a carryback or carryover from another taxable year, is allowed in computing a net operating loss for the loss year. [IRC § 172(d).]

Example: Katie has $50,000 of business income, a $10,000 capital gain, a $13,000 capital loss, $90,000 in business deductions, $4,000 of itemized deductions, and a $2,000 personal exemption. Her net operating loss is $40,000 ($60,000 less $100,000).

Because a taxpayer will have no taxable income in a loss year, the utility of the net operating loss deduction arises in taxable years prior or subsequent to the loss year by means of the carryback or carryforward rules. Generally, a net operating loss is a net operating loss *carryback* to each of the 3 taxable years preceding the loss year, and it is a net operating loss *carryover* to each of the 15 taxable years following the loss year. [IRC § 172(b)(1).] The amount of a net operating loss from a loss year generally must be carried back to the earliest taxable year which is not also a loss year; to the extent that a net operating loss carryback or carryover to a particular taxable year exceeds the taxable income (with certain modifications) of that year, the excess continues to be a net operating loss carryback or carryover to other taxable years. [IRC § 172(b)(2) and (d).] A taxpayer may elect to have a net operating loss for a taxable year carried forward to subsequent taxable years, relinquishing the right to carry it back to prior taxable years. [IRC § 172(b)(3)(C).]

Example: Larry has taxable income of $15,000 in Year One; $10,000 in Year Two; and $5,000 in Year Three. In Year Four, Larry has a net operating loss of $40,000, but in Year Five he has taxable income of $6,000, and in Year Six he has taxable income of $10,000.

The $40,000 net operating loss generated in Year Four is, first of all, a net operating loss carryback to Year One; however, because Year One's taxable income is only $15,000 the net operating loss deduction for that year is also $15,000. Larry may now file an amended return for Year One claiming a refund for the tax paid. The amount of the net operating loss carryback to Year Two is the excess of the net operating loss ($40,000) over the taxable income of the earliest year to which the loss could be carried ($15,000 for Year One), or $25,000. Once again, the amount of the net operating loss carryback to Year Two is in excess of the taxable income of that year and thus the net operating loss deduction for Year Two is $10,000, leaving $15,000 to be carried back to Year Three. For Year Three, the net operating loss deduction is $5,000, the amount of taxable income in that year, and $10,000 of the net operating loss remains to be carried over to subsequent taxable years, $6,000 to Year Five and the remaining $4,000 to Year Six.

In the alternative, Larry could elect to carry his net operating loss deductions forward only, with no carrybacks, and he would wipe out his $6,000 of Year Five and $10,000 of Year Six income and would have $24,000 of remaining net operating loss to be carried forward to Year Seven and later years.

B. PERSONAL DEDUCTIONS AND ALLOWANCES

The preceding section discussed deductions which are allowed for expenditures incurred in deriving income. In addition, Congress has authorized, for varying policy reasons, certain deductions which are not related to income producing activities, collectively referred to as personal deductions and allowances. A deduction is allowed to a taxpayer, however, only if he has an obligation to pay the item; no deduction is allowed to a taxpayer who makes payment of someone else's obligation.

Example: Herman buys a house, borrowing a portion of the purchase price from a local savings and loan. During the current year, Herman is a full time law student and is unemployed, so his mother, Isabel, pays his mortgage payments for him. The payments total $6,000, of which $2,000 is interest. Isabel may not take a deduction for the interest which she pays on behalf of Herman because she does not have an obligation to pay interest. The transaction will be treated as if Isabel made a gift to Herman of $6,000, and Herman, in turn, paid the interest; Herman is entitled to a deduction for the interest. [See *Sheppard v. Comm'r*, 37 B.T.A. 279 (1938); see discussion of deduction for interest, III. B. 2., at page 131, *infra.*]

1. PERSONAL EXEMPTIONS

Deductions are authorized for the "exemptions" provided for a taxpayer, certain dependents of the taxpayer, and, in very limited situations, the taxpayer's spouse. [IRC § 151.] The amount of each exemption is $1,900 in 1987, $1,950 in 1988, and $2,000 in 1989, thereafter the $2,000 amount is to be increased by a cost-of-living adjustment each year in which the Consumer Price Index increases by a prescribed amount. [IRC § 151(d).]

a. Taxpayer and spouse

If spouses file a joint return, each spouse is a "taxpayer," entitled to a personal exemption in his or her own right which is claimed on the joint return. If a married individual files a separate return, however, and her spouse has no gross income and is not a dependent of any other taxpayer, the taxpayer spouse who files the return may claim an additional personal exemption for the nontaxpayer spouse. [IRC § 151(b).]

A taxpayer may not claim a personal exemption for himself, however, if he is able to be claimed as a dependent by another taxpayer, such as his parent. [IRC § 151(d)(2).] Finally, the personal exemptions are effectively phased out by the imposition of a 5% surtax on certain high income taxpayers. [IRC § 1(g); see discussion of computation of tax liability, VII. D., at page 311, *infra.*]

Example: Josephine files a joint income tax return for the current year with her husband, Kalil. They may claim a total of 2 personal exemptions on their joint return; one personal exemption for each of them. In the alternative, if Kalil has no gross income during the current year and if he is not the dependent of another taxpayer, Josephine may file a return as a married individual filing separately, on which she may claim 2 personal exemptions, one for herself as well as one for her nontaxpaying spouse. Note, however, that she will be taxed under IRC § 1(d), which will tax a smaller amount of taxable income at the 15% rate than if a joint return is filed and tax computed under IRC § 1(a).

b. Exemptions for dependents
i. In general

A taxpayer may take an additional deduction for the exemption provided for each of his dependents. [IRC § 151(c).] In order to qualify for the deduction, each dependent must satisfy three tests, relating to gross income, relationship, and support.

ii. Gross income test

A dependent may not have gross income in excess of the exemption amount unless the dependent is a child of the taxpayer who is either under the age of 19 or a full-time student for at least 5 calendar months during the year. [IRC § 151(c). The gross income amount must be adjusted annually by a cost-of-living adjustment; see IRC § 151(d).] A "child" is a son, stepson, daughter, or stepdaughter of a taxpayer; adopted children and foster children are included as well. No deduction may be claimed for a dependent who has filed a joint return with his spouse, unless the return was filed merely to obtain a refund of withheld tax where there was no tax liability. [See Rev.Rul. 65–34, 1965–1 C.B. 86.]

Example: Daughter is a married law student whose parents provide over one half of her support. She and her husband are both students who work part time. They file a joint return claiming 2 personal exemptions. Since they claim personal exemptions on their joint return, they may not qualify as dependents of their respective parents, unless they had no tax liability and their return was filed merely to obtain a refund of withheld taxes. If Daughter files a separate return, she will qualify as a dependent of her parents and they will be able to claim a dependency deduction for her, but she will not be entitled to claim a deduction of the exemption amount for herself on her separate return. [IRC § 151(d)(2).]

iii. Relationship test

A person claimed as a dependent must have one of the following relationships with the taxpayer: (1) a son or daughter (including adopted or foster children), or a descendant of either; (2) a stepson or stepdaughter; (3) a brother or sister (including a brother or sister by the halfblood), stepbrother, or stepsister; (4) the father or mother or an ancester of either; (5) the stepfather or stepmother; (6) a niece or nephew; (7) an aunt or uncle; (8) a son-in-law, daughter-in-law, father-in-law, mother-in-law, brother-in-law, or sister-in-law; or (9) an individual other than the taxpayer's spouse who has his principal place of abode in the home of the taxpayer and is a member of the taxpayer's household, so long as the relationship is not in violation of local law. [IRC § 152(a) and (b).]

Example: Elton supports the following individuals: his stepfather, Felix; Felix' new wife Gwynne (whom Felix married after Elton's mother died); his cousin, Hortense; and Hortense's husband, Irwin. None of these individuals live with Elton. Only Felix may qualify for dependency status with Elton.

iv. Support test

An otherwise qualified individual must receive over one-half of his support from the taxpayer. [IRC § 152(a).] Support includes food, shelter, clothing, education, and medical care but not services provided by the supporter. In determining whether the support requirement is met, the amount of support received from the taxpayer is compared with the entire amount of support which the dependent received from all sources, including support she provides herself. [Reg. § 1.152–1(a) (2)(i).] However, the amount of a scholarship received by a student who is the son, stepson, daughter or stepdaughter of a taxpayer is disregarded. [IRC § 152(d).]

If an individual has the proper relationship to a taxpayer, but the taxpayer does not provide over one-half of that person's support, the taxpayer may claim a dependent exemption if a multiple support agreement is made. To qualify, no one person may contribute over one-half of the dependent's support, but over one-half of the support must be provided by persons with a qualifying relationship to the dependent. In addition, the taxpayer must contribute over 10% of the dependent's support, and each person related to the dependent who furnished over 10% of the dependent's support must file a written declaration that they will not claim an exemption for the dependent for that year. [IRC § 152(c).]

Example: Laura's father, Michael, who has no gross income, was supported last year by Laura, her two brothers, Nick and Oliver, and by Paula, an unrelated friend of the family. A total of $10,000 was spent for Michael's support: $1,500 (15%) was provided by Michael himself out of savings; $2,500 (25%) by Laura; $2,000 (20%) by Nick; $1,000 (10%) by Oliver; and $3,000 (30%) by Paula. Because Laura, Nick and Oliver provide over one half of Michael's support, Laura and Nick are potentially able to claim a dependent exemption for Michael under a multiple support agreement. Oliver is not qualified because he did not provide *more than* 10% of Michael's support, and Paula lacks the proper relationship to Michael. Laura may claim the deduction if Nick files a written statement that he will not claim Michael as a dependent for last year; alternatively, Nick may claim the deduction if Laura files a similar statement.

v. Children of divorced parents

A child who receives over one-half of his support from his parents (including a new spouse of a parent), but whose parents are divorced, separated, or living apart during the last 6 months of a calendar year, and who is in the custody of one or both parents for more than one-half of the year is treated as receiving over one-half of his support from the parent who has custody of the child for a greater portion of the calendar year. [IRC § 152(e)(1).] Exceptions to the general rule are provided if the custodial parent signs a written declaration that he will not claim the child as a dependent for the year, if there is a multiple-support agreement in effect, or for support provided under certain divorce decrees or separation agreements entered into prior to 1985, if the noncustodial parent provides at least $600 for the support of the child during a calendar year. [IRC § 152(e)(2)–(4).]

Example: Paula and Quincy are divorced after 1985; Paula is given custody of their 3 children but Quincy provides all of their support. Unless Paula signs a waiver she may claim the children as exemptions if the gross income test is satisfied.

2.   INTEREST
a.   In general

"Interest" is an amount one pays for the use of borrowed money, and as the compensation paid for the use or forbearance of money. [See *Old Colony Railroad Co. v. Comm'r*, 284 U.S. 552, 52 S.Ct. 211 (1932).] The label which parties to a contract use is not controlling; thus, "points" or a "loan origination fee" may qualify as interest, provided the amount is not a payment for specific services which the lender may perform for the borrower. [See Rev.Rul. 69–188, 1969–1 C.B. 54.]

A deduction is allowed for interest paid or accrued during a taxable year on indebtedness. [IRC § 163(a).] Tempering this general rule, however, are numerous restrictions and limitations which effectively limit the deduction for *individual* taxpayers to interest paid in one of five situations discussed below.

i.   Trade or business interest

Interest may be deducted if the debt was incurred in connection with the conduct of a trade or business, other than the trade or business of performing services as an employee. [IRC § 163(h)(2)(A).]

Example: Michael owns a wine store; he borrows money to buy a truck with which to deliver wine to local restaurants. Michael may deduct the interest paid on the truck loan. Patty is employed as a sales representative for an office supplies wholesaler; she borrows money to buy a car so that she may drive and make sales visits with office supply retailers within a 300 mile radius of her home office. Patty may not deduct the interest on her car loan even though she uses the car exclusively for business.

ii.   Investment interest

A deduction may be taken for interest paid or accrued on indebtedness incurred to purchase or carry property held for investment. [IRC § 163(h)(2)(B).] The amount of investment interest which may be deducted in a taxable year is limited, however, to the amount of net investment income for that year; any investment interest paid or accrued in excess of that limitation may be carried over to succeeding taxable years. [IRC § 163(d)(1) and (2).] "Net investment income" is the excess of gross income and gains from investments (which do not constitute a trade or business of the taxpayer) over deductible expenses directly connected with the production of investment income. [IRC § 163(d)(4).] A somewhat larger amount of investment interest may be deducted in taxable years beginning in calendar years 1987 through 1990 pursuant to special transition rules. [IRC § 163(d)(6).] No deduction is allowed, however, for interest paid on indebtedness incurred or continued to purchase or carry obligations which, in turn, pay interest which is exempt for the Federal income tax. [IRC § 265(a)(2); see discussion, III. C. 4., at page 159, *infra.*]

> ***Example:*** Quincy borrowed money with which to buy corporate stocks and bonds and paid $10,000 interest. During that same taxable year, Quincy had $25,000 of net income from his investments. The $10,000 interest payment is deductible.

iii. **Interest in connection with a passive activity**

Special restrictions on tax credits and deductions, including the deduction for interest, apply to a taxpayer's "passive activities." [IRC § 469; see discussion, III. C. 10., at page 169, *infra.*] To the extent the deduction for interest is allowed under the "passive activity" special rules, it may be deducted under IRC § 163. [IRC § 163(h)(2)(C).]

iv. **Qualified residence interest**

The payment or accrual of interest on indebtedness secured by a residence of the taxpayer may be deducted. [IRC § 163(h)(2)(D).] The residence need not be the principal or primary residence of the taxpayer, but qualifying indebtedness is limited to a maximum of 2 residences, and if there are 2, one must be the taxpayer's principal residence. [IRC § 163(h)(5)(A).] Also, interest is deductible only to the extent it is attributable to an amount of indebtedness secured by a residence up to the lesser of the fair market value of the residence or the residence's basis (adjusted only upwards by the cost of any improvements). [IRC § 163(h)(3)(B).] An additional amount of interest may be deductible if the indebtedness is incurred in excess of this limitation for the purpose of paying medical or educational expenses. [IRC § 163(h)(4).]

> ***Example:*** In Year One, Roxanne paid $50,000 cash for House #1 which she used as her residence. During Year Five, she sold House #1 for $80,000 and several months later she bought a new residence, House #2; she elected to rollover the recognition of the $30,000 gain on House #1 pursuant to IRC § 1034. Roxanne paid $20,000 cash and took out a $80,000 loan, secured by a mortgage on House #2, in order to purchase her new residence. The interest which Roxanne pays on the mortgage on House #2 is deductible. Further, in the future she may borrow up to an additional $20,000 in loans secured by House #2 and the interest will be deductible. This is so even though the adjusted

basis in House #2 is less than $100,000 because of IRC § 1034(e). [See discussion, IV. D. 3. a., at page 226, *infra.*]

v.   Interest payable on estate tax deficiencies
       In certain situations the time for payment of estate tax may be deferred, but interest on the amount of the estate tax due must be paid; these interest payments are deductible. [IRC § 163(h)(2)(E).]

The statutory provisions confining the interest deduction to the five categories described above were enacted in 1986 and prior to that time, deductions could be taken for interest paid or accrued on personal loan, credit cards or on loans to purchase automobiles used for nonbusiness purposes. The new restrictions generally apply to interest paid or accrued after 1986, even though the loan may have been obtained before then. In order to ameliorate the impact of these restrictions, they are phased-in and deductions are disallowed for only 35% of nondeductible personal interest in 1987, but that rises to disallowance of 60% in 1988, 80% in 1989, 90% 1990, and 100% thereafter. [IRC § 163(h)(6).]

Example: In 1991, Harold paid interest on his student loan, his VISA credit card, his automobile loan and his loan from a local furniture store. None of these interest payments is deductible in 1991.

b.   **Year of deduction**
       If a taxpayer uses the accrual method of accounting, the deduction arises in the taxable year in which the interest accrues. [See discussion, IV. B. 2. c., at page 196, *infra.*] If a taxpayer is on the cash method of accounting, the interest deduction is generally available in the year in which the taxpayer actually pays (or is deemed to pay) the interest. [See discussion, IV. B. 1. b., at page 188, *infra.*] However, interest paid by a cash method taxpayer on a loan which extends beyond the taxable year in which the interest is paid is prorated over the period of the loan and is deductible in the taxable years to which it is so apportioned. This rule does not apply to interest in the form of "points" paid on a loan made to purchase or improve a taxpayer's principal residence. [IRC § 461(g); see discussion IV. B. 1. b. ii., at page 189, *infra.*]

Example: Raul, a calendar year, cash method taxpayer, borrows $100,000 to purchase his residence on January 1 of Year One for a period of 3 years. Interest is to be paid at a simple rate of 10% per annum, but on January 1 of Year One he prepays the full $30,000 which will be due over the 3 year period of the loan. Under IRC § 461 (g)(1), Raul may deduct only $10,000 in Year One and he may deduct additional amounts of $10,000 in Year Two and Year Three.

c. Additional restrictions on interest deductions

In addition to the restrictions on the deductibility of interest discussed above, no deduction is allowed for interest paid on indebtedness incurred in order to purchase either certain life insurance policies or annuity contracts [IRC § 264(a)(2)–(4)], or obligations which, in turn, pay interest which is exempt from income tax [IRC § 265(a)(2); see discussion at III. C. 4., at page 159, *infra*]. In addition, restrictions on the timing of the deduction for interest may be encountered if the borrower and the lender are related taxpayers. [IRC § 267(a)(2); see discussion, III. C. 5., at page 159, *infra*.]

> *Example:* Investor borrows $100,000 at 14% interest and uses the loan proceeds to purchase bonds whose 10% interest is exempt from tax. Since the 10% interest is excluded from gross income, the 14% interest on Investor's loan is not deductible.

d. Unstated interest

In addition to allowing a deduction for interest actually paid or accrued, deductions may be allowed for interest which is not actually paid but is merely imputed and is deemed to be paid under: (1) "installment purchases where an interest charge is not separately stated" rules of IRC § 163(b); (2) the "interest on certain deferred payments" rules of IRC §§ 1274 or 483; (3) the original issue discount rules of IRC §§ 1272 and 1273; or (4) the "treatment of loans with below-market rates" rules of IRC § 7872. [See discussion, IV. E., at page 230, *infra*.]

3. TAXES
a. In general

A deduction is authorized for the following categories of taxes which are paid or accrued within a taxable year: (1) state, local, and foreign real property taxes; (2) state and local personal property taxes; (3) state, local, and foreign taxes on income, war profits, and excess profits; and (4) the windfall profit tax imposed by IRC § 4986. [IRC § 164(a).] State or local taxes are taxes imposed by a State, a possession of the United States, a political subdivision (such as a municipality, a county, or a school district), or Washington, DC. [IRC § 164(b)(3).] In addition, other taxes may be deducted if they are incurred in carrying on a trade or business or in activities engaged in for the production of income. [See discussion, III. A. 1. and 2., at pages 70 and 93, *supra*.] However, a tax paid in connection with acquiring or disposing of property may not be deducted, instead it is added to the basis of the property acquired, or it reduces the amount realized in the disposition.

> *Examples:* Irving purchases a $2,500 computer for use in his business and pays $125 in state sales tax. He may not deduct the $125; his basis for the computer is $2,625.

Judy sells the building in which her business is located for
$300,000 and pays $300 in state documentary stamp taxes.
Judy may not deduct the $300; her amount realized for the
sale of the building is $299,700.

A deduction is specifically *disallowed* for certain taxes, even if they
are paid or incurred in a business or profit seeking context. [IRC § 275.]
Some of the more important taxes for which no deduction is allowed
include Federal income taxes, Federal estate and gift taxes, and the
Federal Insurance Contributions Act (FICA or "Social Security") tax
imposed on employees under IRC § 3101. The FICA tax imposed on an
employer, however, is levied under IRC § 3111, and a deduction for this
tax is not disallowed by IRC § 275; thus, an employer may deduct the tax
imposed by IRC § 3111 with respect to his employees as an ordinary and
necessary business expense, under IRC § 162.

Example: J.O.B. pays $10,000 of social security for his employees out of
his funds, and he withholds $10,000 of social security payments
out of their paychecks. The first $10,000 is deductible as a
tax paid in a business context; the second $10,000 is not
deductible as a tax; however, it is part of the compensation
paid to the employees and is deductible by J.O.B. as such
under IRC § 162.

b.   Property taxes

State, local, or foreign *real property taxes* are taxes imposed on
interests in real property and levied for the general public welfare.
Charges imposed on real property for local benefits of a kind tending to
increase the value of the taxed property (special assessments), however,
are not deductible. [IRC § 164(c).] If real property is sold during a
taxable year, the seller and the purchaser may each deduct only the
amount of real property taxes attributable to the portion of the year each
of them owned the property. [IRC § 164(d).]

State and local *personal property taxes* are ad valorem taxes imposed
on an annual basis in respect of personal property. [IRC § 164(b)(1).] An
"ad valorem tax" is, generally, a tax imposed in proportion to the value of
the property.

Example: State X imposes a tax on motor vehicles at a rate of 1% of an
automobile's value, plus 40 cents per hundredweight. An
automobile with an assessed value of $10,000, weighing 2,500
pounds, is subject to a tax of $110.00 (1% of $10,000 = $100,
plus $.40 × 25 = $10.00). Only $100.00 of the tax is a
deductible State personal property tax. [Reg. § 1.164–3(c)(1).]

4. PERSONAL CASUALTY AND THEFT LOSSES

A deduction is authorized, with certain limitations, for losses of property even though *not* connected with a trade or business or a transaction entered into for profit if the loss arises from fire, storm, shipwreck, or other casualty, or from theft. Such losses are known as personal casualty losses. [IRC § 165(c)(3)(B).] As with any loss, a deduction is permitted only to the extent that it is not compensated for by insurance or otherwise. [IRC § 165(a).] Casualty and theft losses on property used in business or in profit-seeking activities are subject to less stringent limitations than casualty losses on personally held property. [See discussion of loss deduction, III. A. 3., at page 96, *supra.*]

a. Nature of the casualty

To qualify for the deduction, the loss must arise from a "fire, storm, shipwreck, or other casualty, or from theft." The phrase "other casualty" is construed in light of the terms which immediately precede it, each of which describes an identifiable event of a sudden, unusual or unexpected nature. Thus, a loss resulting from damage to a dwelling caused over a long period of time by termites is not a "casualty" within the purview of this section.

> **Example:** Pierre discovers termites in his residence, and a thorough inspection reveals that they have caused $10,000 of damage. Damage caused by termites is not the result of an identifiable event of a sudden, unusual or unexpected nature; rather, it is the result of gradual deterioration through a steadily operating cause. The loss due to the termite damage to Pierre's house may not be deducted. [Rev.Rul. 63–232, 1963–2 C.B. 97.]

Generally, only a loss resulting from actual physical damage to property caused by a casualty qualifies for the deduction. [*Pulvers v. Comm'r,* 407 F.2d 838 (9th Cir.1969).] If a taxpayer's residence is located in an area declared by the President to be a "disaster area," however, and if the taxpayer is ordered by state or local government within 120 days of the disaster determination to demolish or relocate the residence because it has been rendered unsafe for use as a residence as a proximate result of the disaster, any loss resulting from the demolition or relocation of the residence is deemed to be a loss arising from a casualty. [IRC § 165(k).]

> **Example:** The President declares the area in which Trent's residence is located to be a "disaster area" because of a hurricane. Although the storm did not directly damage Trent's residence, State authorities determine that the storm rendered the residence unsafe because of nearby mudslides, and they order the residence to be demolished or relocated. Trent's loss upon

demolishing or relocating his residence qualifies as a casualty loss.

A "theft" includes larceny, embezzlement, robbery and other criminal appropriations of one's property. [Reg. § 1.165–8(d).] A taxpayer has the burden of proving that property was lost by theft, and that the property was not merely lost by some mischance or inadvertence.

Example: Mary Frances wore a valuable diamond brooch while visiting an art gallery. When she returned home, the brooch was missing. Because Mary Frances could not prove that the brooch was stolen (or destroyed by some casualty), she may take neither a casualty nor a theft loss deduction. [*Allen v. Comm'r*, 16 T.C. 163 (1951).]

b.   Measure of the loss

Generally, the amount of a loss occasioned by a casualty is the same as losses to property used in business or profit-seeking activities [see discussion, III. A. 3. b. i., at page 97, *supra*]; it is the *lesser* of: (1) the excess of the fair market value of the property immediately before the casualty over its fair market value immediately after the casualty; or (2) the taxpayer's adjusted basis for the property. [IRC § 165(b) and Reg. § 1.165–7(b)(1).] The cost of repairing damaged property may be used as evidence of the amount of loss in value to the property, if the repairs merely fix the casualty damage and restore the property to its pre-casualty condition and value. [Reg. § 1.165–7(a)(2).]

A loss is not sustained and, thus, no deduction is allowed to the extent the taxpayer is reimbursed such as by insurance. If a taxpayer has insurance covering the damaged or stolen property, the deduction is reduced to the extent of the coverage unless he files a timely claim for reimbursement. [IRC § 165(h)(4)(E).]

Example: Tad's automobile, which he uses for personal purposes, is damaged in an accident. The adjusted basis of the automobile is $10,000, the fair market value before the casualty was $14,000, and its fair market value after the accident is $2,000. Although the value of the automobile decreased by $12,000 as a result of the accident, the amount of Tad's loss is limited to $10,000, his adjusted basis for the automobile. If the automobile was worth $6,000 after the accident, the loss would be only $8,000 and the adjusted basis limitation would not affect the amount of his deduction. In either event, if Tad received or could have received $3,000 from his insurance company, the amount of the loss would be reduced by the $3,000 recovery (to $7,000 and $5,000, respectively).

c. **Amount of deduction**

A personal casualty or theft loss for which a deduction is authorized by IRC § 165(c)(3) is allowed only to the extent that the amount of the loss arising from each casualty, or from each theft, exceeds $100. [IRC § 165(h)(1).] The amount of a deduction for personal casualty losses is subject to further limitations.

> **Example:** In the previous Example, Tad's potentially deductible loss would be either $6,900 or $4,900.

i. Definitions of personal casualty gains and losses

A "personal casualty gain" is the recognized gain from any involuntary conversion of property not connected with a trade or business or a transaction entered into for profit arising from a fire, storm, shipwreck, or other casualty, or from theft. [IRC § 165(h)(3) (A).] For purposes of computing whether personal casualty losses exceed personal casualty gains (or vice versa), a "personal casualty loss" is a theft or casualty loss described in IRC § 165(c)(3) reduced by the $100 floor. [IRC § 165(h)(1) and (3)(B).]

ii. Excess of personal casualty losses over personal casualty gains

If the total amount of personal casualty losses for a taxable year exceeds the personal casualty gains for that year, the losses may be deducted only to the extent of the sum of: (1) the amount of the personal casualty gains; plus (2) the amount by which the excess of personal casualty losses over personal casualty gains exceeds 10% of the taxpayer's adjusted gross income for the year. [IRC § 165(h)(2)(A); see discussion of adjusted gross income, VII. A., at page 304, *infra.*] Personal casualty losses, up to the amount of personal casualty gains, are treated as a deduction allowable in computing the taxpayer's adjusted gross income for the taxable year for purposes of computing the 10% threshold. [IRC § 165(h)(4)(A).] The excess is treated as an itemized deduction. [See discussion of itemized deductions, VII. B. 2., at page 307, *infra.*]

> **Example:** Vicky has $200,000 of adjusted gross income including her $50,000 of casualty gains, but not her casualty losses; she has $70,000 of personal casualty losses (after applying the $100 floor). The personal casualty gains and losses are all treated as ordinary. $55,000 of the personal casualty losses are allowed as a deduction [$50,000 personal casualty losses to the extent of personal casualty gains, plus the $5,000 excess of the remaining $20,000 personal casualty losses over $15,000 (10% of $150,000 adjusted gross income which is computed by deducting casualty

losses to the extent of casualty gains)]; the remaining losses are not carried over to any other year.

iii. Excess of personal casualty gains over personal casualty losses

If the amount of personal casualty gains for a taxable year exceed personal casualty losses for that year, all such gains and losses are treated as gains and losses from the sale or exchange of capital assets, and since gains exceed losses, the losses are not subject to the 10% of adjusted gross income floor. [IRC § 165(h)(2)(B).] The deductibility of the resulting capital losses when combined with other capital losses may be limited by IRC §§ 1211 and 1212. [See discussion, VI. B. 2., at page 271, *infra.*]

Example: Vicky, from the preceding Example, still has $200,000 of adjusted gross income (which includes $50,000 of personal casualty gains, but not including her casualty losses). However, she now has only $40,000 of personal casualty losses (after applying the $100 floor). All of Vicky's personal casualty gains and losses for the year are treated as capital gains and losses; the 10% of adjusted gross income floor does not apply.

d. Year of deduction

Generally, a deduction is allowable for the taxable year in which a loss is sustained. A loss arising from theft is considered to be sustained in the year in which the taxpayer discovers the theft, rather than the year in which the theft actually occurs. [IRC § 165(e).] A casualty loss is not sustained, and thus no deduction is allowed to the extent the taxpayer has a claim for reimbursement and there is a reasonable prospect for recovering all or a portion of the loss from insurance or from a tort claim against the person who damaged or destroyed the property. [Reg. § 1.165–1(d)(3).] An exception to the general rule is provided if a loss is attributable to a disaster occurring in an area subsequently declared to be a "disaster area" by the President. In such situations, the taxpayer may elect to take the otherwise allowable loss deduction in the taxable year *preceding* the year in which the loss actually occurs. [IRC § 165(i).] This exception also applies to a loss from the demolition or removal of a residence in a disaster area which has been rendered unsafe by the disaster. [See discussion, III. B. 4. a., at page 136, *supra.*]

5. WORTHLESS NONBUSINESS DEBTS

See discussion of bad debts, generally, and worthless nonbusiness debts, III. A. 4. f., at page 103, *supra.*

6. CHARITABLE CONTRIBUTIONS
a. Qualified donees

A deduction is authorized, subject to certain limitations, for any charitable contribution made within a taxable year. [IRC § 170(a).] A "charitable contribution" is a contribution or gift to or for the use of an entity described in the Code: Federal, state or local government (but only if the contribution or gift is for exclusively public purposes); religious, charitable, scientific, literary, or educational organizations; certain war veterans organizations, domestic fraternal lodge-system societies or orders, and cemetery companies; and amounts paid, within certain limits, to maintain a foreign exchange student as a member of a taxpayer's household. [IRC § 170(c), (g).]

Example: Wealthy is proud of his gardner's son who has done well in school but cannot afford to go on to college. Wealthy pays his college tuition and room and board. Wealthy may not deduct the payments. The gardner's son is not a charitable entity qualifying for a deduction.

b. Contributions
i. In general

A deduction is authorized only for charitable contributions, which are voluntary transfers of money or other property with donative intent and without consideration. [Rev.Rul. 71–112, 1971–1 C.B. 93.] If money or other property is transferred to a qualified donee under circumstances where the transferor receives or expects to receive some benefit other than benefits which will inure to the general public, the transfer is not a "contribution" and no deduction will be allowed under IRC § 170 (although the transfer may qualify for a deduction as an ordinary and necessary business expense under IRC § 162).

Example: S. Company is in the business of manufacturing and selling sewing machines and it has a policy of selling sewing machines at a discount to public and private schools, and to other charitable organizations such as churches, hospitals and the Red Cross. With regard to the machines sold at a discount to the schools, the S. Company expected a return in the nature of increased future sales to the students who would learn to use their machines. This expectation of a *quid pro quo* for the discounts precludes a deduction as a charitable contribution. The S. Company did not expect to receive substantial benefits from the discounts provided to other, non-school charitable organizations, however, and a deduction is allowed for charitable contributions made to them. [*Singer Company v. U.S.*, 449 F.2d 413 (Ct.Cl.1971).]

ii. Partial consideration

If money or other property is transferred to a qualified donee and the transferor receives partial consideration for the transfer, a deduction may be allowable to the extent that the amount of money or the value of the transferred property exceeds the partial consideration.

Example: A charitable organization sponsors a concert performance by a symphony orchestra for the purpose of raising funds for the organization's charitable programs. Tickets for performances by the orchestra normally sell for $25, but the organization sells them for $40. Walter purchases a ticket. The amount of Walter's charitable contribution is $15, the difference between the $40 he pays for the ticket and the $25 consideration he receives in return. [Rev.Rul. 67–246, 1967–2 C.B. 104.]

iii. Bargain sale to a qualified donee

Similarly, if property is sold to (or exchanged with) a qualified donee for an amount which is less than the fair market value of the property, the transaction is a "bargain sale," or "part-gift, part-sale." If a charitable deduction is allowable with respect to a bargain sale of property to a qualified donee [i.e., if the percentage limitations do not preclude a deduction for the contribution, see discussion, III. B. 6. d., at page 146, *infra*], then, in determining the seller/donor's gain, the adjusted basis of the property is apportioned between the gift portion and the sale portion of the transaction according to the following formula:

$$\text{Adjusted basis apportioned to sale} = \text{Adjusted basis} \times \frac{\text{Amount realized}}{\text{Fair market value}}$$

[IRC § 1011(b); Reg. § 1.1011–2(a).] The portion of the property's adjusted basis apportioned to the gift part of the transaction (the remaining adjusted basis) is used to determine any reduction in the amount of the contribution under the rules of IRC § 170(e). [See discussion, III. B. 6. c. ii., at page 143, *infra*.].

Example: In Year One, Walter sells to a church for $4,000 shares of stock which he has held for more than 6 months and which have an adjusted basis of $4,000 and a fair market value of $10,000. Walter makes no other charitable contributions in Year One and his contribution base for the year is large enough that a deduction will be allowable for this bargain sale. The adjusted basis for determining Walter's gain on the transaction is $1,600

[$4,000 adjusted basis $\times$ ($4,000 amount realized/$10,000 fair market value)] Walter has a long-term capital gain from the transaction of $2,400 ($4,000 amount realized − $1,600 adjusted basis) and he makes a charitable contribution of $6,000 ($10,000 fair market value − $4,000 consideration received) of property with an adjusted basis of $2,400. [Reg. § 1.1011–2(c) Example (1).]

c. Amount of charitable contribution

i. Cash

If a charitable contribution is made in money or its equivalent, such as a check or charge to a credit card, the amount of the contribution is the amount of money, less any consideration received for the transfer.

Example: Indebted makes a $100 contribution to the American Cancer Society by having it billed to his American Express Card. This is treated as a $100 contribution at the time the voucher is signed. [Rev.Rul. 78–38, 1978–1 C.B. 67.]

ii. Property

The amount of a charitable contribution of property is the fair market value of the contributed property at the time of the contribution, less the value of any consideration received for the transfer, subject to further reduction under IRC § 170(e). The fair market value of property is "the price at which the property would change hands between a willing buyer and a willing seller, neither being under any compulsion to buy or sell and each having a reasonable knowledge of relevant facts." [Reg. § 1.170A–1(c).] If there is a bargain sale of property to a qualified donee, the amount of the property's adjusted basis which is apportioned to the gift portion becomes relevant in determining any reduction in the amount of the gift under IRC § 170(e). [See discussion, III. B. 6. b. iii., at page 142, *supra.*]

a. Ordinary income and short-term capital gain property

The amount of a charitable contribution of property is reduced by the amount of gain which would have been ordinary income or short-term capital gain if the donor had sold the property at its date-of-contribution fair market value. [IRC § 170(e)(1)(A); see discussion of capital gains, VI. B. 1., at page 270, *infra.*]

Example: Alan makes a charitable contribution of a painting; Alan's adjusted basis for the painting, which he

purchased 5 months ago, is $60,000, and its fair
market value on the date of the contribution is
$80,000. The amount of Alan's charitable contribution
(the fair market value of the painting, $80,000) is
reduced by the amount of gain which would have
been short-term capital gain if, instead of making the
charitable contribution, he had sold it for its fair
market value ($80,000 – $60,000 = $20,000); thus, the
amount of Alan's charitable contribution is $60,000.
Similarly if the property were inventory or personal
or real property subject to $20,000 of IRC § 1245 or
§ 1250 recapture gain, Alan would also have a
$60,000 charitable contribution.

b.   Long-term capital gain property
        The amount of a charitable contribution of property is
reduced by all of the amount of gain which would have been
long-term capital gain (including gains, the character of which is
determined under IRC § 1231 [see discussion, VI. C., at page 291,
infra]) if the donor had sold the property at its date-of-
contribution fair market value, *and* if the contribution is: (1) of
tangible personal property the use of which is unrelated to the
exempt purpose of the donee; or (2) to or for the use of a
nonoperating private foundation. [IRC § 170(e)(1)(B).] The amount
of the contribution to a nonoperating private foundation does not
have to be reduced, however, for contributions of 10% or less of
the shares of stock of a corporation which are traded on an
established securities market. [IRC § 170(e)(5).]

Example: Alan, from the preceding example, has the same
                painting with an adjusted basis of $60,000 and a date-
                of-contribution fair market value of $80,000, but now
                he waits until he has held it for more than 6 months
                before making a charitable contribution of it. If he
                contributes the painting to an art gallery, where it
                will join a collection of other paintings by the same
                artist, the amount of Alan's charitable contribution is
                $80,000; it is not subject to reduction under IRC
                § 170(e)(1)(B). Alternatively, if Alan contributes the
                painting to a nonoperating private foundation, or to
                the American Red Cross (which sells the painting and
                uses the proceeds for its charitable purposes), the
                amount of the contribution will be reduced by the
                $20,000 potential long-term capital gain; thus, the
                amount of Alan's charitable contribution is $60,000.
                If Alan contributes shares of Exxon stock, with the

same fair market value and adjusted basis as the painting, to a nonoperating private foundation or to the American Red Cross, the amount of the contribution is $80,000.

iii. Services

No deduction is allowed for a contribution of services to a charitable organization. One might look at services as appreciated ordinary income property with a zero basis. Unreimbursed expenditures incurred in the course of rendering services to a charitable organization, however, may constitute charitable contributions. [Reg. § 1.170A–1(g).] If a passenger automobile is used in performing donated services, a taxpayer may deduct either the amount of actual expenses (such as fuel costs), or use a standard rate of 12 cents per mile. [IRC § 170(j).] No deduction is allowed for any travelling expenses unless there is no significant element of personal pleasure, recreation or vacation in such travel. [IRC § 170(k).]

Example: Yvonne is the second bassoonist in an orchestra and she agrees to perform in a benefit concert without pay. Yvonne may not deduct the value of her services, but she may deduct either the actual costs of driving her personal automobile to the concert, or 12 cents per mile, plus the cost of any tolls or parking fees.

iv. Partial interests in property

A charitable contribution of a remainder interest, an income interest, or other partial interest in property may be deducted only in certain limited circumstances. [IRC § 170(f).] The limitations do not apply, however, if charitable contributions are made of all the taxpayer's interests in the property. [IRC § 170(f)(2)(D).]

a. Transfers in trust

A charitable contribution of a remainder interest in property transferred in trust is deductible only if the trust is a charitable remainder annuity trust, a charitable remainder unitrust, or a pooled income fund. [IRC § 170(f)(2)(A).] Each of the three types of qualifying trusts is described elsewhere in the Code, but their common characteristic is that the trust property must be adequately preserved for the charitable organization.

A charitable contribution of an income interest in property, or of any partial interest in property other than a remainder interest, is deductible only if the interest is in the form of a guaranteed annuity, or if a specified fixed percentage of the fair market value of the trust property must be distributed annually to a charitable organization. [IRC § 170(f)(2)(B).] Again, both of these alternatives ensure that a readily determinable amount will actually be transferred to a charitable organization annually.

b. Transfers not in trust

   A charitable contribution (other than a transfer in trust) of a partial interest in property, including a right to use the taxpayer's property, is deductible only if it is: (1) a partial interest in property which would be deductible if transferred in trust, i.e., a qualified remainder or income interest; (2) a remainder interest in a personal residence; (3) a remainder interest in a farm; (4) an undivided portion of the donor's entire interest; or (5) a qualified conservation contribution. [IRC § 170(f)(3) and (h); Reg. § 1.170A–7(b).]

   Example: Zeke creates a trust providing simply that the income is to be paid to his son, Abel, for Abel's life and at Abel's death the remainder is to be paid to the American Cancer Society. There is no deduction of the value of the remainder interest at the time the trust is created because the trust is not a charitable remainder annuity trust, a charitable remainder unitrust or a pooled income fund. If Zeke transfers a life estate in his farm to his son, with the remainder to the American Cancer Society, the gift of the remainder interest is deductible.

d. Limitations on contributions amounts
i. In general

   The total amount of deductions for charitable contributions which a taxpayer may take in any taxable year is limited according to the form in which the contribution is made, the nature of the donee, the nature of the property contributed, and the contribution base of the taxpayer. [IRC § 170(b).] To the extent contributions made in a taxable year exceed the applicable percentage limitation, the excess may be carried over and treated as a contribution of the same character and to the same classification of donee in the 5 succeeding taxable years. [IRC § 170(b)(1)(B), (C), (D), and (d)(1); see discussion, III. B. 6. d. v., at page 149, *infra*.]

ii. Contribution base

   A taxpayer's "contribution base" for any taxable year is the amount of her adjusted gross income, computed without any net operating loss carryback to the taxable year. [IRC § 170(b)(1)(F); see discussion of adjusted gross income, VII. A., at page 304, *infra*.]

iii.   Public Charities
   a.   50% limitation

A taxpayer may deduct charitable contributions made during a taxable year *to* (but not "for the use of") certain charitable organizations described in the statute, commonly referred to as "Public Charities," to the extent the total of such contributions does not exceed 50% of the taxpayer's contribution base for the taxable year. [IRC § 170(b)(1)(A).] A contribution of an income interest in property, or a contribution of property to be held in trust for the benefit of a charitable organization is considered to be made "for the use of" the organization, rather than being made "to" the organization; such a contribution is subject to the 30% limitation on contributions to or for the use of Private Foundations. [Reg. § 1.170A–8(a)(2); see discussion, III. B. 6. d. iv. *a.*, at page 147, *infra.*]

Example: Dora's contribution base is $100,000 for a year in which she makes a charitable contribution of $100,000 cash to a Public Charity. Her deduction for charitable contributions is limited to $50,000, 50% of her contribution base.

   b.   Capital gain property—30% limitation

Charitable contributions to Public Charities of property which, if sold, would produce long-term capital gain or gain whose character is determined under IRC § 1231 ("capital gain property") *and* to which the reduction rules of IRC § 170(e)(1)(B) do *not* apply, may be deducted only to the extent the total amount does not exceed 30% of the taxpayer's contribution base. Alternatively, the taxpayer may elect to have the amount of the charitable contribution of capital gain property reduced under the rules of IRC § 170(e)(1)(B) (by the gain), thereby subjecting it to the 50% limitation rather than this 30% limitation. [IRC § 170(b)(1)(C).]

Example: In a year in which her adjusted gross income is $200,000, Fola makes a charitable contribution of shares of stock in XYZ corporation with an adjusted basis to her of $70,000 and a fair market value of $80,000 *to* a Public Charity. The shares of stock would have produced long-term capital gain if Fola had sold them, and the amount of the contribution, $80,000, is not subject to reduction under IRC § 170(e). The maximum deduction allowable for the year of the contribution is $60,000, 30% of her contribution base (the remaining $20,000 would be carried over to the 5 subsequent taxable years). [See discussion of carryovers, III. B. 6. d. v., at page 149, *infra.*] Alternatively, Fola may elect to have the amount of the contribution reduced by the unrealized long-term capital gain ($10,000), and the resulting $70,000 contribution would be allowed as a deduction in the year because it is within the 50% limitation ($100,000).

iv.   Private Foundations
   a.   30% limitation

A taxpayer may deduct charitable contributions made during a taxable year, *other than* contributions *to* Public Charities, only to the extent that the total does not exceed the *lesser* of: (1) 30% of the taxpayer's contribution base; or (2) the excess of 50% of the taxpayer's contribution base over the amount of charitable contributions allowable under the 50% limitation rules (disregarding the capital gain property limitation). [IRC § 170(b) (1)(B).] Thus the maximum deduction to private foundations is 30% of the taxpayer's contribution base. Charitable contributions to which this limitation applies are generally made to or for the use of organizations which are commonly referred to as "Private Foundations."

Example: In a year in which his adjusted gross income is $150,000, Elmer makes charitable contributions totaling $100,000, $60,000 in cash to a Public Charity and $40,000 to a Private Foundation. The $60,000 contribution to the Public Charity may be deducted in full, because it is less than $75,000, 50% of Elmer's contribution base of $150,000. The $40,000 contribution to the Private Foundation may be deducted to the extent it does not exceed the *lesser* of: (1) 30% of his contribution base, $45,000; or (2) the excess of 50% of his contribution base over the amount allowable for contributions to 50% organizations, $15,000 ($75,000 − $60,000). Thus, only $15,000 of the charitable contribution made to the Private Foundation is deductible in the current year. If Elmer had given only $20,000 cash to the Public Charity, then the entire $40,000 contribution to the Private Foundation could be deducted in the current year.

b. Capital gain property—20% limitation

Charitable contributions of capital gain property, other than contributions of such property *to* 50% organizations, may be deducted only to the extent the total amount does not exceed the lesser of: (1) 20% of the taxpayer's contribution base, or (2) the excess of 30% of the taxpayer's contribution base over the amount of contributions of capital gain property to Public Charities. [IRC § 170(b)(1)(D).] "Capital gain property" is property which, if sold, would produce long-term capital gain or gain whose character is determined under IRC § 1231. In addition, the amount of a contribution of capital gain property other than to 50% organizations may be required to be reduced under the rules of IRC § 170(e)(1)(B). [See discussion, III. B. 6. c. ii. *b.*, at page 144, *supra.*]

Example: In a year in which his adjusted gross income is $100,000, Gerard makes a charitable contribution of real property which is capital gain property with an adjusted basis of $6,000 and a fair market value of $12,000 to a Public Charity. In the same year he contributes to a Private Foundation personal property which is capital gain property with an adjusted basis of $10,000 and a fair market value of $20,000, and shares of Exxon common stock which have an adjusted basis of $4,000 and a fair market value of $15,000. The $12,000 contribution of capital gain real property to the 50% organization is not subject to the reduction rules of IRC § 170(e), and it is less than 30% of Gerard's contribution base ($30,000); thus, this contribution is deductible in full. The contribution of personal property which is capital gain property to the private foundation is reduced to $10,000 under IRC § 170(e)(1)(B); the contribution of the shares of Exxon stock, however, is not reduced in amount, but remains $15,000 by virtue of IRC § 170(e)(5). However, the $25,000 of deductions for the two contributions of capital gain property to the Private Foundation are limited to $18,000, the lesser of: (1) 20% of Gerard's contribution base ($20,000), or (2) the excess of 30% of his contribution base over the amount of contributions of capital gain property to Public Charities, $18,000 ($30,000 − $12,000).

v. Carryovers

If the total amount of charitable contributions during a taxable year exceeds any of the applicable limitations, the excess amount may be carried over and treated as a charitable contribution of the same type of property and same classification of charity made in each of the 5 succeeding taxable years. The amount carried over to any of the 5 succeeding years is the excess of the amount initially carried over, less any amount treated as a contribution during an intervening succeeding year. In determining any carryover an actual contribution made in any year is first considered followed by carryover from the earliest carryover years. [IRC § 170(d).]

Example: Dora's contribution base is $100,000 for each of the 3 Years, One, Two and Three. In Year One, she makes a charitable contribution of $100,000 cash to a 50% organization; in Year Two, she makes a charitable contribution of $20,000 cash to a 50% organization; and in Year Three, she does not make any charitable contributions. In Year One, her deduction for charitable contributions is limited to $50,000, 50% of her contribution base. In Year Two, her deduction for charitable contributions is again $50,000, consisting of the $20,000 actually contributed in that year and $30,000 of the excess contribution made in Year One. In Year Three, Dora's deduction for charitable contributions is $20,000, consisting of the remaining portion of the contribution actually made in Year One and not considered as being made in Year Two.

e. Year of deduction

Generally, a deduction for a charitable contribution may be taken only for the taxable year in which it is actually paid, or in a carryover year, even if the taxpayer otherwise uses the accrual method of accounting. [See discussion, IV. B. 2. c., at page 196, *infra.*] Thus, a contribution may not be taken in the year in which a "pledge" is made to contribute a certain amount in a future year. If a taxpayer uses a bank credit card, however, to make a charitable contribution, the deduction is allowable for the taxable year in which the charge is made. [Rev.Rul. 78–38, 1978–1 C.B. 67.]

Example: On December 30 of Year One, Colin charges a $50 contribution to a charitable organization on his VISA card, he mails a check for $100 to another charitable organization, and he pledges to donate $500 to a third charitable organization within the next 6 months. Both the $100 check and the $50 charge are charitable contributions for Colin for Year One.

f. Verification

   A charitable contribution is allowable as a deduction only if verified in accordance with the regulations. [IRC § 170(a)(1).] If a contribution is made of property other than money, the taxpayer must obtain a receipt from the donee, and if the property (other than money or publicly traded securities) has a claimed value in excess of $5,000, the taxpayer must submit a qualified appraisal of the property with the tax return or no deduction will be allowed. [Temp.Reg. § 1.170A–13T(b) and (c).]

7. EXTRAORDINARY MEDICAL EXPENSES

a. In general

   A deduction is allowed for expenses actually paid during a taxable year, not compensated for by insurance or otherwise, for medical care, to the extent that such expenses exceed 7.5% of the taxpayer's adjusted gross income. [IRC § 213(a).] The deduction is available for expenditures for the medical care of the taxpayer, his spouse, and "dependents," as defined in IRC § 152 [see discussion, III. B. 1. b., at page 129, *supra*]; however, for this purpose a child of divorced parents is treated as a "dependent" of each parent. [IRC § 213(d)(5).] If a taxpayer dies, medical expenses paid by his estate for his care within one year of his death are deemed to have been paid by the taxpayer, and thus are potentially deductible when such expenses were *incurred,* rather than when they are actually paid. [IRC § 213(c).]

> *Example:* Father pays $1,000 of his 21 year old Son's medical expenses. Father provides over one half of Son's support even though Son has $10,000 of gross income; Son is not a student. Since Son is a dependent under IRC § 152 (relationship and support tests are met) Father may include the $1,000 as part of his potentially deductible medical expenses.

b. Medical care

   Expenditures for medical care include amounts paid for the diagnosis, cure, treatment or prevention of disease, for transportation primarily for and essential to such medical care, for prescription drugs and insulin, and for insurance covering such medical care. [IRC § 213(b) and (d).] In addition, expenses for lodging, up to $50 per night per individual, while away from home primarily for medical care are treated as amounts paid for medical care if the medical care itself is provided in a hospital and there is no significant element of personal pleasure or vacation in the travel away from home. [IRC § 213(d)(2).] A deduction may also be allowed for an individual accompanying the patient.

> *Example:* Geoffery incurred medical expenses totalling $2,500 ($200 for premiums for medical insurance, $800 for prescription drugs, $1,000 for hospital room, and $500 for doctors' services) during

Year One, prior to his death in December of that year; his adjusted gross income for the year was $10,000. He paid $1,300 of the medical expenses prior to his death, and he was reimbursed for $500 of that amount, and his estate paid the remaining $1,200 within one year of his death. Geoffery's final income tax return, for Year One, may reflect unreimbursed medical expenses of $2,000 ($1,300 less $500 plus $1,200), and a deduction may be allowed for $1,250 ($2,000 less 7.5% of $10,000).

c. Capital expenditures

A capital expenditure is generally not deductible, but if the primary purpose for the expenditure is for medical care, it may be deductible. In addition, a capital expenditure for a permanent improvement to property may qualify as a medical expense to the extent that the expenditure exceeds the amount by which the value of the property is increased. However, the full cost of expenditures made to modify a personal residence for the special needs of a physically handicapped individual, such as wheelchair ramps or bathroom railings, qualify for the deduction.

Examples: Heather pays for eyeglasses, artificial teeth and a wheelchair. Although each of these items is a capital expenditure, they qualify for the medical expense deduction. [Reg. § 1.213–1(e)(1)(iii).]

Raymon's daughter suffers from asthma and upon the recommendation of her physician, he installs central air conditioning in his house at a cost of $1,300. The air conditioning unit increases the value of Raymon's house by $800; the excess $500 of the expenditure qualifies for the medical expense deduction. [*Raymon Gerard*, 37 T.C. 826 (1962).] All operating and maintenance expenses on the air conditioner in the current and subsequent years are considered expenses for medical care. [Reg. § 1.213–1(e)(1)(iii).]

8. ALIMONY

A deduction is allowed for amounts paid during a taxable year for alimony or separate maintenance payments. [IRC § 215; see discussion, V. C. 1., at page 261, *infra.*]

9. MOVING EXPENSES
a. In general

A taxpayer may deduct qualified moving expenses incurred in connection with beginning work as an employee or as a self-employed individual at a new principal place of work. [IRC § 217(a).] Amounts received as payment for or reimbursement of work-related expenses of moving from one residence to another residence are included in gross income as compensation. [IRC § 82; see discussion, II. B. 3. d. at page 43, *supra.*]

b. Conditions for allowance of deduction

A taxpayer must satisfy both a distance requirement and an employment-duration requirement to deduct qualified moving expenses. [IRC § 217(c).]

i. Distance requirement

The distance requirement is satisfied if the taxpayer's new principal place of work is at least 35 miles farther from his old residence than was his old principal place of work. If the taxpayer had no old principal place of work, the new principal place of work must be at least 35 miles from his old residence. Distance is to be measured by the shortest of the more commonly traveled routes between two points. [IRC § 217(c)(1).]

> *Example:* Chance's old residence is 8 miles from his old place of employment. His new principal place of work must be at least 43 miles from his old residence in order to satisfy the distance requirement. If he has not previously been employed his new principal place of work must be at least 35 miles from his old residence to satisfy the distance requirement.

ii. Employment-duration requirement

The employment-duration requirement is satisfied if either the employee test or the self-employed test is met. The employee test is satisfied if, during the 12-month period immediately following the taxpayer's arrival in the general location of his new principal place of work, he is a full-time employee in that general area for at least 39 weeks. The self-employed test is met if, during the 24-month period immediately following his arrival in the general location of his new principal place of work, he is either a full-time employee, or he performs services as a self-employed individual on a full-time basis, in that general area for a period of at least 78 weeks, of which, at least 39 weeks must be during the first 12 months of the 24-month period. [IRC § 217(c)(2).] A "self-employed individual" is someone who performs personal services as a sole proprietor or as a partner in a partnership carrying on a trade or business. [IRC § 217(f)(1).] The employment-duration requirement is waived if the taxpayer is unable to satisfy it because of death or disability, or, if he could have satisfied the test as a full-time employee but his employer involuntarily separates him from his employment. [IRC § 217(d)(1).]

> *Example:* Dawn moves from Dallas to Denver, where she is employed as a physician in a medical clinic for 30 weeks during the first 12 months after her arrival in Denver. After leaving the medical clinic, she opens her own office for the practice of medicine; she engages in private practice for 12 weeks during the first 12 months of her arrival in Denver. Because Dawn changes her status from employee to self-employed prior to satisfying the 39 week test, Dawn must also perform services as a self-employed individual on a full-time basis for at least 36 weeks [78 − (30 + 12)] during the second 12-month period following her arrival in Denver.

c. Qualified moving expenses

Deductible moving expenses include reasonable amounts spent for the following: (1) moving household goods and personal effects from the old to the new residence; (2) traveling from the old to the new residence; (3) traveling from the old residence to the general location of the new principal place of work, after employment has been obtained there, in order to search for a new residence; (4) lodging and 80% of meals in temporary quarters in the general location of the new principal place of work for *any* period of 30 consecutive days after obtaining employment; and (5) qualified residence sale, purchase, or lease expenses. [IRC § 217(b) (1)(A)–(E).] Moving expenses incurred for members of a taxpayer's household also qualify for the deduction. [IRC §§ 217(b)(3)(C) and 274(n) (1).]

The fifth category of qualified moving expenses, "qualified residence sale, purchase, or lease expenses," includes reasonable amounts which are spent for the following purposes: (1) expenses incident to the sale or exchange of the taxpayer's old residence ("selling expenses") which would otherwise offset the amount realized on the sale or exchange (other than "fix-up" expenses incurred to assist in the sale of the residence); (2) expenses incident to the purchase of a new residence in the general location of the new principal place of work ("purchasing expenses") which would otherwise be included in the basis of the new residence, or the costs of obtaining a loan (other than interest) to purchase the new residence; (3) expenses incident to the settlement of an unexpired lease of an old residence ("lease settlement expenses"); and (4) expenses (other than payments of rent) incident to leasing a new residence ("lease acquisition expenses"). [IRC § 217(b)(2).] If a deduction is taken, the amount may not be capitalized, i.e., a "selling expense" amount may not be used to offset the amount realized upon the sale or exchange of the old residence and a "purchasing expense" amount may not be added to the basis of the new residence. [IRC § 217(e).]

The amount of the deduction for expenses in the first two categories may not exceed an amount which is reasonable under the circumstances of the particular move, but there is no absolute limit on the amount of the deduction. In contrast, the maximum deduction for expenses in the second two categories is $1,500 ($750 if the taxpayer is a married individual filing a separate return). This limitation applies even if both the husband and the wife begin work at new principal places of work within the same general location. [IRC § 217(b)(3)(A) and (B).] The maximum deduction for the total amount of the fifth category of "qualified residence sale, purchase, or lease expenses" is $3,000 ($1,500 if the taxpayer is married, filing a separate return), reduced by the total of amounts deducted for travel on house hunting trips plus amounts deducted for meals and lodging in temporary quarters (described as items (3) and (4), *supra*). [IRC § 217(b)(3).]

Example: Bertha incurs the following expenses: (1) $2,500 in moving her family's household goods from their old residence to their new residence; (2) $1,200, including motels and 80% of meals, in transporting her family to the new residence; (3) $500 on an unsuccessful house hunting trip to the new town after obtaining a job there; and (4) $1,800 in motel and 80% of meal expenses for a period of 20 consecutive days 2 months after finding a job in the new town and moving her family there, but before locating permanent housing there. Assuming that Bertha otherwise qualifies for the deduction for moving expenses, the following amounts are potentially deductible: (1) $2,500, under IRC § 217(b)(1)(A); (2) $1,200, under IRC § 217(b)(1)(B); (3) $500, under IRC § 217(b)(1)(C); and (4) $1,800, under IRC § 217(b)(1)(D). Only $1,500 of the $2,300 expenses for house-hunting and for temporary lodging and 80% of meals is deductible, however, because of the limitation of IRC § 217(b)(3)(A).

If, in addition to the above expenses, Bertha paid $1,000 to obtain a release from her lease on her old residence, and $2,600 in closing costs upon purchasing her new residence, the additional $3,600 of expenditures are "qualified residence sale, purchase, or lease expenses." However, the amount which may be deducted is limited to $3,000, reduced by the $1,500 amount deducted for the house-hunting temporary quarters meals and lodging expenses, or $1,500. [See Reg. 1.217–2(b)(9).]

d. Time for deduction

The deduction for qualified moving expenses is to be taken in the taxable year in which the expenses are paid or incurred, in accordance with the taxpayer's method of accounting. If a taxpayer has not satisfied the employment-duration requirement at the time the income tax return is due to be filed for the taxable year in which the moving expenses were paid or incurred, she may either claim the deduction if it is still possible for her to ultimately satisfy the requirement, or she may file the return for that year without claiming the deduction and when she actually does satisfy the requirement, she may file an amended return for that taxable year. [IRC § 217(d)(2).] If she claims the deduction, however, and subsequently *does not* satisfy the employment-duration requirement, she must include in gross income an amount equal to the amount of the earlier deduction in either the subsequent year or the year of the deduction. [Reg. § 1.217–2(d)(3).].

Example: Willamina is an employee who moves from Florida to California in November of Year One and incurs $3,000 of moving expenses. In Year Two, she satisfies the time requirements of IRC § 217(c)(2). She may deduct her expenses in Year One and if she fails to meet the time requirements in Year Two she must include the deduction amount in income in either Year One or Year Two (her choice!). If she files her Year One return in April of Year Two without taking the deduction, waiting until she satisfies the time requirement, she must file an amended return for Year One taking her deduction on that return.

e.   Special rules

Special rules for the allowance of deductions for moving expenses are provided for certain members of the U.S. armed forces, and certain moves to or from foreign countries. [IRC § 217(g)–(i).]

10. RETIREMENT SAVINGS

A deduction is allowed for qualified retirement contributions made during a taxable year. [IRC § 219(a).] These are commonly referred to as Individual Retirement Accounts, or I.R.A.'s. The maximum amount of the deduction for any taxable year is generally the lesser of: (1) $2,000, or (2) the amount of the taxpayer's compensation income for the taxable year. [IRC § 219(b).] Different limitations apply to certain divorced individuals who receive alimony which is included in their gross income under IRC § 71(a) and to certain married individuals who file a joint return if one of the spouses has no compensation income for the taxable year. [IRC § 219(b)(4) and (c).] The deduction is allowed in computing adjusted gross income; thus, a taxpayer does not need to itemize deductions in order to make effective use of this allowance. [IRC § 62(a)(7); see discussion, VII. A. at page 304, *infra.*] The amount of the deduction is phased-out, however, if either the taxpayer or his spouse participate in an employer-maintained or self-employed retirement plan; the phase-out begins when adjusted gross income exceeds $40,000 if the taxpayer and his spouse file a joint return, at $25,000 if the taxpayer is unmarried, and at $10,000 if the taxpayer is married and files a separate return. [IRC § 219(g).]

Self-employed individuals generally may deduct amounts contributed to certain retirement plans, often referred to as "Keogh plans." [IRC § 404.] Amounts properly deductible may be subtracted from gross income in computing adjusted gross income. [IRC § 62(a)(6); see discussion, VII. A., at page 304, *infra.*]

C. RESTRICTIONS ON DEDUCTIONS

Unless the Code specifically provides otherwise, no deduction is allowed for personal expenses; in addition, a number of situations are described in which no deductions are allowed even though a deduction might otherwise seem appropriate. Limitations on deductions in the nature of restrictions on the *amount* which may be deducted or whether the deduction is allowable only if the taxpayer elects to itemize deductions are discussed in VII. B. 2. b., at page 307, *infra.*

1. PERSONAL, LIVING AND FAMILY EXPENSES

No deduction is allowed for personal, living, or family expenses, unless there is specific authorization for a deduction under another provision of the Code. [IRC § 262.]

Example: The following expenditures are illustrations of nondeductible personal expenses: premiums paid for life insurance by the insured; premiums paid for insurance on a personal residence; expenses of maintaining a household, such as rent, food and utilities; commuting expenses; expenses for medical care (other than to the extent a deduction is allowed under IRC § 213); losses sustained on the sale or other disposition of property used for personal purposes, such as one's residence, car, boat, etc. (other than to the extent allowed for "casualty losses" under IRC § 165(c) (3) [see discussion, III. B. 4., at page 136, *supra*]); expenses incurred in obtaining an education (unless they qualify under IRC § 162 and Reg. § 1.162–5 [see discussion, III. A. 1. i., at page 86, *supra*]). [Reg. § 1.262–1(b).]

2. ILLEGAL ACTIVITIES

No deduction is allowed for illegal bribes or kickbacks, any fine or similar penalty paid to a government for violation of any law, or treble damages paid for violation of the antitrust laws. [IRC § 162(c), (f), and (g).] Generally, other business expenses of an illegal business are deductible; however, no deduction is allowed for any amount paid or incurred in carrying on the trade or business of trafficking in illicit drugs. [IRC § 280E.]

> *Example:* Peg runs an illegal basement gambling casino with substantial gross income. She may deduct expenses for rent, salaries, equipment, utilities, etc. She may not deduct payoffs to the local policeman on the beat; however, she may deduct the cost of fees paid to an attorney she hires to defend her criminal prosecution for violating the gambling laws in the conduct of her business even if the defense is unsuccessful. [See *Commissioner v. Tellier*, 383 U.S. 687, 86 S.Ct. 1118 (1966).]

3. ACTIVITIES NOT ENGAGED IN FOR PROFIT
a. In general

No deduction is allowable for expenses attributable to an activity not engaged in for profit. [IRC § 183(a).] The primary function of this Code section is to provide some objective guidelines to differentiate between situations where someone is engaged in an activity as a trade or business and, thus, deductions are allowable, and other situations where someone is engaged in the same activity for personal pleasure and, thus, deductions are not allowable under the general rule of IRC § 262.

b. "Activity not engaged in for profit"

An "activity not engaged in for profit" is any activity other than one for which deductions are allowable under IRC § 162 (a trade or business), or under IRC § 212(1) or (2) (production or collection of income or management of property held for the production of income). [IRC § 183(c); see discussions, III. A. 1. and 2., at pages 70 and 93, *supra*.]

c. Presumptions

In determining whether a particular activity is an "activity not engaged in for profit," the activity is presumed *to be* one engaged in for profit (and, thus, the disallowance rule of IRC § 183(a) does not apply unless the I.R.S. overcomes the presumption) if the gross income from the activity exceeds the deductions attributable to the activity during at least 3 years out of the 5 consecutive years (2 out of 7 consecutive years if the activity involves race horses) ending with the current year. [IRC § 183(d).] A taxpayer may elect to defer a determination of whether the presumption applies with respect to a new activity until the close of the fourth year following the year in which he first engages in the activity. [IRC § 183(e)(1).]

> *Example:* For the 5 taxable Years One through Five, Alphonso is engaged in the activity of farming. In Years One, Four and Five, his deductible expenses exceed his gross income from the activity; in Years Two and Three, he has gross income in excess of deductions (other than net operating loss carryovers and carrybacks). Alphonso is presumed, for taxable Years One, Four and Five, to have engaged in the activity of

farming for profit. [Reg. § 1.183–1(c)(2) Example (1).] If Year One was the first year in which Alphonso engaged in the activity of farming, he could elect to have application of the presumption deferred until after Year Five.

d. Allowable deductions

If an activity is not engaged in for profit, deductions are, nonetheless, allowed as follows: (1) to the extent a deduction would be allowed under the authority of some provision other than IRC §§ 162 or 212 (*e.g.* local taxes, under IRC § 164); and (2) to the extent the expenditure would be allowed under IRC §§ 162 or 212 if the activity *was* engaged in for profit, but only to the extent that the activity produces gross income in excess of the amount of deductions allowed under (1). [IRC § 183(b).]

Example: Brenna's *hobby* is breeding and raising German Shepard dogs. During a taxable year, she pays $2,000 (plus $100 of state sales tax) for dog food, $500 for a veterinarian's services and $300 in local property taxes on the land used for her kennels. Brenna enters one of her best dogs in a regional dog show and wins the first prize of $1,500. If Brenna were legitimately in the dog breeding business, she could deduct a total of $2,900 for her expenses. Since this is a mere hobby, however, she may deduct only the local property taxes of $300 without regard to whether her dog breeding activities constitute "an activity engaged in for profit." In addition, she may deduct $1,200 ($1,500 gross income less $300 local property taxes) of her other expenses because she had gross income from her hobby during this taxable year.

4. EXPENSES AND INTEREST RELATING TO TAX–EXEMPT INCOME

No deduction is allowed for expenditures which would otherwise be allowed as deductions to the extent the expenditures are allocable to income which is exempt from the Federal income tax. In addition, no deduction is allowed for the payment of interest on indebtedness incurred or continued to purchase or carry obligations which, in turn, pay interest which is exempt from the Federal income tax. [IRC § 265(a)(1) and (2).]

Example: Clarence incurs $1,000 of expenses for education which would otherwise be deductible under IRC § 162 and Reg. § 1.162–5; however, he receives a $1,000 scholarship which is excluded from his gross income under IRC § 117. Clarence may not deduct his education expenses. [Rev.Rul. 83–3, 1983–1 C.B. 72.] In addition, Clarence borrows $10,000 in order to purchase municipal bonds which pay interest which is excluded from his gross income under IRC § 103. Clarence may not deduct the interest he pays with respect to the $10,000 borrowed funds.

5. TRANSACTIONS BETWEEN RELATED TAXPAYERS

a. In general

No deduction is allowed for any loss arising from the sale or exchange of property between *related* taxpayers. In addition, a taxpayer on the accrual method of accounting may not take deductions for interest or other expenses to be paid to a *related* taxpayer who is on the cash method of accounting until the amount is actually or constructively paid. [IRC § 267(a).]

b. Relationships

"Related taxpayers" include: (1) an individual and her brothers and sisters, spouse, ancestors, and lineal descendants; (2) an individual and a corporation which the individual owns, directly or indirectly, more than 50% of the value of its outstanding stock; (3) the fiduciary of a trust and the grantor of that trust; (4) various fiduciaries and beneficiaries of 2 or more trusts with respect to which the same person is the grantor; and various other relationships between certain corporations, partnerships, and educational and charitable organizations. [IRC § 267(b).] In determining whether an individual is within the prescribed relationship to a corporation, stock of the corporation actually owned by a corporation, partnership, estate or trust is considered to be owned proportionately by its shareholders, partners, or beneficiaries. In addition, an individual is considered to own stock actually owned by other members of his family, and if an individual is a partner in a partnership, he is considered to own stock actually owned by other partners of the partnership. [IRC § 267(c).]

Example: X Corporation has 100 shares of stock outstanding, 20 are owned by Z Corporation, 35 by Delilah, 10 by Eric, and 35 by Faye. Delilah owns one half of the shares of Z Corporation, and she and Eric are brother and sister; Faye is not related to Delilah or Eric and she owns none of the Z Corporation stock. Delilah is considered to be the owner of (i.e., she "constructively owns") one half of the shares of X Corporation stock actually owned by Z corporation (10 shares) as well as all of the shares owned by her brother Eric (10 shares). Delilah owns, actually and constructively, 55 shares of X Corporation, thus Delilah and X Corporation are related taxpayers.

c. Losses and relief on subsequent sales

No deduction is allowed for any loss incurred on the sale or exchange of property between related taxpayers. [IRC § 267(a)(1).] However, if a loss is disallowed with respect to an item of property, and the property is later sold or disposed of at a gain by the transferee related party, the gain is recognized only to the extent it exceeds the amount of the previously disallowed loss. [IRC § 267(d).]

Example: Greg purchased stock in XYZ Corporation several years ago for $50,000, and he sells it on January 1 of the current year to his daughter, Heather, for its fair market value of $40,000. Greg may not deduct the $10,000 loss. If Heather later sells the stock to an unrelated person for $55,000, her realized gain of $15,000 will be recognized only to the extent it exceeds the previously disallowed loss of $10,000; thus, only $5,000 of gain will be recognized on the subsequent sale.

d. Deferred timing of deductions

A taxpayer on the accrual method of accounting may not take deductions for interest or other expenses to be paid to a related taxpayer who is on the cash method of accounting until the amount is actually or constructively paid. [IRC § 267(a)(2).] The circumstances in which persons are "related taxpayers" is broadened for the purposes of this rule with regard to certain partnerships and S corporations. [IRC § 267(e).]

Example: Ignatius, a cash method taxpayer, is employed by XYZ Corporation, an accrual method taxpayer, at a salary of $4,000 per month; Ignatius owns 75% of the outstanding stock of XYZ. XYZ is normally entitled to deduct the amount of Ignatius' salary as it accrues to him on a monthly basis, and Ignatius includes the salary in his gross income when he actually or constructively receives it. In November and December of Year One, however, XYZ is short on cash and does not pay Ignatius his salary. In January of Year Two, XYZ pays Ignatius the $8,000 arrearage in his salary. XYZ may not deduct the $8,000 in Year One, but may deduct it in the year in which it is actually paid, Year Two.

6. ENTERTAINMENT EXPENSES
a. In general

In addition to satisfying the requirements of IRC §§ 162 or 212, expenditures incurred for business meals, entertainment, amusement, recreation activities or facilities, or for gifts must meet further statutory criteria; if they do not, no deduction will be allowed. [IRC § 274.] This section is strictly a *disallowance* provision; it does not authorize the deduction of any item not otherwise allowed under some other section of the Code. Expenditures which are deductible without regard to whether they are connected with a taxpayer's trade or business or income-producing activity, such as payment of interest or state or local taxes, are not affected by these disallowance rules. [IRC § 274(f).]

b. Activity

No deduction is allowed for an expenditure with respect to an activity which is of a type generally considered to constitute entertainment, meals, amusement, or recreation, unless the taxpayer establishes that the expenditure is "directly related to" the active conduct of the taxpayer's trade or business or income-producing activities or "associated with" the active conduct of the taxpayer's trade or business if the expenditure directly precedes or follows a substantial and bona fide business discussion. [IRC § 274(a)(1)(A).] Generally, an expenditure is "directly related to" the active conduct of a trade or business if business activities go on during the entertainment; an expenditure is "associated with" the trade or business if the taxpayer has a clear business purpose in making the expenditure. [Reg. § 1.274–2(c) and (d).] A deduction is allowed, however, for only 80% of the cost of any otherwise deductible expenditure for food, beverages or for any entertainment activity. [IRC § 274(n).]

Example: Jessica is a sales representative for a corporation which publishes textbooks used in law schools. She attends a law professors' convention in order to talk with professors about adopting the books she sells for use in courses which they teach. In addition, she plans to meet with certain professors about publishing books which they have written or are writing. The afternoon before the convention begins, she spends several hours talking with a professor about publishing a Torts casebook which the professor is writing, and that evening Jessica takes her to dinner. During the three days of the convention, Jessica rents a suite in the hotel where she has copies of law textbooks on display, and snacks and beverages are provided; she extends an open invitation to all of the law professors attending the convention to drop by the suite for a drink and to look at the books. The expenditure for the hospitality suite is "directly related" to Jessica's trade or business, and the expenditure for the dinner following her business discussion is "associated with" her trade or business; thus, 100% of the cost of the hospitality suite is deductible and 80% of the costs of the snacks, beverages and dinner is deductible. [Reg. § 1.274–2(c)(4) and –2(d)(3)(ii).]

c.   **Facility**

No deduction is allowed for any expenditure incurred with respect to a facility used in connection with entertainment, amusement, or recreation. [IRC § 274(a)(1)(B).] However, even though the payment of dues or fees to a social, athletic, or sporting club is treated as an expenditure with respect to a facility, if the taxpayer establishes that the club is used primarily for the furtherance of her trade or business and that the expenditure is "directly related" to the active conduct of the trade or business 80% of the business portion of the dues is deductible. [IRC § 274(a)(2).]

Example: Kevin is a dentist. He owns a yacht and is a member of a yacht club in Newport Beach. The yacht is a "facility" and no deduction is allowed for depreciation or expenses associated with the yacht. In addition, the dues which Kevin pays to the yacht club are treated as expenditures related to a "facility" and, thus, they are not deductible. If Kevin uses the club 60% of the time for business lunches, and 40% of the time for personal use, 48% (60% x 80%) of the dues is deductible, as well as 80% of the cost of the business lunches.

d. Entertainment tickets

No deduction is allowed for an expenditure for an otherwise deductible ticket to an entertainment facility or event in excess of the face value of the ticket, unless it is a ticket to a qualifying charitable sports event. [IRC § 274(*l*)(1).] The deduction is generally further limited to 80% of the face value of the ticket. [IRC § 274(n).]

Example: Vinny purchases 2 tickets to a professional football game, one for himself and one for a business client, in a context that the entertainment is "associated with" Vinny's business. The face value of the 2 tickets is $100, but because the game was sold out, he was able to obtain them only by paying a scalper $200. Vinny may deduct only $80 for the tickets.

e. Skyboxes

Subject to a phase-in rule ending in 1988, the amount which may be deducted for the cost of leasing a skybox or other private luxury box for more than one event is limited to the cost of purchasing the same number of non-luxury tickets available to the general public. [IRC § 274(*l*)(2).] The deduction is generally further limited to 80% of the cost of the non-luxury tickets. [IRC § 274(n).]

Example: Hugh leases a skybox at Home Town Stadium for a post-1988 year's fall football season for $30,000. There are 12 seats in the skybox, 5 home games in the season, and Hugh is careful to invite others to join him in the skybox for the games only in a context that the entertainment is "associated with" Hugh's business. The highest-priced non-luxury seats available for purchase by the general public cost $20 per game. Hugh may deduct only $960 [80% of $1,200 ($20 × 5 games × 12 seats)] of the cost of leasing the skybox.

f. Exceptions to the disallowance rules

The rules which disallow deductions for entertainment, amusement, or recreation activities or facilities do not apply in various situations listed in IRC § 274(e) such as food and beverages furnished to employees by an employer on his business premises, expenses treated as compensation, reimbursed expenses and expenses incurred at business meetings for employees, stockholders or directors.

g. Substantiation

A taxpayer must be able to substantiate entertainment expenses in accordance with the regulations, or no deductions will be allowed. [IRC § 274(d); see discussion, III. A. 1. k., at page 92, *supra.*]

7. BUSINESS USE OF HOME AND RENTAL OF VACATION HOMES
a. In general

Subject to exceptions discussed below, no deduction is allowed with respect to the use of a dwelling unit which is used as a residence by a taxpayer during the taxable year. [IRC § 280A(a).] Expenditures which are deductible without regard to whether they are connected with a taxpayer's trade or business or income-producing activity, such as payment of qualified residence interest or state or local taxes, are not affected by this disallowance rule. [IRC § 280A(b).]

i. "Dwelling unit"

A "dwelling unit" includes a house, apartment, condominium, mobile home, boat, or similar property, but does not include any portion of a unit which is used exclusively as a hotel, motel or inn. [IRC § 280A(f)(1).] A single structure, such as an apartment building or a duplex, may contain more than one dwelling unit and if the owner of the building occupies one of the units, the restrictions of IRC § 280A do not apply to the other units which he does not use as a residence. [See Prop. Reg. § 1.280A–1(c).]

ii. Use as a residence

A taxpayer is considered to use a dwelling unit as a residence if, during a taxable year, he uses it for personal purposes the *greater of* 15 days or a number of days in excess of 10% of the number of days during the year the unit is rented at a fair rental. A taxpayer is deemed to have used a dwelling unit for personal purposes on any day: (1) he or any member of his family uses it; (2) someone uses it and the taxpayer thereby becomes entitled to use some other dwelling unit; or, (3) any individual (other than an employee who is entitled to exclude the rental value of the unit from her gross income under IRC § 119) uses it and pays less than a fair rental for its use. The first two tests apply without regard to whether a fair rental is charged, unless the dwelling unit is rented at a fair rental to someone for use as that person's principal residence. [IRC § 280A(d).]

Example: Lisa's yacht has 2 staterooms which will provide overnight accommodations. During the current year, she uses the yacht herself on 4 days, her sister uses it for 5 days, and her college roommate uses it (without paying a fair rental) for 7 days; thus, Lisa is deemed to use the yacht for personal purposes for a total of 16 days. In addition, Lisa rents the yacht at a fair rental for 163 days during the year. Because the number of days on which Lisa uses the yacht for personal purposes does not exceed 16.3 (10% of 163 days), Lisa has not used the yacht as a "residence" during the current year. [Prop. Reg. § 1.280A–1(d)(2) Example (1).]

b. Business use

The general rule which disallows deductions with respect to the use of a dwelling unit which is used by a taxpayer as a residence does not apply to the extent a deductible item is allocable to a portion of the dwelling unit which is used for certain business purposes, for storing inventory, or in providing day care services. [IRC § 280A(c).] The amount which may be deducted in a taxable year is limited, however, to the excess of the gross income derived from the business use over the sum of the deductions such as mortgage interest and real property taxes allocable to that portion of the unit plus business deductions other than those attributable to the use of the dwelling. The amount of deductions in excess of this limitation may be carried over and treated as deductions in the next taxable year. [IRC § 280A(c)(5).]

Example: Ariel uses one fourth of the house in which he resides as the principal place of his business. In the current year, he pays $12,000 in rent for the building, and $4,000 for utilities and repairs. His gross income from his business for the current year is $3,500 and he pays $1,000 for supplies and other business expenses. Ariel's deductions for the business use of his home are $4,000 (¼ of $12,000 rent plus ¼ of $4,000 utilities and repairs), but he may only deduct $2,500 (the excess of $3,500 of gross income from the business over $1,000 of business expenses unrelated to the use of the dwelling unit) in the current year. The remaining $1,500 of deductions will be treated as a deduction in the next taxable year.

i. Certain business use

Deductions are allowed to the extent they are allocable to a *portion* of a dwelling unit which is *exclusively* used *on a regular basis* as either: (1) the principal place of business for any trade or business of the taxpayer; or (2) a place of business which is used by patients, clients or customers in meeting or dealing with the taxpayer in the normal course of his trade or business; or (3) in connection with the taxpayer's trade or business, if the property is a separate structure not attached to the dwelling unit. If the taxpayer is an employee, the *exclusive* use of the dwelling unit for a qualifying purpose must be "for the convenience of his employer." [IRC § 280A(c)(1).] The rules may not be circumvented by rental of the property by an employee to his employer for use by the employee in performing services as an employee of the employer. [IRC § 280A(c)(6).]

> *Example:*   John is a condominium supervisor. His employer requires him to be available for telephone calls in the evenings and on weekends, so he converted a bedroom in his home into an office. John keeps files relating to condominium matters in his home office and he has a telephone there which he uses strictly for incoming calls from clients; however, clients rarely visit John at his home office. John's home office is not "used by . . . clients" and thus no deduction for the office is allowed. [*Green v. Comm'r,* 707 F.2d 404 (9th Cir.1982).]

ii.   Certain storage use

If a dwelling unit is the sole fixed location of a taxpayer's trade or business and the trade or business involves selling products at wholesale or retail, deductions are allowed to the extent they are allocable to space within the dwelling unit which is used on a regular basis to store the taxpayer's inventory. [IRC § 280A(c)(2).]

> *Example:*   Melvin is an engineering professor at Undergrad University, where he is provided an office. In addition, he operates a small mail-order business from his home, selling items which he has invented to customers who have responded to advertisements which he places in various periodicals. He devotes the exclusive use of one room in his house to conducting his mail-order sales business. Melvin is engaged in two businesses. The principal place of business for teaching is at the University, and the principal place of business for his mail-order business is at his home, and the expenses related to the one room used for that business are deductible. If Melvin also devotes the exclusive use of another room in his house to store his inventory of items which he sells in his mail-order business, deductions are allowable with respect to the storage space. [Prop.Reg. § 1.280A–2(b)(2) and (e).]

iii.   Use in providing day care services

Deductions are allowed to the extent they are allocable to the portions of a dwelling unit which are used on a regular basis in the taxpayer's trade or business of providing day care for children, individuals who have attained the age of 65, and individuals who are physically or mentally incapable of caring for themselves. [IRC § 280A(c)(4).]

c. Rental of dwelling unit

If a dwelling unit is rented, or held out for rental, the deductibility of items attributable to the dwelling unit depends on how many days the dwelling unit is rented, and on how much personal use the taxpayer makes of the dwelling unit.

i. De minimis rule

If a dwelling unit which is used by a taxpayer as a residence is actually rented for less than 15 days during a taxable year, the rental income is excluded from gross income, and *no* deduction otherwise allowable because of the rental use (such as for depreciation or repairs) is allowed. [IRC § 280A(g).]

ii. Dwelling unit rented for more than 14 days, but not used as a "residence"

If a dwelling unit is rented out for more than 14 days during a taxable year, and it is not used "for personal purposes" on any day during the taxable year, the deduction limitation provisions of IRC § 280A(c)(5) and (e) do not apply, but the provisions of IRC § 183 might apply if the rental activity is determined to be an "activity not engaged in for profit." [See discussion, III. C. 3., at page 157, *supra.*]

If a dwelling unit is rented out for more than 14 days, and the taxpayer uses the dwelling unit for personal purposes on one or more days (but not enough days to qualify the dwelling unit as a "residence" under IRC § 280A(d)) during the taxable year, the deduction limitation provisions of IRC § 280A(c)(5) do not apply, but the limitation imposed by IRC § 280A(e) does apply (see Example below), as well as the potential application of IRC § 183.

Example: Norma owns a beach house. Last year, she rented the house, at a fair rental of $100 per day, for a total of 30 days, and she used it for personal purposes on 10 days. During the year, she paid a total of $2,000 for local ad valorem property taxes; she also paid $4,000 in repair and maintenance expenses. IRC § 280A(e) limits the deduction for the repair and maintenance expenses to $3,000 (30 days rented at a fair rental divided by 40 days total use, multiplied by the total amount of repair and maintenance expenses); in addition, she may deduct the $2,000 paid for local taxes. If the rental activity is determined to be an "activity not engaged in for profit" under IRC § 183, that section will further limit her deduction of the repair and maintenance expenses to $1,000 [the amount by which the gross income from rents ($3,000) exceeds the deduction for local property taxes ($2,000)].

iii.   Dwelling unit rented for more than 14 days and used as a "residence"

If a dwelling unit is rented out for more than 14 days, and it is used for personal purposes on enough days to treat the dwelling unit as a "residence," deductions with respect to the dwelling unit are subject to the restrictions of both IRC § 280A(c)(5) and (e); the provisions of IRC § 183, however, are not applicable for such year. [IRC § 280A(f)(3).]

Example: Dorance and his wife Helen own a vacation home in Palm Springs and last year they rented it out for 91 days, used it for personal purposes for 30 days, and left it unoccupied for 244 days. They received $2,700 in rents, and paid $3,475 for qualified residence interest and local taxes, and $2,693 in maintenance expenses. Under IRC § 280A(e), deductions for maintenance expenses are limited to $2,020, which is $91/121$ of the $2,693 spent for maintenance. Under IRC § 280A(c)(5), their deductions are further limited to the amount by which the gross income (rents) exceeds the deductions for interest and taxes which are allocable to the rental use. Because interest and taxes are attributable to the entire year, these are apportioned by a fraction with the number of rental days in the numerator, and 365 as the denominator; thus $868 (which is $91/365$ multiplied by $3,475) of the interest and taxes is subtracted from the $2,700 of rental income, resulting in $1,832 as the maximum amount which may be deducted for maintenance expenses. [*Bolton v. Comm'r*, 694 F.2d 556 (9th Cir.1982); the figures used in the Example were taken from the opinion of the court, as rounded off by the court.]

iv.   Rental of principal residence

The deduction limitation provisions of IRC § 280A(c)(5) do not apply to a taxpayer's principal residence if the only use for personal purposes occurs before or after a qualified rental period. [IRC § 280A(d)(4).] A "qualified rental period" is a consecutive period of 12 months or more, or a shorter period ending with the sale or exchange of the dwelling unit, during which the unit is rented, or is held for rental, at a fair rental.

> *Example:* Mable owns a house in Houston in which she lives with her husband and children until November 15 last year when she moves to Dallas with her family. After they move, they rent the Houston house for 10 months while attempting to sell it; the house is finally sold in August of the current year. The period after November 15 last year until the date the Houston house is sold is a qualified rental period.

8. DEMOLITION OF STRUCTURES

A taxpayer may not deduct any of the cost of demolishing a building or other structure or any loss incurred because of the demolition. Instead, the amount of the demolition expense or loss is added to the basis of the land on which the building was located.

> *Example:* Ned paid $450,000 for a parcel of land with an old warehouse on it; the warehouse was worth $50,000. Sometime later (when the basis of the warehouse was still $50,000), Ned decided to tear down the warehouse and build a motel in its place; he paid $7,000 to have the warehouse demolished. Ned may not deduct the $50,000 loss of the warehouse, nor may he deduct the $7,000 demolition expense. Ned's basis for the land is $457,000.

9. DEDUCTIONS LIMITED TO AMOUNT AT RISK
a. In general

An individual or closely held corporate taxpayer who is engaged in an activity may deduct any loss from the activity only to the extent the taxpayer is "at risk" for the activity at the close of the taxable year. Any loss which is not allowed in a taxable year because of the application of this rule is treated as a deduction attributable to that activity in the next taxable year; whether a deduction will be allowed in the subsequent year depends upon application of the at risk rules in the subsequent year. [IRC § 465(a) and (d).] For purposes of these rules, a "loss" from an activity during a taxable year is the excess of deductions allocable to the activity over the income derived from the activity. [IRC § 465(d).] Generally, these rules apply to any activity in which the taxpayer engages in carrying on a trade or business or for the production of income. [IRC § 465(c).]

b. Amounts considered "at risk"

A taxpayer is considered to be at risk with respect to an activity to the extent of the amount of money and the adjusted bases of other property the taxpayer contributes to the activity as well as amounts borrowed with respect to the activity but only if the taxpayer is personally liable for the repayment of the borrowed funds, or if the taxpayer has pledged property (other than property used in the activity) as security for the borrowed amount, and if he is not protected against loss through nonrecourse guarantees or some similar arrangement. In some situations, a taxpayer may be considered at risk with respect to certain nonrecourse financing secured by real property used in the activity. [IRC § 465(b)(6).] Generally, amounts borrowed from another person who has an interest in the activity, or from a person related to such a person, are not included in the at risk amount.

If a taxpayer has a loss with respect to an activity in a taxable year, and the loss is allowed as a deduction in that year because the amount which the taxpayer is at risk is in excess of the amount of the loss, then, in subsequent taxable years, the taxpayer's at risk amount is reduced by the portion of the loss which was allowed as a deduction. [IRC § 465(b).] A taxpayer's at risk amount with respect to an activity is determined at the close of a taxable year, and takes into consideration events which have occurred during the year, such as repayment of borrowed amounts or the conversion of a liability for which the taxpayer was personally liable into a nonrecourse liability.

Example: In Year One, Oscar is engaged in a business to which he has contributed $10,000 in cash and a truck, which has an adjusted basis of $5,000 and a fair market value of $7,000. In addition, Oscar borrowed $25,000 from a local bank, which took a second mortgage on Oscar's house to secure the loan, and he borrowed $2,000 from a finance company, which took a security interest in the truck; Oscar is not personally liable under either loan, and he contributes all $27,000 of the proceeds from the 2 loans to the business. Assuming that none of the principal is paid on any of the loans at the end of the taxable year, Oscar is at risk with respect to his business in the amount of $40,000 ($10,000 cash + $5,000 adjusted basis of truck + $25,000 amount borrowed for which he has pledged his house as security; the $2,000 amount borrowed for which he pledged the truck is not included in the at risk amount).

In Year One, Oscar's business has $15,000 of income, and $45,000 of deductions are attributable to the business; the business has a "loss" for Year One of $30,000. Because Oscar is at risk in the amount of $40,000, all of the deductions are allowed, but Oscar's at risk amount for Year Two is reduced by $30,000. In Year Two, the business again has $15,000 of income and $45,000 of deductions, and none of the principal is paid on any of the loans. The "loss" for Year Two of $30,000 is deductible only to the extent of $10,000, the at risk amount determined at the end of Year Two. The $20,000 excess loss amount which is not deductible in Year Two is treated as a deduction in Year Three; thus, in Year Three, if the business has $100,000 of income, and $45,000 of deductions actually paid in that year, the $20,000 excess loss amount from Year Two may also be deducted.

c. Recapture

Because the at risk amount is computed at the end of each taxable year it is possible for a taxpayer to have an at risk amount of less than zero especially if an at risk loan is converted to a nonrecourse (not at risk) loan during the year. In such circumstances, the amount by which the at risk amount is less than zero must be included in gross income, and an equal amount is treated as a deduction in the succeeding taxable year. [IRC § 465(e).]

Example: At the end of Year One, Prudence is at risk with respect to her business in the amount of $20,000, $5,000 of cash which she contributed, and a $15,000 loan on which she is personally liable. In that year, the business has $25,000 of income, and $40,000 of deductions; thus, she has a $15,000 "loss" from the business, and as that amount is less than her at risk amount, all of the deductions are allowed. In Year Two, the business breaks even but the loan is converted to a nonrecourse liability; Prudence's at risk amount determined at the end of Year Two is the amount of cash she contributed ($5,000) reduced by the portion of the Year One loss which was allowed as a deduction because it did not exceed the at risk amount computed at the end of Year One ($15,000), for a negative at risk amount of $10,000. Prudence must include $10,000 in her gross income for Year Two as income derived from her business. In addition, $10,000 is treated as a deduction allocable to her business in Year Three; whether the deduction will be allowed in Year Three depends upon application of the at risk rules to her and her business in that year.

10. PASSIVE ACTIVITY LOSSES AND CREDITS

Generally, an individual taxpayer computes his tax liability by aggregating his gross income from all sources and then subtracting allowable deductions from all sources in computing taxable income. Thus, if a taxpayer is engaged in two separate activities, an overall loss (total deductions exceed total gross income) from one activity can effectively offset an overall gain (total gross income exceeds total deductions) attributable to the second activity. Because of Congressional concern that it is inappropriate for a taxpayer to be allowed to offset net income derived from a trade or business (including the performance of services as an employee) in which the taxpayer is actively involved with deductions attributable to a trade or business in which the taxpayer is *not* actively involved, it enacted provisions limiting deductions and tax credits attributable to certain passive activities. [IRC § 469.] Although this Outline focuses on individual taxpayers, it should be noted that these passive activity rules also apply to taxpayers which are estates, trusts, personal service corporations and certain closely held C corporations. [IRC § 469(a)(2).] The rules also apply to an individual who is a partner in a partnership or a shareholder in an S corporation with respect to the activities of the partnership or S corporation.

The provisions of IRC § 469 apply generally to taxable years beginning after 1986, but there are some transition rules and a phase-in of the disallowance rules with respect to a taxpayer's interest in passive activities which were being conducted as of October 22, 1986, the date the Tax Reform Act of 1986 was enacted (referred to as a pre-enactment interest). Under the phase-in rules, if passive investment losses or credits (other than carryforwards) otherwise disallowed under the general rules are attributable to a taxpayer's pre-enactment interest, only the applicable percentage of such passive activity losses or credits is disallowed. The applicable percentage for taxable years beginning in 1987 is 35%; for taxable years beginning in 1988, 1989 and 1990 the applicable percentage increases to 60%, 80% and 90%, respectively. The phase-in rule applies only to taxable years beginning in calendar years 1987 through 1990. [IRC § 469(*l*).]

Example: Harold was engaged in a passive activity prior to 1986 and in 1987 the activity produced a passive activity loss of $100. The phase-in rule permits Harold to deduct $65 (35% of the $100 loss is disallowed) in 1987; the remaining $35 of the passive activity loss is carried over to 1988. If the activity produces no gain or loss in 1988 (other than the $35 passive activity loss carried to 1988 from 1987), no deduction is allowed for 1988 under the phase-in rule. In the alternative, if the activity produces a $15 loss in 1988 in addition to the $35 carryover, the phase-in rule permits Harold to deduct $6 (60% of the $15 loss is disallowed) in 1988.

a. Passive activity
i. In general
A passive activity is one which involves the conduct of a trade or business (or an activity for which deductions would be allowable under IRC § 212) in which the taxpayer *does not* materially participate. [IRC § 469(c).] A taxpayer is considered to be materially participating in an activity only if he is involved in the operations of the activity on a regular, continuous and substantial basis. [IRC § 469(h).] In determining whether the material participation test is met, the participation in the activity by the taxpayer's spouse is also considered, and if the activity involves a farm, special rules may

apply if the taxpayer is retired, disabled or a surviving spouse. [IRC § 469(h)(3) and (5).] A taxpayer is never treated as materially participating in an activity in his capacity as a limited partner in a partnership. [IRC § 469(h)(2).]

> *Example:* Gus is a general partner in a partnership which is engaged in the business of selling tractors and farm implements at retail. Gus spends 35 to 40 hours each week at the partnership's business establishment, making sales to customers, taking inventory and ordering spare parts. Gus is materially participating in the partnership's business. If Gus was a limited partner, however, he would not be treated as materially participating in the partnership's business.

ii. Rental activities

Rental activities are deemed to be passive activities without regard to whether the taxpayer materially participates in the activity. [IRC § 469(c)(2)–(4).] In applying this rule, the Congressional Committee Reports accompanying the Tax Reform Act of 1986 indicate that if a rental activity also involves the rendition of substantial services, it will not be treated as a "rental activity" under the passive loss rules.

> *Example:* An activity involving the daily or weekly rental of automobiles where the lessor provides insurance, repair and maintenance service on the automobiles is not a rental activity under the passive loss rules. If the automobiles are leased for a long term and the lessee is responsible for repairs, maintenance, and so forth, it is a rental activity under the passive loss rules.

iii. Working interests in oil and gas property

Working interests in oil and gas property are excluded from the definition of "passive activity" unless the interest is held indirectly through an entity, such as a limited partnership, which limits the taxpayer's liability. [IRC § 469(c)(3).] This rule applies regardless of the lack of material participation by the taxpayer. [IRC § 469(c)(4).]

b. Passive activity loss or credit

A passive activity loss is the excess of deductions from passive activities over the total income from passive activities for a taxable year. [IRC § 469(d)(1).] A passive activity credit is the excess of the sum of tax credits attributable to passive activities over the taxpayer's tax liability allocable to passive activities. [IRC § 469(d)(2); see discussion of tax credits at VII. F., at page 314, *infra*.] For the purpose of computing passive activity losses or credits, certain items of "portfolio income" (i.e., interest, dividends, annuities and royalties not derived in the ordinary course of business) and related deductions are not taken into account. [IRC § 469(e)(1).]

c. Treatment of passive activity loss or credit
i. In general

To the extent a taxpayer's passive activity losses (or credits) for a taxable year exceed his income from passive activities (or income tax attributable to passive activities) for the taxable year, they may not be deducted (or credited) in that taxable year, but are carried over to subsequent taxable years. [IRC § 469(b), (d) and (e).] Passive activity losses (or credits) disallowed in a taxable year under IRC § 469(a)(1) are not permanently disallowed, but are merely suspended.

> ***Example:*** Casey is a physician whose adjusted gross income for Year One (a Year after 1990) from his medical practice is $150,000. In addition, he owns a partnership interest in two separate partnerships, but he does not materially participate in the business of either partnership. Casey's share of Partnership #1's operations is a net loss of $25,000, and his share of Partnership #2's business is a net gain of $10,000. Casey may deduct only $10,000 of the net loss from Partnership #1 in Year One; the remaining $15,000 net loss from Partnership #1 is carried over to Year Two and may be used then to offset Year Two's passive activity income (and it may be carried on to future years to the extent it is not used in Year Two).

ii. Special rule for rental real estate activities

Although rental activities are generally deemed to be passive activities regardless of the material participation by a taxpayer, an exception applies to rental real estate activities. [IRC § 469(i).] If an individual taxpayer owns at least a 10% (in value) interest and "actively participates" in rental real estate activities, the limitations on passive activity losses (and credits) do not apply to the extent the losses (and deduction equivalents for credits) do not exceed $25,000. The requirement that the taxpayer "actively participate" in the rental real estate activity is less rigorous than the "material participation" standard and can be satisfied without the regular, continuous and substantial participation in the operations of the activity. [See IRC § 469(i)(6)(A).] A taxpayer actively participates in an activity if she is involved in a significant and *bona fide* sense, such as making management decisions concerning rental terms or repair expenditures. On the other hand, a lessor under a net lease is unlikely to satisfy the active participation requirement. A limited partner does not satisfy the active participation requirement, to the extent of the limited partnership interest. [IRC § 469(i)(6)(C).] The active participation requirement does not apply to low-income housing or rehabilitation credits. [IRC § 469(i)(6)(B).]

Congress did not want this special rule to be available to high income taxpayers, so the $25,000 limitation is reduced by 50 cents for every dollar the taxpayer's adjusted gross income (determined without regard to any taxable social security benefits, deductions for retirements savings, or passive activity losses) exceeds $100,000; thus, the special rule is unavailable to a taxpayer whose adjusted gross income exceeds $150,000. The phase-out occurs at a higher adjusted gross income level (between $200,000 and $250,000) with respect to low-income housing and rehabilitation credits. [IRC § 469(i)(3).]

Example: Franklin is employed and has an adjusted gross income of $75,000. Several years ago he bought a small quadraplex apartment building. He does all of the minor repair work on the building, takes care of the landscaping, collects the monthly rents and otherwise manages the operations of the building. During the current year, there are several vacancies in the apartments and deductions exceed income by $8,000. Franklin may deduct the $8,000 loss against his nonpassive income. If Franklin's adjusted gross income was $140,000, he would be allowed to deduct $5,000 of the loss against his nonpassive income in the current year and the remaining $3,000 would be a passive activity loss carried over to the next year.

iii. Treatment of former passive activities
      It is possible that an activity which is a passive activity in one taxable year will not be a passive activity in another taxable year, such as where a taxpayer does not materially participate in the activity in the earlier year but does so participate in the later year. If an activity was a passive activity for any prior taxable year, but is not a passive activity for the current taxable year, it is a "former passive activity." [IRC § 469(f)(2).] Income derived from a former passive activity (or income tax liability attributable to a former passive activity) may be offset by deductions (or credits) which were previously disallowed as passive activity losses (or credits) attributable to that activity and carried forward to taxable years in which the activity is a former passive activity. Any further passive activity losses (or credits) carryforwards attributable to that activity continue to be treated as passive activity losses (or credits). [IRC § 469(f)(1).]

The net effect of the rule regarding former passive activities is to require passive activity losses and credits which were suspended while an activity was a passive activity to remain suspended even though the activity itself is no longer a passive activity. The treatment of former passive activities should be contrasted with the rules discussed below which apply to a taxpayer's disposition of his entire interest in a passive activity.

Example: Casey, the physician in a prior Example who had a $15,000 passive activity loss in Year One with respect to his investment in Partnership #1, begins to materially participate in Partnership #1 in Year Two. In Year Two, Casey's adjusted gross income from his medical practice is again $150,000, his share of Partnership #1's operations is a net gain of $7,000, and his share of Partnership #2's operations is a net gain of $5,000. Casey may offset the net gain from Partnership #1 (the nonpassive activity) with $7,000 of the passive activity loss carried over from Year One, and he may offset the net gain from Partnership #2 (the passive activity) with $5,000 of the passive activity loss from Year One. The remaining $3,000 passive activity loss attributable to Partnership #1 in Year One may not be deducted from Casey's income from his medical practice; it will be carried over to Year Three.

iv. Taxable disposition of passive activity

If a taxpayer disposes of his entire interest in a passive activity to someone other than a related party and the gain or loss realized on the disposition is fully recognized, any passive activity losses (but *not* credits) attributable to that activity which have not been allowed as deductions generally will be allowed to offset both passive and nonpassive income in the year of disposition. [IRC § 469(g)(1).] If a taxpayer makes an installment sale of his entire interest in a passive activity, the passive activity losses may be deducted proportionately as the gain is recognized under the installment method rules. [IRC § 469(g)(3); see discussion of the installment method, IV. B. 3., at page 200, *infra.*]

Example: Casey from the preceding Example sells his interest in Partnership #1 in Year Two (instead of beginning to participate materially in its activities). In Year Two, Casey's adjusted gross income from his medical practice is again $150,000, his gain from the sale of Partnership #1 is $4,000, and his share of Partnership #2's operations is a net gain of $5,000. All of the $15,000 loss generated by

Partnership #1 in Year One is deducted in Year Two; it is deducted to the extent of his gain from the sale of Partnership #1 ($4,000) plus his net income from Partnership #2 ($5,000) plus his other income for the year. If the interest in Partnership #1 is sold at a loss, the loss from the sale may also be deducted as well as the prior passive activity losses attributable to the activity. [If the loss from the sale is a capital loss, other limitations may apply; see discussion in VI. B. 2. b., at page 272, *infra.*]

v.   Nontaxable disposition of passive activity

When a taxpayer disposes of property by gift or bequest, generally no gain or loss results and the rule discussed above which allows the taxpayer to deduct suspended passive activity losses does not apply. If an interest in a passive activity is disposed of by gift, the amount of any passive activity losses allocable to the interest is added to the adjusted basis of the interest immediately before the transfer and thereafter no deduction is allowed for those losses. [IRC § 469(j)(6).] If the interest is disposed of by reason of the death of a taxpayer, however, passive activity losses attributable to the interest are allowed under the rule applicable to taxable dispositions to the extent the losses are not greater than the excess of the transferee's basis in the interest (generally, its fair market value as of the date of the decedent's death) over the decedent's basis in the interest just before he died. [IRC § 469(g)(2).] When a taxpayer disposes of an interest in a passive activity in a transaction to which a nonrecognition provision applies, the suspended passive activity losses remain suspended and continue to be treated as passive activity losses, deductible in the time and manner prescribed under the general rules. [See discussion of nonrecognition rules, IV. D., at page 214, *infra.*]

d.   **Interrelationship with other Code provisions**

Generally, the passive activity rules of IRC § 469 apply to losses *after* other limitations on losses are considered. Thus, the restrictions under IRC § 267 [see discussion, III. C. 5., at page 159, *supra*] imposed on deductions arising from transactions between related taxpayers, the limitation on capital loss deductions under IRC §§ 1211 and 1212 [see discussion, VI. B. 2. b., at page 272, *infra*] and the at-risk rules of IRC § 465 [see discussion, III. C. 9., at page 169, *supra*] are applied *before* applying the limitations on passive activity losses and credits. Deductions for interest paid with respect to a passive activity are not subject to the "investment interest" limitations of IRC § 163(d)(3) [see discussion, III. B. 2. c., at page 134, *supra*] but must run the IRC § 469 gauntlet.

Passive activity credits, on the other hand, are limited first under IRC § 469 before applying the limitation on the maximum amount of general business credits allowable during a taxable year contained in IRC § 38(c). The limitations on the credit for increasing research activities contained within IRC § 41, however, are applied first, and then the limitations of IRC § 469 are imposed. [See discussion of tax credits and limitations, VII. F., at page 314, *infra.*]

11. LOSS FROM WASH SALES OF STOCK OR SECURITIES
a. In general

No deduction is allowed with respect to the loss sustained from the sale or other disposition of shares of stock or securities if, within a 61 day period beginning 30 days before the date of the loss transaction and ending 30 days after that date, the taxpayer acquires (other than in an exchange in which gain or loss is not recognized) or enters into a contract or option to acquire substantially identical shares of stock or securities. [IRC § 1091(a).] This disallowance rule does not apply to a taxpayer who is a dealer in stock or securities if the loss is sustained in the normal course of his business. Similar rules apply to losses realized from closing a short sale of stock or securities. [IRC § 1091(e).]

Example: Ronald bought 100 shares of common stock in XYZ Corporation several years ago for $10,000. On July 1 of the current year he sells them for $8,000, and on July 8, he purchases another 100 shares of common stock in XYZ Corporation. Ronald's $2,000 loss on the sale of the stock is not deductible. The result would be the same if, instead of purchasing the shares on July 8, he had purchased them on June 25, and the result would be the same if he purchased options to acquire common stock in XYZ Corporation, rather than the shares of stock themselves.

b. Substantially identical stock or securities

Shares of stock or securities which are acquired are "substantially identical" to shares of stock or securities disposed of in a loss transaction if they are not substantially different in any material feature. [Rev.Rul. 58–211, 1958–1 C.B. 529.] Shares of common stock in the same corporation are substantially identical, and voting trust certificates for common stock in a corporation are substantially identical to the common stock. [*Kidder v. Comm'r,* 30 B.T.A. 59 (1934).]

Generally, shares of preferred stock in a corporation are *not* substantially identical to shares of common stock in the same corporation. Convertible preferred stock, however, which has the same voting rights as common stock, which sells at prices that do not vary significantly from the conversion ratio, and which is restricted as to its convertibility is substantially identical to common stock in the corporation. [Rev.Rul. 77–201, 1977–1 C.B. 250.] In addition, shares of stock (whether common or preferred) in *different* corporations are not substantially identical, even if the two corporations are engaged in the same line of business.

Securities issued by the same source are substantially identical if they are not substantially different in any material feature, such as maturity date, rate of interest paid, and rights of redemption. Thus, bonds issued by the same municipality which have the same par values, issue dates, interest rates, and unit selling prices, but which differ only in maturity dates by 4 to 10 months, 16 years in the future, are substantially identical. [*Hanlin v. Comm'r,* 38 B.T.A. 811 (1938).] On the other hand, bonds issued by the U.S. Treasury paying 11% interest are *not* substantially identical to U.S. Treasury bonds maturing 10 years later and paying 12% interest, and bonds issued by one municipality are not substantially indentical to those issued by another municipality even though they have the same interest rates and maturity dates. [See Rev. Rul. 76–346, 1976–2 C.B. 247.]

c.   Unadjusted basis

If stock or securities are acquired, and as a consequence a loss deduction is disallowed, the basis of the acquired stock or securities is the same as the basis of the stock or securities disposed of in the loss transaction, increased (or decreased, if appropriate) by the difference between the price of the acquired stock or securities, and the price at which the substantially identical stock or securities were disposed of or sold. [IRC § 1091(d).] The holding period of the old stock is "tacked" on to the new. [IRC § 1223(4); see discussion, VI. B. 5. b. iv., at page 287, *infra.*]

Example: If in the previous Example, Ronald paid $8,500 for the shares of XYZ stock he purchases on July 8 of the current year, their basis is $10,500 [$10,000 basis in the old shares, increased by the difference between the purchase price of the new shares and the selling price of the old shares, or $500 ($8,500 – $8,000)]. Alternatively, if the purchase price of the new shares was $7,000, their basis is $9,000 [$10,000 basis in the old shares, decreased by the difference between the purchase price of the new shares and the selling price of the old shares, or $1,000 ($7,000 – $8,000)]. The simplest way to make the computation is to compute total costs less total receipts.

REVIEW QUESTIONS

Q# 1: David owns a sporting goods store. In the current year, David pays his employees a total of $100,000 in salary, he builds an addition to the store at a cost of $20,000, and he spends $1,000 for advertising expenses. On his return for the current year, David deducted $121,000 in expenses for the above items. Is this treatment correct?

Q# 2: Richard is a certified public accountant who enrolls in law school. Although the program in which he is enrolled leads to the J.D. degree, he does not intend to practice law after graduation, but he believes the law courses will be helpful to him in his accountancy practice. Can Richard deduct the costs of his law school education?

Q# 3: Elizabeth sells her personal residence for $85,000 in the current year. She purchased the house several years ago at a cost of $100,000. What is the amount of Elizabeth's deductible loss on the sale?

Q# 4: John is an attorney who uses the cash method of accounting. During the current year, John is unable to collect $10,000 of amounts he billed to his clients in previous years. Does John have a bad debt deduction and, if so, how much?

Q# 5: Paul is an accountant in South Carolina and he attends a convention for accountants in New York City during the current year. While in New York for three days, Paul incurs the following expenses: Airline tickets, $700; meals, $300; hotel, $450; and taxi fares, $100. How much of the listed expenses can Paul deduct? Does it make any difference that the meals would be a personal expense if Paul was not away from home?

Q# 6: Karen is an attorney who practices law in a state which requires attorneys to take a certain number of continuing professional education classes each year. In the current year, Karen returns to her law school alma mater and enrolls in two courses which she did not have time to take while a J.D. candidate; the courses qualify for continuing professional education credit. Karen spends $500 for tuition and books to take the courses. Can Karen deduct the $500 expense?

Q# 7: Paul receives a bill from his attorney in the current year for a total of $2,000. The bill is broken down into three parts: $1,250 is for representing Paul in a divorce suit against his wife; $500 is for closing a transaction in which Paul purchased some real estate; and the remaining $250 is for representing Paul before the local property tax appraisal board when Paul contested the appraised value of his house. Can Paul deduct the legal fees?

Q# 8: Sally lives in an ocean-front home. One day she notices that the hood of her car has rusted through. This rust is a complete surprise to Sally; can she claim a casualty loss for this damage?

Q# 9: Under the Accelerated Cost Recovery System (ACRS), how is the useful life of property determined? Is salvage value relevant in calculating deductions under ACRS?

Q# 10: Andrew purchases residential rental property in the current year, but Andrew does not want to use ACRS to depreciate this property. Can Andrew elect not to use ACRS for this property?

Q# 11: In the current year Rachel purchases from her father a used machine to use in her business; her father had used it in his business since January 1979. The asset cost Rachel $10,000, it has a 4 year useful life and a $2,000 salvage value. What depreciation methods are avaiable to Rachel? How would she compute depreciation deductions under the straight line method?

Q# 12: Patricia purchases a piece of machinery for use in her business in the current year. The asset cost $10,000 and is 5-year property under IRC § 168(e)(1). What is the maximum amount she may deduct with respect to the machinery in the current year?

Q# 13: Jerry purchases a piece of machinery, an item of 5-year property, in September of the current year. The property cost $10,000 and Jerry planned on using it exclusively in his business for 3 years. The estimated salvage value of the property at the end of the third year is $2,000. Compute Jerry's ACRS deductions for the current year and the succeeding year.

Q# 14: If the property in the Question above was an apartment building, rather than machinery, (and it cost $1,000,000, rather than $10,000), how would ACRS deductions be computed for the current year and the succeeding year.

Q# 15: Greg's boat is totally destroyed by a fire in the current year. The boat cost Greg $20,000 two years ago and it was used exclusively for personal purposes. At the time of the fire the boat had a fair market value of $10,000. Greg's adjusted gross income for the current year is $50,000. Is Greg entitled to any deduction with respect to the damage to his boat, and if so, in what amount?

Q# 16: Tip, whose adjusted gross income in the current year is $100,000, gives some shares of General Motors stock which he bought several years ago for $30,000, and which now have a fair market value of $35,000 to the American Cancer Society. In addition, he gives the American Smithsonian Institution copies of letters which were written to him by various newsworthy people from around the world; the letters have a fair market value of $10,000. What general rules govern the deductibility of these gifts?

Q# 17: Frank, a sole proprietor, sells a business asset at a loss to his brother. Can Frank deduct this loss?

Q# 18: During the current year Paula pays $2,000 in ad valorem property taxes imposed by the local school district, $500 for the state property tax imposed on intangible personal property, $1,500 in state sales tax, state income tax of $1,800 and state gasoline taxes of $250. How much of these state and local taxes may Paula deduct?

Q# 19: Supporter files a joint return with her spouse. Together they have three children who live at home. The value of meals and lodging they provide each child is $3,000 per year. Each child works and earns $2,500 which is also used for their support. One child is a high school student, one a college student and the third is 23 years old and works for a local company. How many exemptions may be filed on the joint return?

Q# 20: Giver transfers some land with a basis of $10,000 and value of $40,000 to a public charity. The land is a capital asset which Giver has held for 10 years. Charity transfers $10,000 of cash to Giver who has a $50,000 contribution base for the year. What is the amount of Giver's charitable contribution if this is his only charitable gift for the year?

Q# 21: Dick buys a computer which is 5-year property for use in his business for $25,000 on July 20 of the current year. He wishes to maximize his deductions in the current year. How much may he be allowed?

Q# 22: Marge moves to a new job and satisfies both the time and distance requirements of IRC § 217. She has $3,000 in moving and traveling expenses including 80% of meals, she spends $2,000 for temporary living quarters after arriving at her new location and $1,700 to buy out the lease on her old apartment. Her new employer reimburses her for the $1,700 expense. How much may Marge deduct under IRC § 217?

Q# 23: Businessman owns a sole proprietorship business in which he incurs the following expenses. To what extent are the expenses deductible?

(1) Salaries of $20,000.

(2) Rent of building, $12,000.

(3) Utility bills, $1,000.

(4) Entertainment of clients for which he has no vouchers, $500.

(5) Legal fees to defend a business defamation suit, $700.

(6) $400 for transportation, $200 for hotels and $100 for food while traveling on an out-of-town business trip.

(7) Dues to a professional organization of $200.

(8) Federal income taxes attributable to the business of $15,000.

(9) State income taxes attributable to the business of $3,000.

(10) Interest of $2,500 on a business loan.

(11) $11,000 for the purchase of a car to be used exclusively in the business.

(12) Newspaper and magazine advertising expenses of $900.

(13) Businessman's business was a new business begun two years ago. He spent $10,000 investigating whether to engage in it and properly elected § 195 with respect to his expenses.

(14) Businessman spent $1,500 to determine whether to expand his business to a neighboring community.

(15) He demolishes a building which has an adjusted basis of $5,000 in order to build a new building for his business.

Q# 24: Brother is an accrual method taxpayer and Sister is a cash method taxpayer. Brother owes Sister rent on a building. The deductible $10,000 rent for the year is not paid until March of the following year. In addition on November 1 Brother sells Sister 100 shares of ATT stock at a loss. A week later he buys 100 shares of ATT stock on the New York stock exchange for himself. Discuss the consequences of the above transactions.

Q# 25: Patience has been ill during the year and has spent $1,000 for medical insurance, $2,000 in doctor bills, $500 for prescription drugs, $400 for nonprescription drugs and $3,000 in hospital bills. What is her medical expense deduction if her adjusted gross income is $20,000?

Q# 26: Darwin invests $40,000 of cash in a real estate tax shelter and his total deductions exceed his total income from the real estate activity in the current year by $100,000. He is "at risk" in the activity to the extent of his $40,000 investment. How much may he deduct?

*

IV

TIMING

Analysis

The Federal income tax is imposed periodically on the basis of events which take place during a taxable period. The taxable period is generally a calendar year or a 12 month fiscal year, and taxpayers determine in which taxable year a particular event is to be considered in determining tax liability according to various rules, or methods, of accounting. Generally, individuals who derive most of their income from salaries use the cash method of accounting, while most businesses use the accrual method. In addition, special accounting rules apply in determining the tax consequences of certain types of transactions, such as the installment sale of property or exchanges of certain types of property.

A. TAXABLE PERIOD

The taxable period for computing the Federal income tax is a taxpayer's taxable year. [IRC § 441(a).] Most individuals use the calendar year as their taxable year, and the Examples in this outline have been drafted on the assumption that the parties involved have the calendar year as their taxable year. A taxpayer may also elect to have his taxable year be a fiscal year (a 12 month period ending on the last day of any month other than December), or an annual period which varies from 52 to 53 weeks, if he regularly keeps his books using either of those methods. [IRC § 441(b) and (f).] If a taxpayer desires to change his taxable year, however, he may do so only if prior approval is obtained from the I.R.S. and, generally, he must demonstrate a substantial business purpose for making the change. [IRC § 442.] A taxpayer may have an annual accounting period of less than 12 months if she changes her taxable year, or if she dies during a taxable year. When a taxpayer dies, her taxable year terminates as of the date of death and her estate may become taxable with respect to income received thereafter. [IRC § 443(a)(1).]

B. METHODS OF ACCOUNTING

A taxpayer is required to compute taxable income using the method of accounting which he regularly uses to compute income in keeping his books. [IRC § 446(a).] The term "method of accounting" includes the over-all method of accounting of the taxpayer as well as the accounting treatment of particular items of income or deductions. The Code specifically authorizes the use of several methods of accounting, including the cash receipts and disbursements method, the accrual method, and the installment method; the regulations authorize other methods in special situations, such as the percentage of completion method for long-term contracts. [IRC § 446(c); see IRC § 460 and Reg. § 1.451–3.] Regardless of the method of accounting selected by a taxpayer, however, the method used must clearly reflect income; if the method the taxpayer selects does not clearly reflect income, the I.R.S. may require the taxpayer to change to a method which does. [IRC § 446(b).] In some situations, a taxpayer is required to use a particular method of accounting, or is precluded from using a particular method. [See, e.g., IRC § 448(a) (certain taxpayers prohibited from using the cash method) and Reg. § 1.446–1(c)(2)(i) (accrual method generally must be used with regard to purchases and sales of inventory).] If a taxpayer is engaged in more than one trade or business, she may use a different method of accounting for each trade or business provided that each method does clearly reflect income for the respective trade or business. [IRC § 446(d).] Once a method of accounting is selected, it may not be changed without prior approval from the I.R.S. and, generally, the taxpayer must demonstrate some business purpose for making the change. [IRC § 446(e).]

1. CASH RECEIPTS AND DISBURSEMENTS METHOD

A taxpayer using the cash receipts and disbursements method ("cash method") generally includes items of gross income in the taxable year in which they are actually or constructively received, and takes into account amounts representing allowable deductions in the taxable year in which they are paid. [Reg. §§ 1.446–1(c)(1)(i) and 1.461–1(a)(1).] Although most individuals use the cash method, certain corporations, partnerships and tax shelters are specifically prohibited from using the cash method. [IRC § 448.]

a. Receipts
i. In general

A taxpayer using the cash method must include items of gross income in the taxable year in which he receives the item, regardless of whether the amount is paid in cash, by check, or with property other than money. [IRC § 451(a); Reg. § 1.451–1(a).] If an item of income is received in the form of a check, it is treated as the equivalent of cash and is included in gross income in the year in which the check is received, not the year in which it is cashed. [*Lavery v. Comm'r,* 158 F.2d 859 (7th Cir.1946).] This rule applies even if the check is received after banks have closed for the day. [*Charles F. Kahler,* 18 T.C. 31 (1952).] If a cash method taxpayer receives a promissory note or contract, rather than a check or other negotiable instrument, as mere evidence of an amount owed to him and the note or contract is not assignable nor is it intended as payment, the note or contract is not treated as the equivalent of cash and no amount is included in gross income because of its receipt. [*Estate of Coid Hurlburt,* 25 T.C. 1286 (1956).] If property other than money is received and is includible in gross income, the amount to be included is the fair market value of the property as of the date of receipt. [See *Paul V. Hornung,* 47 T.C. 428 (1967).]

ii. Constructive receipt

A taxpayer using the cash method must include items of gross income in the taxable year in which they are constructively received, if that is earlier than the year in which they are actually received. An item is constructively received by a taxpayer when it is credited to his account, set apart for him, or otherwise made available so that he may draw on it at any time, but it is not constructively received if its actual receipt is subject to substantial limitations or restrictions. [Reg. § 1.451–2(a).]

Example: A sports magazine selects Paul, a professional football player, as the "outstanding player" in a football game played in Wisconsin on December 31, the last day of his taxable year. The magazine awards Paul an automobile, which is a prize, includible in his gross income under IRC § 74. The decision is announced at 4:30 on the afternoon of December 31. At that time, the automobile is in New York City, and the representative of the magazine in Wisconsin does not give Paul the keys to the automobile, or any other evidence of ownership of the automobile. The automobile is not actually delivered to Paul until the following year on January 3. Paul does *not* constructively receive the prize on December 31 because he does not have unfettered control over it on that date; he must include the fair market value of the automobile in his gross income for the taxable year in which he actually receives it. [*Paul V. Hornung,* 47 T.C. 428 (1967).]

Paul also has a savings account at a bank in New York City. Interest is credited to his account on December 31, and there are no restrictions on his withdrawing the interest at that time. The interest is included in his gross income for that taxable year even though he is in Wisconsin on December 31. [Reg. § 1.451–2(b).]

b. Disbursements
i. In general

A taxpayer using the cash method generally may take allowable deductions in the taxable year in which actual payment takes place. [IRC § 461(a); Reg. § 1.461–1(a)(1).] If payment is made by check, it is considered to be paid when the check is delivered, unless the check is not subsequently honored or paid, or if there are restrictions as to the time and manner of payment on the check. [Rev.Rul. 54–465, 1954–2 C.B. 93.] In addition, payment is considered to be made when a check is mailed, rather than on the date the recipient receives it. If payment is made by charging a deductible expenditure to a credit card, payment is considered to be made when the charge is made, rather than on the date the credit card company is paid. [Rev.Rul. 78–38, 1978–1 C.B. 68.] Unlike the doctrine of constructive receipt of items of income, there is no corresponding doctrine of constructive payment of deductible items; a deduction is available only in the year in which the payment is actually made.

> ***Example:*** V.P., F. & Company, a cash method taxpayer, voted to pay two of its employees salaries for 1942, and unconditionally credited the appropriate amounts to the employees' respective accounts on the company's books. The two employees, also using the cash method, properly reported the amounts as compensation income for 1942, because the amounts were constructively received by them in that year. The corporation, however, could not take a deduction for the salaries in 1942, because there was no actual payment in that year. [*Vander Poel, Francis & Company, Inc.,* 8 T.C. 407 (1947).]

ii. Prepaid expenses

If a deductible expenditure creates an asset with a useful life extending *substantially* beyond the end of the taxable year, the deduction must be spread out, or amortized, over the taxable years in which the asset will be used. Some leniency is permitted if the prepayment does not create an asset or secure an advantage to the taxpayer which has a useful life in excess of one year's duration.

A cash method taxpayer may take a deduction for the payment of interest only in the taxable year to which the interest is properly allocable; thus, a prepayment of interest in one taxable year will be spread out over the taxable years the loan is outstanding. [IRC § 461(g)(1).] An exception to the rule regarding interest applies for the payment of "points" paid in respect of indebtedness incurred to purchase, or to make improvements to, a taxpayer's principal residence. [IRC § 461(g)(2).] "Points" represent interest which relates to the entire term of the loan, but the amount may be deducted in the year in which it is paid under this special rule, rather than being amortized. The "points," however, must be actually paid, rather than simply being added to the principal amount of the loan. [*Cathcart v. Comm'r,* 36 T.C.M. 1321 (1977).]

> ***Examples:*** B.M.A., a cash method taxpayer, paid $1,000 in premiums for insurance coverage related to its business. The full $1,000 is paid in Year One, although the insurance coverage is for three years, Year One, Year Two and Year Three. The deduction of $1,000 may not be taken in Year One, but must be prorated over the three year term of the policy. [*Comm'r v. Boylston Market Ass'n,* 131 F.2d 966 (1st Cir.1942).]
>
> Martin, a cash method, calendar year taxpayer, is in the farming business. He entered into an agreement to lease a parcel of land for use in his business from

December 1 of Year One, through November 30 of Year
Twenty-one; annual rent of $27,000 is payable on
December 20 of each lease year. On December 20 of
Year One, Martin paid $27,000 for the lease year
running from December 1 of Year One through
November 30 of Year Two. Because the lease payment
did not create an asset (a leasehold estate) extending
substantially beyond the end of Year One, and because
the created asset did not have a life of more than one
year, the entire $27,000 payment made in Year One is
deductible in that year. [*Zaninovich v. Comm'r*, 616 F.2d
429 (9th Cir.1980).] If Martin had borrowed money,
instead of leasing land, and the payment had been for
interest, rather than rent, a statute, IRC § 461(g)(1),
specifically provides for timing and only the portion of
the $27,000 interest paid in December of Year One,
which is properly allocable to Year One (roughly ¹/₁₂ of
$27,000) may be deducted in that year.

2. ACCRUAL METHOD

A taxpayer using the accrual method of accounting generally includes
items in gross income in the taxable year in which all events have occurred
which fix his *right* to receive the item and fix the *amount* of the item. An
accrual method taxpayer deducts items in the taxable year in which all events
have occurred which fix his *liability* to pay items, the *amount* payable becomes
fixed, and certain tests of economic performance are satisfied. This is
commonly referred to as the "all events" test.

a. Effect of economic and legal contingencies on income and deductions
i.   Economic contingencies

The all events test is generally considered to be satisfied, thereby
requiring inclusion of an item in gross income (or permitting a
deduction), even though economic considerations or contingencies may
exist which make it uncertain that the taxpayer will *actually* receive
the item of income (or pay the deductible item); it is generally
sufficient that the legal right (or obligation) has been established and
that the amount may be reasonably determined.

Example: S.C.F. uses the accrual method of accounting. Early in a
taxable year, it sells goods to a purchaser; the purchaser
does not pay for the goods at the time of the sale, but the
obligation to pay, and the amount of the obligation,
becomes fixed at that time. Later that same year, and
before any actual payment is made, the purchaser files for
bankruptcy and it is clear that S.C.F. will not be paid the
full amount of the obligation. S.C.F. is required to

include in gross income the full amount of the obligation for the taxable year, notwithstanding the economic contingencies surrounding the prospect of receiving actual payment. [*Spring City Foundry Co. v. Comm'r,* 292 U.S. 182, 54 S.Ct. 644 (1934).]

ii. Legal contingencies

If an accrual method taxpayer's right to an item of income (or deduction) is the subject of litigation, a legal contingency arises and her right to the item (or deduction) generally does not become fixed until the litigation, including appeals, is concluded.

> *Example:* A domestic corporation using the accrual method files suit against the U.S. for damages for breach of contract. The taxpayer wins a judgment in the Court of Claims in 1968, and a petition for writ of certiorari is denied by the Supreme Court in 1969. The taxpayer must include the amount of the damages award in gross income for 1969. [Rev.Rul. 70–151, 1970–1 C.B. 116.]

An exception to application of the legal contingency requirements may arise, however, if cash flows. For example, if an accrual method taxpayer actually receives payment of a legally contested item, the taxpayer will be required to include the item in gross income in the year payment is received even though the taxpayer's right to the item is still subject to a legal contingency. With respect to deductions, the all events test also may be modified if cash flows. If a taxpayer contests an asserted liability, the liability is not "fixed," but if he transfers money or other property to satisfy the asserted liability, if economic performance has occurred [see IRC § 461(h)] and if the contest still exists after the transfer, then he may take the deduction in the year of the transfer. [IRC § 461(f).]

> *Examples:* N.A.O.C., an accrual method taxpayer, became involved in litigation with the U.S. concerning ownership of income produced by certain property. In 1916, a receiver was appointed to operate the property, and income earned by the property was paid to the receiver. In 1917, the District Court ruled in favor of N.A.O.C., and the receiver paid over to N.A.O.C. the profits which had been earned in 1916. The U.S. subsequently appealed the decision of the District Court, and the appeals were finally concluded, in N.A.O.C.'s favor, in 1922. N.A.O.C.'s right to the income produced by the property was not fixed in 1916; thus, it was not required to include the amount in its gross income that year. In 1917, N.A.O.C.

actually received the income, pursuant to the decision of the District Court, under a claim of right; thus, it must include the amount in gross income for 1917 (not 1922) even though it was possible that the U.S. might have won its appeal, requiring the taxpayer to repay the amount in question. [*North American Oil Consolidated v. Burnet,* 286 U.S. 417, 52 S.Ct. 613 (1932).]

X Corporation, which uses the accrual method of accounting, contests $20 of a $100 asserted real property tax liability, but it pays the entire $100 to the taxing authority in Year One. The contest is settled in Year Two when a court determines that $95 was the correct Year One liability; X Corporation receives a refund of $5 of the property tax. X Corporation may properly deduct $100 in Year One, and it must include $5 in gross income for Year Two (assuming that X Corporation received a tax benefit from taking the $100 deduction in Year One). [Reg. § 1.461–2(a)(4) Example (1); see discussion of the tax benefit rule, IV. C. 2., at page 213, *infra.*]

b.   Income
   i.   In general
      The accrual method requires a taxpayer to include items of income in the taxable year in which all the events have occurred which fix the *right* to receive the income, and the *amount* of the income can be determined with reasonable accuracy. [Reg. § 1.451–1(a).] If an accrual method taxpayer earns the right to receive income from the performance of services, he is not required to accrue amounts which he probably will not actually receive, based on previous experience. [IRC § 448(d)(5).]

   ii.   Advance payments for services
      If a taxpayer using the accrual method of accounting actually receives payment for services he must generally include the amount in gross income in the taxable year in which it is received, even though his right to the item is subject to a legal contingency, and thus his right to the item is not fixed in that year. [See discussion, IV. B. 2. a. ii., at page 191, *supra.*] There are some exceptions, however, authorized by judicial decisions, by the I.R.S., and by the Code.

   Example: N.C.H., an accrual method taxpayer, owned a parcel of real property which it agreed to lease for a period of 10 years. The lease agreement called for the lessee to pay annual rent of $30,000, but the payment for the last year was to be made in advance, at the beginning of the 10 year term. The payment was paid as advance rent, not as a security deposit, and there were no restrictions on the taxpayer's use of the $30,000 advance payment. The taxpayer was required to include the $30,000 advance rental payment in the year in which it received it, not in the later year to which it related. [*New Capital Hotel, Inc. v. Comm'r,* 28 T.C. 706 (1957).]

a.   Exceptions under case law

If an accrual method taxpayer receives payment in one taxable year for services which it is obligated to perform in a subsequent taxable year, it is arguable that, in order to "clearly reflect income," the amount received should be included in gross income in the taxable year in which the services are performed, because that is the taxable year in which the taxpayer incurs expenditures in providing the services.   [See IRC § 446(b).]

Examples: A.C.M., an accrual method taxpayer, was in the business of providing emergency road service and travel information to persons who paid an annual membership fee which entitled them to such services. An annual membership ran for 12 months, but did not necessarily coincide with A.C.M.'s taxable year. Although members paid their annual membership fees in full at the beginning of each year's membership, A.C.M. attempted to apportion each member's fees over a 12 month period, including in gross income for a particular taxable year only the portions allocated to that taxable year. The pro rata allocation bore no relation to the services which A.C.M. was obligated to provide to its members, upon their demand. A.C.M. was required to include membership fees in gross income in the taxable year in which they were received. [*Automobile Club of Michigan v. Comm'r,* 353 U.S. 180, 77 S.Ct. 707 (1957); *accord, American Automobile Association v. U.S.,* 367 U.S. 687, 81 S.Ct. 1727 (1961). The results in these cases have now been altered with the enactment of IRC § 456, relating to prepaid dues income of certain membership organizations; see discussion, IV. B. 2. b. ii. *c.,* at page 196, *infra.*]

Mark operated a ballroom dancing studio business, for which he used the accrual method of accounting.

Customers made cash payments to Mark in exchange for his agreement to provide them with a set number of dancing lessons. The contracts were noncancelable and the payments were nonrefundable; although the contracts designated the time period during which the lessons had to be taken, there was no schedule of specific dates on which the lessons would be given. The services which Mark was obliged to perform under the contracts were effectively rendered only on the demand of the customers. The prepayments were required to be included in Mark's gross income in the year in which they were actually received; they could not be allocated over the term of the contracts. [*Schlude v. Comm'r,* 372 U.S. 128, 83 S.Ct. 601 (1963).]

Occasionally, a taxpayer is able to demonstrate that a cash prepayment relates to an obligation to perform services in a future taxable year which is definite and not at the discretion or demand of his customers. In such a case, the taxpayer may defer including the prepayment until the taxable year in which the services are performed, so that the receipt of the income and the corresponding deductible expenses will be properly matched, thereby "clearly reflecting" the taxpayer's net income. The argument prevails over the general rule, described above, that an accrual method taxpayer must include amounts actually received in the year of receipt, even though the absolute right to the item does not become fixed until a later taxable year. It is questionable, however, to what extent this deferral is permitted.

Example: Chicago White Sox Corporation, an accrual method taxpayer, owned and operated a major league baseball team. It sold season tickets, and radio and television broadcasting rights to baseball games scheduled for the 1962 season, and received payment prior to rendering the services (playing the ball games). In that year, however, the taxpayer corporation was liquidated on May 31, prior to completing the season, and, as a consequence, the taxpayer's taxable year terminated. [See IRC § 443(a)(2).] The successor corporation asserted that the portion of the prepaid income which related to the baseball games played after May 31 should not be included in the gross income of Chicago White Sox Corporation on its final income tax return, but should be included in the first income tax return of the successor corporation, beginning June 1, when the income could be matched with the expenses incurred in playing the season's remaining baseball games. The taxpayer's method did "clearly reflect income," whereas application of the general rule did not; thus, Chicago White Sox Corporation was not required to include the full amount of the advance payments in the year in which they were actually received. [See *Artnell Co. v. Comm'r,* 400 F.2d 981 (7th Cir.1968).]

b. Exceptions allowed by the I.R.S.

In certain limited circumstances, the I.R.S. permits an accrual method taxpayer who receives prepaid income for services to defer for one year the inclusion of such income in gross income. [Rev.Proc. 71–21, 1971–2 C.B. 549.] This procedure only applies to prepayments for services which are to be rendered no later than the end of the taxable year which immediately follows the taxable year in which the payment is received; in addition, the procedure does not apply to prepaid interest or rent. It appears that this rule was prescribed to accommodate the facts of the *Artnell* case; thus, it is uncertain what a court would hold if presented with facts which are not within the parameters of Rev. Proc. 71–21, but where deferral of the income would "clearly reflect" the taxpayer's net income.

Example: Agatha, an accrual method taxpayer who is in the business of giving dancing lessons, receives payment on November 1 of the current year for a 1 year contract to provide 48 individual, one-hour lessons. She provides 8 lessons during the current year. She may include $8/48$ (or $1/6$) of the payment in gross income for the current year, and the remaining $40/48$ (or $5/6$) is included in gross income in the following taxable year. [Rev.Proc. 71–21, 1971–2 C.B. 549.]

In the alternative, if Agatha receives payment for a 2 year contract to provide 4 lessons each month for a total of 96 lessons, under Rev.Proc. 71–21, she must include the entire amount of the payment in gross income in the current year because performance of a portion of the services may take place later than the end of the immediately subsequent year. Assuming that Agatha could demonstrate that deferring the inclusion of some portion of the payments would "clearly reflect" her net income as in *Artnell,* it is uncertain whether courts would permit the deferral. [Compare *Boise Cascade Corp. v. U.S.,* 530 F.2d 1367 (Ct.Cl.1976) (deferral of prepaid income for engineering services allowed where obligation to provide services was fixed and certain) with *Union Mut. Life Ins. Co. v. U.S.,* 570 F.2d 382 (1st Cir.1978) (deferral of prepaid interest income not permitted).]

c. Exceptions under statutes
   The general rule requiring an accrual method taxpayer to include prepaid income in the taxable year in which payment is received is modified by statute in a few limited situations. For example, if a taxpayer elects, prepaid income from subscriptions to a newspaper, magazine, or other periodical may be included in gross income in the taxable years in which the liability to deliver the periodical exists, rather than in the taxable year in which the prepaid income is received. [IRC § 455.] If a membership organization elects, prepaid dues income, entitling a member to receive services or membership privileges over a period of time extending beyond the end of the taxable year (but not more than 36 months), may be included in gross income in the taxable years in which the liability to provide the services or privileges exists. [IRC § 456.]

iii. Advance payments for goods
   The regulations authorize, in certain limited circumstances, an accrual method taxpayer who receives advance payments for the sale of goods to defer including the amounts received until a subsequent taxable year. [Reg. § 1.451–5.]

c. **Deductions**
   i. In general
      A taxpayer using the accrual method generally may take allowable deductions in the taxable year in which the all events test is satisfied, but not any earlier than the taxable year in which economic performance with respect to the item occurs. [IRC § 461(h).] The all events test is met if all events have occurred which determine the fact of the liability, and the amount of the liability can be determined with reasonable accuracy. [IRC § 461(h)(4).] Economic performance with respect to various deductible items occurs as follows: (1) if the taxpayer is to pay for someone to perform services, economic performance occurs when the services are performed; (2) if the taxpayer is to pay for property, economic performance occurs when the property is provided; (3) if the taxpayer is to pay for the use of property, economic performance occurs as the taxpayer uses the property; and, (4) if the taxpayer is required to make payments to a

person because of an obligation under a workers' compensation act or because of a tort, economic performance occurs as the person is paid. Exceptions are provided for certain recurring items and cases where other specific provisions, such as an account with respect to liability for accrued vacation pay for employees [IRC § 463], apply. In addition, the I.R.S. is given authority to provide when economic performance occurs in other situations. [IRC § 461(h)(2) and (3).]

An accrual method taxpayer may not take a deduction, however, for a taxable year in which it accrues an expense if payment is to be made to a related taxpayer who uses the cash method and if payment is not actually or constructively made in that taxable year. [IRC § 267(a)(2); see discussion, III. C. 5. d., at page 160, *supra*.]

Example: S.M. Corporation, an accrual method taxpayer, is engaged in the business of strip mining coal. S.M. enters into a contract with R. Corporation under which S.M. agrees to pay R. $1 million, and R. agrees to reclaim an exhausted coal deposit which S.M. has strip mined. Economic performance occurs when R. performs the reclamation (rather than when S.M. and R. enter into the binding contract) and S.M. may not take deductions for the reclamation until that time.

ii. Reserve accounting

Conventional accounting methods attempt to match items of income with the costs of producing the income. If payment is received in one taxable year for services which the taxpayer is obliged to provide in the future, an accrual method taxpayer is generally required to include the amount received in gross income in the year in which it is received. [See discussion, IV. B. 2. b. ii., at page 192, *supra*.] The taxpayer may attempt to match the anticipated costs of providing the services in the future by establishing a "reserve account," deducting in the current year the amount of the future expenses. Although reserve accounting is theoretically appealing, in the past, courts have only occasionally permitted taxpayers to use reserve accounting in computing taxable income. [See *Schuessler v. Comm'r*, 230 F.2d 722 (5th Cir.1956) (reserve allowed for services to be rendered at a set time; decision was rendered prior to the enactment of IRC § 461(h)(2)(B)).] The enactment of IRC § 461(h)(2)(B) now precludes the use of reserve accounting, unless specifically authorized by the Code. The Code authorizes such reserve accounting only in the case of accrued vacation pay for employees. [IRC § 463.]

d.   Inventories

Inventories must be used by taxpayers for whom the production, purchase, or sale of merchandise is an income-producing factor. [IRC § 471; Reg. § 1.471–1.] A taxpayer who is required to use inventories must also use the accrual method of accounting for purchases and sales. [Reg. § 1.446–1(c)(2).] Gross income derived from businesses using inventories includes the total receipts from the sale of inventory items, less the cost of goods sold. [IRC § 61(a)(2); Reg. § 1.61–3(a).]

> *Example:*   Bjorn begins his business of selling tennis balls in January of Year One when he purchases 100 cases of tennis balls for $2,400 ($24 per case). During Year One, he sells all of the tennis balls for a total of $3,600 ($36 per case). When he sells his last tennis ball, in December of Year One, Bjorn decides to discontinue his tennis ball sales business. Bjorn's gross income derived from business in Year One is $1,200 ($3,600 – $2,400).

i.   Cost of goods sold

In computing gross income derived from business, the "cost of goods sold" is, generally, the value of inventory on hand at the beginning of the taxable year, plus the value of inventory items acquired during the taxable year, less the value of inventory on hand at the end of the taxable year. The value of inventory at the end of one taxable year (closing inventory) becomes the value of the inventory at the beginning of the next taxable year (opening inventory). Items should be included in inventory if the taxpayer has title to them; and if the taxpayer is in the business of manufacturing goods for sale, her inventories should include all finished or partly finished goods, as well as raw materials and supplies which will become part of the merchandise intended for sale. [Reg. § 1.471–1.]

> *Example:*   Chrissy begins her business of selling tennis balls in December of Year One when she purchases 100 cases of tennis balls for $2,400 ($24 per case), however she does not sell any tennis balls in Year One. In July of Year Two, she purchases another 100 cases of tennis balls for $2,400 ($24 per case) to add to her inventory. During Year Two, she sells a total of 150 cases of tennis balls for a total of $5,400 ($36 per case); thus, she still has 50 cases on hand at the end of Year Two. Chrissy's "cost of goods sold" for Year Two is $3,600 [($2,400 + $2,400) – $1,200], and her gross income derived from business is $1,800 ($5,400 – $3,600).

ii.   Valuation of inventories

Inventories must be valued by a taxpayer according to a consistent method from year to year and in a manner which will clearly reflect income. Two of the most common methods are to use the cost of the inventory, or to use either the cost or the market value of the inventory, whichever is lower. [Regs. § 1.471–2.] If the lower-of-cost-or-market approach is used, the market value is the wholesale price of a bulk purchase of the goods, not the retail price of individual items. [Reg. § 1.471–4.]

> *Example:* In the previous Example, Chrissy valued her inventory of tennis balls at cost. If the wholesale price of tennis balls had dropped to $20 per case by the end of Year Two, and if she had used the lower-of-cost-or-market approach to valuing her inventory, her cost of goods sold for Year Two would be $3,800 [($2,400 + $2,400 – $1,000]. Chrissy's gross income derived from business for Year Two would be $1,600 ($5,400 – $3,800).

iii.   Last-in, first-out inventories

Generally, closing inventories are valued according to the cost of the items of inventory which were most recently purchased; this is commonly referred to as the "first-in, first-out" (FIFO) convention. In some situations, a taxpayer may elect to value his closing inventory with reference to the items which were in the opening inventory, in the order of their acquisition, and then those items acquired during the year; this is commonly referred to as the "last-in, first-out" (LIFO) convention. [IRC § 472; see Reg. § 1.472–1(a).] The LIFO convention generally produces a lower amount of gross income when the prices of inventory items are increasing; however, if a taxpayer uses the LIFO method to compute gross income, he must also use it for financial accounting purposes, and he must consistently use it from one year to the next. A special "simplified" LIFO method is available for certain small businesses. [IRC § 474.]

> *Example:* Dexter begins his business of selling tennis balls in December of Year One (just as Chrissy did in the previous Example) when he purchases 100 cases of tennis balls for $2,400 ($24 per case). He does not sell any tennis balls in Year One, but becomes more successful in Year Two. In July of Year Two, he purchases another 100 cases of tennis balls to add to his inventory, but the price has gone up and he pays $3,000 ($30 per case). During Year Two, he sells a total of 150 cases of tennis balls for a total of $5,400 ($36 per case). At the end of Year Two, he still has 50 cases of tennis balls on hand. If Dexter

uses the "first-in, first-out" convention for Year Two, his closing inventory is $1,500; his "cost of goods sold" is $3,900 [($2,400 + $3,000) – $1,500]; and his gross income derived from business is $1,500 ($5,400 – $3,900). Alternatively, if Dexter uses the "last-in, first-out" convention for Year Two, his closing inventory is $1,200; his "cost of goods sold" is $4,200 [($2,400 + $3,000) – $1,200]; and his gross income derived from business is $1,200 ($5,400 – $4,200).

3. INSTALLMENT METHOD

A gain or a loss which is *realized* upon the sale or other disposition of property is generally required to be *recognized,* or included in gross income, in the year of the disposition. [IRC § 1001(c).] The installment method, however, permits a taxpayer, in certain circumstances, who has a *realized gain* (but not a loss) from the sale or other disposition of property to spread out the *recognition* of the gain. [IRC § 453.] Special rules apply to dealers who regularly sell personal property on the installment plan. [IRC § 453A.] In addition, rules are provided to govern the tax consequences to a taxpayer who disposes of an installment obligation. [IRC § 453B.]

a. Transactions under IRC § 453

Gain from the installment sale of property is recognized in accordance with the installment method, unless the taxpayer elects to have the installment method *not* apply. [IRC § 453(a).] The installment method is limited in certain circumstances, however, and denied in others. [See IRC §§ 453(k) and 453C, and discussion at IV. B. 3. a. ii. c. and 3. d., at pages 202 and 208, *infra.*]

i. Installment sale

The installment sale of property is the disposition of property under terms where at least one payment is to be received in a taxable year subsequent to the year in which the disposition takes place. [IRC § 453(b).] An "installment sale" does not include the sale of personal property inventory, or the regular sale of personal property on the installment plan; special rules apply to such sales on the installment plan, however, which provide roughly the same treatment as the treatment provided for installment sales. [IRC §§ 453(b)(2) and 453A.]

Example: Demetrius sells a parcel of real estate to Eudora in December of Year One. The contract of sale provides for Eudora to pay Demetrius $1,000 at the time of the sale, and the balance of the purchase price, $9,000, in December of Year Two. The sale is an installment sale. The sale would be an installment sale even if the contract of sale provides that Eudora is not required to make *any* payment in Year One, the full purchase price of $10,000 being payable in January of Year Two.

ii. Installment method
a. In general

The installment method requires a portion of payments received from an installment sale in a taxable year to be recognized gain, included in gross income in the taxable year in which the payments are received. The amount of gain to be recognized is determined by multiplying the total amount of payments received during the taxable year by a fraction, the numerator being the "gross profit" and the denominator being the "total contract price." [IRC § 453(c).]

The "total contract price" is the selling price of the property. The "selling price" is the gross selling price (not including interest). The "gross profit" of an installment sale is the selling price of the property being sold, less its adjusted basis. [Temp. Reg. § 15a.453–1(b)(2).]

Example: The parcel of real property which Demetrius sells to Eudora in the preceding Example has a fair market value of $10,000, and an adjusted basis to Demetrius of $4,000. The contract of sale provides for Eudora to pay Demetrius $1,000 in December of Year One and additional payments of $1,000 (plus interest) each December for the next nine years. Both the "selling price" and the "total contract price" of the property is $10,000. The "gross profit" to Demetrius is $6,000 ($10,000 − $4,000). With respect to each annual payment of $1,000, Demetrius must treat $600 ($1,000 × ($6,000/$10,000)) as recognized gain; the remaining $400 of each annual payment is treated as the recovery of his basis in the property and is not recognized gain.

b. Contingent payment sales

The rules for reporting gain under the installment method apply (unless the taxpayer elects for them to not apply) even if the aggregate selling price cannot be determined as of the date of sale because of contingencies. [IRC § 453(j)(2) and Temp.Reg. § 15a.453–1(c).] If the aggregate selling price is indeterminable, the Regulations provide a series of rules for the application of IRC § 453. First, if there is a *maximum selling price* called for, then the maximum selling price is treated as the "selling price" in determining the amounts of annual payments which must be included in gross income.

Second, if a maximum selling price cannot be determined, but the *maximum period* over which payments may be received is fixed, then the seller's adjusted basis in the property is allocated among the taxable years during which payments may be received.

If there is neither a maximum selling price nor a fixed period during which payments may be made, the transaction will be scrutinized closely to ascertain whether a sale (rather than a lease or a license arrangement) has, in fact, taken place. If it is determined that a sale has occurred, the seller's adjusted basis is allocated, in equal increments, over a 15 year period; if the seller's basis is not fully recovered in 15 years (because the payments received in one or more years are less than the portion of the adjusted basis allocated to that year) then the unrecovered basis is carried over to the succeeding years until it has been fully recovered.

Examples: Freemont sells Gay all of X Corporation's stock, which is *not* traded on an established securities market, for $100,000 plus an amount equal to 5% of the net profits of X Corporation for each of the next 9 years; however, the maximum amount (exclusive of interest) which Freemont may receive is $2 million. The selling price and the total contract price is $2 million. [Temp.Reg. § 15a.453–1(c)(2)(i) Example (1).]

Hubert sells Blackacre to Isis for 10% of Blackacre's gross yield for each of the next 5 years. Hubert's adjusted basis in Blackacre is $5 million. Because the selling price is indefinite and the maximum selling price is unascertainable, Hubert may recover his basis in equal annual increments of $1 million over the 5 year period during which he is to receive payments. [Temp.Reg. § 15a.453–1(c)(3)(ii) Example (1).]

c.   Disallowance and limitations on use of installment method
Use of the installment method is denied for sales pursuant to a revolving credit plan and for sales of stock or securities which are traded on an established securities market, or, to the extent provided in the Regulations, for sales of other property of a kind regularly traded on an established market. [IRC § 453(k).]

Example: Joel sells shares of stock in General Motors Corporation for $1,000, of which $100 is paid in the year of the sale and the remaining $900 is paid in the next year. The installment method does not apply to the sale and Joel is treated as receiving the entire $1,000 in the year of the sale.

d. Property encumbered by indebtedness

The installment method of recognizing gain may be used in the sale of property which is encumbered by indebtedness. The amount of gain to be recognized with respect to payments received during a taxable year is still determined by multiplying the amount of the payments by a fraction whose numerator is the "gross profit" and the denominator is the "total contract price." In determining the "gross profit," the "selling price" is the gross selling price (not including interest) without any reduction to reflect either selling expenses or any existing mortgage on the property. The "total contract price" is the selling price, reduced now by any "qualifying indebtedness" which the buyer takes the property subject to or assumes, but only to the extent the indebtedness does not exceed the adjusted basis of the property.

"Qualifying indebtedness" is, in general terms, a mortgage or other indebtedness encumbering the property, or debt incurred or assumed by the buyer incident to acquiring the property. In addition, to the extent that the qualifying indebtness exceeds the seller's adjusted basis in the property, the amount of the excess is treated as a payment received by the seller in the year of the transfer. [See Reg. § 1.453–4(c).] These rules, in effect, treat the assumption of liabilities as an installment *payment* in the year of sale to the minimum extent possible. Once the total mortgage amount exceeds the basis in the property, however, the installment fraction would exceed 100%; therefore, the excess of the mortgage over basis is treated as a payment in the year of sale.

Example: Jose sells Kerry a parcel of real property which has a fair market value of $10,000, an adjusted basis of $4,000, and it is subject to a mortgage of $2,000; the contract of sale provides for Kerry to assume the mortgage and to pay Jose $1,000 in December of Year One and $7,000 (plus interest) one year later in December of Year Two. Jose has a *realized* gain in Year One of $6,000, but the transaction is an installment sale, and the gain will be recognized in accordance with the installment method. The "selling price" is $10,000; the "gross profit" is $6,000 ($10,000 – $4,000); there is $2,000 of "qualifying indebtedness"; and in making the income inclusion computation the "total contract price" is reduced by the amount of the mortgage to $8,000 ($10,000 – $2,000). Therefore, in Year One, Jose receives a payment of $1,000, and $750 [$1,000 × ($6,000/$8,000)] is recognized gain; in Year Two, he receives a payment of $7,000, and $5,250 [7,000 × ($6,000/$8,000)] is recognized gain, included (plus the interest) in gross income for Year Two; the total amount of recognized gain in Year One and Year Two is $6,000. In effect the regulations have not treated the liability assumption as an installment payment and have only included a portion of the actual cash payments in gross income.

As an alternative, assume that the amount of the mortgage is $6,000 and the adjusted basis is $4,000; Kerry agrees to assume the mortgage and to pay Jose $1,000 in December of Year One, and $3,000 in December of Year Two (plus interest). The "selling price" is $10,000; the "gross profit" is $6,000 ($10,000 – $4,000); there is $6,000 of "qualifying indebtedness"; and the "total contract price" is $6,000 (selling price less the portion of the qualifying indebtedness which *does not* exceed his adjusted basis, $10,000 – $4,000). Since the amount of the liability ($6,000) exceeds the adjusted basis of the property ($4,000) by $2,000, both that amount and the $1,000 of actual payment are treated as payments in the first year. Since the gross profit and total contract price are each $6,000, Jose is taxed on $3,000 ($3,000 × $6,000/$6,000) in Year One. In Year Two, he receives an actual payment of $3,000, and all $3,000 [$3,000 × ($6,000/$6,000)] is recognized gain, included in gross income for Year Two. [See Reg. § 1.453–4(c).] Thus when the mortgage assumption is in excess of Jose's adjusted basis, the excess amount is treated as a payment received in the year of sale; and in addition, the installment fraction is 100% resulting in the full amount of actual and constructive payments being included in gross income in the year of sale or as actually received.

iii. Character of gain

The character of gain recognized on the sale of property under the installment method is governed by the character of the gain which would have been recognized if the property had been sold for its full fair market value in cash. If the sale of property for cash would result in some recognized gain being characterized as ordinary income, however, because of IRC §§ 1245 or 1250 ("recapture income"), then, to that extent, installment treatment is not available and the full amount of the recapture income must be recognized in the year of the disposition; any remaining gain is then recognized in accordance with the installment method. [IRC § 453(i); see the discussion of recapture income, VI. E. 2. and 3., at pages 295 and 298, *infra.*]

> *Example:* Kurt sells a building held for the production of rental income with an adjusted basis of $50,000 for a sales price of $150,000, $50,000 down and payments of $10,000 per year for 10 years. The building is subject to the recapture rules of IRC § 1250, requiring $30,000 of the realized gain on the sale to be characterized as ordinary income. [See discussion, VI. E. 3., at page 298, *infra.*] In the year of disposition, $30,000 of the gain must be recognized (as ordinary income) regardless of the amount of payments actually received in that year or the amount of gain which would otherwise be required to be recognized under the installment method. The remaining $70,000 of gain is spread among the cash payments, $70/150$ of the $50,000 payment ($23,333) being taxed in the first year and $70/150$ of the $10,000 ($4,667) in each of the next 10 years. In total, Kurt will recognize $30,000 of ordinary income under IRC § 1250 and $70,000 of gain whose character is determined under IRC §§ 1221 or 1231. [See discussions, VI. B. and C., at pages 270 and 291, *infra.*]

iv. **Sale of depreciable property to controlled entity**

   The installment method does not apply to the sale of property which is subject to depreciation deductions in the hands of the *buyer,* if the buyer is a corporation or a partnership and if more than 50% of the value of the buyer is owned (actually or constructively) by the seller, nor does it apply if the sale is to a trust in which the seller or her spouse is a beneficiary (other than a remote contingent beneficiary). [IRC § 453(g).] This rule supplements the provisions of IRC § 1239(a) which apply in the same circumstances, requiring any gain recognized on such a sale or exchange to be treated as ordinary income. [See discussion, VI. D., at page 294, *infra.*]

> *Example:* Grover sells his personal truck to his wholly owned corporation which corporation will use in its business. The truck has a $3,000 basis and a $5,000 value and payment is to be made $1,000 per year for 5 years. Grover has $2,000 of income in the year of sale. [IRC

§ 453(g).] That income is characterized as ordinary income. [IRC § 1239(a).]

b.   Second disposition by related person

Under the installment method rules discussed thus far, it would be possible for a taxpayer to sell appreciated property to a related taxpayer, deferring the recognition of gain until the related buyer actually makes payments to the seller. However, the related buyer might resell the property for cash a short time later (for little or no gain because his cost basis is close to the fair market value for which he resells it) with the result that the economic unit of the two related taxpayers has the full amount of the purchase price in hand, but is taxed on the gain under the deferral rules of IRC § 453. [See *Rushing v. Comm'r,* 441 F.2d 593 (5th Cir.1971).] Congress enacted IRC § 453(e) to address this situation.

If a taxpayer makes an installment sale of property to a related person (first disposition), and the related person, in turn, disposes of the property within 2 years (second disposition), then the amount realized by the seller in the second disposition is treated as being received by the seller in the first disposition, with certain limitations. [IRC § 453(e).] A "related person," in general terms, includes the members of the taxpayer's family, and corporations, estates, trusts, and partnerships in which she has an interest. [IRC §§ 453(f)(1), 267(b) and 318(a).] The 2 year cutoff does not apply if the property sold is corporate stock or securities for which there is an established market; second dispositions on such property are taxed whenever they occur. In addition, the 2 year cutoff is suspended for any period that the related person's risk of loss is substantially diminished. [IRC § 453(e)(2).]

If the second disposition is not a sale or exchange, the fair market value of the property is treated as the amount realized. [IRC § 453(e)(4).] The amount which the seller in the first disposition is treated as receiving in the second disposition is limited to the *lesser* of the amount realized in the second disposition or the total contract price for the first disposition; the lesser of these two amounts is further reduced by the sum of the payments received with respect to the first disposition by the *end* of the taxable year in which the second disposition occurs, plus any amount previously treated as received by the first seller under the second disposition rules. [IRC § 453(e)(3).] Payments actually received by the first seller in taxable years subsequent to the second disposition do not result in recognized gain to the extent the gain has already been recognized under these rules. [IRC § 453(e)(5).] These rules do not apply if the second disposition is the result of a compulsory or involuntary conversion, or if either the seller or the buyer in the first disposition dies before the second disposition, or if there is no tax avoidance purpose to either the first disposition or the second disposition. [IRC § 453(e)(6) and (7).]

Example: Leroy agrees to sell stock (which is not traded on an established securities market and which has an adjusted basis of $50,000) to his daughter, Miriam, for $200,000; Miriam is to pay $100,000 cash at the time of the sale (July 1 of Year One), and annual payments of $10,000 (plus interest) for the next 10 years. On March 1 of Year Three, before she makes that year's annual payment, Miriam sells the stock to an unrelated third party for $350,000. In Year Three, Leroy is treated as receiving $350,000 (the amount realized by Miriam in the second disposition), but limited to $200,000 (the total contract price for the first disposition, because that is lesser than the amount realized in the second disposition) and further reduced by $120,000 (the sum of the $110,000 payments received in Year One and Year Two, plus the $10,000 payment for Year Three which will be received before the end of Year Three) down to $80,000. Hence, Leroy is treated as receiving an $80,000 payment in Year Three because of the second disposition and, in addition, he receives the actual payment on July 1 of Year Three, of $10,000; thus, he must recognize $3/4$ (the portion of his gross profit divided by the total contract price) of $90,000 in Year Three. By the end of Year Three, he has received, or is treated as receiving, payments totaling $200,000, the total contract price of the first disposition, and the total amount of his realized gain ($150,000) will have been recognized. Payments which Leroy actually receives in Year Four and subsequent years will not result in any further recognized gain.

c. Disposition of an installment obligation

When there is an installment sale of property, the contract of sale, note or other evidence of the purchaser's obligation to pay the balance of the purchase price is referred to as an "installment obligation." If an installment obligation is subsequently satisfied for less than its face value, if it becomes unenforceable, or if the seller subsequently sells or otherwise disposes of the installment obligation, the seller must recognize gain or loss (if any) with respect to the installment obligation. The amount of the gain or loss is the difference between the basis of the obligation and either the amount realized (if the installment obligation is sold, exchanged or satisfied at other than its face value), or its fair market value (if it is otherwise disposed of, *e.g.,* by gift). [IRC § 453B(a).] The basis of an installment obligation is the excess of its face value over the amount which would be recognized gain if it were satisfied in full. [IRC § 453B(b).] The character of the gain or loss resulting from the disposition of an installment obligation is determined with reference to the sale of the property for which the installment obligation was received. The rules pertaining to the disposition of installment obligations generally do not apply when an installment obligation is transferred at death, transferred between spouses, or transferred by a spouse to her former spouse incident to divorce. [IRC § 453B(c), (g).]

Example: In the preceding Example, Leroy agreed to sell stock with an adjusted basis of $50,000 to his daughter, Miriam, for $200,000; Miriam was to pay $100,000 cash at the time of the sale (July 1 of Year One), and to make annual payments of $10,000 (plus interest) for the next 10 years. The "gross profit" on the installment sale is $150,000, and the "total contract price" is $200,000; therefore, when Leroy receives the $100,000 payment on July 1 of Year One, he has recognized gain of $75,000 [$100,000 × $150,000/$200,000)]. If Leroy sells the installment obligations on January 1 of Year Two, for an amount realized of $90,000, the basis of the installment obligations is $25,000 {the excess of the face value, $100,000, over the amount which would be recognized gain if the obligation were satisfied in full, $75,000 [$100,000 × ($150,000/$200,000)]}. Therefore, Leroy will recognize $65,000 of gain on the disposition of the installment obligations. The character of this gain will be the same as the character of the gain from the sale of the stock.

d. Certain indebtedness treated as payment on installment obligations

Congress enacted IRC § 453C in 1986 for the purpose of effectively limiting the deferred recognition of gain under the installment method for certain taxpayers who have outstanding indebtedness during a taxable year. The rules under IRC § 453C are complex, but they are basically an extension of the notion expressed in IRC § 453(e). Under IRC § 453(e), the seller of property on the installment basis is not permitted to defer recognizing gain on an installment sale made to a related person when the related person resells the property, thereby bringing cash into the economic unit comprised of the seller and the related person. [See discussion at IV. B. 3. b., at page 206, *supra.*]

The problem addressed by IRC § 453C is really quite simple, although the statutory solution to the problem is complex. If a taxpayer sells property on the installment method and no payments are made in the year of sale, no tax is due on the gain realized from the sale that year. If during the same year the taxpayer borrows money, the amount of the loan proceeds is not included in gross income, but the taxpayer has the use of money just as he would have if he had received some payment for the property sale. Further, the loan may have been made because the lendor knew the taxpayer owned the installment sales obligation, whether or not the obligation is actually pledged as collateral for the loan. Congress believes it is inappropriate for the installment method to allow the deferral of recognized gain when, in essence, a taxpayer borrows money to finance the deferral of recognizing gain from an installment sale. Dealing with this problem is troublesome, however, because of the difficulty in establishing a connection between an installment sale made in one transaction to money borrowed in an entirely separate transaction. The approach adopted under IRC § 453C does not attempt to trace loan proceeds to particular installment sales. Instead, in general terms, a taxpayer's overall nonpersonal indebtedness outstanding during a taxable year (whether incurred during that year or prior years) is compared with installment sales made during the year, and a portion of the amount of the indebtedness is then treated as if it was received by the taxpayer as a payment on the installment obligations received during the year.

A taxpayer's "allocable installment indebtedness" (AII) is computed by multiplying the installment percentage times the taxpayer's average quarterly indebtedness for the taxable year. The "installment percentage" is determined by dividing the face amount of "applicable installment obligations" outstanding at the end of the year by the sum of the adjusted basis of all nonpersonal assets plus the face amount of all installment obligations not related to the sale of personal property outstanding at the end of the year. [IRC § 453C(b).] "Applicable installment obligations" are generally obligations arising from the disposition of: (1) personal property by a person who regularly disposes of the same type of personal property on the installment plan; (2) real property which is held by the taxpayer for sale to customers in the ordinary course of business; or (3) real property used in the taxpayer's trade or business if the sales price exceeds $150,000. [IRC § 453C(e)(1).] The average indebtedness includes all nonpersonal indebtedness and the computation is made on a quarterly basis. The AII amount for a taxable year is then treated as the receipt of a payment for applicable installment obligations received during the year; if more than one such obligation is received during the year, the AII amount is allocated among them on a pro rata basis. [IRC § 453C(a).]

Example: During Year One, Janet sells for a gain one item of real property held for the production of rental income for $270,000 and receives only the purchaser's note for the sale; she does not receive any actual "payment" during Year One. As of the end of Year One, the aggregate adjusted basis of her nonpersonal property, other than installment obligations, is $930,000 and her average quarterly indebtedness is $600,000. Janet's allocable installment indebtedness for Year One is $135,000, computed by multiplying her average quarterly indebtedness ($600,000) by her installment percentage (22.5%). The installment percentage is determined by dividing $270,000, which is the face amount of her applicable installment obligations, by $1,200,000, which is the sum of the adjusted basis of her nonpersonal assets ($930,000) plus the face amount of her installment obligations outstanding as of the end of the year ($270,000). Janet is treated as receiving a payment in Year One in the amount of $135,000 from the installment sale of the item of property, even though she does not receive any actual payment in Year One. Assuming that her gross profit margin on the installment sale is 25%, she must recognize gain of $33,750.

When actual payments are made with respect to an installment obligation which has been affected by the IRC § 453C rules, they are received tax-free up to the amount treated as a payment under IRC § 453C. [IRC § 453C(c).]

Example: If Janet, from the preceding Example, makes no additional installment sales, incurs no additional indebtedness and receives an actual payment of $50,000 in Year Two, the payment is not taken into account in computing recognized gain for Year Two under IRC § 453(c). If, in addition, Janet receives an actual payment of $100,000 in Year Three, only $15,000 [$100,000 − $85,000 ($135,000 − $50,000)] is treated as a payment received in Year Three for purposes of computing recognized gain under IRC § 453(c).

e. Transactions elected out of IRC § 453

If an installment sale is made, realized gain must be recognized in accordance with the installment method unless the taxpayer elects to have the installment method not apply.

i. Election

A taxpayer may elect out of the installment method with respect to one or more installment sales made during a taxable year on or before the due date (including extensions) of the income tax return for that taxable year; once made, an election may be revoked only with the consent of the I.R.S. [IRC § 453(d).]

ii. Consequences of election

If a transaction is elected out of IRC § 453, the gain is recognized in accordance with the taxpayer's general method of accounting, *i.e.,* the accrual method or the cash method. If a taxpayer uses the accrual method of accounting, generally, the *face value* of any installment obligation is included in the amount realized from the sale, because the face value is the amount he is entitled to receive under the "all events test." [See discussion, IV. B. 2. b., at page 192, *supra.*] If a taxpayer uses the cash method of accounting, however, she is required to include the *fair market value* of any installment obligation in the amount realized for purposes of computing gain. [IRC § 1001(b).] The fair market value of an installment obligation may be less than its face value, and if so, the obligation itself will take a "cost basis" equal to its fair market value as of the date of the sale of the property. [See discussion, II. B. 2. a. ii. *b.,* at page 25, *supra.*]

The installment obligation itself becomes an independent item of property, which may produce gain or loss upon a subsequent sale or other disposition, or upon being satisfied at its face value; the character of the resulting gain or loss is determined with reference to the installment obligation itself, not with reference to the property for which the installment obligation was received.

Example: Neal sells an item of property which has an adjusted basis of $100 to Odessa under a contract calling for her to pay him $500 (plus interest) 1 year later, and Neal elects out of IRC § 453. As of the date of the sale, the contract has a fair market value of only $450 because of Odessa's poor credit rating. If Neal uses the accrual method, his recognized gain in the year of sale is $400. There is no further gain when the obligation is paid. If Neal uses the cash method, his recognized gain in the year of sale is only $350 and the contract (the installment obligation) has a basis to him of $450. When Neal (cash method taxpayer) collects the $500 under the terms of the obligation, he will recognize $50 of gain which is ordinary income because the obligation is extinguished and so there is no sale or exchange. [See discussion, VI. B. 4., at page 282, *infra.*] If instead of collecting the $500 under the terms of the obligation, Neal (cash method taxpayer) sells the contract which is a capital asset 2 weeks after receiving it for $400, he will recognize a short-term capital loss of $50. [See discussion, VI. B. 5., at page 285, *infra.*]

iii.   Open transaction doctrine

    If a cash or an accrual method taxpayer makes an installment sale and receives an installment obligation which, because of contingencies or other terms, makes it *impossible* to determine the fair market value of the obligation, the transaction may be treated as "open" with the result that she will not recognize *any* gain until she has actually received payments (or property with an ascertainable fair market value) up to the amount of her basis in the property sold in the installment sale. [*Burnet v. Logan,* 283 U.S. 404, 51 S.Ct. 550

(1931).] It is only in extremely rare and unusual circumstances that the fair market value of an installment obligation will not be able to be determined, or approximated with reasonable accuracy, thus, as a practical matter, the "open transaction" doctrine is seldom applied. In addition, for installment sales which are *not* elected out of IRC § 453, the I.R.S. has promulgated regulations to determine the proper amount of recognized gain where the selling price is subject to contingencies such that the gross profit or the total contract price (or both) cannot be readily ascertained. [IRC § 453(j) and Temp.Reg. § 15a.453–1(c); see discussion, IV. B. 3. a. ii. *b.,* at page 201, *supra.*]

C. JUDICIAL DOCTRINES

1. CLAIM OF RIGHT DOCTRINE
a. In general

A taxpayer must include in gross income amounts which he receives during a taxable year if he has a claim to the amount and unrestricted use of it, even though he may become obligated to return the amount in a later year. [*North American Oil Consolidated v. Burnet,* 286 U.S. 417, 52 S.Ct. 613 (1932).] If the taxpayer does repay the amount in a taxable year subsequent to the year in which it was received, he may take a deduction in the year of repayment, but he may not file an amended return for the earlier taxable year. Special treatment is provided, however, if the provisions of IRC § 1341 are applicable. [See discussion, IV. C. 1. b., below.]

Example: Isadora reported $22,000 of gross income in 1944 which she had received that year as an employee's bonus, and she computed and paid her federal income tax liability accordingly. In 1946, it was determined that the bonus which she received in 1944 had been improperly computed, and she returned $11,000 to her employer. Isadora could not recompute her income tax liability for 1944, but she could take a $11,000 deduction in 1946. [*United States v. Lewis,* 340 U.S. 590, 71 S.Ct. 522.]

b. Computation of tax where taxpayer restores substantial amount held under claim of right

Congress has provided special treatment in some situations for taxpayers who repay an amount which was included in gross income in an earlier taxable year under a claim of right. If an item was included in gross income in an earlier taxable year because it appeared the taxpayer had an unrestricted right to it, and if a deduction is allowable in the current taxable year because it was established that the taxpayer *did not* have an unrestricted right to the item, and the amount of the deduction exceeds $3,000, then the taxpayer may compute his tax liability in the year of repayment according to one of two prescribed methods, whichever results in the lower amount of tax liability. The first method simply follows case law and allows one to compute the tax liability for the current year, taking a deduction for the repaid amount. The second method is to compute the amount of his tax liability for the current year *without* taking a deduction for the repaid amount, but then subtracting the amount by which his tax liability in the earlier year would have been reduced if the repaid amount had not been included in gross income in the earlier year. [IRC § 1341(a).] This provision does not apply to income derived from the sale of inventory. [IRC § 1341(b)(2).]

Example: Assume that Isadora, from the preceding Example, had received the $22,000 bonus in Year One and repaid the $11,000 in Year Two. Assume that her tax liability in Year One was $15,000, but if she had not included $11,000 of the bonus her tax liability for Year One would have been $11,920, a reduction of $3,080 (28% of $11,000). Because Isadora satisfies the requirements of IRC § 1341(a)(1), (2) and (3), her Year Two income tax liability is the lesser of: (A) the tax computed on Year Two taxable income taking a deduction for the $11,000 repayment (assume that produces a taxable income of $17,000 and a tax liability of $2,550); or (B) the tax computed on Year Two taxable income without taking a deduction for the repayment (for a taxable income of $28,000 and a tax liability of $5,595), but reducing the tax liability by the amount of the decrease in her Year One tax liability if she had not included the $11,000 bonus in gross income in Year One [for a tax liability of $2,515 ($5,595 − $3,080)]. Using IRC § 1341, Isadora's tax liability for Year Two is $2,515.

2. TAX BENEFIT RULE
a. In general

If a taxpayer takes a deduction for an item in a taxable year which is proper on the basis of the facts which are then known, the I.R.S. may not reopen the tax return for that year in order to disallow the deduction if subsequent facts make the deduction inappropriate. Instead, the courts have recognized that because a tax benefit was obtained from taking a deduction, the taxpayer must include in gross income any amount which is recovered in a later year relating to the earlier deduction.

Example: In 1940, the A.P.S. Corporation transferred real property to a charitable organization on the condition that the property be used for a religious or educational purpose, and A.P.S. took a charitable contribution deduction on that year's return. In

1957, the donee decided not to use the gift property and returned it to A.P.S. Even though A.P.S. has, in a sense, merely had property which it once owned returned to it and thus has had a recovery of capital, it is required to include in 1957 gross income the amount which was previously allowed as a deduction. [*Alice Phelan Sullivan Corp. v. Comm'r*, 381 F.2d 399 (Ct.Cl.1967).]

b. Recovery of tax benefit items

Congress has provided for the exclusion from gross income of amounts which are recovered in a taxable year to the extent the amount was deducted in a prior taxable year but did not reduce the amount of the taxpayer's income tax in the prior year. [IRC § 111(a).] A similar rule applies if a tax credit was taken in a prior taxable year and in the current year there is a downward price adjustment, so that the amount of the tax credit should also be lowered, requiring an increase in the current year's tax liability to the extent the prior credit resulted in a tax benefit. [IRC § 111; see discussion of tax credits, VII. F., at page 314, *infra.*]

Example: In Year One, Jacques elected to itemize his deductions in computing taxable income; his itemized deductions exceeded his standard deduction for Year One by $300. In Year Two, Jacques received a refund of $250 of state income taxes for which a deduction had been taken in Year One. None of the state income tax refund may be excluded from Jacques' gross income in Year Two. Alternatively, if the amount of state income taxes deducted in Year One and refunded in Year Two was $500, $200 would be excluded from gross income in Year Two because that amount did not reduce his income tax liability for Year One.

D. NONRECOGNITION PROVISIONS

Generally, gain (or loss) which is *realized* upon the sale, exchange or other disposition of property must be *recognized,* or included in gross income (or considered for a deduction) in the taxable year in which the transaction occurs. [IRC § 1001(a), (c).] If a realized gain (or loss) is entitled to nonrecognition treatment, it does not give rise to gross income (or a deduction) at that time. The objective of the nonrecognition provisions is merely to *postpone* the recognition of gain, leaving the taxpayer in the same position with the new substituted property as with the old property. Rules are provided, therefore, for substituting the old property's basis into the newly acquired property so that the gain or loss which was realized but not recognized in the earlier transaction may be realized *and recognized* when and if the newly acquired property is subsequently disposed of in a transaction where a nonrecognition provision does not apply. In addition, the holding period of the old property is added, or "tacked" on to the holding period of the new property. [See discussion, VI. B. 5. b. ii., at page 286, *infra.*]

There are various types of nonrecognition provisions. For example, when certain types of property of a "like kind" are exchanged Congress has provided that a realized gain or loss with respect to the property given up in the exchange will not be recognized. [IRC § 1031.] In addition, a gain (but not a loss) which is realized from the compulsory or involuntary conversion of an item of property may not be recognized if new property, which is "similar or related in service or use" to the old property, is acquired within certain time limits. [IRC § 1033.] If a taxpayer sells or exchanges his principal residence, a realized gain will not be recognized if the proceeds of the sale are invested in a new principal residence within certain time limits. [IRC § 1034.]

1. LIKE KIND EXCHANGES
a. In general

No gain or loss is recognized if qualifying property is exchanged *solely* for other qualifying property of a like kind; if property other than qualifying property is *received* in exchange, then some portion of a gain (but not a loss) realized with respect to the relinquished property will be recognized. [IRC § 1031(a)(1), (b), and (c).] A qualifying transaction must be an "exchange," in the sense of transferring property for other property without the intervention of money; an "exchange" is to be distinguished from a "sale," where property is transferred in consideration of a definite price expressed in terms of money. [See *Bloomington Coca-Cola Bottling Co. v. Comm'r,* 189 F.2d 14 (7th Cir.1951).] In determining whether a transaction is an exchange or a sale, the substance rather than the form of the transaction will control. Thus, a transaction denominated as a "sale," but which is accompanied by a purchase of similar property from the transferee, or which is accompanied by a lease of the same property back to the transferor, may be treated as an exchange.

Examples: Justin has a computer which he has used in his business for several years; the computer has an adjusted basis of $2,000 and a fair market value of $1,000. A better computer is now available which the local dealer sells for $9,000. Justin and the dealer enter into two separate contracts; under the first contract, Justin "sells" his old computer to the dealer for $1,000, and under the second contract, Justin "purchases" a new computer for $9,000. Because the sale of the used computer and the purchase of the new computer are reciprocal and mutually dependent transactions (the dealer's acceptance of the old computer is dependent upon Justin's purchase of the new computer, and Justin's purchase of the new computer for $9,000 is dependent upon the dealer's taking his used computer), the substance of the transaction is that Justin has *exchanged* his old computer (plus some cash) for the new computer. [Rev.Rul. 61–119, 1961–1 C.B. 395.]

The C.E. Company owned a foundry, which it used in its business and which had a fair market value of $250,000, and an adjusted basis of $500,000. In December, 1943, the Company "sold" the foundry for $150,000 cash (*which was less than the fair market value of the foundry*), and at the same time the Company agreed to lease the foundry from the purchaser for a term of 95 years. The Company *exchanged* the fee title to the foundry for the cash and the leasehold interest in the foundry. [*Century Electric Co. v. Comm'r*, 192 F.2d 155 (8th Cir.1951).]

The L. Company was in the manufacturing business and needed a new manufacturing plant. As a method of financing the new plant, L. entered into an agreement with an insurance company whereby L. would construct the plant and then sell it to the insurance company for its fair market value of $2,400,000, or the actual cost to L., whichever was less, and at the time of purchase the insurance company would lease the building back to L. at a fair rental value for a term of 30 years, with two 10-year options to renew. The transaction was a *sale* of the plant for its fair market value, rather than an exchange of the fee title for a leasehold interest. [*Leslie Co. v. Comm'r*, 539 F.2d 943 (3rd Cir.1976); *see also Jordan Marsh Co. v. Comm'r*, 269 F.2d 453 (2d Cir. 1959).]

b.   Qualifying property

Property relinquished in an exchange to which the nonrecognition rules of IRC § 1031 apply may be either property held for productive use in a trade or business or it may be property held for investment; property received in such an exchange may be either property held for productive use in a trade or business or property held for investment. [IRC § 1031(a)(1).] Business property, therefore, may be exchanged either for business property or for investment property, and investment property may be exchanged either for investment property or for business property. Qualifying property does not include the following items: (1) stock in trade or other property held primarily for sale, such as inventory; (2) stocks, bonds, or notes; (3) other securities or evidences of indebtedness or interest; (4) interests in a partnership; (5) certificates of trust or beneficial interests; or (6) choses in action. [IRC § 1031(a)(2).]

c.   Like kind property

The nonrecognition rules of IRC § 1031 apply only if the qualifying property received in an exchange is of a "like kind" to the qualifying property relinquished in the exchange. [IRC § 1031(a)(1).] The term "like kind" has reference to the nature or character of the property and not to its grade or quality. Improved real estate, thus, is of a like kind to unimproved real estate, and the fee title to real estate is of a like kind to a leasehold of real estate for a term of 30 years or more. [See Reg. § 1.1031(a)–1(b), (c).]

Example: Kate and her three children owned undivided interests in two parcels of real estate, an improved city lot and a tract of unimproved country land. Kate's children transferred to her their undivided interests in the city lot, and Kate transferred to her children her interest in the mineral rights to the country land; the interests which were transferred were of equal fair market value. Under local law, mineral rights to real property are interests in real property, not personal property. The undivided interest in the fee title to the city lot is of a like kind to the mineral rights to the country land; thus, the transfers constitute an exchange of qualifying property of a like kind and the nonrecognition rules of IRC § 1031 apply. [*Comm'r v. Crichton,* 122 F.2d 181 (5th Cir. 1941).]

d.   Exchanges not solely in kind

If property received in an exchange includes not only like kind qualifying property, but also other property or money (commonly referred to as "boot"), then *gain* realized with respect to the property relinquished will be recognized, but only to the extent of the boot received. [IRC § 1031(b).] If a *loss* is realized with respect to property relinquished in an exchange in which boot is received as well as like kind qualifying property, no loss from the exchange is recognized. [IRC § 1031(c).]

Example: Lyndon has a Cadillac which he uses exclusively in his business which has a fair market value of $15,000 and an adjusted basis to him of $10,000. He exchanges the Cadillac for a Chevrolet with a fair market value of $11,000 (which he will use exclusively in his business) and $4,000 cash. Lyndon has a *realized gain* on the exchange of the Cadillac of $5,000, but only $4,000 of *recognized gain.* [See Reg. § 1.1031(b)–1(b) Example (1).]

i.   Non-simultaneous exchange

The nonrecognition rules of IRC § 1031 may apply even if property which is relinquished in an exchange is transferred in a transaction which occurs at a different time as the transaction in which the property received in the exchange is transferred. Property received is *not* treated as like kind property, however, if it is not *identified* as property to be received by the taxpayer on or before 45 days after the taxpayer transfers the property relinquished in the exchange, *or* if it is *received* more than 180 days after the taxpayer transfers the property relinquished in the exchange (or if it is received after the date the taxpayer's income tax return for the year in which the exchange occurred is due). [IRC § 1031(a)(3).]

Example: Muriel has owned a parcel of unimproved real property for many years as an investment. Recently, an interstate highway was constructed adjacent to her property and a corporation in the business of operating motels is interested in acquiring Muriel's property. Muriel is willing to dispose of the property, but she does not want to have to recognize gain upon selling the property. Therefore, she agrees to transfer her real estate to the corporation in exchange for some other parcel of real estate of equal fair market value which she will hold for investment. Pursuant to the agreement, Muriel transfers her parcel to the corporation on May 31 of Year One. The corporation must *identify* the real estate which it will transfer to her on or before July 14 of Year One, and Muriel must *receive* the property no later than November 27 of Year One, or the property she is to receive will be treated as property which is not like kind property.

ii.   Liabilities

If a taxpayer transfers property which is encumbered by a liability and the transferee assumes the liability or takes the property subject to the liability, the amount of the liability is treated as boot received by the taxpayer in the exchange. However, if the property which the taxpayer receives in the exchange is also encumbered by a liability which he assumes or takes subject to, then the liability encumbering the relinquished property is treated as boot only to the extent it exceeds the amount of the liability encumbering the property received in the exchange.

Examples: Noah owns an apartment building which has an adjusted basis in his hands of $500,000, a fair market value of $800,000, and it is subject to a mortgage of $150,000. On September 1, he transfers the apartment building to Olga, subject to the $150,000 mortgage, receiving in exchange therefor $50,000 in cash and another apartment building with a fair market value of $600,000. Noah has

a realized gain of $300,000 ($800,000 amount realized –
$500,000 adjusted basis) on the exchange, but only
$200,000 of the gain (equal to the cash and assumption of
the liability) must be recognized. [Reg. § 1.1031(d)–2
Example (1).]

Pomeroy owns a convenience store which has an
adjusted basis of $175,000, a fair market value of
$290,000, and it is subject to a mortgage of $150,000. On
December 1, he transfers the convenience store to
Quenby, subject to the $150,000 mortgage, receiving in
exchange therefor another convenience store with a fair
market value of $220,000, but subject to a mortgage of
$80,000. Pomeroy realizes a gain of $115,000 ($290,000
amount realized – $175,000 adjusted basis) on the
exchange. For purposes of IRC § 1031(b), the amount of
boot received by Pomeroy and gain recognized is only
$70,000, because consideration received in the form of a
transfer subject to a liability of $150,000 is offset by
consideration given in the form of a receipt of property
subject to an $80,000 liability. [Reg. § 1.1031(d)–2
Example (2)(c).]

e. **Basis of property acquired in an exchange**
   Items of property acquired in an exchange to which IRC § 1031
applies have a total basis equal to the basis of the property relinquished
in the exchange, decreased by the amount of any money received and
increased by the amount of gain (or decreased by the amount of loss) that
was recognized on the exchange. The total basis of the property received
is allocated among the various items, and if any boot is received, the boot
has a basis equal to its fair market value on the date of the exchange.
[IRC § 1031(d).] If more than one piece of like kind property is received
the remaining basis is allocated between the properties according to their
relative fair market values. Because the basis of the new property is the
same, in whole or in part, as the basis of the old property, the basis is
known as a substituted basis and the holding period of the old property, if
it was a capital asset or section 1231 property, is added, or "tacked," onto
the holding period of the new property. [IRC § 1223(1); See discussion,
VI. B. 5. b. ii., at page 286, *infra.*]

Example: Reginald owns a parcel of unimproved real estate with an
adjusted basis of $150,000 and a fair market value of $250,000
which he holds as an investment. On November 1, he
exchanges it for a truck which has a fair market value of
$10,000, and two smaller parcels of land on the other side of
town; Parcel # 1 has a fair market value of $80,000, and

Parcel # 2 has a fair market value of $160,000. Reginald has a realized gain on the exchange of $100,000 ($250,000 – $150,000), but only $10,000 of the gain is recognized. The aggregate basis of the property received is $160,000 ($150,000 basis of the property relinquished increased by the $10,000 of recognized gain). The aggregate basis of $160,000 is allocated between the properties received first by assigning to the truck (the boot) an amount equal to its fair market value, $10,000; the remaining $150,000 is allocated between the two parcels of real property according to their relative fair market values, or $50,000 to Parcel # 1 and $100,000 to Parcel # 2.

2. INVOLUNTARY CONVERSIONS

a. In general

If property is compulsorily or involuntarily converted, then realized gain (but happily not realized loss) may be entitled to nonrecognition. This nonrecognition provision may apply in two situations: (1) if the property is converted directly into other property which is "similar or related in service or use" (similar property) to the involuntarily converted property; or (2) if the property is converted into money or non-similar property and then the taxpayer purchases similar property (or corporate stock, in some situations) within certain time limits. [IRC § 1033(a)(1) and (2).] Special rules apply if real property is converted as a result of its seizure, requisition, or condemnation, or threat or imminence thereof. [IRC 1033(g).] The extent to which gain is not recognized in an involuntary conversion affects the determination of the basis and holding period of newly acquired similar property. [IRC § 1033(b).]

b. Compulsory or involuntary conversion

A compulsory or involuntary conversion of property into money or other property occurs if it is partially or totally destroyed, if it is stolen, seized, requisitioned, or condemned, or if it is sold or exchanged under the threat or imminence of seizure, requisition or condemnation. [IRC § 1033(a).] Real property sold pursuant to Federal reclamation laws, and certain livestock destroyed by disease or sold on account of drought are treated as disposed of in a qualifying involuntary conversion. [IRC § 1033(c), (d), and (e).] Requisition or condemnation generally describes the governmental taking of private property for a public use, with the payment of just compensation to the owner. If two pieces of property constitute a single economic unit, however, and only one is involuntarily converted, a voluntary sale of the remaining piece may be treated as an involuntary conversion.

Example: Harry operated an interstate trucking business in which he used two parcels of real estate located across the street from each other. Harry's business offices, a bunkhouse and facilities for loading and unloading trucks was located on one parcel, and the other parcel was used for parking trucks while they were waiting to be loaded or unloaded; the two parcels were used together as a single economic unit in Harry's business. The New York city government condemned the parcel used in Harry's business for parking trucks. It became impractical to continue Harry's trucking business from the remaining parcel because there were inadequate parking facilities, so Harry sold the remaining parcel as well. Because the two parcels were used in Harry's business as an economic unit, when one parcel was involuntarily converted by condemnation and the other parcel was sold because it was impractical to continue the business on the remaining parcel, the transaction was considered as a whole and both parcels were involuntarily converted. [*Masser v. Comm'r*, 30 T.C. 741 (1958).]

c. Conversion into similar property

If property is compulsorily or involuntarily converted into other property which is similar property, no gain is recognized, regardless of when the disposition of the converted property occurred; the nonrecognition is mandatory, the taxpayer does not need to make any election. Unlike IRC § 1031, however, this section applies only to gain, thus a realized loss is allowed to be recognized. [IRC § 1033(a)(1).]

Example: Tabitha is engaged in the business of farming and in March she bought a tractor to use in her business. In December of the same year, the tractor had a value in excess of its adjusted basis. While the tractor was in the dealer's garage for maintenance, the garage burned down, and the tractor was totally destroyed. Fortunately, the dealer was fully insured, and Tabitha did not need a tractor until time for spring planting. In February of the next year, the dealer delivered a new tractor to Tabitha to replace the one which had been destroyed; the fair market value of the new tractor was greater than Tabitha's adjusted basis for the old tractor. The gain which Tabitha realized upon the destruction of her tractor is not recognized because it was directly converted into a new tractor, which was similar or related in service or use to the old tractor.

d. Conversion into money or dissimilar property

If property is involuntarily or compulsorily converted into money or property which is *not* similar or related in service or use to the converted property (dissimilar property), then realized gain must be recognized unless, within certain time limits, the taxpayer either purchases similar property, or purchases enough stock to acquire control of a corporation which owns similar property. If a taxpayer does purchase similar property, or qualifying corporate stock, the nonrecognition rule applies only if he so *elects,* and the realized gain will not be recognized only to the extent that the cost of the newly acquired similar property, or qualifying corporate stock, equals or exceeds the amount realized on the involuntary conversion of the old property. [IRC § 1033(a)(2).]

i.   Purchase

A taxpayer is considered to *purchase* similar property, or qualifying corporate stock, only if the unadjusted basis of the property (determined without application of the special rules of IRC § 1033(b)) [see discussion, IV. D. 2. g., at page 225, *infra*] is its cost basis, determined under IRC § 1012. [IRC § 1033(a)(2)(A)(ii).] Thus, property which the taxpayer receives as a gift (with its basis determined under IRC § 1015) does not qualify as replacement property. [Reg. § 1.1033(a)–2(c)(4).]

ii. Qualifying corporate stock

As an alternative to purchasing similar property directly, a taxpayer may purchase stock in acquiring "control" of a corporation which owns similar property. "Control" of a corporation means ownership of stock which has at least 80% of the total voting power and at least 80% of the total number of shares of all other classes of stock of the corporation.

Example: Udell owned a small motel which was condemned by the state highway department. Udell uses the proceeds from the condemnation to purchase 90% of the outstanding shares of XYZ Corporation, which owns a small motel. The purchase of the XYZ stock is a qualified use of the condemnation proceeds.

iii. Period for replacement

In order for the nonrecognition rule to apply, the taxpayer must purchase the replacement property, or the qualifying corporate stock, within the period beginning with the date of the involuntary or compulsory conversion (date of disposition) or the earliest date of the threat or imminence of requisition or condemnation, and ending 2 years after the close of the first taxable year in which any part of the gain upon the conversion is realized (or at a later date if the taxpayer shows reasonable cause for the delay and obtains the approval of the IRS prior to the expiration of the 2 year time limit). [IRC § 1033(a)(2)(B); Reg. § 1.1033(a)–2(c)(3).]

e. Similar property

Property which is "similar or related in service or use" (similar property) to converted property is not defined in the Code or in the regulations, but it has generally been applied by looking at the relationship between the taxpayer and the converted property, and comparing that relationship with the taxpayer's relationship to the replacement property. Different perspectives are taken with respect to property which is owned by a taxpayer and actively used by her in her business (owner-user) and property which is owned merely as an investment (owner-investor).

i.   Owner-users

Replacement property which is to be used by the taxpayer (rather than merely being held as an investment) is similar to converted property which was used by the taxpayer if the properties have a close functional similarity; that is, if the physical characteristics and the ultimate end uses of the converted and replacement properties are closely similar.

> ***Example:*** Vivian owned and operated a manufacturing plant on property which was involuntarily converted, and she acquired replacement property on which she operates a wholesale grocery warehouse. The use of property to operate a wholesale grocery business is not similar or related to the use of property as a manufacturing plant. [Rev.Rul. 64–237, 1964–2 C.B. 319.]

ii. Owner-investors

Replacement property which is to be held as an investment is similar to converted property which was held as an investment if the properties are reasonably similar in their relation to the taxpayer; the ultimate use to which the properties are put is not determinative. Factors to consider include the extent and type of management activities the taxpayer engages in, the amount and kind of services he provides, and the nature of his business risks. [See *Liant Record, Inc. v. Comm'r,* 303 F.2d 326 (2d Cir.1962); and Rev.Rul. 64–237, 1964–2 C.B. 319.]

> ***Example:*** C.I. Corporation was in the real estate investment business and, among other properties, it owned an office building. The office building was sold to the city under the threat of the city's exercising its power of eminent domain, and the Corporation purchased 80% of the outstanding stock of a corporation which owned a hotel. Both the office building and the hotel were, in a sense, investments from which the taxpayer derived rental income. When the

taxpayer owned the office building, it primarily rented space to a variety of long-term commercial tenants and the Corporation needed only 2 employees to provide elevator and janitorial services to the tenants; however, the hotel rented rooms primarily to transients who needed a variety of services and facilities and the Corporation needed between 130 and 140 employees to attend to the guests. Because the extent and type of the Corporation's management activity, the amount and kind of services rendered to the tenants and the nature of the business risks connected with the two properties were so different, the hotel is not "similar or related in service or use" to the office building. [*Clifton Investment Co. v. Comm'r,* 312 F.2d 719 (6th Cir.1963).]

f.   Condemnation of real property

If real property which is held for productive use in a trade or business or for investment is compulsorily or involuntarily converted as a result of seizure, requisition, or condemnation, or threat or imminence thereof, then the nonrecognition rules of IRC § 1033(a) are not as strict. Nonrecognition is allowed if the replacement property is either like kind property or similar property. [IRC § 1033(g)(1).] For purposes of this rule, like kind property is determined under the principles of IRC § 1031. [Reg. § 1.1033(g)–1(a); see discussion, IV. D. 1. c., at page 217, *supra.*] In addition, the period for replacement is extended to the end of 3 taxable years after the first taxable year in which any part of the gain upon the conversion is realized. [IRC § 1033(g)(4).] The replacement property, however, may not be qualifying shares of corporate stock. [IRC § 1033(g) (2).]

Example: Waylon owned a warehouse which he rented to third parties. The warehouse and the land upon which it was built was condemned by the state, and he used the proceeds to build a gas station on land already owned by him in another part of town; the gas station was rented to an oil company when construction was completed. Under IRC § 1033(g), Waylon may acquire replacement property which is of a like-kind. *Improvements to* real property (building the gas station), however, are not of a like kind to *improved* real property (the warehouse and the lot). [Rev.Rul. 67–255, 1967–2 C.B. 270.] The replacement property does not qualify under subsection (g) of IRC § 1033, however, because Waylon's relationship as an investor to the warehouse is similar to his relationship to the gas station, the replacement property qualifies under the similar or related in service or use test of subsection (a) of IRC § 1033. [Rev.Rul. 71–41, 1971–1 C.B. 223.]

g. Basis of replacement property

The basis of property acquired through an involuntary conversion in which gain was not recognized under the rules of IRC § 1033 will reflect the extent to which the gain was not recognized. [IRC § 1033(b).] As was the case of like kind exchanges the replacement property takes a substituted basis. Because the basis of the replacement property is the same, in whole or in part, as the basis of the property which was involuntarily converted, the holding period of the old property is added, or "tacked," onto the holding period of the new property if the old property was a capital asset or section 1231 property. [IRC § 1223(1); see discussion, VI. B. 5. b. ii., at page 286, *infra.*]

i. Conversion into similar property

If property is involuntarily or compulsorily converted *directly* into similar property, the basis of the newly acquired similar property is the same as the converted property. [IRC § 1033(b), first sentence; the remaining language in that sentence addresses situations which might have arisen prior to 1951.]

> ***Example:*** Tabitha, whose tractor was involuntarily converted and replaced in a previous Example, at page 221, *supra,* had an adjusted basis in the converted tractor of $12,000. The adjusted basis of her replacement tractor is also $12,000.

ii. Conversion into money or dissimilar property

If gain realized upon the involuntary conversion of property is not recognized because similar property is *purchased* within the prescribed time period and the taxpayer elects to have the nonrecognition rule apply, then the basis of the similar property is its cost, decreased by the amount of gain not recognized on the conversion. [IRC § 1033(b), last sentence.] If more than one item of replacement property is purchased, the basis determined under this rule is allocated to the purchased properties in proportion to their respective costs.

> ***Example:*** Xaviera's barn was destroyed in January and she received $220,000 in insurance proceeds; the adjusted basis of the barn was $100,000. She spent $200,000 to replace the barn during that year, and she elected to have the provisions of IRC § 1033 apply. Xaviera has a realized gain of $120,000 ($220,000 – $100,000) on the conversion, but only $20,000 of recognized gain. The basis of her new barn is $100,000 ($200,000 cost – $100,000 gain not recognized). If the replacement of the converted barn had been made by the purchase of two smaller barns which were both similar property, and which cost $80,000 and

$120,000, respectively, then the basis of the two barns
would be $40,000 and $60,000, respectively (the total basis
of the replacement property, $100,000, is allocated to the
two barns in proportion to their respective costs). [Reg.
§ 1.1033(b)–1(b).]

3. SALE OF PRINCIPAL RESIDENCE

If a taxpayer sells or exchanges his principal residence, a realized gain
(but not a loss) will not be recognized to the extent the proceeds of the sale
are invested in property used as a new principal residence within certain time
limits. [IRC § 1034.] In addition, certain taxpayers, age 55 or older, may be
eligible to elect to exclude from gross income up to $125,000 of gain which
would otherwise be recognized upon the sale or exchange of their principal
residence. [IRC § 121.]

a. Rollover of gain on sale of principal residence

If a taxpayer sells or exchanges property which has been used by him
as his principal residence, and he purchases (or constructs or acquires in
an exchange) a new residence and actually uses it as his principal
residence within certain time limits, then gain (if any) realized on the
disposition of the old residence is recognized only to the extent the
adjusted sales price of the old residence exceeds the cost of purchasing the
new residence. The pertinent time period begins 2 years before the date
the old residence is sold, and ends 2 years after that date. [IRC
§ 1034(a).] This nonrecognition rule does not apply, however, if within 2
years prior to selling a principal residence, the taxpayer sold another
principal residence and the nonrecognition rule of IRC § 1034 applied to
the gain from that earlier sale; however, this limitation does not apply if
the second sale is connected with the taxpayer's commencing work at a
new place and the conditions of IRC § 217 (relating to the deduction for
moving expenses) are satisfied. [IRC § 1034(d); see discussion, III. B. 9. b.,
at page 152, *supra.*]

Example: Yul owned a condominium apartment which was his principal
residence. In January of Year One, he decided to sell the
condominium and move his principal residence to a houseboat,
which he bought that month. The market for selling
condominiums was sluggish at that time so he rented it, on a
month-to-month basis, after he moved into his houseboat
although he continued his efforts to sell the condo. Finally, in
December of Year Two, he sold the condo at a gain, for an
adjusted sales price which was less than his cost of purchasing
the houseboat. The gain which Yul realized from the sale of
the condo is not recognized.

i.   Principal residence

Both the old residence and the new residence must be actually used by the taxpayer as his principal residence. If a taxpayer has more than one residence, only the *principal* residence will qualify. Determination of whether property is used by a taxpayer as his principal residence ultimately depends on all surrounding facts and circumstances, including the good faith of the taxpayer. The mere fact that property is rented, either prior to the sale of the old residence or prior to occupancy of the new residence, is not determinative that the property is not used as the taxpayer's principal residence. [Reg. § 1.1034–1(c)(3)(i).]

Example: George owned a house in Maine which he used as his principal residence. In November, 1979, he was elected Vice President of the United States, and in January, 1980, he took office and moved with his family to quarters provided to him in Washington, DC. In 1981, George sold his house in Maine at a gain of $600,000, and within 2 years, he purchased a house in Texas. Because George's principal residence was in Washington, DC, the gain from the sale of the Maine house must be recognized.

ii. Adjusted sales price

The adjusted sales price of an old residence is the amount realized from its sale or exchange, reduced by certain expenses for work performed in order to assist in its sale (fixing-up expenses). [IRC § 1034(b).] Fixing-up expenses include expenditures to repair or maintain the property, such as painting or minor repair work, but do not include expenditures properly chargeable to capital, such as replacing the roof. The expenditures must not be otherwise allowable as deductions, or taken into account in computing the amount realized from the sale of the old residence. In addition, the work must be performed within the 90 day period ending on the date the contract to sell the old residence is entered into, and must be paid no later than the 30th day after the date the old residence is sold. [See Reg. § 1.1034–1(b)(6).]

iii. Cost of purchasing new residence

The cost of purchasing a new principal residence includes the total of all amounts attributable to its acquisition, construction, and improvements which constitute capital expenditures, made during the 4 year period beginning 2 years prior to the sale of the old residence and ending 2 years after that date. [IRC § 1034(c)(2); Reg. § 1.1034–1(b)(7).]

Example: On January 1 of Year One, Zsa Zsa bought an undeveloped residential lot at Malibu for $300,000, and on July 1 of Year One, she began construction of a new house which she intends to use as her new principal residence upon its completion. Zsa Zsa owned another house which she was using as her principal residence and which has an adjusted basis to her of $800,000. During Year Two the following events occurred: on January 10 she had the interior and the exterior of the old house painted for which she was billed $10,000; on March 1, she entered into a contract to sell the house; on May 5 the closing occurred and the house was sold for $1,500,000 in cash; and on June 1 she paid the painter. By the date the old house was sold, construction of the new house had been completed enough so that Zsa Zsa was able to move in, although much work remained to be done. By May 5 of Year Four, the new house was still not completed, but construction costs totaled $1 million (plus the $300,000 cost of the lot). Zsa Zsa had a realized gain on the sale of her old residence of $700,000 ($1,500,000 – $800,000). The adjusted sales price of the old residence is $1,490,000 ($1,500,000 – $10,000), and the cost of the new residence, as of the date two years after the sale of the old residence, is $1,300,000. Zsa Zsa, therefore, must recognize a gain of $190,000 from the sale of the old residence. She is allowed nonrecognition on $510,000 of her realized gain.

iv.   Basis of new residence

  If the acquisition of a new principal residence results in the nonrecognition of gain with respect to the disposition of an old principal residence, then, at any time the basis of the new residence is determined, an adjustment to its basis must be made by reducing its basis by the amount of gain which was not recognized upon the disposition of the old residence. [IRC § 1034(e).] In addition, the holding period of the old residence, with respect to which gain was not recognized, is added or "tacked" on to the holding period of the new residence. [IRC § 1223(7); see discussion, VI. B. 5. b. v., at page 287, *infra*.]

Example: Zsa Zsa, from the previous Example, finally completes the construction of her new principal residence by January of Year Five, at a total cost of $1,700,000 (plus $300,000 for the lot). The total basis of her new residence with lot in January of Year Five is $1,490,000 ($2,000,000 cost basis of the new residence – $510,000 gain not recognized on the sale of the old residence).

b. One-time exclusion of gain from sale of principal residence by individual who has attained age 55

If a taxpayer or his spouse has attained age 55, he may elect to exclude from gross income the gain from the sale or exchange of his principal residence if the property has been used as the principal residence of the taxpayer or his spouse for periods totaling at least 3 years during the 5 year period ending on the date of the disposition. [IRC § 121(a), (d).] The maximum amount of gain which may be excluded is $125,000 ($62,500 if the taxpayer is married and files a separate return), and if an election is made by a taxpayer or by his spouse, no further election may be made. [IRC § 121(b).] If the amount of realized gain upon the disposition of an old residence exceeds $125,000, the provisions of IRC § 1034 may apply to provide nonrecognition, in which case, the amount realized on the old residence is reduced by the amount excluded under IRC § 121. [IRC § 121(d)(7).]

> *Example:* Adrian, age 50, and his wife Bernice, age 56, own a house which has been their principal residence for the past 20 years, and its adjusted basis is $20,000. On March 10 they sell the house for $200,000, and two weeks later, they purchase a condominium apartment, which will be their new principal residence, for $80,000. Adrian and Bernice have a realized gain of $180,000 from the sale of the old residence, and they have never previously used the IRC § 121 exclusion. If they elect to have the provisions of IRC § 121 apply, $125,000 of that gain is excluded from their gross income. In addition, because they have satisfied the requirements of IRC § 1034, the remaining $55,000 of the gain will not be recognized (the adjusted sales price of the old residence, $75,000 ($200,000 less the $125,000 exclusion amount), does not exceed the cost of the new residence, $80,000).

4. TRANSFER OF PROPERTY BETWEEN SPOUSES OR INCIDENT TO DIVORCE

No gain or loss is recognized on the transfer of property from one spouse to the other spouse, *or* to a former spouse if the transfer is incident to their divorce. [IRC § 1041(a); see discussion, V. C. 3., at page 265, *infra.*]

5. MISCELLANEOUS

There are a number of other nonrecognition provisions which apply in a variety of factual settings, some of which are beyond the scope of this outline and some of which are simply of relatively less importance than the provisions discussed above. There are special nonrecognition rules, for example, which apply when a shareholder in a corporation transfers property to the corporation [IRC § 351], or when a partner transfers property to his partnership [IRC § 721]. Further examples of special nonrecognition rules include: (1) certain exchanges of insurance policies [IRC § 1035]; (2) certain exchanges of stock in a corporation for stock in the same corporation [IRC § 1036]; (3) certain exchanges of U.S. obligations [IRC § 1037]; (4) certain repossessions of real property [IRC § 1038]; and (5) certain sales of low-income housing projects when the proceeds are reinvested in another such project [IRC § 1039].

Each of these nonrecognition situations also provides for the adjusted basis of the new or replacement property to be the same as the old property, adjusted by the amount of any gain or loss that is recognized in the transaction; in this manner, taxation of the gain (or loss) that goes unrecognized is merely postponed, not forgiven.

E. UNSTATED INTEREST

There are special rules which affect the timing and the character of income in certain situations when money is borrowed under terms which do not nominally call for payment of a reasonable rate of interest while the loan is outstanding or where property is sold under terms calling for payments to be made over an extended period of time.

1. LOANS WITH BELOW–MARKET INTEREST RATES

Loans made under terms which do not provide for the payment of a reasonable rate of interest while they are outstanding are subject to rules requiring both the borrower and the lender to be treated for tax purposes as if interest at a reasonable rate has been paid. [IRC § 7872.] These rules do not apply, however, to loans to which IRC §§ 483 or 1274 apply. [IRC § 7872(f)(8); see discussion, IV. E. 2. and 3., at pages 234 and 238, *infra.*] The borrower will be considered as receiving a gift, additional compensation income, a dividend or other income, depending on the surrounding facts and circumstances, in the amount of the interest which is imputed under these rules. In addition, in some situations the borrower is entitled to a deduction for the amount of foregone interest which he is deemed to have retransferred to the lender. [IRC § 163; see discussion of limitations on interest deduction, III. B. 2. c., at page 134, *supra.*] Correspondingly, the lender will be considered as having made a gift (potentially subject to the gift tax) or as having paid additional compensation, or a dividend or other income to the borrower and she will also have interest income in the amount of the foregone interest she is deemed to receive.

The determination of whether a reasonable rate of interest is called for is made with reference to the rate of interest the U.S. Treasury would have to pay to borrow money (the "applicable Federal rate"). [IRC § 7872(f)(2).] If a loan calls for no interest or interest at a rate less than the applicable Federal rate, it is a "below-market loan," and the extent to which the applicable Federal rate exceeds the interest which is called for under the terms of the loan is "foregone interest." [IRC § 7872(e)(1) and (2).]

Loans which are subject to these rules may be classified either as gift loans or nongift loans, and the rules which govern the tax consequences are further determined by whether the loan is a demand loan (payable in full at any time on the demand of the lender) or a term loan (payable over some set time period). [IRC § 7872(f)(5) and (6).]

a.   Gift loans

A gift loan is a below-market loan made in circumstances where the foregoing of the interest is in the nature of a gift, such as a loan between members of a family. [IRC § 7872(f)(3).] The amount of foregone interest is characterized as a gift from the lender to the borrower, potentially subject to the gift tax. [IRC § 7872(b)(1) and (d)(2).] In addition, foregone interest is considered to be periodically retransferred from the borrower to the lender, included in the gross income of the lender and possibly generating a deduction for the borrower. [IRC § 7872(a)(2).] The tax consequences to the parties are further determined by whether the gift loan is a term loan or a demand loan.

i.   Term gift loans

If a below-market gift loan is made for a specified period of time, the amount of foregone interest is the present value, using a discount rate equal to the applicable Federal rate, of all payments which the borrower is required to make, regardless of whether the payments are for interest or for repayment of the principal amount of the loan. The lender is deemed to make (and the borrower, to receive) a gift equal to the total amount of the foregone interest on the day the loan is made. [IRC § 7872(b)(1) and (d)(2).] In addition, the borrower is deemed to pay (and the lender, to receive) payments of foregone interest attributable to each calendar year the loan is outstanding, on the last day of each calendar year. [IRC § 7872(a)(2).] Different computations must be made for determining the amount of foregone interest which is a gift at the time the loan is made, and the amount of foregone interest which is deemed to be paid by the borrower to the lender at the end of each calendar year the loan is outstanding.

Example: Acting out of a spirit of detached and disinterested generosity, Celeste makes an interest-free loan of $100,000 to her son, Dennis, on January 1 of Year One, when the applicable Federal rate of interest is 14%. Dennis agrees to repay the $100,000 3 years later. The present value of $100,000 to be paid 3 years later, at a discount rate of 14%, compounded semiannually, is approximately $66,630. The difference between that present value and the principal amount of the loan, or $33,370 ($100,000 – $66,630), is considered to be a gift from Celeste to Dennis, because that is the amount which Celeste would

presumably have been willing to give Dennis to enable
him to borrow $100,000 from someone else. On December
31 of Year One, Dennis is deemed to pay Celeste $14,490
of interest [14%, compounded semiannually, on the
outstanding loan of $100,000; this is computed by adding
7% of $100,000 ($7,000) for the first half of the year plus
7% of $107,000 for the second half of the year ($7,490) for
a total of $14,490]; Celeste must include that amount in
her gross income for Year One and Dennis is possibly
entitled to a deduction of the same amount. The same
computation of imputed interest payments is made for
December 31 of Year Two and Year Three.

ii.   **Demand gift loans**
      If a gift loan is a demand loan, which means that the borrower
may be required to repay the loan at any time, it is impossible to
compute an amount of foregone interest at the time the loan is made.
Instead, foregone interest is computed on December 31 of each year
the loan is outstanding; a gift in the amount of the foregone interest
is deemed to be made by the lender to the borrower on that date,
and the interest is deemed to be immediately retransferred by the
borrower to the lender as interest. [IRC § 7872(a).]

   Example: Consider the same facts discussed in the preceding
                Example, except the loan Celeste makes to Dennis is a
                demand loan. No gift of foregone interest is imputed on
                the date the loan is made. On December 31 of Year
                One, Celeste is deemed to make a gift of foregone interest
                to Dennis of $14,490 (14% on $100,000, compounded
                semiannually). In addition, Dennis is deemed to make a
                payment of $14,490 in interest to Celeste on that date;
                Celeste must include $14,490 in her gross income for Year
                One and Dennis possibly may take an itemized deduction
                of $14,490. Similar computations are made on December
                31 of each year the loan is outstanding.

iii. **Exceptions**
      The interest imputation rules do not apply to gift loans on any
day the total amount of outstanding loans between the lender and the
borrower does not exceed $10,000, unless the loan proceeds are used
to acquire income producing assets. [IRC § 7872(c)(2).] In addition, if
a gift loan of less than $100,000 is made directly between individuals,
the amount of interest which the borrower is deemed to retransfer to
the lender may not exceed the borrower's net income from
investments for the taxable year; if the borrower's net income from
investments for the taxable year does not exceed $1,000, no interest

payments are imputed. [IRC §§ 7872(d)(1) and 163(d)(3).] This last limitation does not apply if one of the principal purposes for arranging the below market interest was the avoidance of any Federal tax. [IRC § 7872(d)(1)(B).]

b. Nongift loans

Some below-market loans which are not gift loans are also subject to the imputation of interest rules, and the characterization of the amount of foregone interest is determined by the relationship between the lender and the borrower. [IRC § 7872(c)(1).] If the borrower is an employee of the lender, or if the borrower is an independent contractor who provides services to the lender, the amount of foregone interest is compensation; the loan is a "compensation-related loan." [IRC § 7872(c)(1)(B).] If the lender is a corporation and the borrower is one of its shareholders, the amount of foregone interest is generally treated as a dividend; the loan is a "corporation-shareholder loan." [IRC § 7872(c)(1)(C).] The foregone interest rules also apply to any below-market loan if one of the principal purposes of the interest arrangements is to avoid any Federal tax, or if the interest arrangements have a significant effect on any Federal tax liability of either the lender or the borrower. [IRC § 7872(c)(1)(D) and (E).]

Foregone interest with respect to a below-market nongift loan is considered to be periodically retransferred from the borrower to the lender, included in the gross income of the lender and likely generating a deduction for the borrower. [IRC §§ 7872(b)(2) and 1272.] The tax consequences to the parties are further determined by whether the nongift loan is a term loan or a demand loan.

i.   Term nongift loans

If a nongift below-market loan is a term loan, the amount of foregone interest is deemed to be transferred (as compensation or as a dividend, depending on the surrounding facts and circumstances) on the date the loan is made. [IRC § 7872(b)(1).] Interest is deemed to be repaid annually by the borrower to the lender, however, under the rules applicable to Original Issue Discount on an annual basis. [IRC §§ 7872(b)(2) and 1272; see discussion, IV. E. 2. b., at page 238, *infra.*]

Example: Edsel makes an interest-free loan of $100,000 to his employee, Fiona, on January 1 of Year One, when the applicable Federal rate of interest is 14%. Fiona agrees to repay the $100,000 3 years later. The present value of $100,000 to be paid 3 years later, at a discount rate of 14%, compounded semiannually, is approximately $66,630. The difference between that present value and the principal amount of the loan, or $33,370 ($100,000 – $66,630), is considered to be compensation paid by Edsel to Fiona. Fiona would have $33,370 of compensation income for Year One, and Edsel would be entitled to deduct a like amount if the total compensation paid to Fiona for Year One is not unreasonable. [IRC § 162(a)(1); see discussion, III. A. 1. e. i., at page 76, *supra.*] In addition, $33,370 is treated as original issue discount, which will be accrued in daily portions and the sum of the portions which accrue during each year will be treated as interest paid by Fiona to Edsel, includible in Edsel's gross income and possibly deductible by Fiona.

ii. Demand nongift loans

The imputed interest rules for below-market nongift demand loans are the same as for below-market gift demand loans. The amount of the foregone interest is computed, and is deemed to be transferred to the borrower and immediately retransferred to the lender on the last day of each calendar year the loan is outstanding. [IRC § 7872(a).]

Example: G. Corporation makes an interest-free demand loan of $100,000 to Grady, one of its shareholders, on January 1 when the applicable Federal rate of interest is 14%. If G. Corporation had made a distribution of cash or property to Grady on that date, it would have been treated as a dividend. No payment of a dividend with reference to foregone interest is imputed on the date the loan is made; however, on December 31 of that year, G. Corporation is deemed to pay Grady a dividend of $14,490 (14% on $100,000, compounded semiannually). Grady must include the amount of the dividend in his gross income, but the G. Corporation is not entitled to a deduction for the payment of the dividend. In addition, Grady is deemed to make a payment of $14,490 in interest to G. Corporation on that date; G. Corporation must include $14,490 of interest in its gross income. Grady may possibly take a deduction of $14,490.

iii. Exception

The interest imputation rules do not apply to nongift loans which are compensation-related loans or corporation-shareholder loans on any day the total amount of outstanding loans between the lender and the borrower does not exceed $10,000. [IRC § 7872(c)(3).]

2. ORIGINAL ISSUE DISCOUNT

The Original Issue Discount rules encompass both loans and deferred payments for the sale or exchange of property, and they may affect the timing as well as the character of income in transactions which are within their scope. [IRC §§ 1271–1288.] The basic thrust of these rules is to supply tax treatment which is in accordance with economic reality, recognizing that when a taxpayer buys property, agreeing to pay all or a portion of the purchase price at some point in the future, he has effectively borrowed money from the seller. When money is borrowed, a reasonable rate of interest must be paid for the use of the borrowed funds, the interest should be paid periodically over the period of time the loan is outstanding and, to the extent payments of interest are not actually made, subsequent interest should be computed on the now larger total debt (this is referred to as "compounded interest"). These same concepts apply to transactions involving direct loans as well as to sales or exchanges of property under a deferred payment plan.

a. Deferred payments for property

i. Debt instruments *without* adequate stated interest

A portion of the Original Issue Discount rules potentially apply to debt instruments given in consideration for the sale or exchange of property. [IRC § 1274.] These rules will not apply if there is "adequate stated interest" with respect to a debt instrument, a determination which is made by comparing the interest which the debt instrument calls for with the rate of interest the U.S. Treasury would have to pay to borrow money, the "applicable Federal rate". [IRC § 1274(c)(2), (d).] There is adequate stated interest if the rate which is called for is at least equal to the applicable Federal rate. If the stated interest is not adequate, then a portion of the selling price is recharacterized as interest, imputed at a rate equal to the applicable Federal rate, less any amount of interest which is called for in the instrument. Interest which is imputed under these rules is computed on a daily basis, compounded semiannually, and is included in the gross income of the property seller as interest (or possibly deducted by the property purchaser) in the taxable year in which the imputed interest accrues. [IRC §§ 1272(a)(1), (3); 1274(b)(2), (d)(1).]

> *Example:* Conrad sells Dolly (they are both cash method taxpayers) a parcel of unimproved business real estate for $10 million on January 1 of the current year. Dolly pays nothing down, but she gives Conrad a note, agreeing to make annual payments, on December 31 each year, of interest at a rate of 8% on the note, or $800,000 each year, and to pay the $10 million on December 31 three years later. The applicable Federal rate of interest at this time on a short-term note such as this is 10%. Because the stated rate of interest is less than the applicable Federal rate, interest must be imputed at that 10% rate. The statute requires that the selling price of the property be recomputed by determining the present values of the payments which are called for, discounted at the 10% rate

and compounded semiannually. The present value, determined as of the date of sale, of the $800,000 payment which is to be made one year later is approximately $727,200; the present value of the $800,000 payment to be made two years later is approximately $660,800; and the present value of the $10,800,000 ($10 million principal plus $800,000 interest) payment to be made three years later is approximately $8,110,800. The purchase price of the property, therefore, is recomputed to be $9,498,800 ($727,200 + $660,800 + $8,110,800), rather than $10 million, and Dolly's cost basis for the property is also $9,498,800.

One year's interest at a rate of 10%, compounded semiannually, on the adjusted purchase price of the property of $9,498,800 is $973,627. Even though Dolly only makes an actual payment of $800,000 to Conrad at the end of the first year, she will be deemed to pay an additional $173,627 of interest during that year under these rules (and Conrad will correspondingly be required to include an additional $173,627 of interest income, even though he is a cash method taxpayer). In the second year, interest at a rate of 10%, compounded semiannually, is computed with reference to the adjusted purchase price of the property, increased by the $173,627 which was imputed in the first year (it is as if Conrad received the imputed amount and immediately re-lent the same amount to Dolly, thereby increasing her debt to him); the amount of interest imputed in the second year, therefore, is $191,424 ($991,424 – $800,000, the amount actually paid in the second year). Similarly, in the third year, the amount of interest imputed is $211,045 ($1,011,045 – $800,000).

ii.   Debt instruments *with* adequate stated interest

If a debt instrument which is issued for the purchase of property does provide for an adequate *amount* of stated interest, but does not provide for the *payment* of the interest at appropriate intervals, the Original Issue Discount rules do not impute any additional interest, but they do force both the buyer and the seller to account for the amounts of interest annually under the accrual method. [IRC § 1272(a)(1), (3).] If a debt instrument provides for an adequate amount of stated interest, and payments of interest are actually paid annually, the Original Issue Discount rules will not affect the tax treatment of the transaction.

Example: Return to the facts of the preceding Example, but assume that the contract for sale provides for interest of 14.4%, a rate in excess of adequate stated interest; however, no payments are to be made until the end of the three year period. Because there is adequate stated interest, the selling price of the property is not recomputed. Even though no payments are actually made, interest payments of $1,491,840 (14.4% on $10 million, compounded semiannually) are deemed to be made during the first year; Conrad must include $1,491,840 of interest income during the first year and Dolly may possibly take a deduction for the same amount. During Year Two, the principal amount of the obligation is increased by the $1,491,840 which was accrued during the first year (it is as if Conrad received the accrued amount and immediately re-lent the same amount to Dolly, thereby increasing her debt to him); the amount of interest accrued in the second year is $1,714,399 (14.4% on $11,491,840, compounded semiannually). Finally, in the third year, $1,970,159 [14.4% on $13,206,238 ($11,491,840 + $1,714,399), compounded semiannually] of interest is accrued.

iii. Exceptions

The Original Issue Discount rules do not apply to debt instruments issued for the purchase of property in the following situations: (1) if the property is a farm and the sales price does not exceed $1 million; (2) if the property is the seller's principal residence; (3) if the selling price of the property does not exceed $250,000; (4) if the debt instrument is publicly traded (such as a corporate bond); (5) certain sales of patents; and (6) certain sales of land between related persons. [IRC § 1274(c)(3).]

Two special rules may apply in certain situations which are otherwise within the scope of the Original Discount Rules. If a debt instrument is given in consideration for the sale of property with a stated principal amount of $2,800,000 or less, the applicable Federal rate of interest is effectively capped at 9%, compounded semiannually. [IRC § 1274A(a).] Therefore, the rules of IRC § 1274 will not apply to such a sale if stated interest is at least 9% compounded semiannually. In addition, taxpayers may elect to use the cash method, in order to alter the timing rules of IRC § 1274, if the stated principal amount does not exceed $2 million and other requirements are met. [IRC § 1274A(c).]

b.   Loans

A portion of the Original Issue Discount rules may apply to debt instruments issued for money (i.e., loans) in situations where the borrowed amount is less than the amount to be repaid, such as when a corporation sells, for $900, a bond which will pay $1,000 when it matures several years later.   This situation differs from loans with below-market interest covered by IRC § 7872 where the amount borrowed is the amount to be repaid, but insufficient interest is called for.   [See discussion, IV. E. 1., at page 230, *supra.*]

The "original issue discount" with respect to a debt instrument issued for money is essentially the excess of the amount which is required to be paid at the maturity of the debt instrument over the price for which it was issued.   [IRC § 1273(a)(1).]   The effect is to recharacterize a portion of the amount which is to be paid upon the maturity of the debt instrument (ostensibly, a repayment of principal) as interest.   In addition, the amount of the original issue discount must be accrued on a daily basis, included in the gross income of the lender (and possibly deducted by the borrower) in an amount equal to the sum of the daily portions for each day the loan is outstanding during the year.   [IRC §§ 163(e), 1272(a)(1) and (3).]   Exceptions from these rules are available for tax-exempt obligations, U.S. savings bonds, debt instruments with a fixed maturity date of 1 year or less, and certain loans between individuals.   [IRC § 1272(a)(2).]

Example: H Corporation borrows money from Hilda by selling her a bond on January 1 of Year One.   The bond provides that H Corporation will pay Hilda $10,000 four years later, but it does not call for the payment of any interest.   Hilda pays $6,500 for the bond.   The original issue discount with respect to the bond is $3,500.   The original issue discount will be accrued in daily portions, and the sum of the portions which accrue during Year One will be included in her gross income, and will be deductible by H Corporation in Year One.

3.   INTEREST ON CERTAIN DEFERRED PAYMENTS

If a debt instrument is given in consideration for the transfer of property and the Original Issue Discount rules do not apply because of one of the exceptions under IRC § 1274(c), interest may be imputed under IRC § 483.   If property is sold under terms calling for the payment of all or a portion of the purchase price more than 1 year after the date of the sale, and providing for inadequate interest, then a portion of the deferred payments will be treated as interest, included in gross income as interest to the seller, and possibly deductible as interest by the buyer.   [IRC § 483.]   The amount of imputed interest is determined in the same manner it is computed under the Original Issue Discount rules, with reference to the rate of interest the U.S. Treasury would have to pay to borrow funds.   Unlike the Original Issue Discount rules, however, if interest is required to be imputed, IRC § 483 does not affect the timing of the inclusion (or deduction) of the imputed interest; instead, the accounting method which the taxpayer uses will control. Exceptions to IRC § 483 include sales of the property for $3,000 or less, certain sales of patents and situations where the rules governing Original Issue Discount apply. [IRC § 483(d).] Interest is imputed at a maximum rate of 6%, compounded semiannually, on certain transfers of land between related parties. [IRC § 483(e).] In addition, the maximum discount rate is 9%, compounded semiannually, in the case of debt instruments with a stated principal amount of $2,800,000 or less which are given in consideration for the sale of property other than most items of new tangible personal property used in a trade or business or held for the production of income. [IRC § 1274A(a) and (b).]

Example: Assume that Conrad sells Dolly a new machine for use in her business, rather than a parcel of unimproved real estate, and the selling price is $100,000, rather than $10 million; otherwise, the terms of the sale are the same as in the original Example. The Original Issue Discount rules for imputing interest do not apply because the sale involves total payments of less than $250,000. [IRC § 1274(c)(3)(C).] The amounts of interest which must be imputed are the same as in the original Example, reduced by a factor of 100, but, because they are both cash method taxpayers, Conrad will not include the imputed interest amounts in gross income (and Dolly may not take a deduction) until actual payment occurs, at the end of the third year. If the sale had involved real property, rather than the machine, imputed interest would have been computed at a rate of 9%, compounded semiannually. [IRC § 1274A(a).]

F.   SPECIAL RULES

Income derived from annuities and income under certain deferred compensation plans are subject to special rules governing their inclusion in gross income.

1.   ANNUITIES

An annuity is a contractual arrangement under which payments are made periodically to the purchaser of the contract, or to another designated beneficiary, for a term of years or for the life of the beneficiary. Gross income does not include the recovery of capital; therefore, when an annuity contract is purchased, some portion of the payments received in the future should be excluded from gross income. The amount to be excluded is determined by multiplying the payments received within a taxable year by an exclusion ratio. [IRC § 72(b)(1).] The exclusion ratio is a fraction, the numerator being the taxpayer's investment in the contract, and the denominator being the expected return under the contract. The investment in the contract is, generally, the amount of premiums paid for the contract. [IRC

§ 72(c)(1).] The expected return under the contract is determined by multiplying the amount of the periodic payments either by the number of payments called for under the contract or, if the period for making payments is determined with reference to someone's life expectancy, by an appropriate actuarial value provided in the regulations. [IRC § 72(c)(3).] The total amount which may be excluded over a period of years is limited, however, to the amount of the taxpayer's investment in the annuity contract. [IRC § 72(b)(2) and (4).] On the other hand, if the taxpayer dies before receiving payments equaling or exceeding his investment in the annuity contract, a deduction is allowed for the unrecovered amount. [IRC § 72(b)(3) and (4).]

Example: Errol purchased an annuity for $10,000 which provides for payments of $100 per month for the rest of his life at a time when his life expectancy is 10 years. The exclusion ratio is 83.3% ($10,000/$12,000). If 12 monthly payments are received in the current year, for a total of $1,200, the total amount which Errol may exclude from gross income is $1,000 (83.3% of $1,200); the remaining $200 received in the current year must be included in Errol's gross income. If Errol lives longer than 10 years, no amount received after Year Ten under the annuity contract may be excluded from gross income because he has already excluded amounts totaling his investment in the contract. If Errol should die before recovering his investment in the contract, for instance, in January of Year Nine before receiving any payments that Year, he would be entitled to a deduction on his final income tax return for Year Nine of $2,000, the amount of the unrecovered investment in the contract ($10,000 less $8,000 excluded in Year One through Year Eight). [See Reg. § 1.72–4(a)(2) Example.]

2. DEFERRED COMPENSATION

If an employer transfers money or other property to a qualified deferred compensation plan, the employees are not required to include the amounts set aside until they actually begin receiving payments under the plan. [See IRC § 402.]

Special rules apply if an employer compensates an employee by transferring property, such as corporate stock, which is subject to restrictions on its transfer by the employee, or if the property is subject to a substantial risk of forfeiture, such as if the employee quits or is fired. In those circumstances, the excess of the property's fair market value at the time the property becomes transferable (or the risk of forfeiture lapses) over the amount (if any) the employee paid for the property is included in the employee's gross income. [IRC § 83(a).] The employee, however, may elect to include the property's fair market value (less the amount paid for it) at the time of the transfer, rather than waiting until the property becomes transferable (or the risk of forfeiture lapses). [IRC § 83(b).]

REVIEW QUESTIONS

Q# 1: Steven rents his property to Mark, for use in Mark's business, on January 1 of the current year for a three-year lease term. The annual rent is $1,000, but Mark pays Steven $3,000 for all three years at the beginning of the lease term. Both Steven and Mark use the cash method of accounting. How must Steven and Mark treat the $3,000 payment?

Q# 2: What are the results in Question # 1 if both Steven and Mark are accrual method taxpayers?

Q# 3: Claudia, an accrual method taxpayer, purchases an office machine and separately for an additional $1,000 she purchases a 3-year service contract relating to the machine. The service contract provides that the machine will be serviced and repaired at no additional charge annually within the next three years. When may Claudia deduct the cost of the service contract?

Q# 4: Martina (an accrual method taxpayer) is a tennis pro who, in November of Year One, contracts with Chrissie to provide 50 one-hour tennis lessons within the next 12 months; Chrissie pays Martina the total contract price of $2,500 when the contract is signed. Martina gave Chrissie ten lessons in Year One. How much must Martina include in her gross income for Year One?

Q# 5: Amanda owns a clothing store. At the end of last year, the remaining inventory had a cost of $5,000. During the current year, she purchases an additional $20,000 of inventory, and at the end of the year, her closing inventory had a cost of $3,000. Her gross receipts from the sale of inventory during the year is $33,000. What is Amanda's cost-of-goods-sold for the current year, and what is her gross income from the sale of inventory.

Q# 6: In the current year, Pamela sells a parcel of investment land which has an adjusted basis of $1,000. The terms of sale call for her to receive a $2,000 cash payment, and $1,000 payments (plus a reasonable rate of interest) in each of the next eight years. If Pamela does not "elect out" of IRC § 453, how much gain must she recognize in the current year, and the next year when she receives the $1,000 payment?

Q# 7: What result in Question # 6 if Pamela immediately resells her contractual rights to the $8,000 of payments for $7,500 of cash?

Q# 8: What result in Question # 6 if Pamela is a cash method taxpayer, the $8,000 of obligations are worth $7,000 and she elects out of IRC § 453 under IRC § 453(d)? What result when she subsequently receives the eight $1,000 payments?

Q# 9: Dale sells a painting to Paul, his son, in Year One. Dale has a gain on the property and was reporting this gain under the installment method. In

Year Two Paul sells the painting to his friend Jim. Does this sale by Paul have any effect on Dale's tax return for Year Two?

Q# 10: Kim owns a piece of real property she holds for investment. The property cost her $10,000 and has a fair market value of $50,000. Kim exchanges this piece of property for a similar parcel of real estate that has a $50,000 fair market value. What is Kim's recognized gain and basis in the new property on this transaction?

Q# 11: How would the answer to Question # 10 change if the property Kim received was worth only $40,000 and Kim also received stock worth $10,000?

Q# 12: Dan owns a restaurant. Unfortunately for Dan, the state plans to build a highway and his restaurant is in the path of the new road. In Year One, the state condemns Dan's restaurant and pays him $100,000 for it. The restaurant has a basis to Dan of $20,000. Dan purchases another restaurant in Year Two at a cost of $110,000. Does Dan have to recognize any gain on the money received for his restaurant? What is Dan's basis in the new restaurant?

Q# 13: How would the answer to Question # 12 change if Dan spent only $70,000 on a new restaurant?

Q# 14: Melissa sells her principal residence in Year One for $200,000. Melissa's basis in the house is $35,000. In Year Two Melissa purchases a new residence for $300,000. Does Melissa recognize any gain on the sale of her residence? What is Melissa's basis in the new residence?

Q# 15: How would the answer to Question # 14 change if Melissa was 60 years old and had lived in the old residence for the past 9 years and she elects to use IRC § 121?

Q# 16: In the current year when the applicable Federal rate of interest is 10% Employer makes a $200,000 interest free demand loan to Employee. What are the consequences to both parties?

V

WHO IS THE PROPER TAXPAYER?

Analysis

The U.S. income tax is imposed annually and is computed by multiplying a taxpayer's taxable income for the taxable year by an applicable rate; the rate at which the tax is imposed becomes higher as the amount of the tax base (taxable income) increases. [See IRC § 1.] For taxable years beginning in 1987, there are 5 rate brackets, ranging from 11% to 38.5%. [IRC § 1(h).] There are only 2 rate brackets, 15% and 28%, for taxable years beginning after 1987. [IRC § 1(a)–(d).] However, some high income taxpayers are subject to a 5% surtax which has the effect of phasing-out both the amount of taxable income taxed at the 15% rate and the tax benefit of personal exemptions, leaving such a taxpayer effectively taxed at a flat rate of 28% without the benefit of exemption deductions. [IRC § 1(g); see discussion at VII. D. 2., at page 311, *infra*.] The rate of tax imposed on any one dollar of taxable income, therefore, is determined not only by *when* the item is included in gross income (and by when related deductions may be taken), but also by *who* the proper taxpayer is with respect to the item. Thus, $100 of income derived by an unmarried individual (not a surviving spouse or a head of household) who already has more than $54,000 of taxable income is taxed at a rate of 38.5%, whereas if the taxpayer is a married individual filing a joint return with taxable income of $2,900, an additional $100 of income is taxed at a rate of only 11%. [IRC § 1(h)(2)(A) and (C).] In 1988, the next dollar of taxable income for the unmarried individual described in the preceding sentence is taxed at a rate of 28% while the married taxpayer filing a joint return is taxed at 15% on the next dollar of taxable income. [IRC § 1(a) and (c).]

Individual persons, and separate entities such as corporations, are generally treated as separate taxpayers. Special treatment is made for the husband-wife marital unit, however, and some entities, such as partnerships and sometimes estates and trusts, are not themselves subject to the income tax, but are required to furnish the I.R.S. with information concerning their activities. Generally, income is taxed to the taxpayer who earns the income or to the taxpayer who owns property which produces income, and the right to receive income (and the liability to pay tax on such income) may not be assigned to another taxpayer. Although each individual is usually treated as an independent taxpayer, reporting their own income and taking their own deductions in computing taxable income, and calculating income tax liability with the rates applicable to them, the tax imposed on unearned income of a minor child may be taxed at the rates applicable to the child's parent. [IRC § 1(i); see discussion at VII. D. 3., at page 312, *infra*.] Because of this provision, and the lowering of the maximum rates of tax, there is less incentive than in years past for taxpayers to attempt to shift income from one taxpayer to another. In addition, in some situations deviations from the general rule may be effected by the use of entities such as partnerships, corporations or trusts. In addition, income earned by one taxpayer may be effectively taxed in the hands of another taxpayer if it is paid by the first taxpayer to the second as alimony. [See IRC §§ 71 and 215.]

A. FAMILIES

Each individual is subject to tax with respect to income to which she has a right, and local law is generally pertinent in determining whether a taxpayer has a right to a particular item of income. Under community property laws, for instance, each spouse generally has a vested property right in community property and in income of the community, including wages or salaries of either spouse. Each spouse, therefore, is subject to income tax on one half of community income. [*Poe v. Seaborn*, 282 U.S. 101, 51 S.Ct. 58 (1930); see IRC § 66 for deviations from community property laws in special situations.]

Although each individual is treated as a separate, independent taxpayer, provision is made for a married individual and his spouse to file a joint return. [IRC § 6013; see IRC § 1(a).] If a joint return is filed, the items of gross income and deductions of both spouses are reported on the same return and each spouse must sign the return; even though there is only one income tax return, there are still *two* taxpayers. [See discussion, VII. C. 3., at page 309, *infra.*]

Local law is not always determinative of who the proper taxpayer is with respect to an item of income. The local law of some jurisdictions provides that if a minor child performs services, income which she earns is deemed to be the income of her parents. Under the Code, however, amounts received in respect of the services of a minor child are included in her gross income, not in the gross income of her parents, even though the amount is paid to the parents rather than to the child. [IRC § 73(a).] Unearned income of a child under the age of 14 may be taxed, however, at the rate it would be taxed if the income were taxable to the child's parents. [IRC § 1(i); see discussion at VII. D. 3., at page 312, *infra.*]

B. ASSIGNMENT OF INCOME

Income is generally taxed to the taxpayer who earns it, or to the taxpayer who owns property which produces income. The liability to pay tax on an item of income generally may not be avoided merely by assigning the right to the item of income to another taxpayer either directly or through an entity. In some situations, however, the determination of who is the proper taxpayer may be affected by the use of entities such as partnerships, corporations, or trusts or by the sale of a right to receive income in the future.

1. INCOME FROM SERVICES

Income in the nature of compensation for the performance of services is generally included in the gross income of the person who performs the services. However, as seen above, community property earnings of a spouse are treated as owned one half by each spouse and are taxed accordingly. The general rule applies even though the person performing services: (1) has made a contractual agreement with another person providing that the two of them will share equally income earned by either one of them [*Lucas v. Earl,* 281 U.S. 111, 50 S.Ct. 241 (1930)]; or (2) has arranged for the income payer to transfer the amount directly to someone else [see *Comm'r v. Giannini,* 129 F.2d 638 (9th Cir.1942)]. A taxpayer, however, may avoid being taxed on income which she would otherwise earn from the performance of services if she intends to perform the services gratuitously.

Examples: A.P. served as the President of a bank under a contract which provided that he would be paid 5% of the net profits of the bank each year. The bank was very successful, and in July of 1927, A.P. learned that his compensation under the contract had already exceeded $445,000 for that calendar year, so he informed the directors of the bank that he would not accept any further compensation for 1927 and he suggested that the bank do something worthwhile with the money. Because A.P. unqualifiedly refused to accept any further compensation after July, 1927, and because he did not direct the bank as to how to dispose of the amount he would otherwise have been paid after that date, he was not required to include in his gross income the amount of foregone compensation. [*Comm'r v. Giannini*, 129 F.2d 638 (9th Cir.1942)].

Alastair served as the personal representative of his deceased wife's estate under the terms of her will. Under state law, the personal representative of an estate is entitled to be paid compensation in a reasonable amount. Shortly after first commencing the duties of personal representative, Alastair decided to waive his right to receive the statutorily authorized compensation; he did not claim any compensation in any of the accountings he filed with the probate court, and he did not otherwise take any action inconsistent with his intention to perform the services gratuitously. Alastair is not required to include in his gross income the compensation to which he is otherwise entitled, even though the effect of his action is to increase the amounts which the beneficiaries of the estate (including Alastair himself) will receive under the will. [Rev.Rul. 66–167, 1966–1 C.B. 20.]

If a taxpayer performs services as an employee or as an agent, income derived therefrom is included in the gross income of the employer or principal, not the gross income of the employee/agent. In this manner, it may be possible for a taxpayer to perform services as an employee of a corporation which, in turn, is owned by the taxpayer and other members of the taxpayer's family with the effect of splitting the income among the family members. [See discussion, V. B. 4. c., at page 255, *infra*.]

Examples: Bonita is a member of the faculty of a law school clinical program. As part of her duties, she is appointed to represent indigent defendants in criminal cases, supervising third-year law students while doing so, and she thereby becomes entitled to court-awarded attorney's fees. When she receives a check from the court, she endorses it over to the law school because representation of the indigent clients is part of her duties as a faculty member for which she is compensated by an annual salary from the law school. Bonita is representing the indigent clients, while supervising law students, as an agent of the law school; she collects court-awarded attorney's fees as an agent of the law school; the attorney's fees are not included in her gross income. [Rev.Rul. 74–581, 1974–2 C.B. 25.]

Cassius is a member of a religious order and, as a condition of membership, he takes a vow of poverty by which all claims to earnings are renounced and the earnings belong to the order. Cassius is a licensed attorney and, on the instructions of the order, he obtains employment with a law firm; the law firm makes payments of Cassius' salary directly to the order. The legal services which Cassius performs for clients of the law firm are performed as an employee or agent of the law firm, not as an agent of the religious order; the performance of legal services is not the performance of the type of services ordinarily required to be performed by members of the religious order. Cassius has assigned his salary to the order and he must include in his gross income the amount of compensation paid by the law firm. [Rev. Rul. 77–290, 1977–2 C.B. 26.]

Dinah is a member of the same religious order to which Cassius belongs, and she also takes a vow of poverty. Dinah is a secretary and she is instructed by the order to accept salaried employment with the local business office of the church which exercises general administrative supervision over the order; she accepts the job and remits to the order all compensation received from the church. The services which Dinah performs in the business office of the church are services performed for another agency of the church as an agent of the religious order. Dinah, therefore, is merely performing services gratuitously for the religious order; she is *not* assigning income and she is *not* required to include the remuneration from the church in her gross income. [*Id.;* see also Rev.Rul. 83–126, 1983–2 C.B. 24.]

2. INCOME FROM PROPERTY
a. In general

Income derived from property, such as rents from real property, interest from bonds, or dividends from stock, is generally included in the gross income of the owner of the property. A property owner may not avoid having the income from property included in his gross income merely by directing that the income be paid to another taxpayer.

Example: Paul owned some interest paying negotiable bonds. The bonds were in the physical form of a large sheet of paper; the top portion of the paper reflected the time and manner of payment of the principal amount of the bond, and the bottom portion consisted of a number of smaller segments of paper, or coupons, each of which entitled the holder of the coupon (the "bearer") to payment of a stated amount of interest at a certain specified date. In 1934, and again in 1935, Paul detached from the bond those coupons which called for the payment of interest later in each year and gave them to his son, Robert. When the maturity date of each coupon arrived, Robert collected the interest. The interest income, however, was included in Paul's gross income because Paul still owned the underlying income producing property, the bond, and by transferring the right to the interest payments to his son, Paul enjoyed the economic benefits of the interest income in the same manner as if he had first collected the interest himself and then had transferred the amounts to Robert. "[T]he fruit is not to be attributed to a different tree from that on which it grew." [*Helvering v. Horst,* 311 U.S. 112, 61 S.Ct. 144 (1940).] If Paul had given Robert the bond as well as the interest coupons, then the interest income would be included in Robert's gross income; if Paul had given Robert a one-half interest in the bond, then one-half of the interest income would be included in Robert's gross income and one-half in Paul's gross income.

b.   Income interest in property

Generally, income derived from property is included in the gross income of the taxpayer who owns the property. Ownership of property, however, may be shared by several different taxpayers according to time, such as where one person owns a present interest (an income interest) and another person owns a future interest (a reversionary interest or a remainder interest). If the owner of *all* of the interests in an item of property (the fee owner) transfers the property to two or more other taxpayers, dividing the ownership into present and future interests, income derived from the property is included in the gross income of the transferee of the present interest. If the transferee of the present interest, in turn, transfers all of his present interest to yet another taxpayer (the second transferee), income derived from the property will be included in the gross income of the second transferee. Similarly, he could transfer a coterminous portion (one ending at the same time as his interest) of his interest and that portion would be taxed to the second transferee.

Examples: If Paul, in the preceding Example, had given all of the interest coupons to his son, Robert, and if he also had given the bond itself to his daughter, Emily, then the interest income would be included in Robert's gross income, not Paul's. If Robert then gave the coupons to his son, Junior, then Junior would be taxed on the income.

William died and left his income producing property in a testamentary trust. Under the terms of the trust, William's son, Edward, was entitled to the income from the trust during his life, and the remainder of the trust was to be paid to someone else upon Edward's death. Edward subsequently transferred to his two daughters and to his two sons portions of his life-estate, so that each of them would receive a portion of the income to which Edward was then or might thereafter be entitled to receive during his life. The transfers by Edward to his children were valid under local law. Edward's children became the owners of their respective portions of the present interest in the trust, and income paid to each of them must be included in their respective gross incomes, not Edward's gross income. [*Blair v. Comm'r,* 300 U.S. 5, 57 S.Ct. 330 (1937).]

c.   Ripeness

Generally, income derived from income producing property is included in the gross income of the taxpayer who owns the property at the time the income is paid or when the right to the income becomes fixed. In some situations, however, the right to income from property may have become sufficiently definite that the income may not be diverted to another taxpayer by a transfer of the property. This is the concept of "ripeness," and the person who owns the income when it ripens is taxed on the income, even though he does not actually receive the income. This concept applies both to income from property, such as rents, interest or dividends, as well as to gain from the sale of the property itself.

Examples: Assume that an interest coupon on the bond which Paul owned in the preceding Example matures every 6 months, on January 1 and July 1 of each year. If Paul gives the bond and the coupons to his son, Robert, on April 1, one-half of the interest with respect to the coupon maturing the next July 1 has already been earned, or accrued. Paul must include one-half of the interest paid on July 1 in his gross income; Robert must include in his gross income one-half of the interest paid on July 1 as well as all future interest payments. The same principle applies to other items of income earned ratably over time, such as rents.

Eleanore owns 100 shares of common stock in Xerox Corporation. The Directors of Xerox announce on March 1 (the declaration date) that they will pay a dividend of $1.00 per share to all persons who hold shares on April 15 (the record date). Xerox will pay the dividend by sending checks to each of the appropriate shareholders on May 31 (the payment date), and shareholders usually receive their checks 1 or 2 days later (the date of receipt). Dividend income is not earned ratably, but is paid at the discretion of the corporate Directors. Dividend income generally accrues on the record date. Thus, if Eleanore gives her shares of Xerox stock to her daughter *after* the record date, the dividend will be included in Eleanore's gross income, even though the daughter owns the shares on the payment date and on the date of receipt. [*Bishop v. Shaughnessy*, 195 F.2d 683 (2d Cir. 1962).]

Susie owned an oil and gas service station. She decided to sell the property and she accepted an offer to sell the service station to Texaco, Inc. After entering into the contract *to sell* the service station, but before closing the contract *of sale* and transferring the property to Texaco, Susie transferred an undivided one-half interest in the service station to her children. The right to the income accrued to Susie when there was an agreement (even just in principle) to sell, and Susie must include in her gross income all (not one-half) of the gain from the sale. [*Susie Salvatore*, 29 T.C.M. 89 (1970).]

d. Timing

The principles governing *who* must include an item of income in their gross income generally do not affect the determination of *when* the item must be included.

Example: Assume that Paul and his son Robert, from the preceding Example are both calendar-year, cash method taxpayers, and that in 1935 Paul gives Robert an interest coupon which matures the next year, in 1936; Paul retains ownership of the bond itself. The interest income with respect to the coupon is included in Paul's gross income for 1936, the year the interest is paid to Robert; the interest income is *not* included in Paul's gross income in 1935, the year in which the assignment of the income (the gift of the coupon) is made.

3. ANTICIPATORY ASSIGNMENT FOR VALUE

The assignment of income doctrine generally requires a taxpayer to include in his gross income an item of income which has been *gratuitously* assigned to another taxpayer. If such a right to future income is *sold or exchanged for its present value*, however, there is no gratuitous assignment and the transferor must include the proceeds in his gross income in the year of the sale or exchange. The transferee takes a cost basis in the right to future income. She must include in her gross income in the later year the difference between the amount she receives in the later year and the amount she paid for the right to the future income.

Example: Frank owned 12,500 shares of stock in the Champion Spark Plug Company. In 1964, Frank paid over $750,000 in interest on income tax deficiencies for earlier years. In that year the Code authorized a deduction for the payment of interest on income tax deficiencies, but Frank's gross income for 1964 was not large enough to enable him to deduct the full amount of the interest paid in that year, so in December, 1964, he sold to his son, Duane, the right to receive dividends to be paid in the future with respect to the Champion Spark Plug stock; Frank retained ownership of the stock itself. Under the agreement, Duane became entitled to receive all future dividends paid on his father's stock, up to a total of $122,820, and Duane paid his father $115,000 in cash. Frank must include the $115,000 in his 1964 gross income. Assuming that $122,820 in dividends are paid to Duane in 1965, Duane must include in his 1965 gross income $7,820 (the amount realized less his cost basis in the dividends); Frank does not include any amount in his 1965 gross income with respect to the dividends. [*Estate of Stranahan v. Comm'r,* 472 F.2d 867 (6th Cir.1973).]

4.   INCOME PRODUCING ENTITIES
a.   In general

Within the parameters of the assignment of income doctrine, an individual taxpayer may shift income to an entity, such as a corporation, a partnership, or a trust. As seen below the Code treats these entities differently for tax purposes. A corporation is treated as an entity distinct from its shareholders, a partnership as a mere aggregate of its partners, and a trust as a modified entity.

A corporation is generally treated as a separate taxpayer, distinct from its shareholders and creditors, and its annual taxable income is subject to income tax according to rates specifically applicable to corporations. Income tax is imposed on the taxable income of corporations at rates which rise progressively from 15% to 34% for taxable years beginning after July 1, 1987. [IRC § 11.] Income which is taxable to a corporation, however, is usually subject to tax a second time when it is distributed as dividends to its individual shareholders. [See IRC § 61(a)(7).] Special treatment is provided to the shareholders of a qualifying small business corporation who elect to have the corporation treated as an "S corporation." An S corporation is generally not subject to income tax itself, but its items of income (and its deductions and credits) flow through to the shareholders and are included in the gross incomes of the shareholders (and are deductible or creditable by the shareholders). [IRC §§ 1361–1379.]

A partnership is not subject to income tax itself, but its partners must include in their gross incomes the items of partnership income (and may take deductions or credits for deductions or credits attributable to the partnership) generally in accordance with the terms of the partnership agreement. [IRC §§ 701–761.] The tax treatment of partnerships (and their partners) and S corporations (and their shareholders) is similar, but not identical.

A trust is treated under the income tax law as an entity separate and apart from its grantor and its beneficiaries. Income which is attributable to a trust, however, may be taxable to the grantor, to the beneficiaries, or to the trust itself depending on the terms of the trust and application of special rules. [See IRC §§ 641–683 and discussion, V. B. 4. d., at page 256, *infra.*] When income is taxable to a trust, the first $5,000 is taxed at a rate of 15% and taxable income in excess of $5,000 is taxed at a rate of 28% for taxable years beginning after 1987. [IRC § 1(e).]

Because of the interplay between corporations and their shareholders, between partnerships and their partners, and between trusts and their grantors and beneficiaries it may be advantageous to engage in income producing activities, or to hold income producing property, through a corporation, a partnership or a trust rather than in the name of a single individual.

b. Assignment of income through a partnership
i. Is the partnership valid?
 If members of a family are partners in a partnership, the surrounding facts and circumstances will be closely scrutinized to ensure that the partnership is valid, in substance, and is not being availed of to accomplish mere assignment of income. If the primary source of partnership income is generated by services which are performed by only one of the partners, a partnership agreement which attempts to divide such income between that individual and the other partners will generally not be given effect for tax purposes.

 Examples: Ben operated a cattle ranch in a partnership with an old friend, R.S., for many years. When R.S. decided to retire from the business, he sold his interest in the partnership to Ben. Subsequently, Ben sold an undivided one-half interest in the business to his four sons and the ranch business was conducted in a partnership between Ben and his sons. The four sons paid for their interest in the business with money which had been received as gifts from Ben, and from loans from Ben which were to be repaid with proceeds from operating the ranch. At the time the partnership was created, one son was 24 years old and he lived on the ranch and performed services for the business until he entered active duty with the Army. The second son was 22 years old and a college student, and he went directly into the Army when he finished college without performing any services for the partnership. The two youngest sons, aged 18 and 16, went to school in the winter and worked on the ranch during their summer vacations. Whether the partnership between Ben and his sons will be treated as valid, thereby subjecting Ben and each of his sons to tax on their respective shares of the cattle ranch partnership income, will be determined by findings of fact which demonstrate that there was a bona fide intent that they become partners in conducting the cattle ranch business. Two factors which are significant although not mandatory are whether the sons performed services for the partnership and whether they contributed capital which they, in fact, truly owned. [*Comm'r v. Culbertson,* 337 U.S. 733, 69 S.Ct. 1210 (1949).]

Paysoff is an accountant, and he creates a partnership with himself, his wife (who is not an accountant) and his infant son, Paysoff, Jr., each having a one-third interest in the partnership; the partnership operates an accounting business. Although the partnership agreement provides for one-third of the partnership income to be distributed to each of the partners, Paysoff must include 100% of the partnership income in his gross income; the form of the partnership will not be given legal effect, so far as the income tax laws are concerned, and the income will be taxed to the person who earns the income. [*Tinkoff v. Comm'r,* 120 F.2d 564 (7th Cir.1941).]

ii. Partnership where capital is a material income-producing factor
a. In general
When capital is a material income-producing factor in a partnership, partnership income will be allocated among (and it will be taxable to) the partners in accordance with the partnership agreement, even though one or more of the partners received their partnership interest as a gift from another partner. [IRC § 704(e).] This is in accordance with the general rule that income from property (*viz.,* the partnership interest) is taxed to the real owner of the property. Capital is a material income-producing factor if a substantial portion of the gross income of the business is attributable to the employment of capital in the

partnership business. [Reg. § 1.704–1(e)(1)(iv).] If capital is *not* a material income producing factor in the partnership, and thus IRC § 704(e) is not applicable, consideration must be given to the question of whether the partnership is valid under the *Culbertson* principles discussed above. [See discussion, V. B. 4. b. i., at page 252, *supra.*]

Example: For many years, Jack operated a wholesale shoe distributing company as a sole proprietorship. In 1943, the business was reorganized as a partnership between Jack (40% interest), his wife Rose (30% interest), and trusts established for their two children (15% interest each). In addition, Jack and Rose were paid salaries to compensate them for services they performed for the partnership business. Capital was a material income producing factor in the business of the partnership, and both the form and the substance of the partnership agreement demonstrate that each of the partners, including the two children, is the real owner of his or her respective partnership interest. Each partner, therefore, is taxable on his or her share of partnership income according to the partnership agreement. [See *Smith v. Comm'r*, 32 T.C. 1261 (1959).]

b.   Reallocation of partnership income

If a taxpayer receives a partnership interest by gift, or if a partnership interest is purchased from a member of the taxpayer's family, partnership income will be allocated among the partners in accordance with the partnership agreement. However, reasonable compensation must be paid to the donor (or seller) of such an interest for the value of any services rendered to the partnership by the donor, and the donee's share of income under the partnership agreement must correspond with his proportionate share of his capital interest in the partnership; if these requirements are not met, partnership income will be reallocated. [IRC § 704(e)(2); Reg. § 1.704–1(e)(3).] These rules merely codify the general assignment of income principles seen above.

Example: Porter, the owner of a pizza parlor business conducted as a sole proprietorship, transfers the business to a partnership consisting of himself and his 17 year old daughter, Quintina, as equal partners. Porter works an average of 60 hours each week at the pizza parlor; Quintina works in the business an average of 20 hours a week, after school and on weekends. Porter and Quintina each draw a paycheck every week based on the number of hours worked at the rate of $4.00 per hour. During the current year, Porter is paid $12,000, and Quintina is paid $4,000; the profits of the pizza business (after subtracting these salaries) are $100,000. Considering Porter's experience, responsibilities and the nature and extent of the services he performs for the business, a salary of $12,000 is unreasonably low; a salary of $30,000 would be reasonable. The $100,000 profits of the business may not, therefore, be divided equally between Porter and Quintina. An additional $18,000 of salary will be allocated to Porter as compensation, and Porter and Quintina will each be taxable on their distributive shares of recomputed profits of $82,000 ($100,000 – $18,000), or $41,000 each. Seemingly this result would have been reached even without IRC § 704(e)(2) assistance.

c.   Assignment of income through a corporation

A corporation (other than an "S corporation") is generally subject to tax on its income, and the owners of shares of stock are generally subject to tax on dividends distributed to them by a corporation. If a corporation's income is attributable to the performance of services by one or more of the major shareholders of the corporation, the shareholders, rather than the corporation, may be required to include the income in their gross incomes under the assignment of income doctrine. Similarly, the assignment of income doctrine may require that dividends paid to one class of shareholders must be included in the gross incomes of another class of shareholders where, in substance, the first class of shareholders has no substantial interest in the corporation itself but merely has a right to receive dividend income.

Examples: Frederick is a sales representative for several manufacturers of steel products. In 1966, he incorporated his business in order to obtain limited liability and to provide a better vehicle for planned expansion into other business ventures. Frederick retained 98% of the common stock (his wife and his accountant each received 1%) and the corporation issued preferred stock to each of his four children. After the creation of the corporation, the manufacturers contracted with the corporation to act as their sales representative, and they paid the agreed upon compensation to the corporation. The corporation, in turn, paid Frederick an annual salary ·as a salesman. Because the corporation is a viable entity (not a mere sham) there are non-tax business purposes for doing business in the corporate form, and because the formalities of honoring the corporate form are consistently followed, the assignment of income doctrine will not be applied to disregard the corporation as a separate, independent taxpayer. [*Foglesong v. Comm'r,* 621 F.2d 865 (7th Cir.1980).]

_ C & S Corporation was engaged in the business of buying and selling material with which to make paper, and Carlton and George each owned one-half of the 1,000 shares of common stock, the only class of stock outstanding. In 1936, C & S was recapitalized, changing the 1,000 shares of common stock into 2,000 shares, of which 1,000 were denominated Class A and 1,000, Class B. The Class A shares had virtually all the voting power, and virtually all of the right to assets of the corporation if it were to liquidate. Dividends were to be paid at the rate of $10 per share on Class A stock before any distribution on the Class B shares. After the required distribution had been made on the Class A stock in any year, further distributions were to be divided between the two classes of stock, with the Class A shareholders receiving one-fifth and the Class B shareholders receiving four-fifths of the distributed amounts. Carlton and George each gave their 500 shares of Class B stock to their wives. During the next several years, $77.60 of dividends were paid on the Class A stock, and $150.40 of dividends were paid on the Class B stock. The recapitalization of the C & S corporation did not give the Class B shareholders any significant interest in the corporation; the arrangement effectively just gave the wives of Carlton and George the right to income flowing from property which was retained by Carlton and George. The dividends paid on the Class B shares, therefore, must be included in the gross incomes of Carlton and George. [*Overton v. Comm'r,* 162 F.2d 155 (2d Cir.1947).]

d. Assignment of income through a trust
i.   In general
When property is placed in trust, the ownership of the property is divided between the legal title, which is generally held in the name of the trustee, and the beneficial title, held by the beneficiaries. The grantor of a trust may or may not retain some beneficial interest in the property, and the grantor may or may not retain some power to deal with the property after it has been placed in the trust. Income

earned by property in a trust may be taxable either to the beneficiaries, to the grantor, or to the trust itself, depending on the terms of the trust. [See IRC §§ 641–683.] Although the details of the taxation of income from property held in trust are beyond the scope of this outline, trusts may be an effective means for having income produced by property included in the gross income of someone other than the grantor, while allowing the grantor to retain some powers of control over the property. If the beneficiary is a child under the age of 14 of the grantor, the trust income may be taxed to the child at the rate the income would have been taxed if paid to the parent/grantor. [IRC § 1(i); see discussion at VII. D. 3., at page 312, *infra*.]

ii.   Trusts for the benefit of the grantor

The grantor of a trust generally will be taxed on income earned by a trust if he retains the power to revoke the trust, if he has a 5% reversionary interest in either the income or the corpus of the trust, if he has the power to control the beneficial enjoyment of the trust corpus or income, or if the trust income *may* be distributed to him or used for his benefit. [IRC §§ 671, 673, 674, 675, 676 and 677.]

Example: George creates a trust naming himself as trustee, and providing that all of the income from the trust is to be held for the benefit of his wife. The trust is to terminate after 5 years, or upon the death of either George or his wife, and the corpus and any accumulated income is to be returned to George. During the term of the trust, George has considerable powers over the trust property and its income, including the absolute discretion to determine how much, if any, of the trust income to pay to his wife, and the power to exercise the voting rights of corporate stock in the trust. Although the legal title to the income producing property is transferred to the trust, in substance the cumulative effect of the short duration of the trust and the powers which George could exercise with respect to the trusted property is that George continues to have essentially the same control over the property as before the trust is created. The income from the trust property, therefore, is taxable to George. [*Helvering v. Clifford,* 309 U.S. 331, 60 S.Ct. 554 (1940).]

iii.   Permissible reversions and powers

In response to the *Clifford* decision, Congress enacted some "safe-harbor" provisions, the "Clifford trust provisions." These provisions permitted a grantor to retain a reversionary interest in the trust income or corpus, or certain powers over the trust, without the grantor being taxed on the trust income. Generally, the safe-harbor was available during a period of 10 years or more during which time the grantor did not have the reversionary interest, a power to revoke the trust, or other enumerated powers to control the beneficial enjoyment of the trust corpus or income.

The grantor trust rules were changed significantly by the 1986 Tax Reform Act. Under IRC § 673(a), as amended, the grantor of a trust is taxed on the trust income if he retains a reversionary interest in income or corpus (or a portion thereof) and the value of the reversionary interest, viewed at the time the grantor creates the trust or transfers property to it, has a value of more than 5% of the value of the trust corpus (or portion of trust corpus). Congress drew the dividing line here for income tax purposes by borrowing from the estate tax. An additional exception under the income tax rules provides that the grantor of a trust will not be taxable on trust income if the reversionary interest will take effect only upon the death, before the age of 21, of a beneficiary who is a child, grandchild or other lineal descendant of the grantor. [IRC § 673(b).]

Example: Grantor creates a trust providing for the income to be paid to his granddaughter, then age 12, as needed for her support, with the corpus to be paid to her when she becomes age 21, but if she should die before reaching age 21, the corpus is to be returned to Grantor. Grantor is not treated as the owner of the trust under IRC § 673(b).

In the alternative, Grantor, age 90, creates a trust providing for the income to be paid to her chauffeur, age 23, for life with the remainder to be paid to her maid, age 31, if living, but if the maid is deceased when the chauffeur dies, the corpus is to revert to Grantor. Because of the relative life expectancies of the Grantor, her chauffeur and her maid, the value of the reversionary interest, computed at the time of the creation of the trust, is less than 5% of the value of the trust. Grantor is not treated as the owner of the trust under IRC § 673(a).

Although the grantor may no longer retain any significant reversionary interest and escape income taxation, the grantor may retain certain "safe-harbor" powers over the beneficial enjoyment of the trust corpus or income, or certain administrative powers, if the grantor is required to obtain the consent of an adverse party before she can exercise the power. [See, e.g., IRC §§ 674(a), 675.] An adverse party is a person who has a substantial beneficial interest in the trust which would be adversely affected by the exercise or nonexercise of the power which he possesses regarding the trust. [IRC § 672(a).]

If property is transferred to a trust and it is sold at a gain by the trust within 2 years of the transfer, the trust will be taxed on the gain at the rate (and according to the character) the gain would have been taxed in the hands of the grantor. [IRC § 644.]

Example: Helsa transfers 1,000 shares of IBM stock which she has owned for more than 6 months to a trust; the stock has a fair market value of $90,000 and an adjusted basis to Helsa of $50,000. Helsa's brother, Ira, is the trustee, and the income from the trust is to be paid to their father, Jonah, for the rest of his life. At the end of 11 years, or upon Jonah's death, the trust is to terminate and the stock will go to Granddaughter. Helsa retains the power, exercisable only with Jonah's consent, to have all or a portion of the income paid to Granddaughter, and she may exercise the power to vote the shares of stock with the consent of Jonah. The income from the trust will not be included in Helsa's gross income during the term of the trust. If the trust sells the shares of stock at a gain within 2 years of receiving them from Helsa, the trust will be taxed on the first $40,000 of gain in an amount equal to the tax Helsa would have had to pay on the $40,000 of long-term capital gain if the stock had not been transferred to the trust.

iv. Person other than grantor treated as owner of trust
A person other than the grantor of a trust will be treated as the owner of a trust, and she will be taxed on the income earned by the trust, if: (1) she may unilaterally exercise a power to have either the corpus or the income paid to her; or (2) she has released or modified a power described in (1) and afterwards she has such control over the trust as would require her to be treated as the owner of the trust if she had been the grantor of the trust. [IRC § 678(a).] This rule does not apply if: (1) the grantor is treated as the owner of the trust because of powers or interests which he has retained; or (2) the person is a trustee with the power to apply trust income to support someone whom he is obligated to support (unless, and to the extent, the income actually *is* used to provide such support). [IRC § 678(b) and (c).]

5. ALLOCATION OF INCOME AND DEDUCTIONS AMONG TAXPAYERS
If two or more organizations, trades or businesses are owned or controlled by the same interests, the I.R.S. may distribute, apportion or allocate gross

income, deductions, credits or allowances between or among them if it is necessary in order to prevent tax evasion or to clearly reflect the income of any of them. [IRC § 482.] The authority of the I.R.S. under this provision of the Code is often asserted in conjunction with the assignment of income doctrine. [See *Foglesong v. Comm'r,* 621 F.2d 865 (7th Cir.1980), *on remand,* 77 T.C. 1102 (1981), *rev'd,* 691 F.2d 848 (7th Cir.1982).]

> ***Example:*** Victor was a professional entertainer, and he also operated a poultry business. Victor created Danica Corporation and transferred the poultry business, which consistently produced operating losses, to the corporation. He also entered into a contract with the corporation under which he would receive an annual salary of $50,000 for performing entertainment and promotional services for the corporation. During the current year, the corporation contracted with various third parties to provide entertainment services (which were actually performed by Victor) and it was paid an amount far in excess of $50,000; the corporation paid Victor the agreed upon salary of $50,000, and deducted losses from the poultry business from income derived from the entertainment business. The I.R.S. recognized the valid existence of the Danica corporation, but allocated a greater portion of the corporate income from the entertainment business to Victor, who alone was responsible for the production of that income, because Victor controlled two separate businesses and the reallocation of income was necessary in order to clearly reflect the income of the two businesses. [*Borge v. Comm'r,* 405 F.2d 673 (2d Cir.1968).]

C. ALIMONY, CHILD SUPPORT, AND PROPERTY SETTLEMENTS

Amounts spent for personal, living or family expenses, including amounts spent to satisfy an obligation to support one's spouse or children, are generally not deductible, and no amount is included in the gross income of the spouse or child to whom support is provided. [IRC § 262.] When spouses are separated or divorced, however, alimony or separate maintenance payments may be deductible by the spouse making the payment, and may be includible in the gross income of the spouse receiving the payment. [IRC §§ 71 and 215.] Amounts paid by one spouse to the other spouse (or ex-spouse) for the support of children of the payor spouse are not deductible by the payor spouse, and are not includible in the gross income of the recipient spouse. [IRC § 71(c).] In order to insulate property transfers between spouses (or former spouses) from income tax consequences, Congress has provided that no gain or loss will be recognized when property is transferred from one spouse to the other spouse (or to a former spouse, if the transfer is incident to their divorce) and the recipient will treat the receipt of the property as a gift, taking the property with the same adjusted basis as it had in the hands of the transferor. [IRC § 1041.]

1. **ALIMONY**
    a. **In general**
        A deduction is allowed for amounts paid as alimony or separate maintenance payments, and such payments are included in the gross income of the recipient. [IRC §§ 71 and 215.] The deduction/inclusion provisions are interdependent; the deduction is authorized only for payments which are includible in the gross income of the recipient. In order to strengthen enforcement of these provisions, the recipient spouse is required to furnish the payor spouse with her taxpayer identification number (Social Security number), and the payor spouse must include her number on his income tax return for the taxable year in which payments are made. [IRC §§ 215(c), 6109(d).] The deduction for alimony or separate maintenance payments may be subtracted from gross income in computing a taxpayer's adjusted gross income and are therefore not subject to any limitations on itemized deductions. [IRC § 62(a)(10); see discussion, VII. B. 2. b., at page 307, *infra*.]

    b. **Definition of alimony or separate maintenance payments**
        Congress has enacted a definition of "alimony or separate maintenance payment" (alimony) which does not rely on concepts or requirements of local law. A payment qualifies as alimony if it satisfies *all* of the following requirements: (1) the payment must be in cash (including checks or money orders payable on demand); (2) it must be received under a "divorce or separation instrument;" (3) the payment must be received either directly by a spouse or former spouse, or by a third party for her behalf; (4) the payment must not be designated as non-alimony (not taxable/deductible) in the divorce or separation instrument; (5) if the payments are received under a final decree of divorce or legal separation, the payor spouse and the payee spouse must not be members of the same household at the time the payment is made; (6) there is no liability to make any payment, or substitute for such payments, after the death of the payee spouse; (7) the payment must not be for child support; and (8) if the spouses are still married to each other, they must not file a joint return. [IRC § 71(b), (c)(1), and (e).]

        A "divorce or separation instrument" is: (1) a decree of divorce or separate maintenance or a written instrument incident to such a decree; (2) a written separation agreement; or (3) a judicial decree (other than of divorce or separate maintenance) requiring that support or maintenance payments be made (generally, temporary alimony or alimony pending litigation). [IRC § 71(b)(2).]

        Example: A divorce decree provides that Clarice is to make annual payments to David of $30,000 for a period of 6 years, or until David dies. In addition, the decree requires Clarice to pay David or David's estate $20,000 each year for a period of 10 years. The $30,000 annual payments will qualify as alimony, if David and Clarice do not share the same dwelling unit at the time the payments are made. The $20,000 annual payments, however, do not qualify as alimony because they do not terminate at David's death. [Temp.Reg. § 1.71–1T(b).]

c. **Front-loading rules**

Even though payments made during a taxable year may satisfy all the definitional requirements of alimony, there are two additional limitations which may affect the deduction/inclusion of the payments. These rules are intended to prevent the parties in a divorce from structuring a property settlement so that it will qualify as alimony. A property settlement generally has the hallmarks of being a larger amount than true alimony and of being paid shortly after the divorce is granted; unlike alimony, amounts paid as a property settlement incident to divorce are not deductible by the payor spouse, and are not included in the gross income of the recipient. [See discussion, V. C. 3., at page 265, *infra.*] Hence, "front-loading" refers to making payments shortly after a divorce or separation which are ostensibly "alimony," but which are significantly larger in amount than payments made in later years.

i. General rules

Under the front-loading rules, the amount of excess alimony payments is required to be included in the alimony payor's gross income in the third post-separation year; the alimony recipient is entitled to a deduction in computing adjusted gross income in the same amount for the third post-separation year. [IRC § 71(f)(1).] Excess alimony payments are the sum of excess payments for the first post-separation year plus excess payments for the second post-separation year. [IRC § 71(f)(2).] The first post-separation year is the first calendar year in which the payor spouse pays deductible alimony, and the second and third post-separation years are the next 2 succeeding calendar years respectively. [IRC § 71(f)(6).]

The excess payments for the *second* post-separation year is the excess of alimony payments made in that year over the sum of the alimony payments made in the third post-separation year plus $15,000. [IRC § 71(f)(4).] The excess payments for the *first* post-separation year is computed by comparing the alimony payments made in that year with the average alimony payments made in the second and third post-separation years (after reducing the second year amount by any recapture amount described in the preceding sentence) plus $15,000. [IRC § 71(f)(3).]

Example: Pursuant to a divorce decree rendered in Year One, Lloyd is required to pay alimony to his former spouse, Kim, for

10 years in the amount of $50,000 per year. In Year One, Lloyd makes the first alimony payment of $50,000 to Kim; Lloyd may deduct $50,000 as alimony and Kim must include $50,000 in gross income. In Year Two, however, Lloyd loses his job and is only able to make payments to Kim of $20,000; again, Lloyd may deduct the payment as alimony and Kim must include the amount in gross income. In Year Three, Lloyd is still unemployed and he is unable to make any payment to Kim; Lloyd is not entitled to any deduction under IRC § 215, and Kim is not required to include any amount in gross income under IRC § 71(a).

Under the front-loading rules of IRC § 71(f), in Year Three Lloyd must include $32,500 in gross income, and Kim is entitled to a $32,500 deduction in computing adjusted gross income. The recapture amount ($32,500) is the sum of the excess payments for the first post-separation year, Year One ($27,500, the excess of $50,000 over $15,000 plus $7,500 [the average of alimony payments made in Year Two ($15,000, which is the $20,000 payment actually made reduced by the $5,000 excess payment for the second post-separation year) and Year Three ($0)]), plus the excess payments for the second post-separation year, Year Two ($5,000, the excess of $20,000 over $15,000).

ii.   Exceptions

Payments such as temporary alimony or alimony pending litigation made under a judicial decree (other than of divorce or separate maintenance) requiring that support or maintenance payments be made are not treated as alimony or separate maintenance payments under the front-loading rules. [IRC § 71(f)(5)(B).] The front-loading rules do not apply if the payments cease upon the death of either spouse or upon the remarriage of the recipient spouse. [IRC § 71(f)(5)(A).] In addition, the rules do not apply if payments fluctuate in amount because they are paid pursuant to a continuing obligation over 3 or more years to pay a fixed portion of the income from a business or property or compensation from employment or self-employment. [IRC § 71(f)(5)(C).]

d.   Indirect alimony

Payments to a third party on behalf of a spouse or former spouse may qualify as alimony or separate maintenance payments, if all the other requirements pertaining to alimony are satisfied. However, payments made to maintain or improve property which is owned by the payor spouse and merely used by the payee spouse under the terms of the divorce or separation instrument do not qualify as payments "on behalf of" the spouse, and are not treated as alimony or separate maintenance payments.

Example: Under the terms of a divorce decree, Mitzi continues to live in a house owned by her ex-spouse, Norton, and he continues to make the mortgage payments on the house. The decree also requires Norton to transfer *all* ownership and rights in a $500,000 policy insuring his life to Mitzi, and he continues to make the premium payments. Neither the mortgage payments (Norton owns the house) nor the transfer of the insurance policy (not cash) qualify as alimony. However, the payments of insurance premiums do qualify. [Temp.Reg. § 1.71–1T(b).]

2. CHILD SUPPORT

A payment made under the terms of a divorce or separation instrument is not treated as alimony to the extent it is fixed, in terms of an amount of money or a part of the payment, as an amount payable for the support of children of the payor spouse. [IRC § 71(c).] An amount is treated as "fixed" for child support if a payment is to be reduced, either on the happening of a specified contingency relating to a child, such as reaching the age of majority, marrying or dying, or at a time which can be clearly associated with such a contingency. [IRC § 71(c)(2).] If payments actually made in any year are less than the full amount specified in the divorce or separation instrument, the amount which is paid is treated first as made for child support, up to the amount fixed for that purpose in the instrument, and the remainder is treated as alimony. [IRC § 71(c)(3).]

Example: Orville is obligated under the terms of a divorce decree rendered in Year One to make payments of $15,000 each year to his former spouse, Phoebe. The payments otherwise qualify as alimony under IRC § 71(b), but the instrument provides that the payments are to be reduced to $10,000 each year after their 8 year old daughter, Quinta, reaches her 18th birthday (which will occur on July 1 of Year Ten). Only $10,000 of each year's payments qualify as alimony, deductible by Orville and includible in Phoebe's gross income. The same result would be reached if the instrument did not call for the reduction upon Quinta's 18th birthday, but merely provided for the reduction to take effect on July 1 of Year Ten (or within 6 months of that date). Further, if in Year Three Orville only made payments of $12,000, the first $5,000 would be treated as child support, and only the remaining $7,000 would be treated as alimony, deductible by Orville and includible in Phoebe's gross income. [Temp.Reg. § 1.71–1T(c).]

3. TRANSFERS OF PROPERTY BETWEEN SPOUSES OR INCIDENT TO DIVORCE

No gain or loss is recognized when an individual transfers property to (or in trust for the benefit of) his spouse, or his former spouse (if the transfer to the former spouse is incident to the divorce). [IRC § 1041(a).] The recipient is treated as if the property were acquired by gift, thus the value of the property is excluded from gross income under IRC § 102. In addition, both the basis and the holding period of the property in the transferee's hands will be the same as they were in the hands of the transferor. [IRC §§ 1041(b) and 1223(2); see discussion, II. B. 2. a. v., at page 33, *supra*.] A transfer is incident to the divorce if it occurs within 1 year after the date of the divorce, or is related to the cessation of the marriage. [IRC § 1041(c).] A transfer is treated as related to the cessation of the marriage if it is made pursuant to a divorce or separation instrument and the transfer occurs within 6 years of the date the marriage ceases, or if the parties can demonstrate that the transfer was made to effect the division of property owned by the former spouses at the time the marriage ceased. [Temp.Reg. § 1.1041–1T(b).] The nonrecognition rule of IRC § 1041(a) does not apply, however, if property is transferred to a trust and liabilities on the property exceed the adjusted basis of the property. [IRC § 1041(e).]

> *Example:* In Year Two Rex transfers to his former spouse, Sheila, shares of stock in XYZ Corporation which have a fair market value of $250,000 and an adjusted basis to Rex of $100,000. The transfer is made pursuant to a written agreement between Rex and Sheila which provides that the stock is to be transferred in consideration for Sheila's release of any dower or other marital rights she might have in Rex's property; the agreement is incorporated in their divorce decree, rendered in Year One. Rex has realized gain of $150,000 ($250,000 − $100,000) on the transfer, but because the transfer is incident to the divorce, none of the gain is recognized. Sheila does not include the value of the stock in her gross income; Sheila's adjusted basis for the stock is the same as Rex's adjusted basis, $100,000, and she also tacks his holding period.

REVIEW QUESTIONS

Q# 1: Wealthy works for Corporation but directs that his $100,000 salary be paid to the American Cancer Society. Who is taxed on the salary?

Q# 2: Landlord owns a building and the land underlying it on which rent of $20,000 is due for each year on December 31. On June 30 (½ way through the year) Landlord deeds one half of the building and *all* of the rents to his Son. The $20,000 rent is paid on January 3 of Year Two. To whom and when is the $20,000 of rent taxed if Landlord and Son are both calendar year, cash method taxpayers?

Q# 3: Grantor creates a trust with income to Daughter for 10½ years and a remainder to Grandson at the end of 10½ years. Grantor names himself trustee with general fiduciary powers, but adds that Grantor has the power to accumulate income. In addition Grantor's sister may demand that any of the income for any year during the 10½ year period be paid to her. In each year of the trust the income is paid to Daughter. Who is taxed on the income?

Q# 4: Father gives Son and Daughter each a one third interest in his steel company which becomes a partnership as a result of the gift. Father continues to work for the company and his services are worth $100,000 per year but Father, Son and Daughter each have an equal say in running the company. The company earns $400,000 after expenses for the year but prior to compensating Father. Is the partnership valid under IRC § 704(e)(1)? How does IRC § 704(e)(2) call for the $400,000 to be allocated?

Q# 5: What are the five basic requirements which must be satisfied in order for a payment to qualify as alimony or a separate maintenance payment?

Q# 6: What possible administrative requirements may be imposed upon the person receiving and the person paying alimony?

Q# 7: Pursuant to a divorce decree, Barbara pays George $10,000 a year alimony for George's life. Barbara also agrees to pay child support of $6,000 a year until the children reach 21 years of age. What are the tax consequences of these payments to Barbara and George? What if in one year Barbara pays only $12,000?

Q# 8: Johnny pays Joanna the following amounts of deductible alimony in the 3 years following their divorce:

Year One:	$100,000
Year Two:	$ 90,000
Year Three:	$ 70,000

To what extent do the recapture rules of IRC § 71(f) apply? What if the amounts which are paid are computed as a percentage of the income from Johnny's business?

Q# 9: Unless the facts provide to the contrary, assume that the requirements of IRC § 71(b) are met. In the following alternative facts, which of the situations qualify as deductible alimony to the payor spouse?

(a) Payor allows payee to live rent free in a house he owns; fair rental value is $500 per month.

(b) Payor pays Payee's landlord $500 of rent.

(c) Payor pays $500 on the mortgage of a house he owns and where Payee is living rent free.

(d) Payor pays $500 on the mortgage of a house which Payee owns and in which Payee resides.

Q# 10: Shortly after Robert and Phoebe are divorced, and as part of their divorce settlement, Robert transfers to Phoebe shares of stock in General Motors Corporation which he had owned in his own name, and Phoebe conveys to Robert her interest in their house which they had purchased during their marriage, taking title as joint tenants. The stock has a fair market value of $75,000 and an adjusted basis to Robert of $30,000; Robert and Phoebe paid $100,000 for the house several years ago, and it has a fair market value of $150,000. How much gain do Robert and Phoebe each recognize? What is Robert's basis for the house after the transfer? What is Phoebe's basis in the stock?

Q# 11: Pamela [from Unit IV Question # 6] sells a parcel of land which has an adjusted basis of $1,000. She receives a $2,000 cash payment and a contractual right to $1,000 payments (plus a reasonable rate of interest) in each of the next eight years. If Pamela does not "elect out" of IRC § 453, how much gain must she realize if she sells the land to her husband, Gus? What if she sells the land to an unrelated third party but immediately resells her contractual rights to the $8,000 of payments to Gus for $7,500 cash?

*

VI

CHARACTERIZATION OF INCOME AND DEDUCTIONS

Analysis

A. INTRODUCTION

Capital gains and losses have been provided special treatment for most of the history of the United States income tax laws. When Congress lowered the maximum marginal rate for individuals to 28% in the Tax Reform Act of 1986, however, the preferential treatment which had previously been accorded to long term capital gains was repealed. Under prior law, a deduction equal to 60% of net long-term capital gains was allowed in computing adjusted gross income; thus, only 40% of net long-term capital gains were taxed. Beginning with taxable years starting in 1988, capital gains will be taxed at the same rate as ordinary income. In order to protect net capital gains from being taxed at a rate higher than 28%, however, the definitional provisions and other Code sections dealing with capital gains and losses have been retained and if the maximum marginal rate for individuals is increased in the future, net capital gains will be taxed at a maximum rate of 28%. [IRC § 1(j).] For taxable yars beginning in 1987, when the maximum marginal rate for individuals is 38.5%, net capital gains are taxed at a maximum rate of 28%. [IRC § 1(h) and (j).] Limitations on the deductibility of capital losses have been retained, although in modified form, by the Tax Reform Act of 1986.

A capital gain or loss arises from the "sale or exchange" of property which is a capital asset. A definition of "capital asset" is provided in the Code, but there are important judicial interpretations of the concept as well. The term sale or exchange is also subject to statutory rules and judicial interpretations. A capital gain or loss is "long-term" if the taxpayer's holding period for the property at the time of its sale or exchange is more than 6 months; it is "short-term" if the holding period is 6 months or less. There are special rules for determining the holding period of property in certain situations, and other special rules may specify long-term or short-term treatment in certain situations.

Although capital gain or loss treatment is generally available only for capital assets, there are some types of noncapital asset property which, if disposed of in certain types of transactions, will give rise to capital gain or loss; these items of property are sometimes referred to as "quasi-capital assets." In addition, if depreciation deductions have been taken with respect to an item of property which is sold or exchanged, recognized gain which may otherwise be capital gain may be required to be characterized as ordinary income.

B. TREATMENT OF CAPITAL GAINS AND LOSSES

1. TREATMENT OF CAPITAL GAINS

a. Maximum rate for capital gains

For taxable years beginning after 1987, capital gains are taxed at the same rate as ordinary income. However, for taxable years beginning in 1987, or in any subsequent year in which the maximum rate is increased above 28%, the amount of an individual's net capital gain is taxed at a maximum rate of 28%. [IRC § 1(j).] If the taxpayer is subject to the 5%

surtax imposed on certain high income individuals, that surtax is also levied on net capital gains thus resulting in a maximum rate of 33%. [IRC § 1(g) and (i)(1)(C); see discussion at VII. D. 2., at page 311, *infra*.] The cap on the rate at which capital gains may be taxed applies only to a taxpayer's net capital gain; the cap does not apply to a taxpayer's net short-term capital gain.

b. Definitions

The Code defines a "net capital gain" as *the excess* (if any) of a taxpayer's **net** long-term capital gain for a taxable year *over* the taxpayer's **net** short-term capital loss for the year. [IRC § 1222(11).] A "**net** long-term capital gain" is *the excess* (if any) of a taxpayer's long-term capital gains for a taxable year *over* the taxpayer's long-term capital losses for the year. [IRC § 1222(7).] Similarly, a "**net** short-term capital loss" is *the excess* (if any) of the taxpayer's short-term capital losses for the taxable year *over* the short-term capital gains for the year. [IRC § 1222(6).] These terms may be expressed by the following formulae:

$$
\begin{array}{l}
\text{long-term capital gains} \\
\underline{-\ \text{long-term capital losses}} \\
\textbf{net}\ \text{long-term capital gain}
\end{array}
$$

$$
\begin{array}{l}
\text{short-term capital losses} \\
\underline{-\ \text{short-term capital gains}} \\
\textbf{net}\ \text{short-term capital loss}
\end{array}
$$

$$
\begin{array}{l}
\textbf{net}\ \text{long-term capital gain} \\
\underline{-\ \textbf{net}\ \text{short-term capital loss}} \\
\textbf{net}\ \text{capital gain}
\end{array}
$$

Example: During the current year, Abner sold various capital assets, producing the following results: $16,000 long-term capital gain; $4,000 long-term capital loss; $6,000 short-term capital gain; and $8,000 short-term capital loss. For the current year, Abner has a **net** long-term capital gain of $12,000 ($16,000 − $4,000), a **net** short-term capital loss of $2,000 ($8,000 − $6,000), and a net capital gain of $10,000 ($12,000 − $2,000).

2. TREATMENT OF CAPITAL LOSSES
a. In general

A loss from the sale or exchange of a capital asset is within the definition of a long-term (or short-term) capital loss only "to the extent that such loss is taken into account in computing taxable income." [IRC § 1222(2) and (4).] In other words, the loss is a *capital loss* only if there is statutory authority for a loss deduction, and an individual taxpayer may generally take deductions only for losses incurred in a trade or business, losses incurred in transactions entered into for profit, and casualty losses.

[IRC § 165(c); see discussions III. A. 3. and B. 4., at pages 96 and 136, *supra.*] If a capital loss is otherwise deductible, there are additional limitations imposed on the amount which may be deducted in a taxable year, and if the capital losses exceed the limit, they may be carried over to subsequent taxable years. [IRC §§ 1211 and 1212.]

Example: Bambi sells her principal residence, (which is a capital asset, more than 6 months after she bought it) at a loss of $20,000. The loss may not be deducted. The loss does not have to be characterized because it does not qualify for a deduction; however, technically the loss is *not* a long-term capital loss. If, instead of selling her house, Bambi had a loss from the sale, more than 6 months after the purchase, of a parcel of undeveloped real estate which she always held out for rent (i.e., a transaction entered into for profit; *not* property held for use in her trade or business), the loss deduction would be allowed by IRC § 165(c)(2), and the loss would be a long-term capital loss.

b. Limitation on capital losses

Capital losses may be deducted by an individual taxpayer only to the extent of capital gains recognized during a taxable year plus an additional amount.

i. Losses to the extent of gains

Capital gains must be included in gross income, and a deduction is allowed for capital losses incurred in a taxable year up to the amount of such gains recognized in the taxable year. [IRC § 1211(b).] Accommodation for this part of the limitation on the deduction of capital losses is reflected in the "netting" of losses against gains in the computations of **net** long-term capital gains, **net** short-term capital gains, and **net** capital gains. [See IRC § 1222(5), (7), and (11).] Under the netting process, capital losses, whether short-term or long-term, will ultimately be able to be deducted up to the amount of capital gains, whether short-term or long-term.

ii. Additional amount

Capital losses may be deducted to the extent they exceed capital gains recognized in a taxable year up to the *smallest* of the following amounts: (1) $3,000 (or $1,500 if the taxpayer is married, filing a separate return); or (2) the excess of capital losses over capital gains. [IRC § 1211(b).]

Example: In the current year Chen, an unmarried taxpayer, earns a salary of $25,000, and he does not have any itemized deductions. In addition, he sells various capital assets, producing the following results: $7,000 long-term capital gain; $7,500 long-term capital loss; $2,000 short-term capital gain; and $4,000 short-term capital loss. For the current year, Chen has a **net** long-term capital loss of $500 ($7,500 – $7,000) and a **net** short-term capital loss of $2,000 ($4,000 – $2,000). [Chen must include in his gross income $9,000 of capital gains ($7,000 of long-term capital gain plus the $2,000 of short-term capital gain), and he may deduct $9,000 of the capital losses.] In addition, he may deduct $2,500, which is the smaller of the following amounts: (1) *$3,000;* or (2) *$2,500,* which is the excess of capital losses ($11,500) over capital gains. Whenever the second alternative applies, there will be no capital loss carryovers to the subsequent year.

c. Capital loss carryovers

If a taxpayer has capital losses in a taxable year in excess of the amount which may be deducted in that year because of the limitations of IRC § 1211, the excess amount may be carried over and treated as a capital loss incurred in subsequent taxable years. [IRC § 1212(b).] Excess short-term capital losses will be carried over as short-term capital losses, and excess long-term capital losses will be carried over as long-term capital losses. Although the rules of IRC § 1211 do not specify whether a deduction of the "additional amount" is to be from short-term capital losses or from long-term capital losses (assuming that the taxpayer has some of each), the loss carryover rules of IRC § 1212(b) effectively require that short-term capital losses must be deducted from ordinary income first. This result is accomplished by the "special rule" of IRC § 1212(b)(2) which requires that an amount equal to the "additional amount" allowed as a deduction, be treated as short-term capital gain before the amount of the capital loss carryover is computed; this is referred to as "constructive short-term capital gain."

Example: In the current year Erasmus, an unmarried taxpayer, earns a salary of $25,000, and he does not have any itemized deductions. In addition, he sells various capital assets, producing the following results: $4,000 long-term capital gain; $10,000 long-term capital loss; $1,000 short-term capital gain; and $3,000 short-term capital loss. For the current year, Erasmus has an actual **net** long-term capital loss of $6,000 ($10,000 – $4,000) and an actual **net** short-term capital loss of $2,000 ($3,000 – $1,000). Erasmus must include in his gross income $5,000 of capital gains ($4,000 of long-term capital gains plus $1,000 of short-term capital gains) and he will be allowed to deduct $5,000 of capital losses. In addition, he will be able to deduct $3,000 under IRC § 1211(b)(1), because it is the smaller of the following amounts: (1) *$3,000;* or (2) *$8,000,* which is the excess of capital losses ($13,000) over capital gains ($5,000).

The amount of short-term capital loss to be carried over to the next taxable year is the excess of his **net** short-term capital loss over his **net** long-term capital gain. [IRC § 1212(b)(1)(A).] Before this computation is made, however, he is deemed to have an additional $3,000 (the additional amount allowed by IRC § 1211(b)(1)) of short-term capital gain for the current year. [IRC § 1212(b)(2).] For this purpose, therefore, Erasmus does not have any **net** short-term capital *loss;* he has a **net** short-term capital *gain* of $1,000 (($1,000 actual short-term capital gain + $3,000 constructive short-term capital gain) – $3,000 short-term capital loss). [See IRC § 1222(5).] Erasmus, therefore, will not carry over to the next taxable year any amount of short-term capital loss.

The amount of long-term capital loss which Erasmus may carry over to the next taxable year is the excess of his **net** long-term capital loss over his **net** short-term capital gain. [IRC § 1212(b)(1)(B).] Before this computation is made, however, he is deemed to have an additional $3,000 of constructive short-term capital gain for the current year. [IRC § 1212(b)(2).] For this purpose, therefore, he has a **net** short-term capital *gain* of $1,000 (($1,000 actual short-term capital gain + $3,000 constructive short-term capital gain) – $3,000 actual short-term capital loss). [See IRC § 1222(5).] The amount of long-term capital loss which Erasmus will carry over to the next taxable year is $5,000 ($6,000 **net** long-term capital loss – $1,000 **net** short-term capital gain).

To recapitulate, in the current year Erasmus had an actual **net** short-term capital loss of $2,000 and a **net** long-term capital loss of $6,000. In addition to deducting capital losses up to the amount of capital gains, he deducted $3,000 of capital losses from ordinary income. That $3,000 deduction came first from his **net** short-term capital losses, and then from his **net** long-term capital losses. Therefore, his short-term capital loss carryover to the next taxable year is zero, and his long-term capital loss carryover to the next taxable year is $5,000.

3. DEFINITION OF CAPITAL ASSET

The definitions of a capital gain and a capital loss (whether long-term or short-term) require that there be a sale or exchange of a "capital asset." [IRC

§ 1222(1)–(4).] The term "capital asset" is broadly defined by the Code as "property held by the taxpayer," but then certain categories of property are excluded from the definition. [IRC § 1221.] In addition to the statutory exclusions, capital asset status has been judicially denied, in some situations, to income producing interests in property, and in other situations, to certain items of property because of the relationship of the property to the taxpayer's trade or business.

a.   Statutory definition

The term "capital asset" means property held by a taxpayer, whether or not it is connected with the taxpayer's trade or business, but it does *not* include property described in the five categories discussed below. [IRC § 1221.]

i.   Inventory

Property is not included in the definition of capital asset if it is the taxpayer's stock in trade or other property of a kind which would properly be included in the taxpayer's inventory if on hand at the close of the taxable year, or property held primarily for sale to customers in the ordinary course of the taxpayer's trade or business. [IRC § 1221(1).] "Gross income derived from business" which results from the sale of property, therefore, is treated as ordinary income, not as capital gain. [See IRC §§ 61(a)(2) and 64.]

a.   Property held primarily for sale to customers in the ordinary course of business

In many situations it is clear that property which is sold is stock in trade or inventory, and thus it is properly excluded from capital asset status, but a taxpayer may hold an item of property both for sale and also for some other purpose. The requirement that the property be held for sale "to customers" has generally been ignored by the courts when construing this provision. Property is not a capital asset if it is held "primarily" for sale; "primarily" means "of first importance" or "principally." [*Malat v. Riddell,* 383 U.S. 569, 86 S.Ct. 1030 (1966).] In addition, it is appropriate to look at the time the taxpayer sells or exchanges the property, rather than when he acquires it, to determine if it is being held primarily for sale.

Example: In 1920, C.E. contracted to purchase 160 acres of land near the town of Clovis, New Mexico, with the intention to operate a cattle business on the land. After the purchase of the land was completed in 1921, he decided not to pursue the cattle business and he attempted to sell the land. Even though he had the land platted and subdivided into residential lots, his attempts to sell the land were unsuccessful until 1931, when the city limits of Clovis were extended to incorporate some of the lots. By 1940 C.E. had sold several lots, but at that time he decided to hold the remaining portions for investment purposes and he made no further efforts to sell any of the land. Because of the rapid expansion of the population of Clovis, however, his lots were in demand and he sold a number of lots each year from 1941 through 1948 in response to unsolicited offers when the price was right. C.E. reported the gain from the sale of lots in 1944 and 1945 as long-term capital gain. Although C.E. originally acquired the land for purposes other than holding it for sale in the ordinary course of business, by 1944 and 1945 he was holding the land for sale. The lots were not capital assets and the gain derived from their sale was ordinary income. [*Mauldin v. Comm'r*, 195 F.2d 714 (10th Cir.1952).]

Some courts have held that the issue of whether property is held "primarily for sale . . . in the ordinary course of . . . business" is *not* to be resolved by comparing the taxpayer's intention to sell the property with his intention to rent the property. The statutory test should, instead, be applied by contrasting the taxpayer's intention to make sales of the property as part of the ordinary conduct of his business with his intention to make sales in circumstances outside the normal conduct of his business, such as upon the termination and sale of a business venture.

Example: The I.S.M. Corporation manufactured shoe machinery equipment. The Corporation usually leased the machines which it produced, but occasionally it would sell one of them to a customer. Most of the Corporation's income was derived from leasing the machines; income from selling the machines constituted only from 2% to 7% of its gross revenues. Nonetheless, the selling of its machines was an accepted and predictable, albeit small, part of its business. The machines were held by the Corporation primarily for sale to customers in the ordinary course of business; the gain from their sale was, therefore, ordinary income not capital gain. [*International Shoe Machine Corp. v. U.S.*, 491 F.2d 157 (1st Cir.1974).]

b.   Real property subdivided for sale

Because the issue of determining a taxpayer's intentions with respect to real property which has been subdivided for sale arises frequently, Congress has provided some safe-harbor guidelines which entitle a taxpayer to at least partial capital gains treatment even if she engages in some selling activities. [IRC § 1237.] A lot or parcel which is part of a tract of real property is not to be deemed "held primarily for sale" solely because the taxpayer has subdivided the tract if the land has not previously been held by the taxpayer primarily for sale (and the taxpayer does not hold any other real property primarily for sale), if no substantial improvements have been made to the property by the taxpayer, certain related parties or by lessees, and if the taxpayer has held the property for 5 years (unless she inherited it). On the other hand, if there are more than 5 lots or parcels in the same tract of land, the gain from any sale or exchange (which occurs in the taxable year in or after the year in which the sixth lot or parcel is sold or exchanged) will be treated as ordinary income to the extent of 5% of the selling price; however, all expenses of sale are deducted first from the 5% of the gain which would otherwise be ordinary income. [IRC § 1237(b)(1) and (2).] Additional special rules permit the taxpayer to make certain improvements to the property if she has held it for 10 years or more. [IRC § 1237(b)(3).]

Examples: Felicity meets all of the conditions of IRC § 1237 in subdividing and selling a single tract of land. In Year One she sells 4 lots to four unrelated purchasers, and 3 adjacent lots (which constitute a single parcel) to a fifth unrelated purchaser. Because Felicity has sold only 5 lots or parcels, the gain which she realizes on the sales is capital gain.

Gus meets all of the conditions of IRC § 1237 in subdividing and selling a single tract of land. In Year One he sells 4 lots to four unrelated purchasers, and in Year Two, he sells 2 lots to two additional unrelated purchasers. Five percent of the selling price of each lot sold in Year Two is ordinary income; however, all expenses of sale are deducted first from the gain which would otherwise be treated as ordinary income under this rule. Thus, with respect to each of the 2 lots sold in Year Two, if the selling price is $10,000, the adjusted basis is $5,000, and the expenses of sale are $300, the realized gain, under this special rule, will be $5,000 ($10,000 amount realized – $5,000 adjusted basis). Of the $5,000 gain, $500 is required to be treated as ordinary income. Although the selling expenses were not permitted to reduce the amount realized in computing gain, they may be deducted from the amount of ordinary income, reducing ordinary income to $200. The sale also results in $4,500 of capital gain. [Reg. § 1.1237–1(e)(2) Example (2).]

ii. Depreciable property and real property used in trade or business

Property is not included in the definition of capital asset if it is depreciable property used in the taxpayer's trade or business or if it is real property used in the taxpayer's trade or business. [IRC § 1221(2).] Such property may, however, be treated as "quasi-capital assets," giving rise to capital gain or loss in certain circumstances. [IRC § 1231; see discussion, VI. C., at page 291, *infra*.]

Example: Harriet owns and operates a bicycle sales and repair business which is located on a parcel of improved real estate. Neither the building, which is subject to depreciation deductions, nor the underlying real property are capital assets in Harriet's hands.

iii. Copyrights and similar property

A copyright, a literary, musical or artistic composition, a letter or memorandum, or similar property is *not* a capital asset while it is in the hands of: (1) the person who created it; or (2) the person for whom it was created (but only with respect to a letter, memorandum, or similar property); or (3) a taxpayer who received the property with a transferred basis from a person described in (1) or (2). [IRC § 1221(3).]

Example: Dick was President of the United States, and in that capacity he wrote numerous letters, memorandums, notes and the like. These documents are not capital assets in Dick's hands. If Dick gives these documents to his daughter, Julie, she would hold them with a transferred basis (under IRC § 1015); therefore, they would not be capital assets in Julie's hands either.

iv. Accounts receivable

Accounts or notes receivable acquired in the ordinary course of business for services rendered or from the sale of property which is stock in trade, inventory, or property held primarily for sale to customers in the ordinary course of the taxpayer's business are not capital assets. [IRC § 1221(4).]

> ***Example:*** Isaac is in the business of selling office supplies. He generally sells items from his inventory to local businesses on terms calling for a payment of 20% of the purchase price upon delivery, and the balance of the purchase price to be paid within 30 days of delivery. Isaac's accounts receivable from the sales of inventory are not capital assets.

v. Publications of the U.S. Government

Capital assets do not include publications of the U.S. Government which are received from the U.S. Government, or any of its agencies, which are held either by a taxpayer who received the publication or by a taxpayer who, in turn, received the publication with a transferred basis from the initial recipient. [IRC § 1221(5).] This exclusion does not apply if the publication was purchased from the U.S. Government at the price at which it was offered for sale to the public.

> ***Example:*** Jesse is a U.S. Senator and in that capacity he receives, free of charge, copies of the Congressional Record and other governmental publications. None of these publications are capital assets in Jesse's hands. If Jesse gives these publications to his daughter, Karma, she will hold them with a transferred basis (under IRC § 1015); therefore, they are not capital assets in his daughter's hands either.

b. Income property

The statutory definition of a capital asset broadly refers to the term "property," and it includes various interests in property; therefore, an interest in property less than the fee, such as a leasehold interest, a life estate or a term of years, is a capital asset, unless it falls within one of the statutory or judicial exceptions. [With respect to the *amount* of gain, see discussion of the uniform basis rule, II. B. 2. a. viii., at page 35, *supra.*] However, if the owner of an interest in property (such as a leasehold) creates a lesser interest in the property (such as a subleasehold) for a period of time which is not coterminous with the owner's interest, amounts which he receives for the lesser interest are ordinary income, not capital gain. This is identical in theory to the concepts underlying the assignment of income doctrine. [See discussion, V. B. 2., at page 247, *supra.*]

> ***Examples:*** Walter inherited an office building from his father. At the time he received the building, a portion of it was leased to the Irving Trust Company, where they operated a branch office, for a term of 15 years at an annual rental of $25,000.

Several years later, the Irving Trust Company decided that it was unprofitable to continue to operate a branch office in Walter's building, so Walter and the Trust Company agreed to cancel the remaining portion of the lease in consideration of a payment to Walter of $140,000. The $25,000 annual rental payments which Walter received during the term of the lease were ordinary income. [IRC § 61(a)(5).] The $140,000 payment to cancel the lease was merely a substitute for the rent reserved in the lease, and it is also ordinary income, not capital gain. [*Hort v. Comm'r*, 313 U.S. 28, 61 S.Ct. 757 (1941).]

A parcel of real property was leased by the M.B. Company (lessee) from the University of Washington (lessor) for a term of some 47 years. Subsequently, the lessee subleased the property to The Olympic Corporation (sublessee) for a term ending one day before the expiration of the lessee's lease from the lessor. Several years later, the parties decided to make this cumbersome arrangement simpler by having the lessee sell its leasehold to the lessor, terminating all of the lessee's interest in the property, and then having the lessor lease the property directly to the former sublessee. The consideration for the sale of the leasehold was $137,000, and it was provided by the sublessee as part of its arrangement to subsequently lease the property from the lessor. The $137,000 was paid for the purchase of the M.B. Company's entire leasehold interest; it was not simply a discharge of The Olympic's obligation to pay rent under the sublease. The $137,000 was capital gain to the M.B. Company, not ordinary income. [*Metropolitan Building Co. v. Comm'r*, 282 F.2d 592 (9th Cir.1960).]

c. **The *Corn Products* Doctrine**
    In addition to the statutory removal of certain categories of property from the definition of a capital asset, the Supreme Court has held that ordinary gain or loss will result in circumstances where the sale of property is an integral part of a taxpayer's business, even though the property remains within the statutory definition of a capital asset. This result is necessary because Congress did not intend to extend any special treatment for capital gains and losses to profits and losses arising from the everyday operation of a business.

Examples: The C.P.R. Company was in the business of manufacturing various products, such as starch, syrup and sugar, from grain corn, and it had several long-term contracts to sell large quantities of these products. Normally, the C.P.R. Company would buy the grain corn necessary for its needs on the open market; however, in order to protect itself from sharp increases in the price of grain corn, it would also buy "corn futures," a contractual right entitling the Company to buy a certain quantity of corn at a set price within a future time. If a particular corn growing season yielded a good harvest, some of the corn futures contracts would be sold at a loss, but if shortages in the corn crop appeared, some of the corn futures contracts would be sold at a gain. The C.P.R. Company's transactions in the corn futures contracts were not separate and apart from its manufacturing operations; the futures transactions were an integral part of the C.P.R. Company's business. The corn futures transactions produced ordinary income and ordinary losses, not capital gains and losses. [*Corn Products Refining Co. v. Comm'r,* 350 U.S. 46, 76 S.Ct. 20 (1955).]

The B & S Company was in the business of manufacturing and selling paper making machinery. In 1946, the Company entered into a contract with the Government of Finland to manufacture and deliver two paper making machines, and as part of the contract, the Company was required to purchase U.S. Government bonds in a face amount of $820,000 and deposit them in an escrow account as security for performance of the contract. In 1948, the Company delivered the machines and, in accordance with the contract, the bonds were returned to the Company. A few days after the bonds were returned, the Company sold them at a loss. The bonds were purchased and sold as an incident of carrying on the Company's business; the Company did not intend to purchase or hold the bonds as an investment. The loss from the sale of the bonds was an ordinary loss, not a capital loss. [*Comm'r v. Bagley & Sewall Co.,* 221 F.2d 944 (2d Cir.1955).]

If a taxpayer is motivated to purchase property both for the purpose of investment and also to use the property in his business, at least one court has held that capital gain or loss will result (no *Corn Products*) if the taxpayer has a *substantial,* even though not *principal,* investment motive either at time of acquisition or disposition of the property.

Example: The W.W.W. Company purchased 3600 shares of common stock of Nor-West Corporation and several years later it sold the shares at a loss. The principal motive for purchasing the shares was to acquire a captive customer for the W.W.W. Company, but the Company also had a substantial investment motive for acquiring and holding the stock. The shares of

Nor-West stock were capital assets in the W.W.W. Company's hands, and the loss was a long-term capital loss. [*W.W. Windle Co.,* 65 T.C. 694 (1976).]

4. THE "SALE OR EXCHANGE" REQUIREMENT
a. In general

The Code defines a gain (or a loss) as occasioned by the "*sale or other disposition*" of an item of property. [IRC § 1001(a).] A capital gain (or loss), however, is more narrowly circumscribed, being defined as "gain [or loss] from the *sale or exchange*" of property which is a capital asset. [IRC § 1222(1)–(4).] Thus, the disposition of a capital asset in a transaction which is not a "sale or exchange," will give rise to ordinary gain (or loss), not capital gain (or loss). The abandonment of property which is subject to a liability has been held to be a "sale or exchange" of the property.

Examples: Louise was the beneficiary of a trust established by her aunt. Under the terms of the trust, when Louise reached the age of forty, she was to receive from the trust $5 million. The trustees had the discretion to pay Louise in cash, or to substitute for the payment in cash, payment in marketable securities with a value of $5 million; Louise did not, however, have title or right to any specific securities. When Louise reached the age of forty, the trustees decided to pay her the $5 million partly in cash and partly with securities which had a fair market value higher than their adjusted basis in the hands of the trust. The trust transferred the securities to Louise in exchange for the release of her claim against the trust; therefore, the trust realized a gain, which was a capital gain, upon transferring the securities to Louise. [*Kenan v. Comm'r,* 114 F.2d 217 (2d Cir.1940).]

[handwritten margin: eg of Xng : ① sec ⟷ release claim vs. trust by ben]

In 1929, Mary sued Howard and obtained a judgment against him in the amount of $75,000. Mary subsequently died and Galvin purchased her judgment against Howard from her estate for $11,000 in 1943. In 1945, Howard paid Galvin $21,000 as full settlement of the judgment against him. Although the judgment was a capital asset in Galvin's hands, the $21,000 which Galvin received was not the result of any sale or exchange; instead, the sum was received merely from the collection or settlement of the judgment, and the claim arising from the judgment was extinguished as a consequence. [*Galvin Hudson,* 20 T.C. 734 (1953).]

[handwritten margin: Not Xng : ② $ ⟷ settlement of claim — ord inc b/c ≅ collectn of jdgmt/debt but orig purch of claim (assgnmt) = Xng of cap asset (prop held for investmt/ltw)]

James and his wife Mary purchased some undeveloped land, paying 10% of the purchase price in cash and issuing nonrecourse promissory notes, secured by the land, for the

[handwritten: 900k]

(3)/abn mt = XnG

*dischgd
then debt*

AR   900K
Ab   700K
*   ───────*
cG   200K

balance of the purchase price. Several years later, the fair market value of the property had declined to an amount less than the amount of the outstanding loans, so James and Mary decided to abandon the property and the holder of the promissory notes foreclosed on the property. James and Mary had an amount realized on the disposition (abandonment) of the property equal to the amount of the outstanding nonrecourse indebtedness which encumbered the property, an amount which was less than their adjusted basis for the property; thus, they had a realized loss on the disposition. In addition the abandonment was held to be a "sale or exchange" and because the property was a capital asset, the loss was a capital loss. [*Yarbro v. Comm'r,* 737 F.2d 479 (5th Cir.1984).]

b.   Special rules

Congress has provided special rules to supply the "sale or exchange" requirement in some circumstances where it would otherwise not be satisfied in order to produce capital gain or loss. Some of the more important special rules are described in the following paragraphs.

i.   Worthless securities

If a security which is a capital asset becomes worthless during a taxable year, the security is deemed to be sold or exchanged on the last day of that taxable year, thereby giving rise to a capital loss (long-term or short-term, depending on the taxpayer's holding period for the security as of the last day of the taxable year). [IRC § 165(g) (1); see discussion, III. A. 3. c. ii. *a.*, at page 100, *supra.*]

ii.   Nonbusiness bad debts

If a nonbusiness debt becomes wholly worthless during a taxable year, the resulting loss is deemed to be a loss from the sale or exchange of a capital asset held for not more than 6 months. [IRC § 166(c); see discussion, III. A. 4. f., at page 103, *supra.*] This rule automatically produces a short-term capital loss; the taxpayer's actual holding period for the debt is irrelevant.

iii.   Options

If an option to buy or sell property which is or would be a capital asset in the hands of the taxpayer expires, the option is considered to be a capital asset and it is deemed to have been sold or exchanged on the day it expires. [IRC § 1234(a).]

Example: If Kathleen buys one ounce of gold, which is a capital asset in her hands, for $400, and she sells it at a later date for $350, she has a capital loss of $50. In the alternative, instead of actually buying an ounce of gold when its price is $400, Kathleen pays $50 for an option which entitles her to buy one ounce of gold for an additional payment of $375 at any time within the next 60 days. If the price of gold falls to $350 an ounce, she will let the option lapse at the end of the 60 days. Kathleen is deemed to have sold or exchanged the option on the date it expires and the resulting loss is a capital loss.

iv. **Cancellation of lease or distributor's agreement**

A sale or exchange is deemed to occur with respect to amounts received by a lessee for cancellation of a lease. [IRC § 1241.] This rule also applies to amounts received for the cancellation of a distributor's agreement by a distributor of goods who has a substantial capital investment in the distributorship. If the lease or distributorship agreement is a capital asset in the hands of the lessee or distributor, capital gain or loss will result.

Example: Lance leases a building for a term of 10 years at an annual rental of $12,000. At the end of the fifth year of the lease, the lessor pays Lance $5,000 in consideration for the cancellation of the lease. The payment is considered to be received in exchange for the lease agreement (not its extinction); since the lease is property to Lance and if it is a capital asset, the transaction results in capital gain. [See *Metropolitan Building Co. v. Comm'r, supra.*]

v. **Transfers of franchises, trademarks, and trade names**

The Code provides two negative rules with respect to the disposition of a franchise, trademark or trade name. If the transferor retains any significant power, right or continuing interest with respect to such property, the transfer is *not* to be treated as a sale or exchange of a capital asset. [IRC § 1253(a).] In addition, amounts received with respect to the disposition of such property are *not* to be treated as received from the sale or exchange of a capital asset if the amounts are contingent on the productivity, use, or disposition of the property transferred. [IRC § 1253(c).]

vi. **Amounts received on retirement of debt instruments**

Amounts received by the holder upon the retirement of a debt instrument (other than one issued by a natural person) are deemed to be received in exchange therefor. [IRC § 1271(a)(1).] If the debt instrument is a capital asset in the hands of the holder, capital gain or loss will result (long-term or short-term, depending on the taxpayer's holding period for the debt instrument). A debt instrument is a bond, debenture, note or certificate or other evidence of indebtedness. [IRC § 1275(a)(1).] This rule does not apply, however, to any obligation issued by a natural person. [IRC § 1271(b)(1).] In addition, ordinary income, rather than capital gain, will result to the extent of any original issue discount, or if there was an intention to call a debt instrument before maturity at the time it was issued. [IRC §§ 1271(a)(2) and 1272; see discussion, IV. E. 2., at page 234, *supra.*]

Example: The XYZ Corporation borrowed $1,000 from Melody in Year One and gave her its certificate of indebtedness which called for annual payments of interest at a rate of 10%, and repayment of the principal amount of $1,000 in Year Ten. In Year Five, Nick, who is not a dealer in securities, purchased the certificate from Melody for $900. In Year Ten, the Corporation paid Nick $1,000 in full payment of his claim. Although the transaction might be viewed as a mere extinguishment of Nick's claim under the debt instrument, it is treated as an exchange of the instrument. Nick has a $100 long-term capital gain. If an individual had borrowed the $1,000 from Melody, who then sold the claim to Nick for $900, Nick would have ordinary income of $100 upon payment by the debtor. [*Galvin Hudson,* 20 T.C. 734 (1953).]

5. HOLDING PERIOD

Capital gain (or loss) is long-term or short-term depending on whether the taxpayer has held a capital asset for more than 6 months when it is sold or exchanged. [IRC § 1222(1)–(4).] In addition to the general rules for determining the holding period, special rules may apply in certain situations.

a. In general

The critical aspect of the holding period for a capital asset is determining whether an asset has been held for *more than* 6 months when it is sold or exchanged, thereby resulting in long-term capital gain (or loss). [IRC § 1222(3) and (4).] In computing the holding period with respect to an item of property, the date on which it is acquired is excluded and the date on which it is sold or exchanged is included; the property goes long-term on the date 6 months and 1 day after it is acquired. If a capital asset is acquired on the last day of a calendar month, it must not be sold or exchanged until on or after the first day of the seventh succeeding calendar month in order to have been held *more than* 6 months. [Rev.Rul. 66–7, 1966–1 C.B. 188.]

Example: Olive buys 100 shares of Xerox Corporation common stock on March 30. Olive will have held the stock for more than 6 months on October 1. If Olive purchases the stock on March 29 it will be held long term on September 30.

The last day of a holding period is the date on which a contract to sell the property is made. Thus, the last day of the holding period of securities sold on a registered securities exchange or in the over-the-counter market, is the "trade date," the date on which the contract to sell the securities is made. Similarly, the trade date is the date securities are considered to be acquired. The holding period for securities acquired on a registered securities exchange or in the over-the-counter market, therefore, is determined by excluding the trade date on which they were acquired and by including the trade date on which they were sold. [Rev.Rul. 66–97, 1966–1 C.B. 190.] The "settlement date," the date on which a security is delivered and payment is tendered (generally several days after the trade date) does not affect the holding period of the securities.

b. Special rules

Congress has provided special rules which affect the holding period of certain items of property in certain situations. Some of the more important special rules are described in the following paragraphs.

i. Nonbusiness bad debts

If a nonbusiness debt becomes wholly worthless during a taxable year, the resulting loss is deemed to be a loss from the sale or exchange of a capital asset held for not more than 6 months. [IRC § 166(d); see discussion, III. A. 4. f., at page 103, *supra.*] This rule automatically produces a short-term capital loss; the taxpayer's actual holding period for the debt is irrelevant.

ii. Exchanged or substituted basis property

In determining the holding period of property received in an exchange, if the property received has its basis determined in whole or in part with reference to the basis of the property given up in the exchange (the basis of the old property is substituted for the new property), the holding period of the property given up is added (or "tacked") on to the holding period of the property received if the property given up was a capital asset or section 1231 property. [IRC § 1223(1); see IRC § 7701(a)(44).]

Example: Queenie owned a used car sales business which she operated on a lot which she purchased in 1970 for $10,000. In the current year, the state road department condemned her car lot and paid her $50,000 for it. Queenie used the $50,000 to purchase another lot to which she relocated her used car sales business. The basis of her newly acquired used car lot is $10,000. [IRC

§ 1033(b); see discussion, IV. D. 2. g., at page 225, *supra.*] The holding period for the newly acquired lot includes the holding period for the old lot.

iii. Transferred or carryover basis property

In determining the holding period of property which has a basis in the hands of the taxpayer determined with reference to the basis, in whole or in part, of the property while in the hands of some other person (a transferred or carryover basis), the holding period of the property while in the hands of the other person is added (or "tacked") on to the taxpayer's holding period. [IRC § 1223(2); see IRC § 7701(a)(43).]

Example: Renfred purchased 100 shares of XYZ Corporation stock on January 10 of Year One for $1,000. On March 1 of Year One, when the 100 shares had a fair market value of $1,500, he gave them to his niece, Swanhilda; he was not required to pay any gift tax on the transfer. Swanhilda sold the 100 shares on July 22 of Year One for $2,000. Swanhilda has $1,000 of long-term capital gain from the sale of the stock.

iv. Wash sales of stock or securities

In determining the holding period of stock or securities which were acquired in circumstances which resulted in the nondeductibility of a loss with respect to substantially identical stock or securities under IRC § 1091, the holding period of such substantially identical stock or securities is added (or "tacked") on to the newly acquired stock or securities. [IRC § 1223(4); see discussion of IRC § 1091, III. C. 11., at page 177, *supra.*]

Example: Tarleton bought 100 shares of XYZ common stock on January 31 as an investment for $10,000. On July 1 of the same year, he sells the shares for $8,000 and on July 15 he purchases another 100 shares of XYZ common stock for $9,000. Tarleton sells the second block of 100 shares on August 16 for $15,000. A deduction for the loss realized on the July 1 sale is disallowed under IRC § 1091(a), and the basis of the block of stock purchased on July 15 is $11,000 under IRC § 1091(d). Tarleton has a $4,000 long-term capital gain from the August 16 sale.

v. Principal residence

In determining the holding period of property used by a taxpayer as his principal residence, if it was acquired under circumstances which resulted under IRC § 1034 in the nonrecognition of gain upon the sale or exchange of another residence, there is to be added (or "tacked") on the holding period of the other residence. [IRC § 1223(7); see discussion of IRC § 1034, IV. D. 3. a. iv., at page 228, *supra.*]

vi.   Property acquired from a decedent

If a taxpayer (an heir, legatee, executor, etc.) acquires property from a decedent and its basis is determined under IRC § 1014, the property is deemed to have a holding period of more than 6 months, even if the taxpayer disposes of the property within 6 months of acquiring it from the decedent and even if decedent had not held it for 6 months. [IRC § 1223(11); see discussion of IRC § 1014, II. B. 2. a. iii., at page 26, *supra.*]

Example: Umeko bought a parcel of real estate on August 1 of Year One for $100,000. Umeko died ten days later and her will provided for the real estate to go to her boyfriend, Vito. On December 2 of Year One, Vito sold the real estate, which was a capital asset in his hands, for $125,000. Vito has a $25,000 long-term capital gain from the sale.

vii.   Short sales of property

A "short sale" of property occurs when someone contracts to sell property which he does not actually own. Generally, the seller borrows the property which he has sold short and he is obligated to return the borrowed property within a certain period of time. The short sale is "closed" or "covered" when the borrowed property is returned. If the price of the property has gone down between the date of the short sale and the date he closes the short sale, he will make a profit; if the price of the property has increased, he will have a loss.

The gain or loss from a short sale occurs, not when the short sale itself takes place, but when the short sale is closed. Gain or loss from the short sale of property is a capital gain or loss if the property which is used to close the short sale is a capital asset. [IRC § 1233(a).] If the property is or would be a capital asset, the gain or loss is long-term or short-term depending on how long the taxpayer actually holds the property used to close the short sale.

Example: Wilma, who owns no shares of XYZ stock, sells 100 shares of XYZ common stock on October 7 for $2,000. She borrows the 100 shares from her broker under terms which require her to return 100 shares of XYZ common stock to him within 30 days. On November 4 the price of

100 shares of XYZ common stock has dropped to $1,500, so she buys 100 shares and transfers them to her broker. Wilma has an amount realized from the short sale of $2,000, and the adjusted basis for the stock used to close the short sale is $1,500. Wilma held the stock used to close the short sale for less than 6 months, thus she has a $500 short-term capital gain from the short sale.

6. CORRELATION WITH PRIOR TRANSACTIONS

A capital loss is statutorily defined exclusively as the consequence of "the sale or exchange of a capital asset." [IRC § 1222(2) and (4).] On occasion, however, a taxpayer repays an amount which relates to his receipt of capital gain in an earlier taxable year under circumstances that permit him to deduct the repayment. Normally, a deductible repayment is deducted from ordinary income; however, if a capital gain received preferential treatment in the year of its receipt, tax benefit principles require the repayment to be characterized as a capital loss (even though there is no "sale or exchange of a capital asset"), subject to the limitations on the deductibility of capital losses, in the year of repayment. There is a question whether recharacterization of the loss as a capital loss would occur if no preferential treatment were accorded the prior included capital gain. The above doctrine has been interpreted to require a subsequent deduction to be limited if it is related to a prior inclusion which was allowed some tax benefit. [*U.S. v. Skelly Oil Co.*, 394 U.S. 678, 89 S.Ct. 1379 (1969).]

Examples: Frederick owned stock in a corporation which liquidated in 1937 and distributed its assets to its shareholders. Frederick treated the amounts he received in the corporate liquidation as long-term capital gain. [*See* IRC § 331(a).] In 1944, a judgment was rendered against the old corporation, and Frederick, as a transferee of the corporation's assets, paid the judgment. Frederick was required to treat the repayment as a long-term capital loss in 1944, rather than an ordinary business deduction. [*Arrowsmith v. Comm'r*, 344 U.S. 6, 73 S.Ct. 71 (1952).]

Charles was the vice president and treasurer of Western Nuclear Corporation. In 1966, Charles sold 3,000 shares of Western Nuclear common stock which he had purchased in 1959 and 1960; the sales produced long-term capital gain. Within 6 months of making these sales, Charles exercised some options to purchase additional shares of Western Nuclear common stock. Section 16(b) of the Securities and Exchange Act of 1934 prohibits the purchase and sale of a corporation's stock within a 6-month period by its officers. In 1968, another holder of Western Nuclear stock filed suit against Charles and Western Nuclear to recover the "insider profits" which Charles obtained in 1966, allegedly in violation of the Securities and Exchange Act of 1934. Charles decided to not contest the suit, and to repay the full amount of asserted damages, which he did in 1968, deducting the full amount as an ordinary and necessary business expense. Because the origin and basic measure for the payment in 1968 was the long-term capital gain which he reported from the sale of Western Nuclear stock in 1966, the repayment was required to be characterized as a long-term capital loss in 1968. [*Brown v. Comm'r,* 529 F.2d 609 (10th Cir.1976).]

7. SPECIAL PROVISIONS
a. Options

Gain or loss from the sale or exchange of an option to buy or sell property is capital gain or loss if the property to which the option relates is or would be a capital asset in the taxpayer's hands. [IRC § 1234(a).]

Example: Yoshi, who is not a dealer in real property, pays $1,000 for an option to acquire a parcel of real estate. Instead of exercising the option, she sells it for $1,500. Yoshi has $500 of capital gain from the sale. In the alternative, if Yoshi is a dealer in real estate (i.e., she holds real estate primarily for sale to customers in the ordinary course of her business) the gain from the sale of the option would be ordinary income, not capital gain.

b. Patents

Generally, a transfer (other than by gift, inheritance or devise) of all substantial rights to a patent (or an undivided interest which includes a part of all such rights) by an individual whose efforts created the patent (or by any other individual who purchased the patent from the creator before the invention covered by the patent is reduced to practice) to an unrelated party is deemed to be a sale or exchange of a capital asset held for more than 6 months. [IRC § 1235(a).] This rule provides favorable tax treatment to patents, and it applies regardless of whether payments in consideration for the transfer are: (1) payable periodically over a period coterminous with the transferee's use of the patent, or (2) contingent on the productivity, use, or disposition of the patent.

c. Dealers in securities

Generally, property held by a taxpayer primarily for sale to customers in the ordinary course of business is not treated as a capital asset. [IRC § 1221(1); see discussion, VI. B. 3. a. i. *a.*, at page 275, *supra.*] Congress recognized, however, that certain taxpayers who are dealers in securities (i.e., they are merchants of securities, regularly engaged in the purchase of securities and their resale to customers) might, on occasion, purchase securities as an investment for themselves, rather than as part of their inventory of securities held primarily for sale to customers. Guidelines have been established under which a dealer in securities may effectively treat a security as a capital asset if, before the close of the day on which a security (or an option to acquire a security) is acquired, the security is clearly identified in the dealer's records as a security (or an option) held for investment and if the security is not, at any time thereafter, held by the dealer primarily for sale to customers in the ordinary course of business. [IRC § 1236(a).] A security includes shares of stock of a corporation, certificates of stock or interest in a corporation, notes, bonds, debentures, evidences of indebtedness, or any evidence of an interest in or right to subscribe to or purchase any such items. [IRC § 1236(c).]

C. QUASI–CAPITAL ASSETS

1. IN GENERAL

Property used in a taxpayer's trade or business of a character which is subject to the allowance for depreciation and real property used in a taxpayer's trade or business is excluded from the statutory definition of capital asset; thus, the sale or exchange of such property produces ordinary income (or loss). [IRC § 1221(2); see discussion, VI. B. 3. a. ii., at page 278, *supra*.] In addition, an involuntary conversion (such as by fire or theft) of property does not involve a sale or exchange; thus, an involuntary conversion of a capital asset technically produces ordinary income (or loss). [IRC § 1222(1)–(4); see discussion, VI. B. 4. a., at page 282, *supra*.] Under the special rules of IRC § 1231, however, capital gain (or loss) treatment may be provided to the sale or exchange of property used in a trade or business, and to the involuntary or compulsory conversion of certain capital assets or property used in a trade or business. Thus, these items of property are referred to as "quasi-capital assets."

Under IRC § 1231, gains and losses from the involuntary conversion (not including a condemnation) of "section 1231 assets" which are recognized during a taxable year are netted against each other; this is referred to as the "subhotchpot." If there is an excess of losses over gains in the subhotchpot, then those gains and losses drop out of any further computations to be made under IRC § 1231, and the character of such gains and losses is ordinary. On the other hand, if the gains equal or exceed the losses in the subhotchpot, then the gains and losses from those transactions are placed in the main hotchpot to be netted against the gains and losses from the sale or exchange or compulsory conversion of other section 1231 assets recognized during the taxable year; this is referred to as the "main hotchpot." If, in the main hotchpot, the overall gains exceed the overall losses (a "net section 1231 gain"), then each gain and each loss is treated as a long-term capital gain, or a long-term capital loss, as the case may be. If losses equal or exceed gains in the main hotchpot, however, each gain and each loss is treated as ordinary income, or an ordinary loss, as the case may be, subject to an exception in

IRC § 1231(c). Gains are included in the IRC § 1231 computations only to the extent they have not been treated as ordinary income pursuant to IRC §§ 1239, 1245 or 1250. [See discussions, VI. D. and E., at pages 294 and 295, *infra.*]

2. SECTION 1231 ASSETS

The rules of IRC § 1231 may apply to two categories of property included in the classification of "section 1231 assets": (1) property used in the trade or business, and (2) capital assets held for more than 6 months *and* held in connection with a trade or business or a transaction entered into for profit.

"Property used in the trade or business" is defined to mean property, held for more than 6 months and used in a trade or business, which is either real property or property of a character subject to the allowance for depreciation. [IRC § 1231(b)(1).] However, specifically excluded from the definition of property used in the trade or business are items of property which are excluded from the definition of capital asset under IRC § 1221(1), (3) and (5), i.e., inventory, copyrights and similar property, and publications of the U.S. Government. [IRC § 1231(b)(1)(A)–(D). Accounts receivable which are excluded from the definition of capital asset under IRC § 1221(4) would not be "property used in the trade or business" because they are not subject to the allowance for depreciation, nor are they real property; see discussion of definition of capital asset, VI. B. 3, at page 274, *supra.*] Timber, coal, domestic iron ore, livestock and unharvested crops are also "property used in the trade or business." [IRC § 1231(b)(2)–(4).]

The second category of property treated as section 1231 assets includes capital assets which have been held for more than 6 months *and* held in connection with a trade or business or a transaction entered into for profit. Capital assets which are merely held for personal purposes are not section 1231 assets. [But see casualty losses on such property, IRC § 165(h) and discussion, III. B. 4., at page 136, *supra.*]

3. THE SUBHOTCHPOT

Gains and losses arising from fire, storm, shipwreck, or other casualty, or from theft (involuntary conversion) of section 1231 assets during a taxable year are first netted against each other before any further computations are made under IRC § 1231. [Note that condemnations are not included.] If the losses exceed the gains in the subhotchpot, then IRC § 1231 has no further application in determining the character of such gains and losses, and lacking any sale or exchange, they are ordinary gains and losses. On the other hand, if the gains equal or exceed the losses, then each gain and each loss will enter the main hotchpot.

Example: Zelig has a building in which his business is located which he has owned for more than 6 months. The building has a fair market value of $100,000, and an adjusted basis to Zelig of $75,000;

depreciation deductions have been taken under the straight line method. In the current year, the building is completely destroyed in a fire. The building is not insured and Zelig is not compensated for its loss. This is the only transaction described in the subhotchpot which Zelig has during the current year. IRC § 1231 will not determine the character of the $75,000 loss on the building. The loss is an ordinary loss because the building is not a capital asset; however, even if it was a capital asset, the loss would still be ordinary because there has been no "sale or exchange" transaction.

In the alternative, if the building had been insured for its full fair market value of $100,000, then the gain of $25,000 would exceed the losses within the subhotchpot, and the gain would move into the main hotchpot of IRC § 1231 for determination of its character.

4. THE MAIN HOTCHPOT

The main hotchpot collects all section 1231 gains and section 1231 losses for a taxable year (not thrown out by the subhotchpot), and if the section 1231 gains exceed the section 1231 losses, then each gain is treated as a long-term capital gain, and each loss is treated as a long-term capital loss. [IRC § 1231(a)(1).] On the other hand, if the section 1231 losses equal or exceed the section 1231 gains for a taxable year, then each gain is treated as ordinary income and each loss is treated as an ordinary loss. [IRC § 1231(a)(2).]

A "section 1231 gain" (or loss) is the sum of the recognized gains (or losses) from the sale or exchange of property used in the trade or business, plus the recognized gains (or losses) from the compulsory or involuntary conversion of section 1231 assets. [IRC § 1231(a)(3).] Gains are taken into account only to the extent they are taken into account in computing gross income; losses are taken into account only to the extent they are otherwise deductible (but the limitations of IRC § 1211 do not apply for this purpose). [IRC § 1231(a)(4).]

Example: Zelig, in the alternative facts of the preceding Example (building was insured), had a $25,000 gain from the destruction of the building. If, in addition, he sold a parcel of unimproved real estate which he used in his farming business for a *loss* of $8,000, then the main hotchpot would include section 1231 gains ($25,000) in excess of section 1231 losses ($8,000); the gain would be treated as a long-term capital gain (even though there was no sale or exchange of a capital asset), and the loss would be treated as a long-term capital loss.

In the alternative, if Zelig sold the land for a loss of *$28,000,* then the main hotchpot would include section 1231 losses ($28,000) in excess of section 1231 gains ($25,000); the gain would be treated as ordinary income, and the loss would be treated as an ordinary loss.

5. RECAPTURE

If a taxpayer has a net section 1231 loss for a taxable year, it may affect the character of net section 1231 gains in subsequent taxable years. If a taxpayer has a net section 1231 gain (excess of section 1231 gains over sections 1231 losses) in a taxable year, it is treated as ordinary income to the extent of the taxpayer's nonrecaptured net section 1231 loss. [IRC § 1231(c).] A "non-recaptured net section 1231 loss" is the excess of the total amount of net section 1231 losses for the 5 most recent preceding taxable years over the portion of such losses previously recaptured. [IRC § 1231(c)(2).]

Example: Anabelle has net section 1231 losses of $2,000 in Year One, $4,000 in Year Two, $3,000 in Year Three, $5,000 in Year Four, and $1,000 in Year Five. In Year Six, she has $13,000 of main hotchpot gains and $5,000 of main hotchpot losses, for a net section 1231 gain of $8,000. Normally, the Year Six gains and losses would be treated as long-term capital gains and losses. However, in Year Six she must recharacterize all $8,000 of the *net* section 1231 gain as ordinary income (the net section 1231 gain ($8,000) *does not exceed* the non-recaptured net section 1231 losses ($15,000)).

In Year Seven, Anabelle has a net section 1231 gain of $10,000; she must treat $7,000 of that amount as ordinary income [the amount of the net section 1231 gain for the taxable year which *does not exceed* the non-recaptured net section 1231 losses, or $7,000 (the aggregate net section 1231 losses for Years Two through Six or $13,000, over the portion of such losses already recaptured, in Year Six, or $6,000 ($4,000 from Year Two plus $2,000 from Year Three))].

D. SALE OF DEPRECIABLE PROPERTY BETWEEN RELATED TAXPAYERS

Gain from the sale or exchange of property which would otherwise be capital gain, or gain subject to the characterization rules of IRC § 1231, is treated as ordinary income if: (1) the sale or exchange is between certain related persons, and (2) the property is of a character which is subject to the allowance for depreciation in the hands of the *transferee*. [IRC § 1239(a).] For purposes of this rule, "related persons" means: (1) a person and all "controlled entities" with respect to that person; (2) a taxpayer and any trust in which she or her spouse has a beneficial interest (other than a remote contingent interest); and (3) an employer and any person related to the employer. [IRC § 1239(b) and (d).] With respect to any person, a "controlled entity" includes a corporation, if more than 50% of the value of its outstanding stock is owned, directly or indirectly, by or for that person, and a partnership, if more than 50% of the capital interest or profits interest is owned, directly or indirectly, by or for that person. [IRC § 1239(c).] In determining whether the 50% owned entity tests are met, constructive ownership rules apply which, in general terms, treat a person as the owner of shares of stock (or partnership interests) which are actually owned by members of that person's family or by other corporations, partnerships and other entities in which that person has an interest. [IRC §§ 1239(c)(2) and 267(c).] In addition, a "controlled entity" includes any entity which is treated as a related person under certain provisions of IRC § 267, relating to the limitations on losses and deductions with respect to transactions between related taxpayers. [IRC §§ 267(b)(3), (10), (11), (12) and 1239(c)(1)(C); see discussion of IRC § 267 at III. C. 5., at page 159, *supra*.]

E. RECAPTURE OF DEPRECIATION

1. IN GENERAL

Depreciation deductions taken with respect to property used in a trade or business, or property held for the production of income, are ordinary deductions and are subtracted from ordinary income in computing taxable income, and the basis of the property is correspondingly reduced by the amount of the deductions taken. [See discussions, II. B. 2. a. vi. and III. A. 5. a. v., at pages 33 and 110, *supra*.] In addition, such property may be treated as a "quasi-capital asset," and thus any gain realized upon its disposition may be treated as long-term capital gain. [See discussion, VI. C., at page 291, *supra*.] The "recapture" provisions of IRC §§ 1245 and 1250 bring symmetrical treatment to such property by characterizing as ordinary income all or a portion of the gain realized from the disposition of property with respect to which deductions for depreciation have been taken. [See IRC § 64.] These recapture rules override other provisions of the Code which might otherwise provide capital gain treatment, such as IRC § 1231. Sometimes the recapture gain does not have to be recognized but only if there is an exception contained within the recapture sections themselves.

2. RECAPTURE UNDER SECTION 1245

a. In general

If section 1245 property is disposed of, *the excess* of the *lower* of either (a) the recomputed basis of the property, or (b) the amount realized (if the property is sold, exchanged or involuntarily converted) or the fair market value of the property (if it is otherwise disposed of) *over* the adjusted basis of the property is required to be treated as ordinary income. [IRC §§ 1245(a)(1) and 64.] The amount of gain required to be treated as ordinary income under this provision is required to be recognized, unless an exception is provided within IRC § 1245 itself.   The general effect of IRC § 1245 is to require any recognized gain to be treated as ordinary income to the extent of any previously allowed depreciation deductions.   Although the recapture rules are triggered broadly by any "disposition" of covered property, statutory exceptions are provided for certain dispositions [see discussion, VI. E. 2. d., at page 297, *infra*], and a taxpayer's mere conversion of property from business use to personal use is not a "disposition" [Rev.Rul. 69–487, 1969–2 C.B. 165].

b.   Section 1245 property

The term "section 1245 property" generally includes tangible and intangible personal property which is or has been property of a character subject to the allowance for depreciation under IRC § 167. [IRC § 1245(a)(3).]   Section 1245 property generally does not include real property, although some items of property which may be treated as real property under local law, such as a "single purpose agricultural or horticultural structure" (i.e., a greenhouse), are included as section 1245 property.   [IRC § 1245(a)(3)(D).]

Example: In Year One, Brent purchased a truck which he used in his business until he disposed of it in Year Seven.   The truck is "section 1245 property."   In the alternative, Brent used the truck in his business until Year Four when he began using it solely for personal purposes.   When he disposed of the truck in Year Seven it was still "section 1245 property" because it was subject to depreciation deductions while in Brent's hands even though it did not qualify for depreciation deductions at the time he disposed of it.

c.   Recomputed basis

The recomputed basis of an item of section 1245 property is the property's adjusted basis *plus* all adjustments reflected in the adjusted basis on account of depreciation or amortization deductions allowed or allowable to the taxpayer or any other person with respect to the property.   [IRC § 1245(a)(2).]   For this purpose, depreciation deductions include the additional, bonus deductions taken pursuant to IRC § 179.   [See discussion, III. A. 5. d. ii., at page 113, *supra*.]   If a taxpayer can demonstrate that the amounts actually *allowed* as deductions for depreciation with respect to an item of property are less than the amount *allowable* as deductions, only the amount allowed must be added to the property's adjusted basis to arrive at its recomputed basis.

Examples: Cherie purchased a machine in Year One for use in her business for $10,000 cash.   She deducted $2,000 with respect to the machine under IRC § 179, and a total of $7,360 under IRC § 168, prior to selling the machine in Year Four.   The adjusted basis of the machine in Year Four is $640, and its recomputed basis is $10,000.

Derwin purchased a machine in Year One for use in his business for $10,000 cash. In Year Two, the machine was damaged in an accident, and Derwin deducted the $1,500 loss in value of the machine. In addition, Derwin deducted a total of $8,120 under IRC § 168 prior to selling the machine in Year Five. The adjusted basis of the machine in Year Five is $380, and its recomputed basis is $8,500.

Enid purchased a machine in Year One for use in her business for $10,000 cash; however, she neglected to take any depreciation deductions with respect to the machine. Assuming that she would have been allowed depreciation deductions of $1,000 per year, and that her taxable income would have been reduced in each year on account of such deductions, the machine would have an adjusted basis of $2,000 when she sells it in Year Eight. Because Enid can establish that the amount *allowed* for depreciation ($0) was less than the amount *allowable* ($8,000), the recomputed basis of the machine is $2,000.

d. Exceptions

The recapture rules of IRC § 1245 do not apply if property is disposed of by gift, or if it is transferred at death. [IRC § 1245(b)(1) and (2).] In addition, the recapture rules apply to certain transactions with corporations and partnerships only to the extent gain is recognized pursuant to specifically cited provisions of the Code. [IRC § 1245(b)(3).] If section 1245 property is disposed of in a transaction to which the nonrecognition rules of IRC §§ 1031 (like-kind exchange) or 1033 (involuntary conversion) apply, gain must be recognized as ordinary income under IRC § 1245(a)(1) only to the extent of the sum of: (1) the gain required to be recognized under IRC §§ 1031 or 1033, plus (2) the excess of the fair market value of property acquired which is not section 1245 property over the amount determined under (1). [IRC § 1245(b)(4); see discussions of IRC §§ 1031 and 1033, IV. D. 1., and 2., at pages 215 and 220, *supra,* respectively.]

Examples: Fidel purchases an automobile in Year One which he uses in his business. In Year Three, Fidel gives the automobile to his daughter, Gratia. The gift of the automobile is not a "disposition" and IRC § 1245(a) does not apply; the automobile is still "section 1245 property" in Gratia's hands.

Hector purchases a machine in Year One which he uses in his business. In Year Three, when the machine has an adjusted basis of $4,000, a recomputed basis of $6,000 and a fair market value of $10,000, Hector exchanges it for another machine of a like kind, which has a fair market value of $7,000, plus $3,000 in cash. Hector must recognize, as ordinary income, $3,000 under IRC § 1245(a)(1).

3. RECAPTURE UNDER SECTION 1250
a. In general

If section 1250 property is disposed of, a portion of the realized gain may be required to be treated as ordinary income, rather than capital gain. The amount of ordinary income is determined by multiplying one or more of three "applicable percentages" (determined according to three successive periods of time) by the lower of: (1) generally, the excess of accelerated depreciation over straight line depreciation, known as the portion of the "additional depreciation" with respect to the property which is attributable to each of the three time periods; or (2) the gain on the property, i.e. *the excess* of the amount realized (if the property is sold, exchanged or involuntarily converted) or the fair market value of the property (if it is otherwise disposed of) *over* the adjusted basis of the property. [IRC § 1250(a)(1), (2) and (3).]

b. Section 1250 property

"Section 1250 property" means any <u>real</u> property which is or has been property of a character subject to the allowance for depreciation under IRC § 167; however the term does not include real property which is treated as "section 1245 property." [IRC § 1250(c); see discussion, VI. E. 2. b., at page 296, *supra.*] As a practical matter, most types of depreciable real property are section 1250 property.

c. Additional depreciation

With respect to section 1250 property, "additional depreciation" means *the excess* of depreciation adjustments, attributable to each of three pertinent periods of time after December 31, 1963, reflected in the adjusted basis of the property on account of deductions allowed or allowable for depreciation or for rehabilitation expenditures *over* the amount of such deductions which would have been allowed if the straight line method had been used. [IRC § 1250(b).] In determining the amounts which would have been allowed under the straight line method, the taxpayer must use the useful life and salvage value which was used in computing the depreciation deductions actually taken, or, if it was depreciated under ACRS, then the comparison is made with the adjustments which would have resulted if the taxpayer had used the straight line method using the property's recovery period. [IRC § 1250(b) (5).] If a taxpayer has a holding period (after applying the rules of IRC

CHARACTERIZATION OF INCOME AND DEDUCTIONS

§ 1223) for section 1250 property of one year or less, then "additional depreciation" means *all* depreciation adjustments, not just the amount in excess of the straight line amount.

> *Example:* Imogene purchased improved residential real property in 1978, and sold it on January 1, 1983. She computed depreciation using the 200% declining balance method, and, for the period from January 1, 1979 through December 31, 1982, she took deductions totalling $4,723; if she had used the straight line method to compute depreciation, her deductions would have totalled only $3,600 for that time period. The additional depreciation for Imogene's property is $1,123 ($4,723–$3,600). [Reg. § 1.1250–2(b)(7) Example (1).]

d. Applicable percentage

In determining the amount of gain required to be characterized as ordinary income under IRC § 1250, adjustments for depreciation taken during three successive time periods must be considered, and an appropriate "applicable percentage" must be ascertained for each relevant time period. The applicable percentage for a particular item of section 1250 property, for each of the pertinent time periods, is based upon the specific type of property involved and the taxpayer's holding period for the property. For this purpose, the taxpayer's holding period for the property is determined *without* applying the special rules of IRC § 1223. [IRC § 1250(e).] The applicable percentage for most real property depreciated since 1975 is 100%. [IRC § 1250(a)(1)(B)(v).]

e. Exceptions

The recapture rules of IRC § 1250 are subject to the same general exceptions applicable to the recapture rules of IRC § 1245. [IRC § 1250(d); see discussion of the exceptions to IRC § 1245, VI. E. 2. d., at page 297, *supra.*]

REVIEW QUESTIONS

Q# 1: Terry owns several parcels of real estate. Over the last few years Terry has made a living buying and selling real estate and in the current year he sells 2 parcels of land which he bought 3 years ago. Terry bought these parcels with the intention of quickly reselling them. What is the character of the gain on the sale of these properties?

Q# 2: In the current year, Lynn sells certain capital assets, held for more than 6 months, at a gain of $2,000. Other capital assets, held for less than 6 months, are sold by Lynn at a loss of $1,000. How much is included in Lynn's net income for the current year?

Q# 3: In the current year, Art sells certain long-term capital assets for a gain of $2,000 and other long-term capital assets for a loss of $20,000. Art also has $100,000 of ordinary income. How much of the long-term capital loss may Art deduct in the current year?

Q# 4: In Question # 3 above, what happens to the remaining loss and what is it's character?

Q# 5: What result if Art, from Question # 3, has $100,000 of ordinary income and a $10,000 short-term capital gain in Year Two?

Q# 6: Kathy sells a rental apartment building that she had used in her trade or business for 5 years. The building was depreciated under the straight-line method and was sold for a gain of $50,000. Is the building a capital asset? What is the character of the gain?

Q# 7: In order to qualify for capital asset treatment certain requirements must be met. What requirement of the capital asset transaction treatment does IRC §§ 165(g) and 1234 provide?

Q# 8: Sally exchanges a plot of investment land for a similar tract in a transaction that qualifies for nonrecognition of gain under IRC § 1031. Sally held the land she exchanged for one year and subsequently sold the land she received one month after acquiring it. What is the holding period for the land Sally acquired in the exchange?

Q# 9: Adam receives 10 shares of stock from his father as a gift. Adam's father had a basis in the stock of $10 and its fair market value on the date of the gift was $100. Adam's father held the stock for 10 years before giving it to Adam. Three months after receiving the stock, Adam sells it for $175. What is Adam's holding period and gain for the stock?

Q# 10: The following gains and losses take place during the current year: $1,000 gain from the involuntary conversion of business property held more than 6 months; a $2,000 IRC § 165(c)(1) loss from the involuntary conversion of business property held more than 6 months; and $500 gain from sale of business property held more than 6 months. How does IRC § 1231 characterize these gains and losses?

Q# 11: In Question # 10, if the gain on the involuntary conversion of the business property was $3,000 instead of $1,000, how would the gains and losses be characterized under IRC § 1231?

Q# 12: In Question # 10, if all of the property was *sold* instead of being involuntarily converted and the same gains and losses resulted, how would IRC § 1231 characterize the gains and losses?

Q# 13: Richard and Elizabeth, husband and wife, each own 50% of the stock of Corporation. Elizabeth sells a building which she has depreciated using the straight-line method and which she has held for 5 years to Corporation at a gain of $50,000. Corporation plans on renting the building and depreciating it immediately. What is the character of Elizabeth's $50,000 gain?

Q# 14: What result in Question # 13 if Richard is Elizabeth's brother-in-law rather than her husband?

Q# 15: How is Elizabeth's $50,000 IRC § 1231(a) main hotchpot gain in Question # 14 characterized if she has no other IRC § 1231 transactions in this or any other year except that two years ago she had $20,000 of net section 1231 losses (excess of section 1231 losses over section 1231 gains)?

Q# 16: On January 2 of the current year, Vanessa sells a piece of business equipment for $9,000. Vanessa purchased this equipment on January 1 two years ago (but after 1986) at a cost of $10,000 and she has taken $5,200 of depreciation on the equipment (it is 5-year property under ACRS). What is the character of the gain on the sale of the equipment?

Q# 17: What results in Question # 16 if Vanessa sells the equipment for $20,000 rather than $9,000?

Q# 18: Determine Businessman's adjusted gross income for the year in which he has $100,000 salary and the following transactions occur:

(1) Businessman sells a building used in his business and acquired in 1975. His gain on the building is $30,000, $10,000 of which is ordinary income under IRC § 1250(a).

(2) He sells some depreciable business equipment at a $4,000 loss.

(3) Businessman sells some stock at a $1,000 long-term capital gain.

(4) He has a nonbusiness bad debt of $2,000.

Q# 19: Lessee's 8 year lease on a residence has 5 years to run and his landlord pays him $5,000 to buy him out so he can construct a new apartment building on the property. What result to Lessee?

Q# 20: Creditor bought Debtor's $10,000 note for $9,000 from the original creditor 2 years ago. The note is a capital asset to Creditor. Debtor pays off the note with a bond ($7,000 fair market value, $4,000 adjusted basis, held for 2 years) and some stock ($3,000 fair market value, $5,000 adjusted basis, held for 5 months). The stocks and bond are both investment properties. What consequences to Creditor and Debtor?

*

VII

COMPUTING TAX LIABILITY

Analysis

F. Tax Credits—Continued
   3. Nonrefundable General Business Credit
   4. Nonrefundable Credit for Prior Year Minimum Tax Liability
   5. Refundable Credits

An individual's income tax liability involves a series of computations according to the following *general* schematic:

	Gross Income
Less	IRC § 62 Deductions
	Adjusted Gross Income
Less	Personal Exemptions & either the Standard Deduction or Itemized Deductions
	Taxable Income
Times	Tax Rate
	Gross Tax Liability
Less	Tax Credits
	Net Tax Liability

Previous sections of this outline have considered what is included in, or excluded from, gross income and what items may be properly deducted in computing taxable income. For individual taxpayers, the computation of taxable income is a two step process, in which certain deductions are subtracted from Gross Income to arrive at Adjusted Gross Income. Taxable Income is then computed by subtracting from Adjusted Gross Income the deductions for Personal Exemptions and *either* the standard deduction *or* the amount of allowable itemized deductions, in general whichever is the larger amount. The Tax Rate, which is multiplied by the Taxable Income to arrive at the Gross Tax Liability, is determined by the taxpayer's filing status or classification and the amount of the taxpayer's Taxable Income for the year. The taxpayer will likely have Tax Credits, which are subtracted from the Gross Tax Liability in arriving at the Net Tax Liability, the amount which he must remit to the Internal Revenue Service. However, a taxpayer may be required to compute an Alternative Minimum Tax, especially if he has a substantial amount of items of tax preference for the year.

A. ADJUSTED GROSS INCOME

Adjusted gross income is computed by subtracting from gross income certain deductions which are otherwise allowable and which are described in IRC § 62(a). Although IRC § 62 does not *authorize* any deductions (it merely determines *whether* a deduction may be taken in computing adjusted gross income), the deductions which are described in the section are often referred to as "section 62 deductions." Deductions which are not section 62 deductions are "itemized deductions." [IRC § 63(d).] Section 62 deductions are generally the types of expenditures which have been made in order to produce income, such as *all* employer trade or business deductions and deductible expenses incurred by an employee which are reimbursed by his employer. In addition, section 62 deductions include deductions attributable to property held for the production of rents or royalties [IRC § 62(a)(1) and (4)]; deductions for contributions to pensions and retirement accounts [IRC § 62(a)(6) and (7); see discussion, IV.F.2., at page 240, *supra*]; and the deduction for alimony [IRC § 62(a)(10); see discussion, V.C.1., at page 261, *supra*].

Adjusted gross income plays a role in determining the deduction for casualty and theft losses [IRC § 165(c)(3); see discussion, III.B.4., at page 136, *supra*]; the deduction for charitable contributions [IRC § 170(b); see discussion, III.B.6., at page 140, *supra*]; the deduction for extraordinary medical expenses [IRC § 213; see discussion, III.B.7., at page 150, *supra*]; the extent to which Social Security benefits are required to be included in gross income [IRC § 86; see discussion, II.B.3.f., at page 44, *supra*] and the amount of miscellaneous itemized deductions which may be allowed in computing taxable income [IRC § 67(a); see discussion, VII.B.2., at page 307, *infra*.]

> **Example:** Otis, an employee, has $25,000 of gross income and the following deductions: an IRC § 162 expense of $200 for uniforms; an IRC § 162 expense of $300 for tuition in a course to update him in his work; an IRC § 162 expense of $150 to attend a business meeting in another city that was reimbursed by his employer; $5,000 in alimony deductible under IRC § 215; a $2,000 payment to his I.R.A. deductible under IRC § 219; and a $500 charitable contribution deductible under IRC § 170. Otis' adjusted gross income is $17,850 ($25,000 less: $150 reimbursed travel expense, $2,000 I.R.A. deduction and $5,000 alimony deduction).

B. TAXABLE INCOME

1. STANDARD DEDUCTION

a. Background

The standard deduction was enacted in 1944 to simplify both compliance with the income tax law by taxpayers and enforcement of the income tax law by the I.R.S. If a taxpayer elected, she could take a deduction in the amount of the standard deduction *in lieu of* listing all of her deductions for state and local taxes, interest, charitable contributions, and other non-section 62 deductions ("itemized deductions"). Taxpayers who elected the standard deduction did not need to substantiate the various deductions they were otherwise entitled to, and the I.R.S. did not need to scrutinize income tax returns which used the standard deduction as closely as returns which itemized deductions. If a taxpayer had itemized deductions in a taxable year in excess of the standard deduction, he could simply not make the election to use the standard deduction and, instead, itemize all of his deductions.

The standard deduction is subtracted from a taxpayer's adjusted gross income to arrive at taxable income subject to tax.

b.   Basic standard deduction

The amount of the basic standard deduction is determined with reference to a taxpayer's filing status, and for taxable years beginning in 1987 (figures for 1988 are in parentheses) the following amounts are allowable:

Married, filing joint return $3,760   ($5,000)
Surviving spouse $3,760   ($5,000)
Head of household $2,540   ($4,400)
Unmarried (not surviving spouse or head of household) $2,540   ($3,000)
Married, filing separate return $1,880   ($2,500)

[IRC § 63(c)(2) and (h).]   For taxable years beginning after 1988, the standard deduction amounts are adjusted annually with reference to fluctuations in the cost-of-living.   [IRC § 63(c)(4).]

c.   Additional standard deduction for aged and blind

An "additional standard deduction" is added to the amount of the basic standard deduction in computing the standard deduction amount for a taxpayer who has attained the age of 65 or who is blind at the end of the taxable year.   [IRC § 63(c)(3) and (f).]   A taxpayer who is entitled to a personal exemption for her spouse [see discussion at III.B.1.a., at page 128, *supra*] may claim additional standard deductions if her spouse is age 65 or blind.   The amount of the additional standard deduction is $600 ($750 if the taxpayer is not married and is not a surviving spouse) and it is adjusted annually in taxable years beginning after 1988 to reflect fluctuations in the cost-of-living.   [IRC § 63(c)(4) and (f).]

> *Example:*   In 1988, Ashley, who is age 68, and his wife Beverly, who is age 69 and blind, file a joint return.   Their standard deduction for 1988 is $6,800 ($5,000 basic standard deduction plus 3 times the additional standard deduction amount of $600 allowed for age and blindness).

d.   Limitations

The amount of the standard deduction allowed to a taxpayer for whom a dependency exemption deduction may be claimed by another taxpayer is limited to the greater of $500 or the individual's earned income.   [IRC § 63(c)(5).]   For taxable years beginning after 1988, the $500 amount is adjusted to reflect changes in the cost-of-living.   [IRC § 63(c)(4).]

> *Example:*   Chris, age 23, is a full-time student and receives over half of his support from his parents.   During the current year he earns $1,000 from a part time job.   A dependency exemption deduction may be claimed for Chris by his parents on their

return for the current year; Chris' standard deduction is limited to $1,000; the amount of his earned income. Recall, as well, that Chris may not claim a personal exemption for himself because of IRC § 151(d)(2). See discussion at III.B.1.a., at page 128, *supra*.

The standard deduction was enacted under the assumption that an average taxpayer would have expenditures during a taxable year which would otherwise qualify for deductions. However, this assumption does not apply to certain individuals, such as alien individuals who do not reside in the U.S. and thus are unlikely to pay U.S. state and local taxes or to make contributions to U.S. charitable organizations. The amount of the standard deduction is limited to zero for the following individual taxpayers: (1) a married individual filing a separate return whose spouse itemizes deductions; (2) a nonresident alien; and (3) an individual filing a return for a short period of less than 12 months because of a change in his taxable year. [IRC § 63(c)(6).] Such individuals may still itemize their other deductions.

2. ITEMIZED DEDUCTIONS
a. In general

A taxpayer computes taxable income *either* by subtracting from adjusted gross income the standard deduction *or* by electing to list (itemize) all allowable deductions and subtracting the total amount (subject to some limitations) from gross income. [IRC § 63(a) and (b).] Itemized deductions are all allowable deductions *other than* Section 62 deductions which are allowable in computing adjusted gross income and the personal exemption deductions. [IRC § 63(d); see discussion of adjusted gross income at VII.A., at page 304, *supra*.] A taxpayer must affirmatively elect to itemize deductions, but she should do so only if the total allowable amount of itemized deductions exceeds her standard deduction. [IRC § 63(e).]

b. Miscellaneous itemized deductions

If a taxpayer elects to itemize deductions, certain "miscellaneous itemized deductions" may be deducted only to the extent the total amount thereof exceeds 2% of the taxpayer's adjusted gross income. [IRC § 67(a).] The term "miscellaneous itemized deductions" is defined as all itemized deductions *other than* certain enumerated deductions, some of the most significant of which are the deductions for interest, taxes, casualty losses, charitable contributions, extraordinary medical expenses and moving expenses. [IRC § 67(b).] Deductions allowable under IRC § 162 for unreimbursed expenses incurred by a taxpayer in his capacity of being an employee (commonly referred to as employee business expenses) and deductions allowable under IRC § 212 for expenses incurred for the production of income (other than those attributable to property held for the production of rents or royalties, see IRC § 62(a)(4)) are significant categories of miscellaneous itemized deductions.

Example: Dan, who is employed as a computer programmer, has adjusted gross income of $50,000 in the current year and he elects to itemize deductions in computing taxable income. His itemized deductions are: *$500 educational expense for improving his computer programming skills;* $2,500 ad valorem property taxes on his home; *$1,000 for expenses incurred in looking for a job as a computer programmer with a different employer;* $1,500 in interest on the mortgage on his home; *$100 annual dues for a professional computer programmer society; $75 fee for a safe deposit box in which he keeps corporate securities held for investment;* $3,000 charitable contributions; and *$350 paid to an accountant for preparing last year's Federal income tax return.* Dan's miscellaneous itemized deductions (italicized above) total $2,025, but he may subtract only $1,025 ($2,025 less $1,000, 2% of $50,000) from adjusted gross income in computing taxable income.

3. DEDUCTIONS FOR PERSONAL EXEMPTIONS

A taxpayer may subtract deductions allowable under IRC § 151 for personal exemptions in computing taxable income regardless of whether he uses the standard deduction or elects to itemize deductions. [IRC § 63(a) and (b)(2); see discussion of personal exemption deductions at III.B.1., at page 128 *supra.*]

C. CLASSIFICATION OF TAXPAYERS

1. IN GENERAL

A taxpayer's filing status, or classification, determines which tax rate schedule or table must be used in determining his income tax liability. [See IRC §§ 1(a)–(e) and 3.] Although the tax rates are set forth in IRC § 1, the I.R.S. is authorized to prescribe tax tables, based upon the IRC § 1 rates, for many taxpayers to use in determining tax liability. [IRC § 3.] The tax tables make the computation of tax liability easier and less complicated.

The filing status of an individual who is not married, or who is treated as not married, at the end of a taxable year is "unmarried," but special circumstances may qualify such an individual for the filing status of either "surviving spouse" or "head of household." The filing status of two individuals who are married to each other at the end of their taxable year is either "married filing separate returns" or "married filing a joint return," depending on whether they have elected to file a single return jointly under IRC § 6013.

2. DETERMINATION OF MARITAL STATUS
a. In general

The determination of whether a taxpayer is married is made at the close of her taxable year, unless her spouse dies during the taxable year, in which case, the determination is made as of the time of the spouse's death. [IRC § 7703(a)(1).] If, on the applicable date, an individual is legally separated from his spouse under a decree of separate maintenance or divorce, he is not considered as married. [IRC § 7703(a)(2).] State law is generally applied to ascertain whether individuals are legally married (or whether they are legally separated or divorced).

b. Certain married individuals living apart

Under the "deserted spouse rule," a married individual is treated as *not* married if: (1) he does not file a joint return with his spouse; (2) he maintains as his home a household which is the principal place of abode of a child with respect to which he is entitled to a dependent's deduction under IRC § 151(c); (3) he furnishes over one-half the cost of maintaining the household; and (4) his spouse is not a member of the household during the last 6 months of the taxable year. [IRC § 7703(b).] Application of this rule to a couple generally results in only one of the two spouses qualifying as "not married;" the filing status of the other spouse is generally "married filing separate return."

3. MARRIED TAXPAYERS FILING JOINT RETURNS

Two individuals who are married to each other as of the close of a taxable year may file a single return jointly, on which items of gross income, deductions and credits of each spouse are reported. [IRC § 6013(a).] A joint return may be filed even though one of the spouses had no gross income for the taxable year. A taxpayer whose spouse dies during a taxable year is still considered as married for that taxable year [IRC § 7703(a)(1)], and a joint return may be made for that taxable year (or for a prior taxable year) if the deceased spouse has not already filed a return for that year and if no personal representative for the deceased spouse's estate has been appointed. If a personal representative has been appointed, that person may make the joint return with the surviving spouse on behalf of the decedent spouse. [IRC § 6013(a)(3).]

If a joint return is filed, a larger amount of taxable income is taxed at the 15% rate than if a married individual files a separate return; therefore, it is generally advantageous for married couples to file jointly. [*Compare* IRC § 1(a) *with* IRC § 1(d).] However, if a joint return is made, each spouse is jointly and severally liable for the tax liability for that taxable year. [IRC § 6013(d)(3).] Some relief from joint and several liability is provided under limited circumstances to an "innocent spouse," who is able to demonstrate she did not know, and she had no reason to know, that her spouse had substantial amounts of unreported income or that he claimed deductions or credits for which there was no legal basis. [IRC § 6013(e).]

4. SURVIVING SPOUSES

A taxpayer's filing status is that of "surviving spouse" if: (1) her spouse died during either of her two taxable years immediately preceding the current taxable year, and (2) she maintains (by furnishing over one-half of the costs of maintaining) her home as a household which constitutes the principal place of abode (as a member of the household) of a son, stepson, daughter, or stepdaughter with respect to which she is entitled to a dependent's deduction under IRC § 151(c). [IRC § 2(a)(1).] A taxpayer does not qualify as a surviving spouse if she remarries before the close of the current taxable year, or if she and her deceased husband were not entitled to file a joint return for the taxable year in which he died. [IRC § 2(a)(2).] In addition, note that an individual does not qualify as a surviving spouse for the taxable year in which her spouse dies; she is considered to be married for the taxable year in which her spouse dies, and she may file a joint return for that taxable year. [See discussion, VII.C.3., at page 309, *supra.*]

A surviving spouse computes her income tax liability by using the same tax rate schedule or table used by married individuals filing joint returns. [IRC § 1(a)(2).]

5. HEADS OF HOUSEHOLD

The head of household filing status is available to an unmarried taxpayer who does *not* qualify as a surviving spouse, and who maintains (by furnishing over one-half of the costs of maintaining) his home as a household which constitutes the principal place of abode (as a member of the household) for certain enumerated individuals with respect to whom he is entitled to a dependent's deduction under IRC § 151(c). [IRC § 2(b).]

The amount of a head of household's taxable income which is taxed at the 15% rate ($23,900 for 1988) is roughly half way between the amounts taxed at the 15% rate for unmarried taxpayers ($17,850 for 1988) and married individuals filing a joint return ($29,750 for 1988). [IRC § 1(a)–(c).]

6. UNMARRIED INDIVIDUALS

Individual taxpayers who are not married at the close of a taxable year (other than surviving spouses or heads of a household) are subject to tax on their taxable incomes according to the rates prescribed in IRC § 1(c).

7. OTHER CLASSIFICATIONS OF TAXPAYERS

A married individual who does not elect to file a joint return with his spouse must compute his tax liability under the rates prescribed for married taxpayers filing separately in IRC § 1(d). Estates and trusts which are subject to income tax must compute their tax liability under the rates prescribed in

IRC § 1(e). Corporations subject to the income tax are taxed according to the rates set forth in IRC § 11.

D. TAX RATES

1. IN GENERAL

Tax liability is computed by multiplying a taxpayer's taxable income by the applicable tax rates prescribed for the taxpayer's classification. For taxable years beginning in 1987, taxable income is taxed at 5 progressively higher rates, ranging from 11% to 38.5%. [IRC § 1(h)(2).] Tax is imposed at a maximum rate of 28%, however, on the amount of a taxpayer's net capital gain. [IRC § 1(j).]

For taxable years beginning after 1987, generally only 2 rates are applicable, 15% and 28%. The amount of taxable income subject to tax at the 15% rate is determined by the taxpayer's classification, and the amounts are subject to adjustment in taxable years beginning after 1989 to reflect fluctuations in the cost-of-living. [IRC § 1(a)–(d) and (f).]

Example: Taxpayer has $40,000 of taxable income in 1988. If he is married and files a joint return with his spouse, or if he is a surviving spouse, his tax liability is $7,332.50. [IRC § 1(a).] If he is a head of household, his tax liability is $8,093.00. [IRC § 1(b).] If he is unmarried, his tax liability is $8,879.50. [IRC § 1(c).] If the taxpayer is married filing a separate return, his tax liability is $9,266.25. [IRC § 1(d).] If the taxpayer is an estate or a trust, the tax liability is $10,550.00. [IRC § 1(e).] If the taxpayer is a corporation, the tax liability is $6,000.00. [IRC § 11(b)(1).]

2. 5% SURTAX

A 5% surtax is imposed on the amount by which a taxpayer's taxable income exceeds an applicable dollar amount in taxable years after 1987. [IRC § 1(g)(1) and (3).] The 5% surtax is limited in such a manner that its effect is to reduce, or eliminate entirely, the amount of taxable income taxed at the 15% rate, and then to reduce, or eliminate entirely, the effect of the personal exemption deductions in reducing taxable income. [IRC § 1(g)(2).] A taxpayer who is subject to the 5% surtax to its maximum extent is effectively taxed at a flat rate of 28% on the sum of his taxable income plus the amount of his personal exemption deductions. For taxable years beginning in 1988 the applicable dollar amounts for individual taxpayers are as follows:

Married filing joint returns and Surviving Spouses $71,900
Heads of Households $61,650
Unmarried (other than Surviving Spouse or Head of Household) $43,150
Married filing separate returns $35,950

The applicable dollar amounts are adjusted annually for taxable years beginning after 1988 to reflect fluctuations in the cost-of-living. [IRC § 1(g)(3) and (4).] Net capital gains are also subject to the 5% surtax. [IRC § 1(j)(1)(C).]

Example: In 1988, Mr. and Mrs. Calhoun file a joint return claiming four personal exemptions and reporting taxable income of $250,000. The tax imposed under IRC § 1(a) is $66,132.50 [$4,462.50 plus $61,670.00 (28% of $220,250, which is the excess of $250,000 over $29,750)]. In addition, IRC § 1(g)(1) imposes a surtax of $8,905.00 [5% of $178,100 (excess of $250,000 over $71,900)]. The amount of the surtax is limited by IRC § 1(g)(2) to $6,051.50 [13% of $29,750 plus 28% of $7,800 ($1,950 times 4)]. The total tax liability for 1988 is $72,184.00 ($66,132.50 plus $6,052.50); this amount is 28% of $257,800, which is the sum of taxable income plus the amount of four personal exemption deductions.

3. TAX RATE FOR CHILDREN UNDER AGE 14

Net unearned income of a child under age 14 who has either parent alive at the end of the taxable year may be taxed at the rates applicable to the parent rather than the child. [IRC § 1(i).] A child's income tax liability is the greater of the amount computed using the rates applicable to the child, or the amount computed by adding to the parent's taxable income the amount of the child's net unearned income and using the rates applicable to the parent (the "allocable parental tax"). This special rule, enacted as part of the 1986 Tax Reform Act, upset the family tax planning technique of transferring securities or other income producing assets to a minor child so that the income derived therefrom would be taxed at the lower tax rates applicable to the child. "Net unearned income" is the excess of income which is not income received as compensation for rendering services over the sum of the child's standard deduction amount plus, if the child itemizes deductions, the deductions directly connected with producing the unearned income. [IRC § 1(i)(4).]

Example: During the current year, Gregory, age 10, has some earned income as well as $100 of net unearned income. Gregory's tax liability, computed with reference to *all* of his income, is $250; his tax liability computed with reference only to income *other than* his net unearned income is $235. If Gregory's parents had had an additional $100 of unearned income during the current year, their income tax liability would increase by $28. Gregory's income tax liability is $263 ($235 plus $28) instead of $250.

E. ALTERNATIVE MINIMUM TAX

Individual taxpayers are generally subject to an alternative tax (if it is higher than the tax computed according to the general rules) if they have a substantial amount of "items of tax preference" during a taxable year and they may be subject to the tax even if they have no preference items. [IRC § 55; see *Huntsberry v. Comm'r,* 83 T.C. 742 (1984).] The policy underlying the alternative minimum tax is to ensure that taxpayers who reduce their tax liability by taking advantage of certain tax preferences, such as accelerated depreciation deductions under ACRS [IRC § 168], should, nonetheless, pay a share of income taxes.

Computation of the alternative minimum tax begins with determining a taxpayer's alternative minimum taxable income (AMTI). AMTI is a taxpayer's taxable income, adjusted as provided in IRC §§ 56 and 58, and increased by the amount of items of tax preference. [IRC § 55(b)(2).] Adjustments to taxable income include recomputing depreciation deductions generally using the longer life straight line alternative depreciation system under ACRS, disallowing miscellaneous itemized deductions and the standard deduction, and disregarding the effect of the installment method in reporting gain from Section 453C installment sales and installment sales of inventory. [IRC § 56(a)(1), (a)(6) and (b)(1).] Items of tax preference include deductions for depletion and intangible drilling costs, incentive stock options, limited tax-exempt interest and deductions for charitable contributions of appreciated capital gain property. [IRC § 57(a).]

A tentative minimum tax is then computed at a rate of 21% of the excess of a taxpayer's alternative minimum taxable income (AMTI) over the exemption amount. [IRC § 55(b)(1).] The exemption amount ranges from $20,000 for a married individual filing a separate return to $40,000 for married individuals filing a joint return, but it is phased-out for certain taxpayers with large amounts of AMTI. [IRC § 55(d)(1) and (3).] The alternative minimum tax is then the excess of the tentative minimum tax for a taxable year over the regular tax for the year. [IRC § 55(a).] The alternative minimum tax may not be offset by some otherwise allowable tax credits. [See IRC §§ 26(a), 28(d)(2), 29(b)(5) and 38(c), and discussion of tax credits, VII.F., at page 314, *infra.*]

Example: Elmo has gross income for 1988 of $120,000 and $30,000 of interest income from qualified private activity bonds excluded from gross income under IRC § 103(a). His deductions are: $5,000 local ad valorem property taxes on his home; a charitable contribution deduction of $20,000 for a gift of corporate stock held more than 6 months for which he had a $4,000 basis; $2,600 for attorney's fee for tax advice and preparation of last year's income tax return; and $40,000 of depreciation deductions on property used in his business computed under ACRS (the ACRS alternative depreciation system would have allowed a deduction of only $32,000). Elmo is married and files a joint return with his wife on which they claim two personal exemptions and elect to itemize deductions.

Elmo's adjusted gross income for 1988 is $80,000 ($120,000 gross income less $40,000 depreciation deductions on business property). Elmo's miscellaneous itemized deductions total $2,600 ($2,600 attorney's fee for tax advice), but only $1,000 may be deducted (the amount in excess of 2% of his adjusted gross income, or $1,600). Elmo's taxable income for 1988 is $50,100 ($120,000 gross income less allowable Section 62 deductions, of $40,000, itemized deductions of $26,000 and two times the personal exemptions amount for 1988 of $1,950), and his tax liability computed under IRC § 1(a) is $10,160.50.

In computing the alternative minimum tax, Elmo's AMTI is $110,100 ($50,100 taxable income plus adjustments for depreciation of $8,000, miscellaneous itemized deductions of $1,000, ad valorem property taxes of $5,000 and items of tax preference consisting of $30,000 of interest income on qualified private activity bonds and $16,000 appreciated property charitable contribution deduction). The tentative minimum tax is 21% of AMTI less the $40,000 exemption amount applicable to Elmo and his spouse for 1988, or $14,721.00 (21% of $70,100). Elmo's regular tax for 1988 is $10,160.50, so an alternative minimum tax of $4,560.50 is imposed (excess of tentative minimum tax, $14,721.00, over regular tax, $10,160.50). Elmo's total 1988 tax liability is $14,721.00 of which $10,160.50 is imposed under IRC § 1(a) and $4,560.50 is imposed under IRC § 55(a).

F. TAX CREDITS

The final step in computing a taxpayer's net tax liability is to subtract from the amount of tax which is otherwise due any tax credits to which the taxpayer is entitled. Tax credits offset tax liability on a dollar-for-dollar basis, while deductions reduce a taxpayer's tax liability in relation to the marginal rate at which her taxable income is taxed; thus, a tax credit of a certain dollar amount is more advantageous to a taxpayer than a deduction of an equal dollar amount. In addition, because a deduction is relatively more helpful to a taxpayer who is subject to tax at a high marginal rate than to his sister who is subject to tax at a low marginal rate, while a tax credit is equally advantageous to both taxpayers, tax credits are considered to be more equitable and fair in many situations.

Provisions for tax credits have been collected in Part IV of Subpart A of the Code, subdivided into five classifications, and prioritized according to the order in which they may be taken. [IRC §§ 21–53.] One class of tax credits, refundable tax credits, permit a taxpayer whose credits in this class exceed his tax liability (reduced by the amount of nonrefundable tax credits), to receive a refund from the government. The other four classes of tax credits contain nonrefundable tax credits; thus a taxpayer may not obtain a refund even if the amount of these credits exceeds his tax liability, but sometimes the excess amount may be able to be carried forward or back to another taxable year under special rules. The four classes of nonrefundable tax credits are nonrefundable personal credits, miscellaneous nonrefundable credits, the general business credit and the credit for minimum tax liability.

The sum of business related credits and the foreign tax credit attributable to passive activities may be subject to the passive activity credit disallowance rules of IRC § 469. [See discussion at III. C. 10., at page 171, *supra*.] A passive activity credit is defined as the amount by which the sum of business related credits [IRC §§ 38–42] and the foreign tax credit [IRC § 27(a)] attributable to passive activities exceeds the taxpayer's regular tax liability allocable to his passive activities for the taxable year. [IRC § 469(d)(2).] Passive activity credits which are disallowed in a taxable year may be carried forward to subsequent taxable years. [IRC § 469(b).]

1. NONREFUNDABLE PERSONAL CREDITS

Several nonrefundable tax credits are available to individual taxpayers. These tax credits are used to reduce a taxpayer's tax liability before any of the other classes of tax credits.

a. Expenses for household and dependent care services necessary for gainful employment

A taxpayer who maintains a household which includes one or more qualifying individuals is allowed a tax credit in an amount equal to the applicable percentage of his employment-related expenses paid during a taxable year. [IRC § 21.] Employment related expenses taken into account for purposes of the credit are limited to $2,400 if there is one qualifying individual and to $4,800 if there are two or more qualifying individuals. Qualifying individuals include a taxpayer's dependents who are under the age of 15, and dependents or a spouse who are physically or mentally incapable of caring for themselves. The applicable percentage is 30%, reduced (but not below 20%) by 1% for each $2,000 by which the taxpayer's adjusted gross income exceeds $10,000 for the taxable year. Employment-related expenses include amounts paid for household services and for the care of a qualifying individual, but only if the expenses are incurred to enable the taxpayer to be gainfully employed.

b. Credit for the elderly and the disabled

A qualified individual is allowed a tax credit in an amount equal to 15% of his eligible income. [IRC § 22.] A taxpayer who is 65 or older, or who has retired on disability and who, when she retired, was totally and permanently disabled is a qualified individual. The maximum amount of eligible income (credit base) is $5,000 (and, thus, the maximum credit is $750) for unmarried taxpayers who are age 65 or over. Alternative limits may apply according to the qualifications of the taxpayer and his spouse and their filing status. The credit must be reduced, dollar-for-dollar, by amounts received as pension, annuity or disability benefits which are excluded from gross income under the Social Security Act or certain other provisions. In addition, the credit *base* is reduced by one-half of the taxpayer's adjusted gross income which exceeds $7,500 for unmarried taxpayers ($10,000 for married taxpayers filing a joint return, and $5,000 for a married taxpayer filing a separate return).

c. Interest on certain home mortgages

Taxpayers may be entitled to a tax credit with respect to a portion of the interest paid on a mortgage obtained under certain programs established by State and local governments for qualified first-time homebuyers. [IRC § 25.]

2. MISCELLANEOUS NONREFUNDABLE CREDITS

The tax credits in the second classification may be used to offset a taxpayer's tax liability after the credits in the first classification have been used, and they must be used in the numerical order in which they appear in the Code. These credits are not limited to individuals, but are available to corporate taxpayers as well as estates and trusts which are taxpayers.

a. Foreign tax credit

A credit is authorized, within certain limitations, for income taxes paid to the government of a foreign country or a U.S. possession. [IRC §§ 27 and 901.] In lieu of the credit, a taxpayer may take a deduction for the payment of such taxes. [IRC §§ 164(a)(3) and 275(a)(4).] If the amount of the foreign taxes exceeds certain limitations, the excess amount of credit may be carried back or forward to other taxable years under special rules. [IRC § 904(a) and (c).]

b. Clinical testing of certain drugs

A tax credit equal to 50% of qualified clinical testing expenses is authorized in order to encourage research and the development of drugs to treat rare diseases or conditions. [IRC § 28.]

c. Producing fuel from a nonconventional source

Because of a concern that the U.S. was importing excessive quantities of oil and gas from foreign sources, Congress enacted this tax credit to encourage the production, within the U.S. or possessions of the U.S., of alternative fuels. [IRC § 29.]

3. NONREFUNDABLE GENERAL BUSINESS CREDIT

A tax credit is allowed in an amount equal to the sum of business credits for the current taxable year, plus the business credits carried to the current year from prior or subsequent years. [IRC § 38(a).] The current year business credit is the sum of the credits for that year provided for the investment tax credit, the targeted jobs credit, the alcohol fuels credit, the research credit and the low-income housing credit. [IRC § 38(b).] The general business credit for a taxable year may not exceed the lesser of: (1) the amount of the regular tax liability (after reduction for the other nonrefundable tax credits) up to $25,000 plus 75% of such tax liability in excess of $25,000; or (2) the excess of the regular tax liability (after reduction for the other nonrefundable tax credits) over the tentative minimum tax. [IRC § 38(c)(1) and (2).] If the sum of the general business credits carried forward to a taxable year plus the general business credits generated during the year exceeds the dollar limitation for that year, the excess shall be carried back to the 3 preceding taxable years, and carried forward to the subsequent 15 taxable years, until the excess amount can be utilized within the dollar limitations applicable to those carry-back or carry-forward years. [IRC § 39.]

> *Example:* Hogan has a $55,000 tax liability and no credits other than $53,000 of general business credit. Hogan may reduce his tax liability by $25,000 plus 75% of the remaining $30,000 of tax liability, or $22,500. Thus, he owes $7,500 of tax and he may carry-over or back his $5,500 remaining general business credit.

a. Investment tax credit

A credit is authorized for certain rehabilitation expenditures and investment in certain alternative energy sources. [IRC § 46.] Historically, a general investment tax credit has been provided on an on-again, off-again basis for tangible personal property used in a trade or business or held for the production of income, but it has been repealed for most property placed in service after December 31, 1985. [See IRC §§ 46(a) and 48(a).]

b. Targeted jobs credit

A credit is authorized to taxpayers who employ individuals who are in certain "targeted groups" of disadvantaged individuals, such as economically disadvantaged youths, Vietnam-era veterans, or ex-convicts. [IRC § 51.]

c. Alcohol fuels

A credit is authorized to encourage taxpayers to use alcohol as a fuel, either alone or in a mixture with other fuels. [IRC § 40.]

d. Increasing research activities

A credit is authorized in the amount of 20% of the excess of qualified research expenses for a taxable year over the average amount spent for such endeavors during the previous three years. [IRC § 41(a)(1).] An additional credit in the amount of 20% of basic research payments is also authorized. [IRC § 41(a)(2).]

e. Low-income housing

Incentives to construct, rehabilitate or acquire housing for low-income individuals are provided in the form of tax credits, ranging up to 9% per year for a 10 year period. [IRC § 42.]

4. NONREFUNDABLE CREDIT FOR PRIOR YEAR MINIMUM TAX LIABILITY

A taxpayer who is subject to the alternative minimum tax in a taxable year after 1986 may be allowed a credit against his regular income tax liability (after reduction by other nonrefundable credits) in subsequent years in an amount computed with reference to the alternative minimum tax previously paid. [IRC § 53(a); see discussion of the alternative minimum tax at VII. E., at page 313, *supra.*]

5. REFUNDABLE CREDITS

In addition to nonrefundable tax credits, several refundable tax credits are authorized; if the amount of the credit exceeds the taxpayer's tax liability (after being offset by the nonrefundable credits), the excess amount will be refunded to the taxpayer or credited against his future tax liabilities. Some of the more significant refundable tax credits available to individual taxpayers are discussed in the following paragraphs.

a. Tax withheld on wages

A taxpayer who is an employee is subject to having a portion of his wages withheld by his employer and remitted to the I.R.S. at regular intervals during a taxable year. [See IRC § 3402.] The amounts are in essence a prepayment of tax and the taxpayer is entitled to a tax credit for the amounts so withheld, and if the credit exceeds his income tax liability for the taxable year, he may elect to have the excess amount either refunded to him or credited against his income tax liability for the next taxable year. [IRC § 31(a).] Similarly, if an excess amount of Social Security tax is withheld during a taxable year, the taxpayer is entitled to a tax credit for the excess amount. [IRC § 31(b).]

b. Earned income

An eligible individual is entitled to a tax credit equal to 14% of her earned income up to $5,714 (for a maximum credit of $800). [IRC § 32.] An eligible individual is someone who is married, a surviving spouse, or a head of household and who is entitled to a dependent's deduction for a child. In order to restrict the relief of this credit to low-income individuals, the maximum amount of the credit is reduced by 10% of the taxpayer's adjusted gross income (or, if greater, her earned income) in excess of $9,000; thus the credit is totally phased out for a taxpayer whose adjusted gross income exceeds $17,000. The dollar limitations are adjusted annually to reflect fluctuations in the cost-of-living. [IRC § 32(i).]

c. Overpayments of tax

Amounts which are treated as overpayments of income tax may be refunded or credited against a taxpayer's income tax liability. [IRC §§ 35, 6401 and 6402.] Amounts paid as estimated tax [IRC § 6654; see discussion, VIII. A., at page 322, *infra*] are treated as payments of income tax [IRC § 6315], and if the total amount paid as estimated tax exceeds the actual liability for the year, the excess amount is an overpayment of tax.

REVIEW QUESTIONS

Q# 1: In 1988, Ralph (an unmarried individual) receives $20,000 in salary, deposits $2,000 in his deductible I.R.A. account and pays $5,000 interest on his home mortgage. What is Ralph's adjusted gross income? What is his taxable income?

Q# 2: Robert and Carol were married on December 30 of the current year. May they file a joint return? What other filing status is available to them?

Q# 3: When will an individual who is considered married under the general rule of IRC § 7703(a) be treated as not married? What will be the filing status of such an individual?

Q# 4: Jim is a married taxpayer with a minor child whom he supports and who lives at home with Jim and his wife. What is Jim's tax liability in 1988 in the following alternative situations if his taxable income is $35,000:

(a) He files a joint return?

(b) His wife dies during the year but he files a joint return?

(c) His wife died in 1987?

(d) His wife died in 1980?

(e) His wife died in 1980 but their child is now 22 years old and does not qualify as his dependent?

Q# 5: Is the alternative minimum tax a substitute for or an addition to the regular tax in a taxable year to which it applies?

Q# 6: Alternator is an unmarried taxpayer with $10,000 of salary and $100,000 of interest from qualified private activity bonds in 1988, but no other items of income nor any itemized deductions. What is Alternator's 1988 tax liability?

Q# 7: Evelyn is a single, cash method, calendar year taxpayer who is an employee with $30,000 of salary income in 1988. She takes a deductible continuing education course in a nearby town incurring $300 of tuition and $700 of deductible transportation, lodging and 80% of meals; $500 in deductible moving expenses; $1,000 in interest on the loan on her residence; $1,000 in state income taxes; $400 in charitable contributions; and $200 in interest on her credit cards. Her employer has withheld $4,500 in income taxes on her account. How much tax must she remit with her return for 1988?

Q# 8: What is Evelyn's taxable income in Question # 7 if she had paid only $500 in state taxes?

VIII

PROCEDURE

Analysis

A. Pay as You Earn
B. Income Tax Returns
   1. Annual Returns
   2. Penalties
C. Refunds
D. Deficiencies
E. Court Structure
   1. Trial Forums
   2. Appellate Forums

The procedural rules governing taxpayers and the I.R.S. are numerous and often complex. This section of the outline summarizes the more important features of the system for the payment and collection of income taxes through withholding and installment payments of estimated tax, the filing of annual returns, penalties, the procedures for filing a claim for refund if too much tax is paid or for the I.R.S. to assert a deficiency if too little tax is paid, and the administrative and judicial avenues for resolving conflicts between the I.R.S. and taxpayers.

A. PAY AS YOU EARN

Payment of the income tax by the vast majority of taxpayers is virtually assured by the requirement that an employer withhold a portion of each employee's salary as an advance payment of that employee's Federal income tax liability. [IRC §§ 3401–3406.] The amount of income taxes withheld is paid by the employer to the U.S. Treasury at regular intervals during the year, and when an employee files his annual income tax return, he is entitled to a refundable tax credit for the amount of income tax withheld with respect to his salary. [IRC § 31; see discussion, VII. F. 5. a., at page 318, *supra*.] In addition to the withholding requirements imposed on employers, other income-payers are required to withhold income taxes in certain situations, such as payers of gambling winnings and interest-paying financial institutions in some situations. [See IRC §§ 3402(q) and 3406.]

In addition to the withholding requirements, collection of the income tax is enhanced by provisions which require some taxpayers to make installment payments during a taxable year of the amount estimated to be their income tax liability for that taxable year, commonly referred to as estimated tax payments. [IRC § 6654.] The rules with respect to such payments generally affect self-employed taxpayers and others who have income from sources which are not subject to the withholding rules. If the installment payment rules apply, they generally require a taxpayer to pay, 4 times a year, an amount estimated to be the tax which will be imposed for the year on the basis of the amount of income earned up to that point during the year. Certain exceptions and safe-harbors are provided, and taxes withheld by an employer or another withholding agent up to that time may be subtracted from the amount of any installment payment due. Penalties are imposed for the underpayment or failure to pay required installment payments. [See discussion, VIII. B. 2., at page 323, *infra*.]

B. INCOME TAX RETURNS

1. ANNUAL RETURNS

A taxpayer who has gross income during a taxable year in excess of the sum of her exemption amount (the amount allowed as a personal exemption under IRC § 151(a), or 2 personal exemptions if a joint return) plus the basic standard deduction amount is required to file an annual income tax return. [IRC § 6012(a); see discussion of basic standard deduction, VII. B. 1., at page 305, *supra*.] The income tax return for a taxable year which is the calendar year is due on or before April 15th of the following year; if a taxpayer uses a fiscal year as his taxable year, the return is due on or before the 15th day of the fourth month following the close of his taxable year. [IRC § 6072(a); see discussion of taxable year, IV. A., at page 186, *supra*.] Payment of income tax is generally due at the time the return is due. [IRC § 6151(a).] Extensions of time for filing returns and paying the tax may be applied for in various situations. [IRC §§ 6081 and 6161.]

Example: Marge, a unmarried calendar-year taxpayer, who is not the dependent of another taxpayer has gross income of $4,440 in 1987 and $4,950 in 1988.   Marge is not required to file a return for either year because her gross income in each year does not exceed the sum of her personal exemption ($1,900 in 1987 and $1,950 in 1988) and her standard deduction ($2,540 in 1987 and $3,000 in 1988).   If Marge's gross income in 1988 is more than $4,950, she must file a return for 1988 no later than April 15, 1989.

2.   PENALTIES

Separate penalties are imposed for failure to file tax returns, for failure to pay tax due when the return is filed, and for failure to pay estimated taxes. [IRC §§ 6651 and 6654.]   The penalty for failure to file a return is 5% of the amount required to be shown as tax on the return if the failure is for not more than 1 month, with an additional 5% penalty for each additional month or fraction thereof that the return is delinquent, not exceeding 25% in the aggregate.   [IRC § 6651(a)(1).]   The penalty for failure to pay the tax when it is due is 0.5% of the unpaid amount of tax shown on the return (or required to be shown on the return) if the failure is for not more than 1 month, with an additional 0.5% for each subsequent month or fraction thereof during which the tax remains unpaid, not exceeding 25% in the aggregate.   [IRC § 6651(a)(2).]   If the I.R.S. has issued the taxpayer a notice of levy or a notice and demand for immediate payment of tax, the penalty for failure to pay the tax is increased to 1% per month.   [IRC § 6651(d).]   The failure to file and failure to pay penalties will not be imposed if the failures were due to reasonable cause and not due to willful neglect.   In addition, the amount of the failure to file penalty is reduced by the amount of the failure to pay penalty for any month in which both penalties apply.   [IRC § 6651(c)(1).]

Further penalties may be imposed for negligence and civil fraud.   [IRC § 6653.]   Criminal penalties, in addition to civil penalties, may also be imposed.   [IRC §§ 7201–7207.]

If any amount of income tax is not paid when it is due, the taxpayer is charged interest on the amount of the underpayment at the underpayment rate.   [IRC § 6601(a).]   Interest is compounded daily at a rate determined with reference to the average market yield of U.S. government securities and it is adjusted 4 times each year.   [IRC §§ 6621 and 6622.]   The taxpayer will also be charged interest on the amount of penalties imposed if they are not paid within 10 days of receiving notice and demand for payment of the penalty. [IRC § 6601(e).]

Example: Nikki files her Year One tax return and pays the $500 balance of tax due on May 20 of Year Two.   The return shows a total tax liability of $1,000, but she is entitled to credit for $500 of tax withheld during the year.   The due date for a Year One return and additional tax due is April 15 of Year Two; thus, Nikki's return and tax payment are late by 2 months (or fractions thereof). The *failure to file penalty* is 10% of $500, or $50. [IRC § 6651(a)(1).] The penalty is 10% (because the return is 2 months late) of $500 (the $1,000 tax required to be shown on the return less the $500 paid by April 15 of Year Two). [IRC § 6651(b)(1).] In addition, Nikki will be subject to a *failure to pay penalty* of 1% of $500, or $5. [IRC § 6651(a)(2).] The penalty is 1% (because the payment is 2 months late) of $500 (the $1,000 tax shown on the return less the $500 payment made by April 15 of Year Two). [IRC § 6651(b)(2).] Because both penalties applied to the same $500 amount for the same 2 month period, the amount of the failure to pay penalty ($5) must be subtracted from the failure to file penalty ($50) leaving a net failure to file penalty of $45 and a failure to pay penalty of $5. [IRC § 6651(c)(1).]

C. REFUNDS

If a taxpayer feels she has overpaid her tax, she may file a claim for a refund. [IRC § 6511.] A refund claim generally must be filed within 3 years after the return was filed, or within 2 years after the tax was paid, whichever is later (unless the I.R.S. and the taxpayer have agreed to an extension of time). [IRC § 6511(a) and (b).] If the 3-year limit applies, the taxpayer may claim a refund up to the amount of tax paid within that period; if 2-year limit applies, the amount of the refund may not exceed the amount of income tax paid during the 2 years prior to filing the refund claim. [IRC § 6511(b)(2).]

A taxpayer may be entitled to be paid interest at the overpayment rate on overpayments of tax. [IRC § 6611.] The overpayment rate of interest is 1% lower than the rate charged to the taxpayer on penalties and underpayments of tax; interest is compounded daily at a rate determined with reference to the average market yield of U.S. government securities and it is adjusted 4 times each year. [IRC §§ 6621 and 6622; see discussion, VIII. B. 2., at page 323, *supra*.] Interest on overpayments starts accruing from the date of overpayment to a date preceding the date of the refund check by not more than 30 days. [IRC § 6611(b)(2).] Interest will not be paid on income tax refunds if the amount is refunded within 45 days after the taxpayer files her return, or within 45 days of the due date for the return if she files the return early. [IRC § 6611(e).]

D. DEFICIENCIES

When a taxpayer files his annual return, it is initially checked for mathematical errors and for the payment of any tax due as shown on the return; if the return indicates a refund is due to the taxpayer, it is generally sent to him within a few weeks. Some returns are checked more carefully, however, either because the return has been selected at random or because one or more items on a particular return are in categories which the I.R.S. has selected for closer scrutiny. The closer examination of a return by the I.R.S. may simply involve written correspondence with the taxpayer, or it may include visits to the taxpayer's home or place of business by agents of the I.R.S. The I.R.S. has broad authority to seek information from a taxpayer, and from others who might have information regarding her income tax liability. [IRC §§ 7601–7612.]

If the I.R.S. determines that the amount of tax shown on the return is too low, a letter is sent to the taxpayer indicating the amount of the underpayment and the reasons the I.R.S. has for asserting the deficiency, i.e., whether certain deductions the taxpayer took were disallowed or whether there were additional items of gross income which the taxpayer failed to include in the return. At this point, the taxpayer may still discuss the issues, in a relatively informal manner, with local I.R.S. personnel in an attempt to resolve the conflict and, if the controversy is not resolved, the taxpayer may be entitled to further administrative review within the I.R.S. at the Appeals Office for the region of the country in which the taxpayer lives.

If the I.R.S. still asserts that there is a deficiency upon conclusion of the administrative process (or earlier, if the taxpayer decides not to use the process) the I.R.S. will send a formal Notice of Deficiency to the taxpayer by certified or registered mail. [IRC § 6212.] This Notice is commonly referred to as a "90-day letter" because the taxpayer has 90 days from the date it is sent to file a petition for review of the matter by the Tax Court. [See discussion, VIII. E., at page 326, *infra*.] If the taxpayer does not challenge the Notice of Deficiency in the Tax Court (or if he does so, but loses) the I.R.S. may then formally make an assessment of the amount of additional taxes due, and give the taxpayer notice and demand for payment. [IRC §§ 6201 and 6303.] The I.R.S. generally has 6 years to collect the taxes. [IRC § 6502.] The I.R.S. has a panoply of powers available to aid in the collection of the tax, including placing a lien on the taxpayer's property and the outright seizure and sale of the taxpayer's property in certain circumstances. [See IRC §§ 6321, 6331 and 6332.]

The I.R.S. generally must assess any amount of an alleged underpayment within three years after a taxpayer files her annual return. [IRC § 6501(a).] When a return is filed before the due date, it is deemed filed on the last day prescribed for filing the return for statute of limitations purposes. [IRC § 6501(b).] In the case of a false or fraudulent return or when no return is filed, the statute of limitations does not begin to run and the tax may be assessed at any time. In certain situations, generally involving a taxpayer's failure to report substantial amounts of gross income, the limitations period is extended to 6 years. [IRC § 6501(e).]

Example: Margie files her Year One return and pays the tax due on April 15 of Year Two. The last day the I.R.S. may assess a tax (or the last day

Margie may file a claim for a refund) with respect to Margie's Year
One taxable year is April 15 of Year Five.

E. COURT STRUCTURE

1. TRIAL FORUMS

When a taxpayer disagrees with an administrative determination made by
the I.R.S., he has a choice of three trial forums in which to litigate: the Tax
Court, the Claims Court, and the District Court. The Tax Court has
jurisdiction over cases in which the taxpayer refuses to pay an asserted tax
deficiency. In order to litigate in the Tax Court, the taxpayer must receive a
Notice of Deficiency from the I.R.S., and within 90 days of the mailing of that
Notice, the taxpayer must file a petition with the Tax Court. [IRC §§ 6211–
6213.] The Tax Court has special summary proceedings to deal with cases
where the amount in dispute is $10,000 or less. [IRC § 7463.] The principal
office of the Tax Court is located in Washington, DC, but the court hears cases
in numerous designated offices around the country.

If a taxpayer decides to pay a proposed deficiency and to seek a refund of
what he now asserts to be an overpayment (which he might want to do in
order to avoid paying interest on the disputed amount if he loses the
litigation), or if he decides to litigate a disallowed refund claim, then he may
file suit in either the Claims Court or the District Court. Like the Tax Court,
the headquarters of the Claims Court is in Washington, DC, but proceedings
are held at various locations around the country, at a place relatively
convenient for the taxpayer. The proper venue for District Court litigation is
generally in the district where the liability for the tax accrues, in the district
in which the taxpayer resides, or in the district where the return was filed.
A taxpayer may wish to pay a proposed deficiency and litigate in one of these
courts, as opposed to the Tax Court, if she feels there is "friendlier" precedent
in these courts. Another factor to consider in deciding upon the appropriate
trial forum is that a jury trial is available in a District Court, but not in
either the Claims Court or in the Tax Court.

2. APPELLATE FORUMS

Decisions of the Tax Court and the Claims Court, as well as District
Courts, are appealable to the Federal Appeals Courts and ultimately to the
Supreme Court. A Circuit Court of Appeal will hear appeals from decisions of
the District Courts which are within its geographical jurisdiction, as well as
decisions of the Tax Court affecting taxpayers who reside within the Circuit.
Because of this rule of appellate jurisdiction governing the Tax Court, the Tax
Court decides cases on the basis of the law in the Circuit to which an appeal
will lie. [*Jack E. Golsen,* 54 T.C. 742 (1970), *aff'd* 445 F.2d 985 (10th Cir.
1971).] Appeals from the Claims Court are heard by the Court of Appeals for
the Federal Circuit in Washington, DC. Finally, the Supreme Court may
review tax cases, by writ of certiorari, from the Courts of Appeal.

APPENDIX A

ANSWERS TO REVIEW QUESTIONS

PART II

Q# 1: Clint's employer pays Clint $20,000 a year in cash and gives him a new car worth $10,000. How much gross income does Clint have and what is his basis in the car?

A# 1: Total gross income of $30,000; fair market value of car, $10,000, plus $20,000 cash. Clint's tax cost basis in the car is $10,000.

Q# 2: Burt buys a painting for $10,000 and he sells it several years later for $12,000. What sections of the IRC are relevant in determining the amount of gain or loss from the sale?

A# 2: Burt's basis is $10,000 under IRC § 1012, the amount realized on the sale is $12,000, IRC § 1001(b), and the realized gain is $2,000, IRC § 1001(a).

Q# 3: Assume Burt, from Question # 2, receives the painting as a gift from his father, who bought the painting several years ago for $10,000. The painting is worth $5,000 when father gives it to Burt. What is Burt's gain (or loss) when he sells the painting several years later for $12,000? What if he sells it for $4,000? What if he sells it for $8,000?

A# 3: Burt's basis in the painting is $10,000 under the general rule of IRC § 1015(a). When Burt sells the painting for $12,000, his gain is $2,000. When Burt sells the painting for $4,000, the "except" clause of IRC § 1015(a) applies,

327

requiring Burt to compute basis using the fair market value of the painting as of the date of the gift because Burt is computing a loss, not a gain. Thus, his basis for determining loss is $5,000, and the amount of his loss is $1,000 ($5,000 basis less $4,000 amount realized). When Burt sells the painting for $8,000, however, he has neither a gain nor a loss because the basis under the general rule ($10,000 transferred basis) does not produce a gain (it is in excess of the amount realized) and the basis under the "except" clause ($5,000) does not produce a loss (it is less than the amount realized). [Reg. § 1.1015–1(a)(2).]

Q# 4: Sally bought a house in Year One for $50,000. In Year Three, she had a swimming pool built behind the house at a cost of $8,000 and she also repaired a portion of the roof at a cost of $2,000. What is Sally's basis in the house?

A# 4: Sally's total basis in the house is $58,000. The IRC § 1012 cost basis of $50,000 is increased by the capital improvement of $8,000 under IRC § 1016(a)(1). The $2,000 roof repair is not a capital expenditure and, thus, it is not added to the basis of the house. If the entire roof had been replaced, however, the cost would be a capital expenditure, added to the basis of the house.

Q# 5: Susan operated an ice cream business as a sole proprietor until she sold it to Meryl for a total purchase price of $10,000. The assets of the business consisted of equipment worth $5,000, inventory of $4,000 and goodwill of $1,000. How is Meryl's basis in the ice cream business calculated?

A# 5: The purchase price of $10,000 must be apportioned among the component assets of the business. Meryl has a basis of $5,000 in the equipment (which is depreciable), $4,000 in the inventory and $1,000 in the goodwill. [IRC § 1012 and *Williams v. McGowan*, 152 F.2d 570 (2nd Cir.1945).]

Q# 6: In the current year, Tom receives the following amounts: $2,000 interest from a money market account; $1,500 interest on a New York state bond; $5,000 from an inheritance; $20,000 salary from his job; and a $30,000 damage award to compensate him for personal injuries sustained in an automobile accident. What is Tom's gross income for the current year?

A# 6: $22,000. The $2,000 of interest and $20,000 of salary are included in gross income under IRC § 61(a)(1) and (4). The $1,500 of interest on the New York state bond is excluded from gross income under IRC § 103; the $5,000 inheritance is excluded from gross income under IRC § 102; and the $30,000 damages for personal injuries is excluded under IRC § 104(a)(2).

Q# 7: Rodney receives a $10,000 scholarship from a local university where he is enrolled in a program leading to a bachelor's degree in business administration. What additional information is needed to determine the proper tax treatment of this scholarship?

A# 7: Amounts received as a "qualified scholarship" by a candidate for a degree at an educational institution are excluded from gross income under IRC § 117(a). In order to determine the proper tax treatment of Rodney's scholarship it is necessary to know whether Rodney can establish that the amounts received were spent only for tuition, fees, books, supplies and equipment required by the courses at the University. [IRC § 117(b).] In addition, the exclusion from gross income does not apply to any portion of the amount Rodney receives as payment for teaching, research or other services he may be required to perform as a condition for receiving the scholarship. [IRC § 117(c).]

Q# 8: Ron rents an office building from Nancy for an annual rental of $5,000. Ron decides to build an additional office onto the building which increases the fair market value of the building by $5,000. Ron continues to pay his $5,000 annual rental to Nancy. Is the value of the improvement included in Nancy's gross income? What is the effect on Nancy's basis?

A# 8: Nancy does not have gross income attributable to the value of the improvements. Even in the year the lease terminates Nancy does not have gross income under IRC § 109, under IRC § 1019, Nancy's basis in the property is not increased by the value of the nontaxable improvements.

Q# 9: Madeline works for an insurance company; all employees are allowed to buy insurance at a 30% discount from the normal premiums charged to customers. In the current year, Madeline obtains liability insurance for her automobile, a homeowners policy for her house, and a life insurance policy insuring her own life. She pays a total of $700 in premiums, while a nonemployee customer would have been charged $1,000. Is this discount taxable to Madeline in the current year, and if so, to what extent?

A# 9: Generally, gross income includes, as compensation income, all economic benefits provided to an employee by his employer; however, IRC § 132(a) excludes certain fringe benefits from gross income. A "qualified employee discount" is excluded from gross income to the extent the discount does not exceed certain limits. In the case of property which an employee is permitted to purchase at a discount, the limit is the gross profit percentage of the price at which the property is being offered by the employer to customers. An insurance policy, however, is considered to be a service, and the limit with respect to services provided at a discount is 20% of the price at which the services are offered to customers. Madeline received a discount of 30%, or $300; therefore, she must include $100 in gross income (the excess of the 30% discount over the amount a 20% discount would have provided, or $300 – $200).

Q# 10: Gene inherits stock from his mother in the current year. The basis of the stock to Gene's mother was $20,000 and the fair market value of the stock as of the date of her death was $10,000. If Gene later sells the stock for $5,000 what is the amount of Gene's gain or loss?

A# 10: Gene's basis for the stock, determined under IRC § 1014(a), is its fair market value at the date of his mother's death, or $10,000. Gene has a loss on the sale of $5,000 ($5,000 amount realized – $10,000 basis).

Q# 11:   Terri sells a building for $75,000 cash down payment and she accepts a note from the purchaser for an additional $50,000, to be paid one year later (plus a reasonable rate of interest).   In addition, the building is mortgaged for $100,000 (Terri is not personally liable under the mortgage) and the purchaser agrees to assume the mortgage.   What is Terri's amount realized on the sale?

A# 11: $225,000.   Under IRC § 1001(b), the amount realized on the sale or other disposition of property includes the amount of money received plus the fair market value of any other property received in the transaction.   The $100,000 mortgage assumed by the purchaser is also included in the amount realized, because Terri has received an economic benefit by being relieved of having to pay the liability.

Q# 12:   Although Marty is solvent, he owes various business creditors a total of $50,000.   Marty's creditors agree to accept $40,000 in complete satisfaction of Marty's debts to them.   What are the tax consequences of this transaction?   What additional information is relevant?

A# 12:   It is not a taxable event when someone borrows money, because the borrower incurs an obligation to repay the borrowed sum.   However, if the borrower is subsequently relieved of all or a portion of the repayment obligation, he has received an economic benefit which generally is included in gross income; thus, Marty has $10,000 of gross income from the discharge of indebtedness under the general rule.   [IRC § 61(a)(12).]   If the lender intends to make a gift of the forgiven debt, however, the amount is excludable under IRC § 102.   In addition, IRC § 108 excludes from gross income any income generated by a discharge of indebtedness in bankruptcy or when the taxpayer is insolvent.

Q# 13:   Dudley works as a waiter at a restaurant.   Dudley's employer requires Dudley to eat his evening meal at the restaurant in order to keep dinner breaks for employees as short as possible.   Dudley is paid a $10,000 salary and he receives $3,000 in tips and $2,000 in meals.   What is his gross income?

A# 13: $13,000.   The salary and tips are gross income.   IRC § 119(a) excludes the value of his meals because they are furnished to him as an employee and they are furnished: (1) for the convenience of the employer, and (2) on the business premises of the employer.   The meals in this problem satisfy this test.

Q# 14:   Rosie entered a sweepstakes contest and won the grand prize of $200,000.   In the same year, Rosie also received an award of $10,000 in recognition of her literary talents, evidenced by the best selling novel she wrote a few years ago.   Rosie did not seek to enter literary competition, and she is not required to perform any services as a condition of receiving the $10,000.   How much is included in Rosie's gross income?

A # 14: $210,000.   The value of all prizes and awards are included in gross income under the general rule of IRC § 74(a).   There are 3 exceptions to the general rule, and a prize or award is not included in the gross income of the recipient if: (1) the prize is a qualified scholarship excludable from gross income under IRC § 117;   (2) the recipient was selected to receive the prize without any action to enter the contest, is not required to render any future services as a condition of receiving the award, and if the prize is transferred to a governmental or charitable organization designated by the recipient; or (3) the prize is an employee achievement award. Therefore, if the $10,000 literary achievement prize is transferred to a governmental or charitable organization at Rosie's direction, that prize will not be included in her gross income.

Q# 15: Perry takes out a $100,000 whole-life insurance policy on his life. Several years later, at a time when Perry has paid a total of $15,000 in premiums, he sells the policy to his wife, Sadie, for $20,000; in January of the next year, Perry dies and the insurance company pays the $100,000 to Sadie. How much must Sadie include in her gross income?

A# 15: Nothing. The general rule of IRC § 101(a) excludes the proceeds of life insurance policies from gross income, but there is an exception (requiring life insurance proceeds to be included in gross income) if the policy has been transferred for a valuable consideration, IRC § 101(a)(2). An exception to the exception (thus, permitting exclusion from gross income, under the general rule) applies if the policy has a transferred basis in the hands of the transferee, IRC § 101(a)(2)(A). Sadie has a transferred basis for the insurance policy of $15,000 under IRC § 1041(b)(2), because she received the policy from her spouse.

Q# 16: Joseph is a minister at a protestant church. As compensation for the services he performs as a minister, the church pays Joseph $1,500 per month, plus a housing allowance of $500 per month. Joseph rents an apartment for $450 per month and pays utility bills of $100 per month. How much must Joseph include in his gross income each month?

A# 16: $1,500. IRC § 107 excludes the rental allowance paid to Joseph, to the extent he uses it to obtain a home, including expenses such as utilities which are directly related to providing the home.

Q# 17: Earl's business is defamed by a malicious competitor and Earl receives a $100,000 recovery. This recovery represents $25,000 in lost profits, $40,000 to injured goodwill of the business (in which Earl had a $30,000 basis), and $35,000 in punitive damages. What is Earl's gross income as a result of the recovery?

A# 17: Earl has $70,000 of gross income; $25,000 of lost profits, $10,000 gain on the goodwill, and $35,000 of punitive damages.

Q# 18: Jan purchases a piece of depreciable property paying $20,000 of cash and incurring a nonrecourse liability of $80,000. When the property appreciates in value, she takes out another $50,000 liability on the property. Several years later, when she has properly taken $40,000 of depreciation on the property and the liabilities on the property are $45,000 and $25,000, she sells it for $60,000 of cash and the buyer assumes the liabilities. What is Jan's gain on the sale?

A# 18: Jan's amount realized is $130,000, the total of the cash ($60,000) and the relief of the liabilities ($45,000 + $25,000). Her adjusted basis in the property is her $100,000 original cost which includes the liability of $80,000; there is no change in her basis as a result of the second liability (she liquidated out but she has an obligation to repay that $50,000); and she reduces her basis by the $40,000 depreciation deductions (assuming it resulted in a tax benefit) to $60,000. Her gain is $70,000, the difference between her $130,000 amount realized and $60,000 adjusted basis.

Q# 19: Al operates an illegal loan-sharking business from which he derives a profit of $100,000 in the current year. Is Al subject to income tax on this profit? Are Al's expenses deductible?

A# 19: The profits are taxable under the general rule of IRC § 61. Al's expenses are deductible providing they meet the tests of IRC § 162. Also see IRC § 280E.

Q# 20: Richard, an accountant, has the following tax realizations during the year; what is his gross income for the year:

(1) He is paid a $35,000 salary, receives a $10,000 cash bonus, and a $5,000 car to be used for personal purposes.

(2) He sells for $10,000 some stock purchased for $2,000, and he sells for $9,000 some municipal bonds whose interest is tax exempt which he purchased for $6,000.

(3) He wins a $1,000 vacation in a raffle.

(4) He has an income interest in a trust established by his deceased mother and he collects $5,000 of dividends from the trust.

(5) His uncle wills him $2,000 as agreed compensation for services he rendered to the uncle prior to his death.

(6) He recovers $5,000 of damages for defamation to his personal character.

(7) He collects on a $2,500 loan he made to a friend along with $500 of interest.

(8) He fills out his family's income tax return; H & R Block would have charged $300 to do it.

(9) His employer pays $50 a month for a parking space for Richard in the basement of the building in which they rent their offices.

(10) He buys a $10,000 boat and gets a $1,000 rebate.

A# 20: His gross income is $69,500; the individual items are treated as follows:

(1) The cash salary and the bonus are included in gross income, as is the fair market value of the car. [IRC § 61(a)(1).]

(2) He must include both the $8,000 gain from the sale of the stock, as well as the $3,000 gain from the sale of the bonds; the provision which excludes interest paid on the bonds does not exclude gain derived from selling them. [See IRC § 103.]

(3) The $1,000 prize is included in gross income. [IRC § 74.]

(4) The $5,000 of dividend income from the trust is included in gross income. [IRC § 102(b).]

(5) The $2,000 received under his uncle's will is compensation income; it is not excluded from gross income as an inheritance. [See IRC § 102(a).]

(6) The damages for defamation to personal character is excluded from gross income. [See IRC § 104(a)(2).]

(7) The repayment of the principal amount which he loaned to his friend is a recovery of capital, not included in gross income; the receipt of $500 interest is included in gross income. [IRC § 61(a)(4).]

(8) The value of preparing his own family's income tax returns is imputed income, which is not included in gross income.

(9) The value of parking space provided by his employer is a nontaxable "working condition" fringe benefit. [IRC § 132(a)(3) and (h)(4).]

(10) The rebate is a reduction in the purchase price of the boat, it is not gross income.

PART III

Q# 1: David owns a sporting goods store. In the current year, David pays his employees a total of $100,000 in salary, he builds an addition to the store at a cost of $20,000, and he spends $1,000 for advertising expenses. On his return for the current year, David deducted $121,000 in expenses for the above items. Is this treatment correct?

A# 1: David may take deductions for the salaries and the advertising expense under IRC § 162. The addition to his store, however, is a capital expenditure under IRC § 263, added to the basis of the building under IRC § 1016(a)(1), and it may not be deducted. Deductions for depreciation may be claimed with respect to the building and the improvements under IRC § 168.

Q# 2: Richard is a certified public accountant who enrolls in law school. Although the program in which he is enrolled leads to the J.D. degree, he does not intend to practice law after graduation, but he believes the law courses will be helpful to him in his accountancy practice. Can Richard deduct the costs of his law school education?

A# 2: No deduction is allowed. Even though the law classes may help him in his accounting practice, the J.D. degree will qualify him to enter a new trade or business (the practice of law) and thus the education expenses are not deductible. [Reg. § 1.162–5(b)(3).]

Q# 3: Elizabeth sells her personal residence for $85,000 in the current year. She purchased the house several years ago at a cost of $100,000. What is the amount of Elizabeth's deductible loss on the sale?

A# 3: No deduction for the loss is allowed under IRC § 165(c) which limits losses for individuals to losses incurred in a trade or business, in a transaction entered into for profit, or certain casualty losses. The loss on the residence does not qualify under any of these three classifications.

Q# 4: John is an attorney who uses the cash method of accounting. During the current year, John is unable to collect $10,000 of amounts he billed to his clients in previous years. Does John have a bad debt deduction and, if so, how much?

A# 4: No deduction is allowed under IRC § 166(b) which limits the bad debt deduction to the adjusted basis of the debt. John has a zero basis in the accounts receivable because he is on the cash method of accounting. If John were an accrual method taxpayer he previously would have taken the $10,000 into income and he would have a $10,000 basis in the receivable and would be allowed a $10,000 ordinary deduction for a business bad debt.

Q# 5: Paul is an accountant in South Carolina and he attends a convention for accountants in New York City during the current year. While in New York for three days, Paul incurs the following expenses: Airline tickets, $700; meals, $300; hotel, $450; and taxi fares, $100. How much of the listed expenses can Paul deduct? Does it make any difference that the meals would be a personal expense if Paul was not away from home?

A# 5: Paul can deduct all the travel expenses, but only 80% of the amount spent for meals; it is doubtful that the amounts would be disallowed as "lavish or extravagant under the circumstances." [IRC § 162(a)(2).] It doesn't matter that the meal expense would be a non-deductible personal expense if Paul was not in a business travel status. [IRC § 262.] In order to take the deductions, however, Paul must properly substantiate the expenditures. [IRC § 274(d).]

Q# 6: Karen is an attorney who practices law in a state which requires attorneys to take a certain number of continuing professional education classes each year. In the current year, Karen returns to her law school alma mater and enrolls in two courses which she did not have time to take while a J.D. candidate;

the courses qualify for continuing professional education credit. Karen spends $500 for tuition and books to take the courses. Can Karen deduct the $500 expense?

A# 6: The expenses incurred by Karen are deductible education expenses. [Reg. 1.162–5(a).] The expenses meet the requirements imposed by the state as a condition to the retention by Karen of her license. In addition, unless they were unrelated to her practice, they would be deductible regardless of whether they qualify for continuing professional education credit.

Q# 7: Paul receives a bill from his attorney in the current year for a total of $2,000. The bill is broken down into three parts: $1,250 is for representing Paul in a divorce suit against his wife; $500 is for closing a transaction in which Paul purchased some real estate; and the remaining $250 is for representing Paul before the local property tax appraisal board when Paul contested the appraised value of his house. Can Paul deduct the legal fees?

A# 7: Paul can deduct $250 of the legal fees, the portion attributable to the determination of his local property taxes. [IRC § 212(3).] Legal fees for his divorce representation are non-deductible personal expenses. [IRC § 262.] To the extent they are attributable to *tax consequences* of the divorce or to produce alimony to be paid to him, they are deductible. [IRC § 212(3) and (1), respectively.] The legal fees incurred in the acquisition of property are part of the cost of the property, and, thus, are not deductible but are added to the property's basis. [IRC § 263.]

Q# 8: Sally lives in an ocean-front home. One day she notices that the hood of her car has rusted through. This rust is a complete surprise to Sally; can she claim a casualty loss for this damage?

A# 8: No. Sally cannot claim a casualty loss for the rust damage. IRC § 165(c)(3) allows a deduction for casualty losses, but casualties must be of a sudden and unexpected nature. The damage done to Sally's car is a result of gradual deterioration, not a sudden or unexpected event.

Q# 9: Under the Accelerated Cost Recovery System (ACRS), how is the useful life of property determined? Is salvage value relevant in calculating deductions under ACRS?

A# 9: Under ACRS, IRC § 168, property is divided into various classifications, based in part on the property's "class life". The I.R.S. issues tables listing numerous types of properties and assigning a class life to these properties. The class life to which an item of property is assigned does not necessarily have any relation to the useful life of the property to the taxpayer. Salvage value is treated as zero under ACRS.

Q# 10: Andrew purchases residential rental property in the current year, but Andrew does not want to use ACRS to depreciate this property. Can Andrew elect not to use ACRS for this property?

A# 10: No. ACRS is mandatory with respect to most tangible property; however, Andrew may elect to use the alternative depreciation system under ACRS, using a recovery period of 40 years rather than 27.5 years. [IRC § 168(g)(2).] Andrew would probably not want to use the alternative depreciation system, but may be required to do so if, for example, the property is used predominantly outside the U.S.

Q# 11: In the current year Rachel purchases from her father a used machine to use in her business; her father had used it in his business since January 1979. The asset cost Rachel $10,000, it has a 4 year useful life and a $2,000 salvage value. What depreciation methods are available to Rachel? How would she compute depreciation deductions under the straight line method?

A# 11: ACRS is not available to her; old ACRS is generally applicable to property placed in service after December 31, 1980, and current ACRS is generally applicable to property placed in service after December 31, 1986, but the "anti-churning" rules deny "recovery property" status to property owned or used by a taxpayer or a related party at any time during 1980. [IRC § 168(f)(4).] Rachel may take depreciation deductions under IRC § 167 using the straight line method or the 150% declining balance method. [IRC § 167(b) and (c); see Reg. § 1.167(b)–0(b) and Rev.Rul. 57–352, 1957–2 C.B. 150.] Deductions under the IRC § 167 straight line method are computed by multiplying the excess of the cost or other basis of the property over its salvage value, or $8,000 ($10,000 – $2,000) times a fraction, with 1 as the numerator and the denominator is the number of years of the property's useful life, or 4. Thus, deductions of $2,000 may be taken in each of the four years the property is used in Rachel's business. Anti-churning rules may also apply to property (other than residential rental property and nonresidential real property) owned or used by a taxpayer or related person at any time during 1986, requiring depreciation deductions to be computed under old ACRS if that method produces a smaller amount of deduction than does current ACRS. [IRC § 168(f)(5).]

Q# 12: Patricia purchases a piece of machinery for use in her business in the current year. The asset cost $10,000 and is 5-year property under IRC § 168(e)(1). What is the maximum amount she may deduct with respect to the machinery in the current year?

A# 12: IRC § 179 authorizes a deduction for all or a portion of "section 179 property" purchased and placed in service in a trade or business during a taxable year. The aggregate cost of section 179 property which may be deducted is $10,000, potentially subject to two limitations. [IRC § 179(b)(1).] The first limitation reduces the amount which may be deducted under IRC § 179 dollar-for-dollar by the amount the total cost of section 179 property placed in service during the year exceeds $200,000. [IRC § 179(b)(2).] Under the second limitation, the amount deducted under IRC § 179 in a taxable year may not exceed the amount of taxable income derived from the active conduct of a trade or business during that year, with any excess amount otherwise deductible under IRC § 179 carried over to subsequent taxable years. [IRC § 179(b)(3).] Assuming neither of these limitations apply, Patricia may deduct the entire $10,000 cost of the machine under IRC § 179; Patricia may not use IRC § 179 on any other property in the year.

Q# 13: Jerry purchases a piece of machinery, an item of 5-year property, in September of the current year. The property cost $10,000 and Jerry planned on using it exclusively in his business for 3 years. The estimated salvage value of the property at the end of the third year is $2,000. Compute Jerry's ACRS deductions for the current year and the succeeding year.

A# 13: The 3-year useful life estimate and the salvage value figure are not relevant in computing ACRS deductions. The ACRS deduction for the current year is $2,000, computed using the 200% declining balance method, a 5 year recovery period, the half-year convention, and treating the salvage value as zero. The ACRS deduction for the succeeding year is $3,200.

Q# 14: If the property in the question above was an apartment building, rather than machinery, (and it cost $1,000,000, rather than $10,000), how would ACRS deductions be computed for the current year and the succeeding year?

A# 14: This is residential rental property and ACRS deductions are computed using the straight line method, a recovery period of 27.5 years (unless the taxpayer elects or is required to use the alternative depreciation system), the mid-month convention and treating the salvage value as zero. Assuming the $1 million purchase price is for the building alone, not the underlying land, the deduction for the current year is approximately $10,620, and for the succeeding year it is approximately $36,400.

Q# 15: Greg's boat is totally destroyed by a fire in the current year. The boat cost Greg $20,000 two years ago and it was used exclusively for personal purposes. At the time of the fire the boat had a fair market value of $10,000. Greg's adjusted gross income for the current year is $50,000. Is Greg entitled to any deduction with respect to the damage to his boat, and if so, in what amount?

A# 15: The casualty results in a $4,900 itemized deduction. Individual taxpayers are authorized to take deductions for casualty losses, even though the damaged, destroyed or stolen asset was used solely for personal purposes. [IRC § 165(c)(3).] Greg has a personal casualty loss of $10,000, which is the lower of the property's basis ($20,000) or its change in fair market value as a result of the fire ($10,000). Two additional limitations are imposed on the amount of the loss deduction. The loss is limited to the extent the amount is in excess of $100, or $9,900. [IRC § 165(h)(1).] In addition, since Greg has no personal casualty gains, a deduction is authorized only to the extent the reduced loss exceeds 10% of his adjusted gross income, or $5,000 (10% of $50,000). Greg's casualty loss deduction with respect to the boat is $4,900 [($10,000 – $100) – $5,000] and it is an itemized deduction.

Q# 16: Tip, whose adjusted gross income in the current year is $100,000, gives some shares of General Motors stock which he bought several years ago for $30,000, and which now have a fair market value of $35,000 to the American Cancer Society. In addition, he gives the American Smithsonian Institution copies of letters which were written to him by various newsworthy people from around the world; the letters have a fair market value of $10,000. What general rules govern the deductibility of these gifts?

A# 16: The American Cancer Society is a qualifying charity under IRC § 170(b)(1)(A). If Tip were to sell the letters, the gain would be ordinary income [IRC § 1221(3)(B)]. The amount of a deduction for the charitable contribution of property which, if sold, would produce ordinary income must be reduced by the amount of ordinary income. [IRC § 170(e)(1)(A).] Thus, Tip is not entitled to any deduction with respect to the letters. If Tip were to sell the General Motors stock, however, the gain would be long-term capital gain. The amount of the contribution, $35,000, does not have to be reduced in this situation, [see IRC § 170(e)(1)(B)(i)]; however, the contribution may be deducted only in an amount not exceeding 30% of his contribution base. [IRC § 170(b)(1)(C).] Tip's contribution base is $100,000, therefore he may deduct only $30,000 during the current year; the remaining $5,000 will be treated as a contribution of capital gain property to a Public Charity made in the next year, deductible in accordance with the limitations applicable in that year. [IRC § 170(b)(1)(C)(ii).] In the alternative, Tip may elect under IRC § 170(b)(1)(C)(iii) to reduce the amount of the contribution with respect to the stock by the $5,000 gain to $30,000; the contribution is now within the 50% limit of IRC § 170(b)(1)(A) and the full $30,000 would be deductible in the current year.

Q# 17: Frank, a sole proprietor, sells a business asset at a loss to his brother. Can Frank deduct this loss?

A# 17: No. IRC § 267(a)(1) disallows losses from the sale of property between related taxpayers; brothers are related under IRC § 267(b)(1) and (c)(4). However, if the brother subsequently sells the property at a gain, the gain will not be required to be recognized to the extent of the previously disallowed loss. [IRC § 267(d).]

Q# 18: During the current year Paula pays $2,000 in ad valorem property taxes imposed by the local school district, $500 for the state property tax imposed on intangible personal property, $1,500 in state sales tax, state income tax of $1,800 and state gasoline taxes of $250. How much of these state and local taxes may Paula deduct?

A# 18: Deductions are authorized under IRC § 164(a) for the state and local property taxes and income taxes; deductions are not authorized for the state sales tax or for the state gasoline tax. If Paula elects to itemize deductions, the total amount of deductions for state and local taxes which she may take is $4,300.

Q# 19: Supporter files a joint return with her spouse. Together they have three children who live at home. The value of meals and lodging they provide each child is $3,000 per year. Each child works and earns $2,500 which is also used for their support. One child is a high school student, one a college student and the third is 23 years old and works for a local company. How many exemptions may be filed on the joint return?

A# 19: Four. There are two taxpayers filing the return who qualify for two exemptions. In addition the two children who are *students* each qualify for a dependency exemption even though each of their gross incomes exceeds the exemption amount. They bear the necessary relationship and support requirements. The meals and lodging provided by taxpayers constitute more than half of their support. The non-student child is over 18, has excess gross income and does not qualify for a dependency exemption.

Q# 20: Giver transfers some land with a basis of $10,000 and value of $40,000 to a public charity. The land is a capital asset which Giver has held for 10 years. Charity transfers $10,000 of cash to Giver who has a $50,000 contribution base for the year. What is the amount of Giver's charitable contribution if this is his only charitable gift for the year?

A# 20: This is a part gift, part sale. Giver has a $7,500 long-term capital gain on the sale. He also makes a transfer of long-term gain property with a basis of $7,500 and value of $30,000 to the public charity. Giver may deduct the gift to the extent of 30% of his contribution base or $15,000 in the current year with a $15,000 carryover or he may elect to reduce the gift by his $22,500 gain to $7,500 and deduct the full $7,500 in the current year.

Q# 21: Dick buys a computer which is 5-year property for use in his business for $25,000 on July 20 of the current year. He wishes to maximize his deductions in the current year. How much may he be allowed?

A# 21: Dick may take a $10,000 § 179 deduction (assuming neither of the limitations of IRC § 179(b)(2) or (3) are triggered) and reduce his adjusted basis to $15,000. The property would then be allowed an ACRS deduction of $3,000.

Q# 22: Marge moves to a new job and satisfies both the time and distance requirements of IRC § 217. She has $3,000 in moving and traveling expenses including 80% of meals, she spends $2,000 for temporary living quarters after arriving at her new location and $1,700 to buy out the lease on her old apartment. Her new employer reimburses her for the $1,700 expense. How much may Marge deduct under IRC § 217?

A# 22: The $1,700 reimbursement is included in Marge's gross income § 82. She may deduct a total of $6,000: $3,000 for moving and traveling; $1,500 [$2,000 but limited to $1,500 IRC § 217(b)(3)(A)] for the temporary quarters; and $1,500 for the lease buy out ($3,000 less $1,500) under IRC § 217(b)(3)(A).

Q# 23: Businessman owns a sole proprietorship business in which he incurs the following expenses. To what extent are the expenses deductible?

(1) Salaries of $20,000.

(2) Rent of building, $12,000.

(3) Utility bills, $1,000.

(4) Entertainment of clients for which he has no vouchers, $500.

(5) Legal fees to defend a business defamation suit, $700.

(6) $400 for transportation, $200 for hotels and $100 for food while traveling on an out-of-town business trip.

(7) Dues to a professional organization of $200.

(8) Federal income taxes attributable to the business of $15,000.

(9) State income taxes attributable to the business of $3,000.

(10) Interest of $2,500 on a business loan.

(11) $11,000 for the purchase of a car to be used exclusively in the business.

(12) Newspaper and magazine advertising expenses of $900.

(13) Businessman's business was a new business begun two years ago. He spent $10,000 investigating whether to engage in it and properly elected IRC § 195 with respect to his expenses.

(14) Businessman spent $1,500 to determine whether to expand his business to a neighboring community.

(15) He demolishes a building which has an adjusted basis of $5,000 in order to build a new building for his business.

A# 23: Businessman will be able to deduct the following expenses: (1) the salaries, under IRC § 162(a)(1); (2) the rent for the building used in the trade or business IRC § 162(a)(3); (3) the utility bills, IRC § 162(a); (5) legal fees under IRC § 162(a); (6) the $400 transportation and $200 hotel expenses incurred on the business trip may be deducted in full under IRC § 162(a)(2) but only $80 (80% of $100) may be deducted for the meals because of the limitation of IRC § 274(n)(1); (7) dues to the professional organization under IRC § 162(a); (9) state income taxes under IRC § 164(a)(3); (10) interest under IRC § 163(a); (11) depreciation deductions will be allowed for the car under IRC § 168; (12) advertising expenses under IRC § 162(a); (13) assuming that he elected to deduct his start-up expenditures of $10,000 over a period of 60 months (5 years), the deduction this year will be $2,000 under IRC § 195(b); (14) deduction under IRC § 162(a). The following amounts may *not* be deducted: (4) entertainment expenses because he does not have proper substantiation, IRC § 274(d)(2); (8) Federal income taxes are not deductible, under IRC § 275(a)(1); (15) the demolition loss is not deductible, under IRC § 280B.

Q# 24: Brother is an accrual method taxpayer and Sister is a cash method taxpayer. Brother owes Sister rent on a building. The deductible $10,000 rent for the year is not paid until March of the following year. In addition on November 1 Brother sells Sister 100 shares of ATT stock at a loss. A week later he buys 100 shares of ATT stock on the New York stock exchange for himself. Discuss the consequences of the above transactions.

A# 24: Brother and Sister are § 267 related parties under § 267(c)(4). As a result Brother is allowed no $10,000 rental deduction until March when the rent is actually paid. § 267(a)(2). In addition the loss on the sale of Brother's ATT stock is denied both under § 267(a)(1) and § 1091(a). Sections 267(d) and 1091(a) both provide relief provisions, but since there is only one loss there should be only one relief provision. Sister is denied § 267(d) relief and only § 1091(d) applies. The last sentence of § 267(d) so states.

Q# 25: Patience has been ill during the year and has spent $1,000 for medical insurance, $2,000 in doctor bills, $500 for prescription drugs, $400 for nonprescription drugs and $3,000 in hospital bills. What is her medical expense deduction if her adjusted gross income is $20,000?

A# 25: $5,000. Her total medical expenses under IRC § 213 are $6,500 (nonprescription drugs do not qualify) and she may deduct those expenses to the extent they exceed $1,500 (7.5% of adjusted gross income) or $5,000.

Q# 26: Darwin invests $40,000 of cash in a real estate tax shelter and his total deductions exceed his total income from the real estate activity in the current year by $100,000. He is "at risk" in the activity to the extent of his $40,000 investment. How much may he deduct?

A# 26: He may deduct only $40,000 under the limitations of the "at risk" rules of IRC § 465. The amount he may deduct during the current year may be limited further, however, by the passive activity loss rules of IRC § 469.

PART IV

Q# 1: Steven rents his property to Mark, for use in Mark's business, on January 1 of the current year for a three-year lease term. The annual rent is $1,000, but Mark pays Steven $3,000 for all three years at the beginning of the lease term. Both Steven and Mark use the cash method of accounting. How must Steven and Mark treat the $3,000 payment?

A# 1: Steven must include the entire $3,000 in gross income for the current year, the year in which he receives the payment. Mark, on the other hand, may only deduct $1,000 in the current year, because the lease is to run for three years, a period extending substantially beyond the current year. Mark will be able to deduct $1,000 next year, and $1,000 the year after that.

Q# 2: What are the results in Question # 1 if both Steven and Mark are accrual method taxpayers?

A# 2: The results would likely be the same. The prepaid rent would likely be included in Steven's gross income under Rev.Proc. 71–51, 1971–1 C.B. 549, unless a court extended the *Artnell* case rationale beyond a two year period. Mark's deductibility under the "all events" test is deferred until economic performance occurs. [IRC § 461(h).] Thus he is allowed a deduction of $1,000 per year as use of the property occurs.

Q# 3: Claudia, an accrual method taxpayer, purchases an office machine and separately for an additional $1,000 she purchases a 3-year service contract relating to the machine. The service contract provides that the machine will be serviced and repaired at no additional charge annually within the next three years. When may Claudia deduct the cost of the service contract?

A# 3: The "all events" test is modified with respect to deductions of accrual method taxpayers; no deduction is allowed until economic performance has occurred. Economic performance occurs when the services are provided under the contract; she may not deduct the cost of the contract until the services are actually provided to her.

Q# 4: Martina (an accrual method taxpayer) is a tennis pro who, in November of Year One, contracts with Chrissie to provide 50 one-hour tennis lessons within the next 12 months; Chrissie pays Martina the total contract price of $2,500 when the contract is signed. Martina gives Chrissie ten lessons in Year One. How much must Martina include in her gross income for Year One?

A# 4: $500. Generally, an accrual method taxpayer is required to include advance payments in gross income in the year in which they are received, even though she will be providing services in subsequent taxable years. However, Martina receives payment in one taxable year for services which she is required to perform before the close of the next taxable year. In this situation, she may include in gross income for the year in which the advance payment is received only the portion she earns that year, or $500 (50 lessons for $2,500, or $50 per lesson). Martina must include the remaining $2,000 in gross income for Year Two regardless of how many tennis lessons she actually gives in that year. [Rev.Proc. 71–51, 1971–1 C.B. 549.]

Q# 5: Amanda owns a clothing store. At the end of last year, the remaining inventory had a cost of $5,000. During the current year, she purchases an additional $20,000 of inventory, and at the end of the year, her closing inventory had a cost of $3,000. Her gross receipts from the sale of inventory during the year is $33,000. What is Amanda's cost-of-goods-sold for the current year, and what is her gross income from the sale of inventory.

A# 5: Amanda's cost-of-goods-sold is $22,000, which is the sum of her beginning inventory (the closing inventory from last year, $5,000) plus the purchases of additional inventory during the year ($20,000) less the closing inventory for the year ($3,000). Her gross income from the sale of inventory is $11,000, the amount of gross receipts ($33,000) less her cost-of-goods-sold ($22,000).

Q# 6: In the current year, Pamela sells a parcel of investment land which has an adjusted basis of $1,000. The terms of sale call for her to receive a $2,000 cash payment, and $1,000 payments (plus a reasonable rate of interest) in each of the next eight years. If Pamela does not "elect out" of IRC § 453, how much gain must she recognize in the current year, and the next year when she receives the $1,000 payment?

A# 6: Pamela has $1,800 of recognized gain in the current year, and $900 of recognized gain next year. The "gross profit" on the sale is $9,000, the selling price of the stock ($10,000) less its adjusted basis ($1,000); the "total contract price" is, on these facts, the same as the selling price ($10,000). The ratio of the gross profit to the total contract price ($9,000/$10,000 or 90%) is multiplied times the aggregate amount of payments received during a taxable year to determine the amount of gain which must be recognized during that year. Thus, in the current year, there is recognized gain of $1,800 (90% of $2,000), and in the next year, there is recognized gain of $900 (90% of $1,000). These gains would be characterized by the sale of the land.

Q# 7: What result in Question # 6 if Pamela immediately resells her contractual rights to the $8,000 of payments for $7,500 of cash?

A# 7: Pamela would have a gain of $6,700, the difference between her $7,500 amount realized and $800 basis in the obligations. The basis of the obligations is their face amount, $8,000, reduced by the gain which would be recognized if they were recovered in full, $7,200. [IRC § 453B(b).] The $6,700 gain would be characterized by the original land sale. [IRC § 453B(a).]

Q# 8: What result in Question # 6 if Pamela is a cash method taxpayer, the $8,000 of obligations are worth $7,000 and she elects out of IRC § 453 under IRC § 453(d)? What result when she subsequently receives the eight $1,000 payments?

A# 8: Pamela has $8,000 of recognized gain in the year of sale (cash and fair market value of the obligations yield an amount realized of $9,000 less $1,000 adjusted basis). All the gain is characterized by the original sale of the land. On collection of each of the obligations she has a $1,000 amount realized and a $875 basis for a $125 gain which, lacking a sale or exchange, is characterized as ordinary income.

Q# 9: Dale sells a painting to Paul, his son, in Year One. Dale has a gain on the property and was reporting this gain under the installment method. In Year Two Paul sells the painting to his friend Jim. Does this sale by Paul have any effect on Dale's tax return for Year Two?

A# 9: Yes, IRC § 453(e) provides special rules for second dispositions of property by related persons when the original seller, Dale, uses the installment method. Because Dale and Paul are related and Paul disposes of the painting within 2 years of its purchase, Dale must accelerate his reporting of the original sale and treat the amount realized by Paul as received by Dale, subject to some special limitations.

Q# 10: Kim owns a piece of real property she holds for investment. The property cost her $10,000 and has a fair market value of $50,000. Kim exchanges this piece of property for a similar parcel of real estate that has a $50,000 fair market value. What is Kim's recognized gain and basis in the new property on this transaction?

A# 10: Kim's realized gain is $40,000 but IRC § 1031 provides non-recognition treatment for like kind exchanges. Because the property given up and the property received are investment real estate, no gain is recognized. The basis of the property received is the same as the basis of the property given up or $10,000. IRC § 1031(d). In addition, because the property which was exchanged was a capital asset, the new property takes an IRC § 1223(1) tacked holding period.

Q# 11: How would the answer to Question # 10 change if the property Kim received was worth only $40,000 and Kim also received stock worth $10,000?

A# 11: Kim would have a recognized gain of $10,000. IRC § 1031(b) provides that gain shall be recognized but in an amount not in excess of the sum of such non-like kind property received. Since stock is not like kind property and its value, $10,000, is less than the realized gain, $40,000, only $10,000 of the gain is recognized. The basis of all the property received is $20,000 which is the basis of the property given up ($10,000) plus the gain recognized ($10,000). IRC § 1031(d). The basis is allocated between the stock (boot) and the real property (like kind) with the boot stock taking a $10,000 fair market value basis under IRC § 1031(d) and no tacked holding period and the real property taking a $10,000 "substituted" basis under IRC § 1031(d) with a tacked holding period under IRC § 1223(1).

Q# 12: Dan owns a restaurant. Unfortunately for Dan, the state plans to build a highway and his restaurant is in the path of the new road. In Year One, the state condemns Dan's restaurant and pays him $100,000 for it. The restaurant has a basis to Dan of $20,000. Dan purchases another restaurant in Year Two at a cost of $110,000. Does Dan have to recognize any gain on the money received for his restaurant? What is Dan's basis in the new restaurant?

A# 12: Dan does not have to recognize any gain. IRC § 1033(a) allows non-recognition treatment for gains resulting from involuntary conversions if similar property to that so condemned is acquired within 2 years after the close of the first year any gain is realized. Gain is recognized only to the extent the amount realized on the conversion exceeds the cost of the newly acquired property. Dan's amount realized on the conversion was $100,000 and he reinvested $110,000; thus no gain is recognized. Dan's basis in the new restaurant is the cost of the new restaurant ($110,000) less the gain not recognized on the old restaurant ($80,000) or $30,000. The new restaurant has a tacked holding period under IRC § 1223(1).

Q# 13: How would the answer to Question # 12 change if Dan spent only $70,000 on a new restaurant?

A# 13: Dan would recognize a gain of $30,000. The gain realized by Dan on the original conversion was $80,000 ($100,000 amount realized less $20,000 adjusted basis). IRC § 1033(a)(2)(A) provides that gain shall be recognized to the extent the amount realized on the conversion, $100,000, exceeds the cost of the new restaurant, $70,000, for a total of $30,000. The gain will be characterized by the gain on the old restaurant. Dan's basis in the new restaurant would be $20,000

($70,000 cost of replacement property less $50,000 unrecognized gain). IRC § 1033(b). Again the new property has a tacked holding period under IRC § 1223(1).

Q# 14: Melissa sells her principal residence in Year One for $200,000. Melissa's basis in the house is $35,000. In Year Two Melissa purchases a new residence for $300,000. Does Melissa recognize any gain on the sale of her residence? What is Melissa's basis in the new residence?

A# 14: Melissa does not recognize any of the $165,000 realized gain from the sale of the residence. IRC § 1034 provides for the non-recognition of gain from the sale of a principal residence if the 2-year time requirement is met. Gain is recognized only to the extent the adjusted sales price, $200,000, exceeds the cost of the new residence, $300,000; thus Melissa does not recognize any gain. The basis of the new residence is it's cost, $300,000, reduced by the amount of gain not recognized on the sale of the old residence, $165,000, for a total basis of $135,000. Its holding period is tacked under IRC § 1223(7).

Q# 15: How would the answer to Question # 14 change if Melissa was 60 years old and had lived in the old residence for the past 9 years and she elects to use IRC § 121?

A# 15: IRC § 121 allows a taxpayer who meets certain conditions to elect to exclude up to $125,000 of gain from the sale of a principal residence. Melissa meets the condition of IRC § 121 and thus could exclude $125,000 of the gain. In addition, IRC § 1034 will apply, but first the amount realized ($200,000) is reduced by the gain not recognized under IRC § 121 ($125,000) to $75,000. [IRC § 121(d) (7).] Melissa's realized gain is $40,000 ($75,000 less $35,000), none of which is recognized under IRC § 1034(a) because the cost of her new residence ($300,000) is greater than $75,000. Melissa's basis in the new residence is $260,000 ($300,000 cost of the new residence less $40,000 gain not recognized under IRC § 1034). [IRC § 1034(e).] Possibly since Melissa was not required to recognize gain in Question 14, above, she would not use her IRC § 121 election until some point when under IRC § 1034 she might recognize some gain. Note however, her higher basis in Question # 15's replacement property as a result of the IRC § 121 election. Again the replacement property would have a tacked holding period under IRC § 1223(7).

Q# 16: In the current year when the applicable Federal rate of interest is 10% Employer makes a $200,000 interest free demand loan to Employee. What are the consequences to both parties?

A# 16: Since the loan is a demand loan all consequences occur during the year. In addition interest is imputed at a 10% rate compounded semiannually. Interest compounded semiannually at 10% on $200,000 is 5% of $200,000, or $10,000, plus 5% of $210,000, or $10,500, for total of $20,500. Employer is deemed to pay that amount to Employee at the end of the year and Employee is deemed to repay the $20,500 as interest to Employer. Employer has $20,500 of interest income and a $20,500 IRC § 162 deduction for compensation. Employee has $20,500 of compensation income and possibly a $20,500 interest deduction.

PART V

Q# 1: Wealthy works for Corporation but directs that his $100,000 salary be paid to the American Cancer Society. Who is taxed on the salary?

A# 1: Wealthy. He has attempted to assign his income from services; such income is nonassignable. However, he has made a gift to the American Cancer Society and some or all of the gift will qualify as a charitable contribution deduction under IRC § 170.

Q# 2: Landlord owns a building and the land underlying it on which rent of $20,000 is due for each year on December 31. On June 30 (½ way through the year) Landlord deeds one half of the building and *all* of the rents to his Son. The $20,000 rent is paid on January 3 of Year Two. To whom and when is the $20,000 of rent taxed if Landlord and Son are both calendar year, cash method taxpayers?

A# 2: Since one half of the rent is ripe on June 30 and since Landlord transfers only one half of the income producing property the ripe rent ($10,000) and the income from the unripened retained one half of the building and land ($5,000) is taxed to Landlord as it is collected in Year Two. Son is taxed on the remaining $5,000 of rent in Year Two.

Q# 3: Grantor creates a trust with income to Daughter for 10½ years and a remainder to Grandson at the end of 10½ years. Grantor names himself trustee with general fiduciary powers, but adds that Grantor has the power to accumulate income. In addition Grantor's sister may demand that any of the income for any year during the 10½ year period be paid to her. In each year of the trust the income is paid to Daughter. Who is taxed on the income?

A# 3: Grantor has a power to accumulate the income and add it to the remainder interest. Thus IRC § 671 will tax the income to Grantor as a result of IRC § 674(a). Although Sister would be taxed under IRC § 678 if Grantor was not taxed under § 671, Grantor's taxation under § 671 precludes taxation to Sister. [IRC § 678(b).]

Q# 4: Father gives Son and Daughter each a one third interest in his steel company which becomes a partnership as a result of the gift. Father continues to work for the company and his services are worth $100,000 per year but Father, Son and Daughter each have an equal say in running the company. The company earns $400,000 after expenses for the year but prior to compensating Father. Is the partnership valid under IRC § 704(e)(1)? How does IRC § 704(e)(2) call for the $400,000 to be allocated?

A# 4: Because the children own a capital interest in a partnership in which capital is a material income producing factor, this is a valid partnership under IRC § 704(e)(1). Under IRC § 704(e)(2) Father must be adequately compensated for his services ($100,000) and must have a rate of return on his ⅓ of the capital worth at least ⅓ of the partnership income, or $100,000. Thus the $400,000 would be allocated: Father, $200,000; Son, $100,000; and Daughter, $100,000.

Q# 5: What are the five basic requirements which must be satisfied in order for a payment to qualify as alimony or a separate maintenance payment?

A# 5: The payment must be: (1) in cash; (2) pursuant to a divorce or separation instrument; (3) the instrument must not designate the payment as a non-includible payment; (4) the payee spouse and the payor spouse must not be members of the same household at the time payment is made; and (5) there must be no liability to make any payment after the death of the payee spouse. [IRC § 71(b)(1).]

Q# 6: What possible administrative requirements may be imposed upon the person receiving and the person paying alimony?

A# 6: IRC § 215(c) authorizes regulations which may require a payee spouse to furnish his or her taxpayer identification number (social security number) to the payor spouse and the payor spouse may be required to include that number on her or his return for the taxable year in which payments are made.

Q# 7: Pursuant to a divorce decree, Barbara pays George $10,000 a year alimony for George's life. Barbara also agrees to pay child support of $6,000 a year until the children reach 21 years of age. What are the tax consequences of these payments to Barbara and George? What if in one year Barbara pays only $12,000?

A# 7: The $10,000 payments are alimony under IRC § 71(b) (assuming George and Barbara do not continue to reside in the same household); therefore, they are included in George's gross income and are deductible by Barbara. [IRC §§ 71 and 215.] The $6,000 payments for child support are not included in George's gross income (nor are they deductible by Barbara). [IRC § 71(c)(1).] If Barbara pays only $12,000 of her $16,000 annual obligation, child support takes priority and $6,000 is child support and only $6,000 is alimony. [IRC § 71(c)(3).]

Q# 8: Johnny pays Joanna the following amounts of deductible alimony in the 3 years following their divorce:

Year One:	$100,000
Year Two:	$ 90,000
Year Three:	$ 70,000

To what extent do the recapture rules of IRC § 71(f) apply? What if the amounts which are paid are computed as a percentage of the income from Johnny's business?

A# 8: In Year Three, the amount of excess alimony payments must be computed; excess alimony payments is the sum of excess payments for the first post-separation year (Year One) plus the excess payments for the second post-separation year (Year Two). [IRC § 71(f)(2).] The excess payments for Year Two is $5,000, the excess of the amount of alimony paid in Year Two ($90,000) over the amount of alimony paid in Year Three plus $15,000 ($85,000 = $70,000 + $15,000). [IRC § 71(f)(4).] The excess payments for Year One is $7,500, the excess of the amount of alimony paid in Year One ($100,000) over $92,500, which is the sum of

$15,000 plus $77,500, the average of the amount of alimony paid in Year Two reduced by the excess payments for that year ($85,000 = $90,000 – $5,000) and the alimony paid in Year Three ($70,000). [IRC § 71(f)(3).] The $12,500 ($5,000 + $7,500) of excess alimony payments must be included in Johnny's gross income for Year Three, and Joanna is allowed a $12,500 deduction in computing adjusted gross income for the same year. [IRC § 71(f)(1).] If the amounts paid are a set percentage of income from Johnny's business, the front-loading recapture rules are inapplicable. [IRC § 71(f)(5)(C).]

Q# 9: Unless the facts provide to the contrary, assume that the requirements of IRC § 71(b) are met. In the following alternative facts, which of the situations qualify as deductible alimony to the payor spouse?

(a) Payor allows payee to live rent free in a house he owns; fair rental value is $500 per month.

(b) Payor pays Payee's landlord $500 of rent.

(c) Payor pays $500 on the mortgage of a house he owns and where Payee is living rent free.

(d) Payor pays $500 on the mortgage of a house which Payee owns and in which payee resides.

A# 9: Both (b) and (d) would qualify as indirect alimony payments. Since Payor owns the property in (a) and (c), they do not qualify as alimony payments. In addition, there is no cash payment in (a).

Q# 10: Shortly after Robert and Phoebe are divorced, and as part of their divorce settlement, Robert transfers to Phoebe shares of stock in General Motors Corporation which he had owned in his own name, and Phoebe conveys to Robert her interest in their house which they had purchased during their marriage, taking title as joint tenants. The stock has a fair market value of $75,000 and an adjusted basis to Robert of $30,000; Robert and Phoebe paid $100,000 for the house several years ago, and it has a fair market value of $150,000. How much gain do Robert and Phoebe each recognize? What is Robert's basis for the house after the transfer? What is Phoebe's basis in the stock?

A# 10: Neither Robert nor Phoebe recognize any gain because the transfers of property are between former spouses, incident to their divorce. [IRC § 1041(a).] Robert has a basis of $100,000 in the house ($50,000 in his one half and $50,000 in the one half received from Phoebe) and Phoebe has a basis of $30,000 in the stock. [IRC § 1041(b)(2).] Note that if Phoebe immediately sells the stock, she would have $45,000 gain, while if Robert immediately sells the house, he would have $25,000 of gain attributable to the one half interest which he received from Phoebe and $25,000 of gain attributable to his one half.

Q# 11: Pamela [from Unit IV Question # 6] sells a parcel of land which has an adjusted basis of $1,000. She receives a $2,000 cash payment and a contractual right to $1,000 payments (plus a reasonable rate of interest) in each of the next eight years. If Pamela does not "elect out" of IRC § 453, how much gain must she realize if she sells the land to her husband, Gus? What if she sells the land to an unrelated third party but immediately resells her contractual rights to the $8,000 of payments to Gus for $7,500 cash?

A# 11: If Pamela sells the land to her husband, Gus, she will not recognize any gain on the sale and Gus will have a $1,000 basis in the land even though he has paid $2,000 cash and is committed to make $8,000 in further payments over the next eight years. [IRC § 1041(a) and (b).] Similarly, she will not recognize any gain on the sale of the contractual rights to Gus; Gus will have recognized gain as payments are made to him under the contract pursuant to the installment method under IRC § 453. [See IRC § 453B(g).]

PART VI

Q# 1: Terry owns several parcels of real estate. Over the last few years Terry has made a living buying and selling real estate and in the current year he sells 2 parcels of land which he bought 3 years ago. Terry bought these parcels with the intention of quickly reselling them. What is the character of the gain on the sale of these properties?

A# 1: This is probably ordinary income because of Terry's history of buying and selling property. The property would probably be treated as being held primarily for sale to customers in the ordinary course of Terry's business, and thus not a capital asset. [IRC § 1221(1).]

Q# 2: In the current year, Lynn sells certain capital assets, held for more than 6 months, at a gain of $2,000. Other capital assets, held for less than 6 months, are sold by Lynn at a loss of $1,000. How much is included in Lynn's net income for the current year?

A# 2: $1,000. The $2,000 long-term gain is included in gross income, but IRC § 1211(b) authorizes a deduction for the capital loss to the extent of her capital gains ($1,000).

Q# 3: In the current year, Art sells certain long-term capital assets for a gain of $2,000 and other long-term capital assets for a loss of $20,000. Art also has $100,000 of ordinary income. How much of the long-term capital loss may Art deduct in the current year?

A# 3: $5,000. IRC § 1211 allows capital losses to the extent of capital gains plus the lesser of: (1) $3,000, or (2) the excess of capital losses over the capital gains. Art can offset the $2,000 long-term capital gain with $2,000 of the long-term capital losses, plus Art can deduct an additional $3,000 because it is the lesser of the two limitation amounts.

Q# 4: In Question # 3 above, what happens to the remaining loss and what is it's character?

A# 4: IRC § 1212(b) provides for a carryover of unused capital losses to succeeding taxable years and characterizes the loss in this case as a long-term capital loss. The amount carried over is $20,000 less the $2,000 which reduced capital gains and less $3,000 which reduced ordinary income or $15,000. [IRC § 1212(b)(1)(B) and (2)(B).]

Q# 5: What result if Art, from Question # 3, has $100,000 of ordinary income and a $10,000 short-term capital gain in Year Two?

A# 5: The $15,000 of long-term capital loss carryover first wipes out the $10,000 of short-term capital gain under IRC § 1211(b), and in addition it reduces ordinary income by $3,000 under IRC § 1211(b)(1). The remaining $2,000 long-term capital loss is carried over to Year Three under IRC § 1212(b)(1)(B).

Q# 6: Kathy sells a rental apartment building that she had used in her trade or business for 5 years. The building was depreciated under the straight-line method and was sold for a gain of $50,000. Is the building a capital asset? What is the character of the gain?

A# 6: The building is not a capital asset because IRC § 1221(2) excludes real property used in a trade or business from the definition of a capital asset. Since the building has been depreciated using straight line depreciation there is no recapture gain under IRC §§ 1245 or 1250. The gain will be treated as a main hotchpot gain under IRC § 1231(a) because the building is real property used in Kathy's business and it was held for more than 6 months. If main hotchpot gains exceed losses, the gain on the building will be long-term capital gain; if main hotchpot losses exceed gains, it will be ordinary income.

Q# 7: In order to qualify for capital asset treatment certain requirements must be met. What requirement of the capital asset transaction treatment does IRC §§ 165(g) and 1234 provide?

A# 7: IRC § 1222 requires a capital asset to be disposed of in a "sale or exchange" in order to provide capital gain or loss. IRC § 165(g) provides sale or exchange treatment for a worthless security and IRC § 1234 provides sale or exchange treatment for the failure to exercise an option. Since worthless securities generate a loss, one would prefer an ordinary loss which would wipe out ordinary income without being subject to the limitations of IRC § 1211. However under § 165(g) Congress adds a sale or exchange as well as generally a long-term holding period. Since there is a loss, both potentially work to a taxpayer's detriment. IRC § 1234 can apply to both gains and losses and therefore cuts both ways.

Q# 8: Sally exchanges a plot of investment land for a similar tract in a transaction that qualifies for nonrecognition of gain under IRC § 1031. Sally held the land she exchanged for one year and subsequently sold the land she received one month after acquiring it. What is the holding period for the land Sally acquired in the exchange?

A# 8: Sally is considered to have held the land for one year and one month. Since the old land is a capital asset and since the new land has a substituted basis, IRC § 1223(1) allows Sally to tack the holding period of the land she gave up on to the holding period of the land she acquired.

Q# 9: Adam receives 10 shares of stock from his father as a gift. Adam's father had a basis in the stock of $10 and its fair market value on the date of the gift was $100. Adam's father held the stock for 10 years before giving it to Adam. Three months after receiving the stock, Adam sells it for $175. What is Adam's holding period and gain for the stock?

A# 9: Adam's holding period for the stock will be 10 years and 3 months under IRC § 1223(2) which allows the tacking of the father's 10 year period because the stock has a transferred basis, i.e. the basis of the stock in Adam's hands is determined by the basis of the stock in the hands of Adam's father. Adam's gain is $165, his amount realized ($175) less his adjusted carryover basis under IRC § 1015 ($10).

Q# 10: The following gains and losses take place during the current year: $1,000 gain from the involuntary conversion of business property held more than 6 months; a $2,000 IRC § 165(c)(1) loss from the involuntary conversion of business property held more than 6 months; and $500 gain from sale of business property held more than 6 months. How does IRC § 1231 characterize these gains and losses?

A# 10: The involuntary conversions are in the sub hotchpot and since the losses from the involuntary conversions exceed the gains by $1,000 the sub hotchpot rejects them for IRC § 1231 treatment. [IRC § 1231(a)(4)(C).] Both the $2,000 loss and the $1,000 gain will be characterized as ordinary. The $500 gain is from the *sale* of a section 1231 asset and thus is treated as a main hotchpot gain; this gain is not affected by the sub hotchpot. Since gains exceed losses in the main hotchpot, it is a long-term capital gain.

Q# 11: In Question # 10, if the gain on the involuntary conversion of the business property was $3,000 instead of $1,000, how would the gains and losses be characterized under IRC § 1231?

A# 11: As in Question # 10, the involuntary conversions are first dealt with in the sub hotchpot. Since gains now exceed losses in the sub hotchpot, IRC § 1231(a)(1) applies to determine the character of the gains and losses. The total section 1231 gains are $3,500 and the total losses are $2,000, thus the gains are treated as long-term capital gains and the losses are treated as long-term capital losses.

Q# 12: In Question # 10, if all of the property was *sold* instead of being involuntarily converted and the same gains and losses resulted, how would IRC § 1231 characterize the gains and losses?

A# 12: All gains and losses would be in the main hotchpot. Since the section 1231 main hotchpot gains of $1,500 are less than section 1231 losses of $2,000, IRC § 1231(a) treats all gains and losses as ordinary.

Q# 13: Richard and Elizabeth, husband and wife, each own 50% of the stock of Corporation. Elizabeth sells a building which she has depreciated using the straight-line method and which she has held for 5 years to Corporation at a gain of $50,000. Corporation plans on renting the building and depreciating it immediately. What is the character of Elizabeth's $50,000 gain?

A# 13: Ordinary income. IRC §§ 1245 and 1250 do not apply to the transaction because straight line depreciation was used and the property was held more than one year. IRC § 1231 does not apply to this transaction because IRC § 1239 overrides IRC § 1231. IRC § 1239 treats the gain on the sale of depreciable property between "related persons" as ordinary income. The parties are "related" because Elizabeth actually owns 50% of the stock in Corporation and she is considered as owning the other 50% by attribution; thus she is treated as owning 100% of the stock in Corporation. [IRC §§ 267(c)(4), 1239(b) and (c).]

Q# 14: What result in Question # 13 if Richard is Elizabeth's brother-in-law rather than her husband?

A# 14: The $50,000 is a main hotchpot gain under IRC § 1231(a). Again the recapture rules of IRC §§ 1245 and 1250 do not apply. IRC § 1239 does not apply because the Corporation is not a controlled entity since Elizabeth is not considered to own more than 50% of the stock of Corporation. Richard's stock is not attributed to his sister Elizabeth under IRC § 267(c) because of the modification made by IRC § 267(c)(5).

Q# 15: How is Elizabeth's $50,000 IRC § 1231(a) main hotchpot gain in Question # 14 characterized if she has no other IRC § 1231 transactions in this or any other year except that two years ago she had $20,000 of net section 1231 losses (excess of section 1231 losses over section 1231 gains)?

A# 15: Since in the current year Elizabeth has an excess of gains over losses in the main hotchpot, the gain would ordinarily be characterized as long-term capital gain. However, Elizabeth must recapture her net section 1231 losses from two years ago; her current year's $50,000 section 1231 gain will be characterized as $20,000 of ordinary income and only $30,000 of long-term capital gain. [IRC § 1231(c).]

Q# 16: On January 2 of the current year Vanessa sells a piece of business equipment for $9,000. Vanessa purchased this equipment on January 1 two years ago (but after 1986) at a cost of $10,000 and she has taken $5,200 of depreciation on the equipment (it is 5-year property under ACRS). What is the character of the gain on the sale of the equipment?

A# 16: The gain realized and recognized is $4,200 ($9,000 amount realized less $4,800 adjusted basis). The property is section 1245 property and thus IRC § 1245(a) characterizes the gain as ordinary income. The recomputed basis of the property is $10,000, its adjusted basis ($4,800) plus depreciation adjustments under IRC § 168 $5,200. [IRC § 1245(a)(2).] The amount by which the lower of the recomputed basis ($10,000) or the amount realized ($9,000) exceeds the adjusted basis of the property ($4,800) is treated as ordinary income. [IRC § 1245(a)(1).] Thus the entire $4,200 gain is ordinary income.

Q# 17: What results in Question # 16 if Vanessa sells the equipment for $20,000 rather than $9,000?

A# 17: The gain realized and recognized is $15,200 ($20,000 amount realized less $4,800 adjusted basis). Only $5,200 of the gain (the amount of the previously allowed depreciation) is characterized as ordinary income under IRC § 1245(a) because the recomputed basis ($10,000) is less than the amount realized ($20,000). The remaining $10,000 gain is a main hotchpot gain under IRC § 1231(a).

Q# 18: Determine Businessman's adjusted gross income for the year in which he has $100,000 salary and the following transactions occur:

(1) Businessman sells a building used in his business and acquired in 1975. His gain on the building is $30,000, $10,000 of which is ordinary income under IRC § 1250(a).

(2) He sells some depreciable business equipment at a $4,000 loss.

(3) Businessman sells some stock at a $1,000 long-term capital gain.

(4) He has a nonbusiness bad debt of $2,000.

A# 18: Businessman's adjusted gross income is $116,000. The $10,000 ordinary income under IRC § 1250 is added to his $100,000 salary income. In addition the nonbusiness bad debt is characterized as a short-term capital loss. [IRC § 166(d).] To determine his capital gain and loss consequences we must first determine the results in his IRC § 1231 main hotchpot (note there are no sub hotchpot consequences). In the main hotchpot he has a $20,000 gain on the business building and a $4,000 loss on the equipment; because gains exceed losses in the main hotchpot both are long-term capital gains and losses which then must be combined with his other $1,000 long-term capital gain and $2,000 short-term capital loss. Thus, Businessman has a total of $21,000 long-term capital gains, $4,000 long-term capital losses, and $2,000 of short-term capital losses. His net capital gain is $15,000 (net long-term capital gain of $17,000 less net short-term capital loss of $2,000). The capital losses may be deducted to the extent of his capital gains under IRC § 1211(b)(1) and the deduction may be taken in arriving at adjusted gross income. [IRC § 62(a)(3).] In summary:

Gross Income:		
(The sum of $100,000 + $10,000 + capital gains of $21,000)		$131,000
Less deduction for capital losses [IRC § 62(a)(3)]	6,000	
		–6,000
Adjusted Gross Income:		$125,000

Q# 19: Lessee's 8 year lease on a residence has 5 years to run and his landlord pays him $5,000 to buy him out so he can construct a new apartment building on the property. What result to Lessee?

A# 19: Lessee has a $5,000 gain on the lease buyout, the difference between his $5,000 amount realized and zero adjusted basis. Lessee sells his entire underlying property interest which is a capital asset to him, IRC § 1241 treats the transaction as an exchange, and the lease has been held more than 6 months; thus the $5,000 gain is a long-term capital gain.

Q# 20: Creditor bought Debtor's $10,000 note for $9,000 from the original creditor 2 years ago. The note is a capital asset to Creditor. Debtor pays off the note with a bond ($7,000 fair market value, $4,000 adjusted basis, held for 2 years) and some stock ($3,000 fair market value, $5,000 adjusted basis, held for 5 months). The stocks and bond are both investment properties. What consequences to Creditor and Debtor?

A# 20: Creditor has $1,000 of ordinary income. He receives property worth $10,000 in return for the note in which he has a $9,000 basis. Although the note is a capital asset, it is *extinguished* in the transaction; because there is no sale or exchange, there is no capital gain. [See IRC § 1222(3).]

Debtor satisfies $7,000 of the $10,000 obligation with the bond and $3,000 of the obligation with the stock. Debtor has a $3,000 gain on the stock and a $2,000 deductible loss on the stock. [IRC §§ 61(a)(3) and 165(c)(2).] The $3,000 bond gain is a long-term capital gain; the bond is a capital asset, it is exchanged (it is not extinguished in the transaction), and it is held long term. The stock loss is a short-term capital loss. Again there is an exchange of a capital asset but the stock has not been held for more than 6 months.

PART VII

Q# 1: In 1988 Ralph (an unmarried individual) receives $20,000 in salary, deposits $2,000 in his deductible I.R.A. account and pays $5,000 interest on his home mortgage. What is Ralph's adjusted gross income? What is his taxable income?

A# 2: Ralph's adjusted gross income is $18,000 and his taxable income is $11,050. Ralph's $2,000 I.R.A. deposit, deductible under IRC § 219, is subtracted from gross income in computing adjusted gross income. [IRC § 62(a)(7).] The interest expense, deductible under IRC § 163, does not affect Ralph's adjusted gross income, it is an itemized deduction. [See IRC § 63(d).] Because Ralph's itemized deductions ($5,000) exceed the amount of his standard deduction ($3,000 in 1988), he should elect to itemize deductions; his taxable income is $11,050, gross income ($20,000) less the sum of allowable deductions ($2,000 + $5,000 + $1,950 = $8,950). If Ralph does not itemize deductions, his taxable income is $13,050, adjusted gross income ($18,000) minus the standard deduction ($3,000 in 1988) and the personal exemption deduction ($1,950 in 1988).

Q# 2: Robert and Carol were married on December 30 of the current year. May they file a joint return? What other filing status is available to them?

A# 2: Marital status is determined at the close of the taxable year, thus Robert and Carol may file a joint return. [IRC §§ 7703(a) and 6013(a).] If they file a joint return, the rate schedule of IRC § 1(a) will apply. Alternatively, they may each file separate returns, however if they do so they must each use the rate schedule of IRC § 1(d) which is applicable to married individuals filing separate returns and will in all likelihood result in greater tax liability. They might opt for the higher alternative because, except for the innocent spouse rule, there is joint and several liability on a joint return. [IRC § 6013(d)(3).]

Q# 3: When will an individual who is considered married under the general rule of IRC § 7703(a) be treated as not married? What will be the filing status of such an individual?

A# 3: An individual is not considered to be married if: (1) she files a separate return and maintains a household which constitutes for more than one-half of the taxable year the principal place of abode of a dependent child; (2) she furnishes over one-half of the cost of maintaining the household during the taxable year; and (3) during the last 6 months of the taxable year her spouse is not a member of her household. [IRC § 7703(b).] The filing status of an individual who is treated as not married under this provision will either be as unmarried or, if the requirements of IRC § 2(b) are satisfied, as a head of household.

Q# 4: Jim is a married taxpayer with a minor child whom he supports and who lives at home with Jim and his wife. What is Jim's tax liability in 1988 in the following alternative situations if his taxable income is $35,000:

(a) He files a joint return?

(b) His wife dies during the year but he files a joint return?

(c) His wife died in 1987?

(d) His wife died in 1980?

(e) His wife died in 1980 but their child is 22 years old and does not qualify as his dependent?

A# 4: Jim's 1988 tax liability in the alternative situations is as follows:

(a) $5,932.50. The tax is determined under the IRC § 1(a) as they are married filing a joint return.

(b) $5,932.50. In the year of Wife's death a joint return may still be filed with her executor's approval. [See IRC § 6013(a)(3).] If so, the tax liability is again determined under IRC § 1(a).

(c) $5,932.50. Since Wife died in the prior year and Jim has a dependent child in his household, he is a surviving spouse who may use the IRC § 1(a) joint return rates. [See IRC § 2(a).]

(d) $6,693.00. Wife died more than 2 years prior to the current year, so Jim does not qualify as a surviving spouse, but since he has responsibilities for a dependent he qualifies as a head of household under IRC § 2(b). Jim's tax liability is computed under IRC § 1(b).

(e) $7,479.50. Jim is unmarried, the child is not Jim's dependent, and no other person qualifies as his dependent. Thus his tax liability is computed under IRC § 1(c) as an unmarried taxpayer.

Q# 5: Is the alternative minimum tax a substitute for or an addition to the regular tax in a taxable year to which it applies?

A# 5: The alternative minimum tax is *in addition to* the regular tax for the taxable year. [IRC § 55(a).]

Q# 6: Alternator is an unmarried taxpayer with $10,000 salary and $100,000 of interest from qualified private activity bonds in 1988, but no other items of income nor any itemized deductions. What is Alternator's 1988 tax liability?

A# 6: Alternator's gross income is only $10,000 because the interest income is excluded from gross income under IRC § 103(a). Her taxable income is $5,050 ($10,000 adjusted gross income less $3,000 standard deduction and $1,950 personal exemption) and her regular tax liability under IRC § 1(c) is $757.50.

Alternator's alternative minimum taxable income (AMTI) is $108,050, computed by adding to her taxable income the amount of the standard deduction and the interest on the private activity bonds. [IRC §§ 55(b)(2), 56(b)(1)(E) and 57(a)(5)(A).] A tentative minimum tax of $16,390.50 is then computed (21% of the amount by which the AMTI exceeds the $30,000 exemption amount applicable to unmarried taxpayers). The alternative minimum tax is the amount by which the tentative minimum tax exceeds the regular tax for the year, or $15,633.00. Alternator's total tax liability for the year is $16,390.50, the sum of the regular tax of $757.50 imposed under IRC § 1(c) plus the alternative minimum tax of $15,633.00 imposed under IRC § 55(a).

Q# 7: Evelyn is a single, cash method, calendar year taxpayer who is an employee with $30,000 of salary income in 1988. She takes a deductible continuing education course in a nearby town incurring $300 of tuition and $700 of deductible transportation, lodging and 80% of meals; $500 in deductible moving expenses; $1,000 in interest on the loan on her residence; $1,000 in state income taxes; $400 in charitable contributions; and $200 in interest on her credit cards. Her employer has withheld $4,500 in income taxes on her account. How much tax must she remit with her return for 1988?

A# 7: Evelyn's gross income is $30,000. She has no section 62 deductions so her adjusted gross income is also $30,000. The total of $1,000 spent for tuition and travel to the continuing education course is her only miscellaneous itemized deduction, thus only $400 is deductible (the extent it exceeds 2% of her adjusted gross income, or $600). Her itemized deductions total $3,300, consisting of deductible portion of miscellaneous itemized deductions ($400), IRC § 217 moving expenses ($500), IRC § 163 interest ($1,000; the interest paid on her credit cards is not deductible), IRC § 164 state income taxes ($1,000) and IRC § 179 charitable contributions ($400). Because her itemized deductions ($3,300) exceed her standard deduction amount ($3,000 for 1988) she will elect to itemize deductions; her taxable income is $24,750 ($30,000 gross income less $3,300 of allowable deductions and $1,950 personal exemption). Her pre-credit tax liability is $4,609.50. [IRC § 1(c).] Evelyn's net tax liability, the amount she must remit with her return, is $109.50, $4,609.50 reduced by a credit of $4,500 for the tax withheld on her salary. [IRC § 31(a).]

Q# 8: What is Evelyn's taxable income in Question # 7 if she had paid only $500 in state taxes?

A# 8: Again, Evelyn's gross income and adjusted gross income is $30,000. However, her total allowable itemized deductions are now only $2,800, an amount which is lower than her standard deduction. She should not elect to itemize deductions and her taxable income is $25,050 ($30,000 adjusted gross income less $3,000 standard deduction and $1,950 personal exemption) producing a pre-credit tax liability of $4,693.50 resulting in $193.50 of tax due with her return.

*

PRACTICE EXAMINATION

Question One:

Taxpayer, a calendar year, cash method taxpayer, owns a triplex residential rental property with a basis of $50,000 and a value of $100,000 in each of the three rental units in the building. Each unit generates $12,000 of rent annually. Taxpayer purchased the building in 1979, but he does not own the land on which the triplex is built. Taxpayer has used accelerated depreciation on each unit and the amount of depreciation on each exceeds the amount which would have been allowed if straight line depreciation had been used by $10,000. Discuss all the tax consequences in the current year to Taxpayer when Taxpayer does the following:

(1) On January 1 he sells Unit #1 to Buyer who pays $50,000 down and agrees to pay $50,000 in annual payments of $10,000 (plus a reasonable rate of interest) over the next 5 years.

(2) On January 1 he exchanges Unit #2 for a commercial building without the land worth $95,000 and $5,000 of cash.

(3) On April 30 (⅓ of the way through the year) he deeds to his son one half of Unit #3 along with the right to *all* rents from the unit in this and subsequent years. The annual rent is paid in December.

Answer to Question One:

First, note that the triplex units are *not* ACRS recovery property because they were placed in service in 1979; therefore, depreciation deductions have been taken under IRC § 167. Further, the units are section 1250 property with $10,000 of recapture gain on each parcel. The results of the three transactions are as follows:

(1) Taxpayer makes an installment sale of Unit # 1 to which IRC § 453 will apply, unless he elects to have those provisions *not* apply. The section 1250 gain of $10,000, however, must be immediately recognized. [IRC § 453(i).] Thus Taxpayer has $10,000 of ordinary income in the current year. Note that this is *not* an "applicable installment obligation" as defined in IRC § 453C(e)(1); thus even if Taxpayer had any outstanding quarterly indebtedness, none would be treated as a payment received on the installment obligation from this sale. [See IRC § 453C(a) and (b).] In addition, the installment method of IRC § 453 applies to the remaining gain in the current and subsequent years. After the recapture gain recognition the remaining gross profit on the property is $40,000 and the total contract price is $100,000. Thus ⁴/₁₀ of the $50,000 payment or $20,000 is recognized gain on the sale in the current year. That $20,000 gain is a section 1231 main hotchpot gain. (If Taxpayer has no other section 1231 transactions in the year and no non-recaptured net section 1231 losses, the gain will be a long-term capital gain). Any interest paid on the installment sales obligations during the year must be included in gross income as ordinary income.

(2) This is a like kind exchange and although Taxpayer has a $50,000 realized gain, IRC § 1031(a) requires recognition of only the $5,000 cash boot because the other property received is "like kind" property. Although the transferred property has $10,000 of section 1250 gain, the exception of IRC § 1250(d)(4) allows only the $5,000 gain attributable to the boot to be recognized as ordinary income. The new commercial building received has a basis of $50,000 ($50,000 less $5,000 plus $5,000). [IRC § 1031(d).] The new property also has a tacked holding period [IRC § 1223(a)] and $5,000 of IRC § 1250 taint [IRC § 1250(b)(3)]. The commercial building would qualify for depreciation deductions under IRC § 167 using the $50,000 substituted basis; it would not qualify for ACRS because of the anti-churning rules. [IRC § 168(f)(5)(A).]

(3) Unit # 3 involves an assignment of income problem. Taxpayer is attempting to assign *all* the income from Unit # 3 even though he has transferred only one half of the underlying property. He can successfully assign only one half of the rents. In addition, one third of the annual rents are ripe at the time of the transfer. Thus although Son receives the $12,000 rent in December, the ripe rents ($4,000) and one half of the $8,000 of remaining rents ($4,000) are gross income to Taxpayer; one half of the rent attributable to the last two thirds of the year ($4,000) is income to Son. In effect Taxpayer makes a gift to Son of $8,000, the amount of the excess rents Son receives. Taxpayer also makes a gift of $50,000 value of Unit # 3 to Son. Although there is $5,000 of section 1250 gain on that

portion of the unit, IRC § 1250(d)(1) provides an exception to Taxpayer from the recapture rule of IRC § 1250(a); the section 1250 taint, however, carries over to Son. Depreciation would be allowed in the current year, two thirds (one third of 100% plus two thirds of 50%) to Taxpayer and one third (two thirds of 50%) to Son.

Question Two:

Compute the amount of tax Taxpayer, a calendar year, unmarried, cash method taxpayer, must pay when she files her annual return for 1988 when the following events occur:

(1) She is employed as an accountant and receives a salary of $50,000. Her employer withholds $10,000 of her wages as tax under IRC § 3402.

(2) She bought some stock several years ago for $10,000. She sells the stock for $25,000 after receiving $1,000 of dividends during the current year.

(3) A bona fide $5,000 loan she made two years earlier to a friend becomes worthless.

(4) She attends an accounting convention in New York City paying $600 for travel, $125 for meals and $300 for lodging expenses; her employer does not reimburse her.

(5) She buys $100 worth of books on accounting at her own expense.

(6) She owns a piece of commercial real estate which she purchased after 1981 on which she properly took $15,000 of accelerated depreciation (the amount of depreciation deductions taken under old ACRS exceeds by $5,000 the amount which would have been allowed if the straight line method had been used); the property has an adjusted basis of $75,000 and she sells it on January 1 for $100,000.

(7) Taxpayer's residence is hit by lightning which does $5,000 of damage. Although the damage is covered by her homeowner's insurance policy, she does not file a claim. Her basis in the home prior to the damage was $50,000.

(8) Taxpayer pays $2,000 interest on her home loan, $700 in state income taxes and she makes a $500 charitable contribution. She also gives $200 to her favorite political party.

Answer to Question Two:

Taxpayer has the following consequences from the above transactions:

(1) The salary is $50,000 of gross income characterized as ordinary income. [IRC § 61(a)(1).] The withholding qualifies for a $10,000 tax credit. [IRC § 31(a).]

(2) The sale of the stock results in a $15,000 long term capital gain. [IRC §§ 61(a)(3) and 1222(3).] Taxpayer will include $1,000 of dividends as ordinary gross income. [IRC § 61(a)(7).]

(3) The nonbusiness bad debt results in a $5,000 short-term capital loss. [IRC § 166(d).]

(4) The expenses to attend the accounting convention are deductible under IRC § 162, but only $100 (80% of $125) of the meals is deductible under IRC § 274(n). The remaining $1,000 of expenses are unreimbursed employee business expenses, deductible only if Taxpayer itemizes deductions and, under IRC § 67(a), only to the extent they, plus all other "miscellaneous itemized deductions," exceed 2% of Taxpayer's adjusted gross income.

(5) The books are a business expense deductible under IRC § 162; however, it is also a miscellaneous itemized deduction, limited under IRC § 67(a) as described above.

(6) She has a $25,000 gain on the sale of the real estate. The property is subject to $5,000 of section 1250 ordinary income recapture; the remaining $20,000 is characterized by the main hotchpot of IRC § 1231(a).

(7) Taxpayer has a $5,000 uninsured personal casualty loss of which only $4,900 is potentially deductible. [IRC § 165(h)(1).] Further consequences depend upon the amount of her adjusted gross income. Since there are no other personal casualty gains or losses this loss will be deductible as an ordinary itemized deduction only to the extent it exceeds 10% of Taxpayer's adjusted gross income. [IRC § 165(h)(2).]

(8) Taxpayer has $3,200 of ordinary itemized deductions. [IRC §§ 163, 164 and 170.] There is no deduction or credit for the political contribution.

We must first consider section 1231. There are no sub hotchpot transactions, and in the main hotchpot there is only the $10,000 gain from the real estate sale, which is characterized as a long-term capital gain.

Next, capital gains and losses are netted:

LTCG:	$15,000	STCG	0
	$20,000		
LTCL	0	STCL	$5,000
NLTCG	$35,000	NSTCL	$5,000

This results in a net capital gain of $30,000.

Gross income includes:

Salary	$50,000
Capital gains	35,000
Dividends	1,000
Section 1250 gain	5,000
Total	$91,000

Deductions taken in arriving at adjusted gross income:

Capital loss [§ 62(a)(3)]	5,000
Total section 62 deductions:	$ 5,000
Adjusted Gross Income:	$86,000

Since Taxpayer's potentially deductible personal casualty loss is only $4,900, it does not exceed 10% of her $86,000 adjusted gross income ($8,600) and is not deductible.

Taxpayer's miscellaneous itemized deductions are:

Traveling Expenses	$ 1,000
Books	100
Total	$ 1,100

Because the aggregate amount of Taxpayer's miscellaneous itemized deductions is only $1,100, they do not exceed $1,720 (2% of $86,000 adjusted gross income) and thus may not be deducted in computing taxable income.

Taxpayer's itemized deductions, other than miscellaneous itemized deductions, are:

Interest	$ 2,000
State income tax	700
Charitable contribution	500
Total	$ 3,200

Because the amount of the standard deduction available to Taxpayer in 1988 is only $3,000, she will elect to itemize deductions in computing taxable income. In addition, she is entitled to a personal exemption deduction in 1988 of $1,950. Taxpayer's taxable income and tax liability is computed as follows:

Adjusted gross income		$86,000
Less itemized deductions	$3,200	
personal exemption	1,950	
		5,150
Taxable income		$80,850
Tax under IRC § 1(c)		$20,317.50

Because Taxpayer's taxable income exceeds the applicable dollar amount, a 5% surtax is imposed under IRC § 1(g):

Taxable income	$80,850
Less applicable dollar amount	43,150
	$37,700
	X 5%
5% Surtax	$ 1,885

The 5% surtax is potentially limited to the sum of $2,320.50 (13% of the maximum amount of taxable income taxed at the 15% rate under IRC § 1(c)) plus $546 (28% of the personal exemption deduction), or $2,866.50. However, the amount of surtax is within this limit and so the full $1,885 is imposed.

Taxpayer's total tax liability of $22,202.50 ($20,317.50 under IRC § 1(c) and $1,885.00 surtax under IRC § 1(g)) is offset by the credit of $10,000 for withheld taxes, leaving a balance due of $12,202.50.

Question Three:

On July 1, 1988, Edwin (a calendar year, cash method taxpayer) purchased a new Rolls Royce automobile for exclusive use in his business at a cost of $132,000. In computing his 1988 income tax liability, he chose to make maximum use of the bonus depreciation deduction deduction under IRC § 179 before turning to depreciation deductions under IRC § 168. An automobile is 5-year property under ACRS. From the date he purchased the automobile until March 31, 1991, he used the Rolls exclusively in his business and he took depreciation deductions to the maximum extent permissible. On March 31, 1991, when the automobile had a fair market value of $150,000, he sold it to Alma Mater, which intended to use it to provide transportation for hot recruiting prospects for the football team. Alma Mater paid Edwin $75,000 cash for the Rolls.

Discuss Edwin's tax consequences from the purchase of the Rolls Royce on July 1, 1988, and upon its disposition to Alma Mater on March 31, 1991.

Answer to Question Three:

The Rolls Royce is 5-year property under ACRS [IRC § 168(e)(3)(B)(i)] and section 179 property [IRC § 179(d)(1)]; therefore, it qualifies for ACRS deductions and the bonus depreciation under IRC § 179, but they are limited under IRC § 280F. In 1988, the maximum deduction allowed under IRC § 179 is $10,000, but IRC § 280F treats the section 179 deduction as a depreciation deduction allowable under IRC § 168 thereby subject to a maximum of $2,560. [IRC § 280F(a)(2)(A)(i) and (d)(1).] Because the maximum depreciation deduction is taken under IRC § 179, no further depreciation deduction under IRC § 168 is allowable for 1988.

In 1989, IRC § 280F again limits the amount of depreciation deduction otherwise allowable under IRC § 168 to $4,100. [IRC § 280F(a)(2)(A)(ii).] In 1990, the depreciation deduction is limited to $2,450 and in 1991, to $1,475. [IRC § 280F(a)(2)(A)(iii) and (iv).]

The transfer of the Rolls to Alma Mater is a bargain sale because the fair market value of the automobile is greater than the consideration Edwin receives. Edwin's amount realized is $75,000. The adjusted basis of the Rolls is $121,415 ($132,000 less total depreciation deductions of $10,585). Because this is a bargain sale to a charitable organization, he must apportion the adjusted basis of the Rolls under IRC § 1011(b) by multiplying the adjusted basis times a fraction, with the amount realized in the numerator and the fair market value of the Rolls in the denominator: $121,415 × ($75,000/$150,000) = $60,707.50 adjusted basis allocated to the sale portion of the transaction, producing a realized gain of $14,292.50 ($75,000 less $60,707.50). [IRC § 1001(a).]

The Rolls is section 1245 property, and its recomputed basis is $132,000 ($121,415 adjusted basis plus depreciation deductions allowed of $10,585). [IRC § 1245(a)(2).] If the automobile had been sold for its full fair market value of $150,000, $10,585 ($132,000 less $121,415) of the gain would be ordinary income. [IRC § 1245(a)(1).] Because the disposition of the Rolls was a bargain sale to a charitable organization, the amount of ordinary income required to be recognized under IRC § 1245 is only $5,292.50 (the full amount of potential section 1245 gain, $10,585, times the IRC § 1011(b) basis apportionment fraction, $75,000/$150,000). [Reg. § 1.1011–2(b).] The remaining $9,000 ($14,292.50 less $5,292.50) of the gain recognized on the sale portion of the transaction will have its character determined by the main hotchpot of IRC § 1231(a).

With respect to the gift portion of the transfer of the automobile to Alma Mater, the amount of the gift is $75,000 (fair market value of $150,000 less consideration received of $75,000). The amount of the contribution must be reduced by the extent to which ordinary income would have resulted if the gift portion had also been sold ($5,292.50 under IRC § 1245), resulting in the amount of the contribution being $69,707.50. [IRC § 170(e)(1)(A).] There is some question whether Alma Mater is using the Rolls for a purpose related to the basis for its exemption under IRC § 501. If the use *is* related, no further reduction in the amount of the contribution is necessary, but the amount which may be deducted in 1991 is limited to 30% of Edwin's contribution base for that year. [IRC §§ 170(b)(1)(C) and (e)(1)(B)(i).] If the use *is not* so related, the amount of the contribution must be further reduced by $9,000, the amount of capital gain attributable to this portion of the property, for a contribution of $60,707.50; this contribution is deductible in 1991 to the extent it is within 50% of Edwin's contribution base for that year. [IRC § 170(b)(1)(A).]

*

TEXT CORRELATION CHART

	Andrews (3rd ed. 1985)	Bittker, Stone & Klein (6th ed. 1984)	Dodge (1985)	Freeland, Lind & Stephens (6th ed. 1987)	Graetz (1985)	Guerin & Postlewaite (1986)	Gunn (1981)	Kragen & McNulty (4th ed. 1985)	Solomon & Hesch (1987)	Surrey, McDaniel, Ault & Koppelman (Successor ed. 1986)
I. Introduction										
A. Perspective	1–7	1–3	1–38	1–5	1; 6–27	4–19	1–2	2–3; 11–23	1–2	45–72
B. History of the U.S. income tax	13–15	4–8	143–147	5–20	2–6	1–4	2–5	3–10	2–4	1–17
C. Sources of tax law	15–16	46–55	39–65	20–31	52–56; 64–68	30–43	10	23–25	4–9	17–26
II. Gross income										
A. The nature of gross income										
1. Economists' concept of income	80–83; 124–125	10–11; 113–121	124–125; 135–143	43–44	89–90; 123–127	47–49; 86–90	11–12; 105–107	60–66	53–54; 64–69	73–74; 106–110
2. Tax law concept of income										
a. Realization requirement	89–129	47–48; 283; 298	125–127	52–59	90–91; 144–148	81–86	81–87	49–52	105–123	110–124
b. Receipt of an economic benefit	29–42	111	1; 475–476	44–52; 59–62	95–99; 142–144	60–66	12–19; 49–55	29–40	48–53; 60–64; 181–201	74–110; 212–218
B. Examples of Gross Income										
1. Compensation for services	29–42; 239–267	67–113	333–355	88–89	91–123	49–50	19–49	66–74	70–104	78–105; 193–196

	Andrews (3rd ed. 1985)	Bittker, Stone & Klein (6th ed. 1984)	Dodge (1985)	Freeland, Lind & Stephens (6th ed. 1987)	Graetz (1985)	Guerin & Postlewaite (1986)	Gunn (1981)	Kragen & McNulty (4th ed. 1985)	Solomon & Hesch (1987)	Surrey, McDaniel, Ault & Koppelman (Successor ed. 1986)
B. Examples of Gross Income (Cont'd)										
2. Gains derived from dealings in property										
a. Basis	20; 214–224; 271–273; 291–329; 1067–1073	48–50; 254–265; 296	3–4; 63; 269–271	123–138	159–167	90–95; 123–135	55–59; 134–139; 143–144; 520–522	16; 235–236; 515–517; 584–585	257; 261; 496; 759–809	125–126; 709–726
b. Amount realized	20; 291–329; 1067–1073	254–265; 283–298	2; 547–556; 747–755	138–165	10; 173–183	90–93; 103–114	522	49; 56; 580–598	496; 752–759; 765–792	125–126; 727–728; 741–769
c. Realized gain (loss) vs. recognized gain (loss)	1127	47–48	126–127; 215; 756; 779–780	890–892	160–161	407	81–87	491; 580	846–847	787–788
3. Items specifically included in gross income by statute										
a. Prizes and awards	224–231	154–160	44–56; 63–64	106–112	148–149	143–152	158–160	113–116	296–299	197–201
b. Alimony and separate maintenance payments	912–924	470–485	248–249; 259–262	206–219	466–475	282–288	184–195	547–552	626–629	1076–1082
c. Services of a child	—	—	364–365	940	—	227–229	432	154	703	1073
d. Reimbursement for expenses of moving	421–422	—	291	511–516	119	490–495	364	154; 208	415	298
e. Transfer of appreciated property to a political organization	—	150; 297	230; 270	—	—	—	179	51; 529; 585	—	—
f. Social security payments	267	145–146	246–247	243	231–233	215	105	154	358–359	230–231
g. Unemployment compensation	—	145	—	243	—	215	—	—	359	230–231
h. Annuities	189–199	69–77; 185–189	508–511	166–173	183–186	212–213	73–74	122–129	152–156	137–141
C. Items specifically excluded from gross income by statute										
1. Death benefits										
a. Proceeds of life insurance	199–203	179–184	396–398	166–168	186–190	135–136	144–145	106–113	289–296	141–146
b. Employees' death benefits	263	—	56	168	118	136–143	132–133	97; 109	332–341	191–192
2. Gifts and inheritances										
a. Gifts	205–224	122–154	50–54; 393–395	63–78	128–139	116–123	120–139	92–106	257–278; 282–289	164–169; 177–197
b. Inheritances	262–265	144	53	78–87	140–141	116–123	139–144	99–101	257–264; 278–282	169–171
3. Interest on state and local bonds	339–345	274–282	110–111	244–252	233–241	214–215	108–112	146–153	355–358	233
4. Compensation for injuries or sickness and damages	133–152	226–242	1; 291–300	181–205	218–229	187–201	99–104	129–136	123–152; 156–159	127–137
5. Income from discharge of indebtedness	269–274	242–268	673–677	174–180	190–195	201–208	87–93	46–49	235–243	147–148; 732–741
6. Scholarships, tuition reductions and educational assistance programs	231–239	160–171	44–57	112–121	150–156	152–162	146–158	116–122	299–307	201–212

	Andrews (3rd ed. 1985)	Bittker, Stone & Klein (6th ed. 1984)	Dodge (1985)	Freeland, Lind & Stephens (6th ed. 1987)	Graetz (1985)	Guerin & Postlewaite (1986)	Gunn (1981)	Kragen & McNulty (4th ed. 1985)	Solomon & Hesch (1987)	Surrey, McDaniel, Ault & Koppelman (Successor ed. 1986)
C. Items specifically excluded from gross income by statute (Cont'd)										
7. Meals and lodging	394–422	78–88	309–327	101–105	99–109	163–177	23–30	136–146	308–332	96–100
8. Miscellaneous items excluded from income by statute	28	302–304	1; 58–60; 244–247; 781–782	88–101; 243–244	117–121	178–187; 215	36–43	154–155	349–355	100–106
III. Deductions and allowances										
A. Profit related deductions and allowances										
1. Trade or business expenses										
a. In general	363–389; 422–430	555–563; 575–587; 639–647	273–279	334–355	244–248	441–468	317–337	156–164	360; 482–490; 500–509	272–279
b. Salaries	389–394	643–644	418	355–363	249–255	446–449	337–342	187–193	461–467	394–397
c. Traveling expenses	394–422	511–530; 533–544	309–327	363–377; 478	278–295	469–490	342–356	193–206	385–415; 433–441	280–297
d. Meals	394	78–88	309	399–404; 478	278	509–517	342	193	380–385; 406–407	274–279
e. Rentals	856–864	587–591	381–390	377–390	948–950	—	465–470	221; 259; 630	852–883	809–815
f. Expenses for education	237–238; 709–718	550–554	279–291	390–398	329–336	518–528	364–367	229–234	509–524	375–384
g. Miscellaneous business deductions	—	—	336–337	399–406	295–301	529–534	—	277–280	375–380; 478–482	308–325
h. Substantiation requirements	674–686	542–544	310–311	403–404	299–300	506–509	356	208; 319	427–432	307–308
2. Nonbusiness expenses										
a. Production or collection of income	430–454	—	13–18; 62; 272–273; 307	410–419; 426–434	244; 318	698–707	317–337; 368–373	162–170	360–363; 441–448	271–273
b. Management of income producing property	439–454	—	244; 271; 273; 620	420–434	244; 317	698–707	317–337; 368–373	170	441–448	271–273
c. Expenses in connection with taxes	—	—	238–244	435	334	698	371–372	171; 186	448–457; 640	372–375
3. Losses	491–498	495–504	127; 276–277; 289	406–409; 435–444	370–377; 389–392	707–709	392–398	301–325	458–461	449–460
4. Bad debts	507–519	—	3; 15; 669–673	787–802	392–397	729–737	401–412	338–352	1015–1020	460–464
5. Property										
a. Depreciation deductions (non-ACRS)	549–550	—	4; 511–517	725–732	346–353	534–538; 553–555	271–278	234–245	557–569; 593–614	464–472; 480–483
b. Accelerated Cost Recovery System (ACRS)	597–610	605–633	517–521	732–737	353–357	538–545	—	245–261	569–574	472–480
c. Related concept of depletion	634–643	633–639	534–535	737–738	368–370	—	287–294	271–277	—	501–505
d. Special rules for personal property	613–617	615–620	517–530	744–753	353–357; 365–367	543	276–277; 294	234–249; 261–271	574–577	473–475; 498
e. Special rules for real property	—	618–619	519–520	753–756	356	542	276; 282	241–242; 247–248	571	475–476
6. Net operating loss deduction	157; 168–169	207–208	647–649	641–643	767–772	—	704	307; 505–509	174–175	702–707

	Andrews (3rd ed. 1985)	Bittker, Stone & Klein (6th ed. 1984)	Dodge (1985)	Freeland, Lind & Stephens (6th ed. 1987)	Graetz (1985)	Guerin & Postlewaite (1986)	Gunn (1981)	Kragen & McNulty (4th ed. 1985)	Solomon & Hesch (1987)	Surrey, McDaniel, Ault & Koppelman (Successor ed. 1986)
B. Personal deductions and allowances										
1. Personal and dependency exemptions	924–927	493–494	8; 205; 212; 249–252	534–537	449–452	920–930	194–195	357; 395–402	638–639	564–567
2. Interest	455–467	485–491	213–215	447–471	398–415	737–748	379–392	283–299	641–669	516–518
3. Taxes	477–481	491–493	233–238	471–476	415–421	748–756	179–183	299–301	669–694	519–527
4. Personal casualty and theft losses	519–525	439–442	215–223	825–836	384–389	757–770	398–401	326–338	694–700	559–563
5. Worthless nonbusiness debts	507–519	835–836	669–673	792–802	395–397	730–737	406–412	347–348	1016–1018	—
6. Charitable contributions	721–759	447–470	223–233	802–825	422–442	770–780	167–179; 257–258	358–387	623–626; 1020–1026	528–546
7. Extraordinary medical expenses	177–188	442–447	206–213	520–534	442–448	780–787	160–167	387–395	615–623	547–558
8. Alimony	912–924	470–485	259–262	206–219	466–475	282–288	184–195	547–552	626–629	564; 1074–1082
9. Moving expenses	421–422	530	3; 290–291	511–516	119	490–495	364	208–209; 214	415–416	297–298
10. Retirement savings	—	380	—	—	—	—	—	—	168–170	564
C. Restrictions on deductions										
1. Personal, living and family expenses	645–653	—	4–5; 10	445	265–268	788–791	317	158; 162; 176	362–363; 375–380	272–273
2. Illegal activities	377–389	644–647	276–277	504–510	255–262	562–568	74–80; 378	176–182	467–478	515
3. Activities not engaged in for profit	696–709	495–504	300–307	485–486	377–384	707–717	317–322	214–221	363–368	325–335
4. Expenses and interest relating to tax exempt income	467–474	649; 654	57–63; 110–111	477	407–411	747–748	111–112	165; 287; 300	647–648	436–444
5. Transactions between related taxpayers	1046–1052	340–341	270; 380	603–610; 880–887	371–372; 376–377	839–845	625–626	307–308	745–747	455–457; 655–665
6. Entertainment expenses	664–686	533–544	327–333	399–404; 478	295–301	495–509	352–356	209–210	417–427; 432–433	298–310
7. Business use of home and rental of vacation homes	687–696; 704–709	505–507	307–309	486–492	301–306	717–729	327; 333	211–214	368–371; 900–902	314–315; 333–334
8. Demolition of structures	—	—	—	—	—	—	—	—	—	—
9. Deductions limited to amount at risk	626; 1299	654–655	743–746	481–485	216–217; 357–358	861–864	757–763	254; 257; 309–310; 595–596	887–888	1019–1029
10. Passive activity losses and credits	—	—	—	492–504	—	—	—	—	888–902	—
11. Loss from wash sales of stock or securities	502–507	—	783	887–889	376–377	845–852	415	306–307	—	458–459
IV. Timing **A. Taxable period**	156	—	643–644	544–545	748–751	807–809	602	409–420	171	673–678
B. Methods of accounting										
1. Cash receipts and disbursements method	157–158; 538–539; 545–546	46; 76	463–485	548–573	779–819	809–821	603–622	420–437	211–225; 490–496	586–615
2. Accrual method	157–158; 993–1039	46; 76; 409–424	454–463	574–603	820–855	821–832	622–625	437–448	226–232; 525–556	615–641
3. Installment method	1082–1093	363–371	550–557	837–855	856–861	383–407	666–673	448–453	817–826; 1054–1055	777–781

	Andrews (3rd ed. 1985)	Bittker, Stone & Klein (6th ed. 1984)	Dodge (1985)	Freeland, Lind & Stephens (6th ed. 1987)	Graetz (1985)	Guerin & Postlewaite (1986)	Gunn (1981)	Kragen & McNulty (4th ed. 1985)	Solomon & Hesch (1987)	Surrey, McDaniel, Ault & Koppelman (Successor ed. 1986)
C. Judicial doctrines										
1. Claim of right doctrine	274–279	209–217	692–701	611–624	762–767	832–836	49–54; 626–629; 712–715	74–82; 419–420	171–181	690–694
2. Tax benefit rule	158–176	217–220	707–722	624–627	752–761	208–212	705–712	41–43	201–211	678–690
D. Nonrecognition provisions 1. Like kind exchanges	1118–1129	305–333	758–763	892–910	727–735	408–422	547–555	491–497	848–852	788–801
2. Involuntary conversions	1127	311–315	779–784	910–924	735–742	422–427	561–565	497–498	143; 148; 847	801–806
3. Sale of principal residence	1129–1134	315	777–778	924–935	742–745	428–440	554	498–501	847–848	807–808
4. Transfer of property between spouses or incident to divorce	910–912	333–354	269–271	219–230	466; 471–472	288–292	187–188	545–547	631–638	1082–1089
5. Miscellaneous	—	315–316	—	890–892; 935–939	—	407	—	—	—	801
E. Unstated interest	870–875; 1040–1046; 1093–1110	121	677–688	871–879	861–868	673–689	386	63–64; 297–298	747–749; 830–846; 995–1003	1160–1166
F. Special rules 1. Annuities	189–199	69–77; 185–189	508–511	166–173	183–186	212–213	73–74	479–483	152–156	137–141; 785–787
2. Deferred compensation	931–975	377–404	475–485	636–641	119; 791–804	320–336	734–741	461–479	159–170; 243–256	593–598; 603–607
V. Who is the proper taxpayer A. Families	761–763	30–34	6; 356	253–255	457–466	227–229	432–433	330	701–703	1068–1074
B. Assignment of income 1. Income from services	783–790	708–724	364–376	255–265	476–488	227–243	421–432	517–520	707–712	1090–1103; 1123–1128
2. Income from property	791–805	724–738	364–376	265–283	488–495	243–255	434–457	521–537	703–706; 712–722; 731–745	1103–1123
3. Anticipatory assignment for value	—	—	—	283–288	546–551	255–258	565–585	412; 519	717; 983–984	1122
4. Income producing entities	835–870	744–753; 755–767; 773–791	376–380; 398–445	289–310; 314–333	501–546	239–243; 258–264	483–512	537–545	722–731	1177–1202
5. Allocation of income and deductions among taxpayers	842–851; 857	781–782; 787–788	406–407; 442–443	—	514–516	—	483–504	510; 545; 814–821	—	—
C. Alimony, child support, and property settlements 1. Alimony	912–924	472–485	259–262	206–219	466–475	282–288	184–195	547–551	626–629	1076–1081
2. Child support	923	470–472	259–262	230–236	468–469	288	184	549	629–631	1081–1082
3. Transfers of property between spouses or incident to divorce	905–912	333–354	266–272	219–230	471–472	288–292	184–189	545–547; 550–551	631–638	1082–1089
VI. Characterization of income and deductions A. Introduction	1137; 1187–1189	803–807	148–149	644	592–595	569–571	196–200	580–598	903–909	839–841
B. Treatment of capital gains and losses 1. Treatment of capital gains	1138	805	148–157	644–649; 651–655	595–599	571–574	196–199	598–604	909–937	839–841
2. Treatment of capital losses	498–502	805–806	652–666	649–651; 655–662	597; 599	574–576	232–233	603–606	936–937	839–841

	Andrews (3rd ed. 1985)	Bittker, Stone & Klein (6th ed. 1984)	Dodge (1985)	Freeland, Lind & Stephens (6th ed. 1987)	Graetz (1985)	Guerin & Postlewaite (1986)	Gunn (1981)	Kragen & McNulty (4th ed. 1985)	Solomon & Hesch (1987)	Surrey, McDaniel, Ault & Koppelman (Successor ed. 1986)
B. Treatment of capital gains and losses (Cont'd) 3. Definition of capital asset a. Statutory definition	1142–1143; 1164–1185	807–828	160–182	662–671	605–628	577–597	221–237	607–614	945–967; 983–984	842–875
b. Income property	1153–1164; 1215–1276	838–865	568–577	671–680	652–683	632–650	565–601	621–624	989–995	891–905
c. The *Corn Products* Doctrine	1148–1152; 1200–1212	829–838	658–666	681–688	638–652	597–605	238–255	614–621	967–975	883–891
4. The "sale or exchange" requirement	1141	903–907	157–160	689–709	695–723	605–616	200–221	628–644	937–943; 1004–1015	920–929
5. Holding period	1143	805	148–154; 489; 762	718–724	724–726	616–624	264–270	644–647	943–945	929–932
6. Correlation with prior transactions	1191–1200	899–903	701–707	709–718	687–695	836–839	415–420	624–627	985–989	944–957
7. Special provisions	1186; 1257–1261	811; 891	185–186; 581; 587	—	636–638	669–673	204; 221–231	647–649	946–963	941–943
C. Quasi-capital assets (IRC § 1231)	610–612; 1140–1141	804	182–186	757–769	626–633	624–631	555–560	649–656	975–983	933–941
D. Sale of depreciable property between related taxpayers	—	428	181–182; 380; 766	769–775	—	—	256–257	657–658	984	—
E. Recapture of depreciation	612–613	610–611	530–533	775–786	633–636	650–660	255–256	656–661	1026–1032	936–937
VII. Computing tax liability A. Adjusted gross income	765–766	40	7–8	516–520	10; 242	442–444	166	11; 281–282	12	65
B. Taxable income	765	41	8	537–543	242	44–45	166	281	12; 482–483	65
C. Classification of taxpayers	762	31	8–13; 253–259	940–952	460–466	939–942	11–12; 432–433	399; 580	639–640	69
D. Tax rates	766	30–34	8	940–952	242	930–939; 942–963	166	281	1–2	68
E. Alternative minimum tax	766–769	700–703	544–547; 630; 722	960–967	13–14; 963–964	973–976	199–200; 748–753	664–666; 679	1032–1034	574–578
F. Tax credits	18; 478; 613–617; 766	43; 491; 494; 605–620	9; 35–36; 65–66; 230; 255; 408; 460; 526–530; 709	952–960	450–455	976–991	294–295; 333	13; 277–280; 352; 402	13	65; 505–515
VIII. Procedure	7–13	34–39	65–81	968–1015	43–88	19–25	5–9	10–11	7–9	26–35

GLOSSARY

This glossary is intended to provide the reader with a brief definition of some of the terms frequently encountered in Federal income taxation. Many terms, however, do not lend themselves to a brief definition because they are conceptual or highly technical. If a term does not appear in this Glossary, the reader should consult the Index to this Outline in order to turn to the complete discussion of the term in the body of the Outline.

A

Accelerated Cost Recovery System (ACRS): The method of computing depreciation deductions for most items of real property and tangible personal property used in a trade or business or held for the production of income. The label describes the effect of the system which allows the cost of items of depreciable property to be deducted (recovered) at a faster rate than the rate at which the property is actually, physically being used up in the process of producing income.

Accrual Method of Accounting: A method of determining the taxable year for reporting items of income or taking deductions in which, generally, items are included in gross income in the taxable year in which all events have occurred which: (a) fix the taxpayer's right to receive the item and (b) fix the amount of the item. Deductions may be taken in the taxable year in which all events have occurred which: (a) fix the taxpayer's liability to pay the item, (b) fix the amount payable, and (c) satisfy certain tests of economic performance. A taxpayer using this method is referred to as an accrual method taxpayer.

Additional Standard Deduction: The sum of the additional amounts to which a taxpayer is entitled if he (and sometimes his spouse) has attained age 65 before the close of his taxable year and the additional amount to which a taxpayer is entitled if he (and sometimes his spouse) is blind at the close of the taxable year. [IRC § 63(c)(3).] The additional amount is $600 ($750 for unmarried taxpayers other than surviving spouses) and may be increased annually to reflect adjustments in the cost-of-living. The amount of the additional standard deduction, if any, is added to the amount of the basic standard deduction to compute the standard deduction; the standard deduction is subtracted from adjusted gross income in computing taxable income only if the taxpayer does not itemize deductions.

Adjusted Basis: The basis of property after adjustment to account for events described in IRC § 1016 such as capital expenditures, losses, and deductions for depreciation.

Adjusted Gross Income: Gross income less certain deductions specified in IRC § 62.

Alternative Minimum Tax: A tax which may be imposed under IRC § 55 in addition to the regular income tax computed under IRC § 1 if a taxpayer's regular tax has been computed using a substantial amount of adjustments and items of tax preference.

Amount Realized: The amount of money plus the fair market value of property, including the relief of liabilities, received from the sale or other disposition of property. [IRC § 1001(b).]

Assignment of Income: The transfer of income and the incidence of taxation from one taxpayer (usually in a relatively high tax rate bracket) to another taxpayer (usually in a relatively low tax rate bracket).

Audit: A term commonly used to refer to the review of a taxpayer's return by the IRS.

B

Basic Standard Deduction: An automatic amount of deduction which is allowed to most taxpayers as a deduction from adjusted gross income in computing taxable income if they do not elect to itemize deductions. For taxable years beginning in 1987 (1988) the basic standard deduction is determined by the taxpayer's filing status as follows: married filing joint return, $5,000 ($3,760); surviving spouse, $5,000 ($3,760); head of household, $4,400 ($2,540); unmarried other than head of household or surviving spouse, $3,000 ($2,540); and married filing separate return, $2,500 ($1,880). The amount of the basic standard deduction may be increased for taxable years after 1988 to reflect fluctuations in the cost-of-living. The basic standard deduction plus the additional standard deduction constitute the total standard deduction which is compared with itemized deductions in determining whether to elect to itemize deductions.

Basis: The amount which a taxpayer has invested, in a tax sense, in property; the term is generally modified by words such as "cost," "adjusted," "gift," "stepped-up," "substituted" and "carryover."

Boot: Money or other property which is *not* permitted to be received without the recognition of gain or loss under a nonrecognition provision.

C

Capital Asset: Property held by a taxpayer, whether or not it is connected with her trade or business, other than certain categories of property enumerated in IRC § 1221 such as inventory and depreciable property used in a trade or business, and other than property which is judicially held to not constitute a captial asset such as under the *Corn Products* doctrine.

Carryovers (Carrybacks): Provisions which allow certain items which would ordinarily be given effect for tax purposes in a particular taxable year instead to be considered in a subsequent (or earlier) taxable year; examples include the net operating loss provisions [IRC § 172], the deductions for net capital losses [IRC § 1212] and excess charitable contributions [IRC § 170(d)], and passive loss and credit carryovers [IRC § 469(b).]

Cash Receipts and Disbursements Method of Accounting (Cash Method): A method of determining the taxable year for reporting items of income or taking deductions in which, generally, items of gross income are included in the taxable year in which they are actually or constructively received and deductions are taken in the taxable year in which they are paid. A taxpayer using this method is referred to as a cash method taxpayer.

Claim of Right Doctrine: A rule which requires a taxpayer to include in gross income amounts which he receives during a taxable year if he has a claim to the amount and unrestricted use of it, even though he may become obligated to return the amount in a subsequent year.

Classifications of Taxpayers: The five categories into which individual taxpayers are divided for the purposes of determining the filing status and the tax rate schedule applicable to a particular taxpayer. The classifications are: married filing a joint return, surviving spouse, head of household, unmarried (other than surviving spouse or head of household) and married filing a separate return.

Constructive Receipt Doctrine: A rule which requires a cash method taxpayer to include an item in gross income prior to its actual receipt if it is credited to his account, set apart for him, or otherwise made available so that he may draw on it at any time, unless the subsequent actual receipt of the item is subject to substantial limitations or restrictions.

Cost Basis: The basis of property acquired by purchase or on a taxable exchange. The fair market value of property received on a taxable exchange is its cost basis; the amount of money paid for property in an arms length transaction is its cost basis.

Cumulative Bulletin (C.B.): A hard-bound collection of Revenue Rulings, Revenue Procedures, legislative history of tax legislation and other materials published by the IRS every six months.

D

Deficiency: The amount by which the tax properly due exceeds the sum of the amount of tax shown on a taxpayer's return plus amounts previously assessed or collected as a deficiency, less any credits, refunds or other payments due the taxpayer; i.e., the amount a taxpayer is deficient in his tax payments.

Dependency Exemption: An amount which may be subtracted in computing taxable income for each person who qualifies as a dependent of the taxpayer and whose gross income is less than the exemption amount or who is a child of the taxpayer and who has either not attained the age of 19 or who is a student. [IRC § 151(e).] The amount of the dependency exemption, and the exemption amount, is $1,900 for 1987, $1,950 for 1988, $2,000 for 1989, and it is indexed for years after 1989.

Depreciation Deductions: Deductions allowable for property which is used in a trade or business or held for the production of income and which is of such a nature that it is consumed, wears out or becomes obsolete in the process. Deductions for most items of tangible personal property and real property are computed under the Accelerated Cost Recovery System (ACRS), although the IRC § 167 rules apply to some property including intangible personal property.

E

Exclusions: Generally refers to provisions which authorize omitting from gross income certain economic benefits which would otherwise be within the concept of gross income; examples include gifts [IRC § 102] and qualified scholarships [IRC § 117].

F

Fair Market Value: The price at which property would change hands between a willing buyer and a willing seller, neither being under any compulsion to buy or to sell and both having reasonable knowledge of relevant facts.

G

Gain: The excess of the amount realized from the sale or other disposition of property over its adjusted basis.

Gross Income: Realized accessions to wealth over which a taxpayer has control. Examples of items included in gross income are enumerated in IRC § 61 and include compensation for services, gains derived from dealings in property, interest and dividends. The list of items in IRC § 61 is not exclusive.

H

Head of Household: A taxpayer classification which, generally, describes an unmarried individual (other than a surviving spouse) who provides a home for his dependent(s). [IRC § 2(b).]

I

Imputed Income: The monetary value of goods and services which someone produces and is consumed within the immediate family unit as well as the monetary value of using property which someone within the family unit owns. Imputed income is not included in gross income.

Indexing: The process of automatically adjusting for inflation items such as the amount of the personal exemption and the amount of taxable income taxed at the 15% tax rate; the adjustments are made annually with reference to the Consumer Price Index. [IRC § 1(f).]

Internal Revenue Code of 1986 (IRC): The codification, as amended, of federal statutes pertaining to taxation; it is a common reference to statutes contained in Title 26 of the United States Code.

Itemized Deductions: Deductions *other than* deductions allowable in computing adjusted gross income and the deductions for personal exemptions (including dependency exemptions). [IRC § 63(d).]

J

Joint Return: A single income tax return filed by a taxpayer and her spouse together. [IRC § 6013.] The tax rates on such returns are prescribed by IRC § 1(a).

Judicial Process: The development of tax law by the various courts which interpret and apply provisions of the IRC in litigated cases.

K

"Kiddie Tax:" The tax imposed under IRC § 1(i) on the unearned income of a child which is computed as if the income were taxed in the hands of the child's parent, rather than the child, if that results in a higher tax.

L

Legislative History: Reports of Congressional committees, transcripts of committee hearings, Congressional debates and other material dealing with the enactment of statutes; this material is often useful in interpreting a statute after it becomes law.

Legislative Process: The development of tax law by Congress, often beginning with holding public hearings prior to the introduction of a bill in either the House or the Senate and ending with the signing of an Act by the President.

Loss: The excess of the adjusted basis of property which is sold or otherwise disposed of over the amount realized in the transaction.

M

Married Taxpayer: A taxpayer who is married at the end of his taxable year, or whose spouse dies during the taxable year. [IRC § 7703(a).] The taxpayer classification, or filing status, of a married taxpayer is either married filing a joint return, or married filing a separate return, depending on whether the taxpayer files a joint return with his spouse.

Miscellaneous Itemized Deductions: Deductions *other than* those allowable in computing adjusted gross income, personal exemptions and those enumerated in IRC § 67(b). Significant examples of miscellaneous itemized deductions include unreimbursed employee business expenses otherwise allowable under IRC § 162, deductions to the extent of gross income derived from activities not engaged in for profit (hobbies) otherwise allowable under IRC § 183(b)(2), and deductions for expenses for producing or collecting income (other than rents or royalties) otherwise allowable under IRC § 212(1). Miscellaneous itemized deductions may be used in computing taxable income only if a taxpayer elects to itemize deductions [IRC § 63(e)] and only to the extent the total amount of miscellaneous itemized deductions exceeds 2% of the taxpayer's adjusted gross income [IRC § 67(a).]

N

Net Capital Gain: The excess of a taxpayer's net long-term capital gain for a taxable year over his net short-term capital loss for the year. [IRC § 1222(11).]

Nonrecognition Provisions: Statutory rules which allow or require all or a portion of gain (and sometimes loss) realized on the sale or other disposition of property to not be recognized. Most nonrecognition provisions serve to merely postpone the recognition of gain or loss by the application of rules for determining the basis of newly acquired property with reference to the basis of the property disposed of in the nonrecognition transaction; the holding period of the old property is also generally added (or tacked) on to the holding period of the newly acquired property.

O

Ordinary Income: Items of gross income, including gains from the sale or exchange of property, *other than* gain which is characterized as long-term or short-term capital gain. [IRC § 64.]

P

Passive Activity Losses and Credits: Losses (deductions in excess of income) and tax credits attributable to certain "passive activities." Generally, under IRC § 469 such losses (and credits) may be used in a taxable year only to offset income (or income tax attributable to income) from passive activities. Thus, losses (or credits) attributable to a passive activity during a taxable year may not be deducted from income (or offset tax liability attributable to income) derived as compensation for performing services during that taxable year. Passive activity losses and credits which are disallowed in a taxable year are carried over to subsequent taxable years.

Personal Exemption: An amount which a taxpayer may subtract for herself (and sometimes her spouse) in computing taxable income. [IRC § 151(b).] The exemption amount is $1,900 for 1987, $1,950 for 1988, $2,000 for 1989 and is indexed thereafter. Additional exemption amounts are allowed for each qualifying dependent; see definition of Dependency Exemption.

Procedure: The administrative and judicial method or manner of determining a taxpayer's tax liability and otherwise enforcing the tax laws.

Progressive Rates: Tax rates which generally increase as the amount of the tax base (taxable income) increases. They are sometimes also referred to as accelerated rates.

R

Realized Gain (or Loss): Gain (or loss) resulting from an identifiable event, such as a sale or an exchange of property. The amount of realized gain from the sale or other disposition of property is the excess of the amount realized over the adjusted basis of the property; the amount of realized loss is the excess of the property's adjusted basis over the amount realized.

Recognized Gain (or Loss): A realized gain not covered by a nonrecognition provision is a recognized gain and must be included in gross income; a realized loss not covered by a nonrecognition provision is a recognized loss and may qualify for a deduction.

Refund: An amount a taxpayer is entitled to have paid to him on account of an overpayment of his tax liability.

Revenue Procedure (Rev. Proc.): An administrative statement by the IRS concerning a matter of procedure that affects the rights or duties of taxpayers under the IRC.

Revenue Ruling (Rev. Rul.): An official interpretation by the IRS of the proper application of the tax law, generally furnished in response to a question raised by a taxpayer concerning the tax consequences of a particular transaction or event.

S

Sixteenth Amendment: The constitutional authority for Congress to impose an income tax without having to comply with the rule of apportionment.

Standard Deduction: The sum of the basic standard deduction and the additional standard deduction. [IRC § 63(c)(1).] The standard deduction is limited in the case of an individual with respect to whom a dependency exemption is allowable to another taxpayer and it is zero in the case of certain taxpayers. [IRC § 63(c)(5) and (6).] The standard deduction may not be used in computing taxable income if the taxpayer elects to itemize deductions.

Surtax of 5%: A tax imposed under IRC § 1(g) in addition to the regular tax imposed under IRC § 1(a)–(d) at the rate of 5% on the amount of taxable income in excess of an applicable amount. The maximum amount of surtax which may be imposed is limited in such a fashion that it has the practical effect of rducing, or totally eliminating, the amount of taxable income otherwise taxed at the 15% rate and then reducing, or again perhaps totally eliminating, the amount of deductions for personal exemptions otherwise allowable. For this reason, the 5% surtax is sometimes referred to a phase-out of the 15% rate and personal exemptions.

Surviving Spouse: A taxpayer classification which, generally, describes an unmarried taxpayer whose spouse died within either of the past two taxable years and who provides a home for his dependent(s). [IRC § 2(a).]

T

Tax Accounting: The accounting (timing) rules and methods used in determining a taxpayers tax liability.

Tax Credit: An amount which may be subtracted from the amount of the tax liability which a taxpayer would otherwise owe to determine tax payments (or sometimes refunds) which must actually be made.

Tax Liability: The amount which a taxpayer owes under the tax law after properly computing gross income and deductions, using the appropriate tax rate and subtracting any applicable tax credits.

Tax Rates: The portion, expressed as a percentage, of a taxpayer's tax base (taxable income) which produces her tax liability prior to subtracting any available tax credits. [See IRC § 1.]

Taxable Income: For taxpayers who elect to itemize deductions, taxable income is the excess of gross income over the amount of all deductions allowable under the Code including personal exemptions. [IRC § 63(a).] Taxable income, for individuals who do *not* elect to itemize deductions, taxable income is adjusted gross income minus the standard deduction and the deductions for personal exemptions. [IRC § 63(b).]

Taxable Year: The taxable period for computing the Federal income tax; generally it is either the calendar year or a fiscal year of 12 months ending on the last day of a month other than December. [IRC § 441(b).]

Taxpayer: Any person subject to any internal revenue tax, regardless of whether he actually pays or is required to pay any tax. [IRC § 7701(a)(14).]

Treasury Regulations (Regs.): Administrative pronouncements by the Treasury Department which either interpret, construe or explain various provisions of the IRC ("interpretative regulations") or supply rules in accordance with statutory guidelines and Congressional directives ("legislative regulations").

U

Unmarried Taxpayer: A taxpayer who is not married at the end of her taxable year and whose spouse did not die during the taxable year. A taxpayer who is legally separated from her spouse under a decree of divorce or separate maintenance is considered unmarried, and certain married individuals separated from their spouses and maintaining a household for their dependent children may be treated as unmarried. [IRC § 7703.] If an unmarried individual otherwise qualifies, his taxpayer classification and filing status may be surviving spouse or head of household; otherwise his taxpayer classification and filing status is "unmarried taxpayer."

*

APPENDIX E

TABLE OF CASES, IRC SECTIONS, TREASURY REGULATIONS, REVENUE RULINGS AND PROCEDURES

Table of Cases

Table of Internal Revenue Code Sections

392   APPENDIX E

Table of Treasury Regulations

Table of Revenue Rulings and Procedures

†